The Black Experience in Design

T0004227

The Black Experience in Design

Identity Expression &

Reflection

ANNE H. BERRY
KAREEM COLLIE
PENINA ACAYO LAKER
LESLEY-ANN NOEL
JENNIFER RITTNER
KELLY WALTERS

Allworth Press books may be purchased in bulk at special discounts for sales promotion, corporate gifts, fund-raising, or educational purposes. Special editions can also be created to specifications. For details, contact the Special Sales Department, Allworth Press, 307 West 36th Street, 11th Floor, New York, NY 10018 or info@skyhorsepublishing.com.

26 25 24 23   5

Published by Allworth Press, an imprint of Skyhorse Publishing, Inc. 307 West 36th Street, 11th Floor, New York, NY 10018. Allworth Press® is a registered trademark of Skyhorse Publishing, Inc.®, a Delaware corporation.

www.allworth.com

Editor: Caroline Russomanno

Managing Editor: Anne H. Berry
Developmental Editor: Jennifer Rittner
Creative Director: Kelly Walters
Cover Design: renald Louissaint
Interior Design: renald Louissaint
Copy Editor: Jamie McGhee

Library of Congress Cataloging-in-Publication Data is available on file.

Print ISBN: 978-1-62153-785-4
eBook ISBN: 978-1-62153-786-1

Printed in the United States of America

*To our ancestors, to those who
are with us in the present, and
to those who will follow long
after we are gone: this book, a
labor of love, is for you.*

SECTION	CONTENTS	PAGE
FOREWORD	Emory Douglas	13
	Ruha Benjamin	16
0 – 0.4	INTRODUCTION	
	Why Is This Book Needed? Anne H. Berry	22
	Searching for a Black Aesthetic in American Graphic Design Sylvia Harris	27
	On Sylvia Harris: The Contributions of Black Designers Anne H. Berry & Steven Heller	33
	Designing with Complexity: An Intersectional View Jennifer Rittner	37
1 – 1.7	DESIGN PRACTICES	
	Chapter Introduction Kareem Collie	48
	An Exhibition by Black Designers Dorothy Hayes	52
	In Conversation: Darhil Crooks, Ian Spalter & Dantley Davis on Practicing Design While Black, with Kareem Collie	64
	Another Brick in the Wall R. Vann Graves	74
	The Four Pillars Jon Key	78
	To Be Just . . . *Steward: Some Life Lyrics* Quinlin B. Messenger	84

SECTION	CONTENTS	PAGE

In Conversation: Annika Hansteen-
Izora on Identity, Community &
Authenticity, with Jennifer Rittner — 100

2 – 2.7   DESIGN EDUCATION

Chapter Introduction — 116
Anne H. Berry

In Conversation: Maurice Woods & Anne H. — 120
Berry on Meeting the Demands of the Future

The New Visual Abnormal — 128
Colette Gaiter

Unvisible (What's the Scenario?) — 140
Steve Jones

The Strong Black Woman — 148
Terresa Moses

A Reading List for the Politics of Design — 160
Chris Rudd

Beyond the Universal: Positionality — 170
& Promise in an HBCU Classroom
Kaleena Sales

3 – 3.6   DESIGN SCHOLARSHIP

Chapter Introduction — 178
Lesley-Ann Noel

Follow the Golden Ratio from Africa — 182
to the Bauhaus for a Cross-Cultural
Aesthetic for Images
Audrey G. Bennett

SECTION	CONTENTS	PAGE

The Pause: Reflecting on a   204
Righteous Consciousness that Informs
Our Design as Afrikans
Nii Kommey Botchway

Finding Anthony: Establishing   214
a Research Trajectory
Cheryl D. Miller

Bondage by Paper: Devices   218
of Slaveholding Ingenuity
Alicia Olushola Ajayi

At the Jim Crow Museum, We Use Racist Objects   232
to Engage Hearts & Heads in Social Justice
David Pilgrim

4 — 4.9   ACTIVISIM, ADVOCACY &
COMMUNITY-ENGAGED DESIGN

Chapter Introduction   244
Kareem Collie & Penina Laker

Participatory & Emanicipatory   246
Aspirations in Afrika
Mugendi K. M'Rithaa

From the Black Anti-Ableist Diary: A Tribute   258
to My Black Disabled Son from a Black
Disabled Mother
Jennifer White-Johnson

The Infrastructure of Care: Community Design,   264
Healing & Organizational Post-Traumatic Growth
Sloan Leo

The Center in the Margins: Locating Intimacy   270
in Multi-Communities
June A. Grant

SECTION	CONTENTS	PAGE

Biophilia Patterns in Black & Brown Spaces
Michele Y. Washington — 278

In Conversation: Amos Kennedy
& Kareem Collie on Advocating for Humanity — 288

The Preconditions to Healing
Liz Ogbu — 296

In Conversation: Raja Schaar &
Jennifer Rittner on Sustainability
as a Historically Black Practice — 300

5 — 5.6   AFROFUTURISM IN DESIGN

Chapter Introduction
Lesley-Ann Noel — 320

*From Algorithms to Afro-Rithms in
Afrofuturism*
Lonny Avi Brooks — 324

*A Black-Centered Design Ethos:
Engaging Afrofuturism in Catalyzing
More Inclusive Technological Futures*
Woodrow W. Winchester III — 342

What Type of Ancestor Do You Want to Be?
Adah Parris — 348

Black Secret Technologies
John Jennings — 358

Dark Matter's Magic in Design
Folayemi Wilson — 364

SECTION	CONTENTS	PAGE

6 — 6.8 JOURNEYS IN DESIGN

Chapter Introduction — 374
Kelly Walters

The Black Designer's Journey: Theory of Change — 376
Yocasta Lachapelle

In Pursuit of a Prismatic Profession — 384
Forest Young

&&&: Provoking Type — 392
Schessa Garbutt

1 Word / 1 Object — 402
Former and Current Design Students

Curating My Way into Design: A Work in Progress — 420
Michelle Joan Wilkinson

My Journey to Design — 438
Sabine Maxine Lopez

Moving On: Interview with White Male Academic — 446
Aisha Richards

7 — 7.6 DESIGN = ART ≠ DESIGN

Chapter Introduction — 456
Kelly Walters

In Conversation: Nontsikelelo Mutiti & — 458
Kelly Walters on Image Making, Conceptual
Process, and the Tools of Design

In Conversation: Cey Adams & Kelly Walters — 466
on Design Detours & Artistic Possibilities

Design (Is) Art. If You Want It to Be. — 474
Rick Griffith

SECTION	CONTENTS	PAGE

In Conversation: Mimi Ọnụọha & Romi
Morrison on Unsettling the Equivalents — 484

In Conversation: Rhea L. Combs & Anne H. Berry — 496
on Representing Everyday Black Lives through
Film & Photography

8 — 8.7   COLLECTIVE, RADICAL &
LIBERATORY SPACES IN DESIGN

Chapter Introduction — 504
Lesley-Ann Noel

for colored girls who feel trapped — 506
in white institutions
Lauren Williams

The Black Student Union — 510
Terrence Moline

Make the Path by Talking — 518
Maurice Cherry

Building BADG: The Guild as a Model for — 524
Liberatory Space
Malene Barnett

Designer Profile: Ari Melenciano — 532
Lesley-Ann Noel & Anne H. Berry

This Is Our Time! adrienne maree brown — 538
on Design, Liberation, and Transformation
as told to Lesley-Ann Noel

GUIDING QUESTIONS — 545

GLOSSARY — 560

SECTION	CONTENTS	PAGE

	Letter to Future Designers	567
	Penina Laker	
	On Writing & Editing this Book	570
	Jennifer Rittner & Anne H. Berry	
AFTERWORD	Eddie Opara	573
	BIOS	576
	ACKNOWLEDGMENTS	591
	INDEX	596

FOREWORD:
EMORY DOUGLAS

PAST IS PROLOGUE: EMORY DOUGLAS'
BLACK EXPERIENCE IN DESIGN

As told to Colette Gaiter

The editors of this anthology celebrate the historic contributions of Black designers across the African diaspora who have inspired and informed us. Their unique experiences—and the many identities, expressions, and reflections they contain—offer invaluable insights into the possibilities for understanding our collective experiences. These stories also inform action, specifically about how design will be taught, researched, practiced, curated, critiqued, and created in the future.

Before introducing the sixty-five contributions to the Black Experience in Design, we are honored to share a brief reflection from Emory Douglas, from an interview conducted by Colette Gaiter in October 2021 for this book. Douglas's work as the renowned graphic designer for the Black Panther Party has found new resonances in the 21st century. Here he reflects on his experiences as a commercial art student in San Francisco in the early 1960s.

Through his conversation with Colette Gaiter, we witness many threads woven throughout this book: encouragement, opportunity, disappointment, isolation, ingenuity, artistry, excellence, vision, and resilience. We thank Mr. Douglas for his tremendous contributions to liberation art, the discipline of design, and this book. *This interview was edited for clarity. —The Editors*

EMORY DOUGLAS: I consider myself a manufacturer of art, of creativity. Starting out at the City College of San Francisco in the mid-1960s, I learned techniques and processes, including figure drawing, concept design, typography, and understanding the basic printing concepts behind publishing.

My teachers were supportive. They observed all of us students closely to see what we were doing and what our skill level was. They encouraged us to work as if we were professionals, and if we showed improvement, we got referred to freelance jobs. Our instructors wanted to see us get to the next level. They looked at our work from a professional perspective and compared it to what was going on in the field.

One professor noticed how I was improving and referred me to a paid illustration job for a science instructor at the college. Later I was sent for a job at a silkscreen factory doing T-shirts and other printing; and to another doing paste-up for Dorfman's Fine Wine Goblets and Silverware in downtown San Francisco. I worked on newspaper ads that ran two or three times a week and made signs for the products displayed in the windows.

In class, I worked on a fashion design project, where I designed shoes and clothing using images from *Ebony* magazine as my references. The people in my drawings were Black. When I showed my professor the work, he praised it. But he also said, "I have to be honest with you. It will be another ten years before this will be accepted in the field." Ten years later, in the 1970s, sure enough, you started to see it—Black people, regularly, in advertisements and design. That instructor was being truthful to the reality of institutional racism and bigotry that existed at the time.

At another point, our class had to create a short, animated film from storyboard to frames. We wrote the story, made storyboards, then used rolls of butcher paper to draw the animation. My story was about an African dignitary who came to the United States dressed in traditional clothing and was treated with respect and honor. Later he came back dressed like an American Black person and was told he was not welcome and was denied entry to the country. The professor's reaction was, "This doesn't seem to be provocative enough; you need to emphasize this a little bit more." I took that to mean that he thought I should make the racism and double standard more obvious.

I was lucky to go to the City College of San Francisco with the teachers who were there at that time and encouraged me to do the work necessary to become a professional. That training helped me improve my advertising and creative skills, which I used at the same time for a variety of promotional materials in the Black Arts Movement. I designed flyers and posters for events—even stage props and simple sets for theater productions.

For young designers starting out today, I would encourage them to understand the fundamentals and be open to having their work critiqued. Critique helps take the work to the next phase, the next level—for any kind of design they are doing. Part of design is being open to criticism and evaluation because you are always creating for someone other than yourself. You can be frustrated by requests for changes, but that is the reality of working in this business.

You can't design in an ivory tower. You have to have your ears and eyes open, stay alert and aware of what ideas and goals are progressive. And even if you work a nine-to-five job, know that you can still do work for social movements. It is possible.

This book, *The Black Experience in Design*, provides guidance and context that was not available to me when I started in the field. It gives young people entering design an opportunity to hear from Black designers, educators, scholars, and thinkers whose experiences overlap in some ways and are unique in other ways. All of the essays add up to a way of seeing design that was not possible in the past. I am happy that this book will support design educators and help students find their way into meaningful design work. That way has been paved by those who came before and generously share their memories and thinking with those who are entering the field, who have more opportunities than ever to shape their individual experience in design.

FOREWORD:
RUHA BENJAMIN

PARABLE OF THE BLACK DESIGNER

Thou art like unto
the pupil of the eye
which is dark in colour,
yet it is the fount of light
and the revealer of the
contingent world.

—'Abdu'l-Bahá[1]

In her 1993 novel, *Parable of the Sower*, famed writer Octavia E. Butler imagines a dystopian world plagued with every imaginable crisis: disease, environmental collapse, authoritarianism, corporate greed, and violence born of deep-seated inequities. It is a world, in short, that resembles our own. At one point, the Black teenage protagonist at the heart of the story, Lauren Oya Olamina, contends,

All struggles are essentially
power struggles. Who will rule?
Who will lead? Who will define,
refine, confine, design?[2]

Design. Prescient as always, Butler's words echo across the decades, from the 70-pound Adler manual typewriter she chained to her desk because three previous typewriters had been stolen, to the sleek device on which you are likely reading this text.[3] The technologies may have changed dramatically over time—faster, more networked, and rapacious in consuming every, last bit of data they can manage—but the deadly hierarchies that animated Butler's writing have only grown starker. Innovation, after all, breeds inequity, not inevitably, but predictably.

The pursuit of seamless and "frictionless" technology too often covers up social frictions, like the racist and sexist harassment many of us experience online in the name of "free speech" and "connection." But connection is no straightforward good when we are being connected to those who despise us. Too often, technological ease and speed are inversely related to social progress, because only a small sliver of humanity currently shapes the digital worlds which the rest of us inhabit.

16

The Jamaican philosopher Sylvia Wynter notes that there are different genres of humanity, but that we too often conflate the dominant genre, Man, with humanity as a whole.[4] The Man is cisgendered, raced, classed, able-bodied, and so on, standing in for the wide variety of ways that people move in the world, the many ways of being human. The imperative, as I see it, is to not only approach design from the perspectives of those who are routinely written out of Humanity—those who are type-cast or get no speaking parts—but to draw on their insights, imagination, and expertise from the very beginning.[5]

Similar to frictionless design, minimalist design has its own history and politics. In 2020, as monuments to white supremacy were being toppled in the wake of protests for racial justice, the renowned graphic designer Cheryl D. Miller was asked, "So, what is the rebel flag or Confederate monument of design, to you?" She responded that the dominant aesthetics associated with minimalist sophistication have an altogether different meaning to her:

I would like to retire the Paul Rand look. I would like to retire mid-century Helvetica. I want to retire flush left. I want to retire white space. It is the look of my oppressor . . . a mid-century era when it wasn't easy to enter the New York marketplace as a Black designer. When I see that look, the only thing it says to me is, "You cannot enter. You don't belong. You're not good enough."[6]

To wit, the white space of design aesthetics reflects the white space of professional design worlds. This, moreover, was a political choice intended to reinforce hierarchies which then became naturalized as simply "good design" over time.

Indeed, science, technology, and design are powerful tools for naturalizing racist and sexist hierarchies. But we can also appropriate them to denaturalize social hierarchies.[7] As a first step, we need to know how these hierarchies were constructed in the first place. In "Graphic Designers Have Always Loved Minimalism. But At What Cost?" (2021), Jarrett Fuller reminds us that,

In 1910, the architect and essayist Adolf Loos wrote his famous treatise "Ornament and Crime," which decried the excessive ornamentation he saw in Art Nouveau and foreshadowed the upcoming Modernist movement. He called ornamentation "primitive" and wrote that decoration was for "degenerates." His entire essay, based on a racist cultural

*superiority, repeatedly uses words
like "criminal," "amoral," and "barbar-
ian" to describe ornament, comparing
the arts and crafts from indigenous
populations to that of children.*[8]

Loos called for society to move beyond these old ways into modernity: "The evolution of culture is synonymous with the removal of ornament," he claimed. There is also a parallel history of early architects of scientific thinking working to remove ornamental or flowery writing from scientific texts. Any hint of the first-person subjectivity of the author was seen as a distraction, delegitimizing scientific claims for an already ambivalent public.[9]

In the same way that scientific writing eschews ornamental writing, science has eschewed non-white, feminized, and working-class people. How convenient—the very humans science has objectified are deemed "not objective." Only one genre of humanity, Man, could be trusted to give us scientific facts by ventriloquizing nature, in the same way that only one genre of humanity has monopolized the white space of technological design.

Fortunately, a critical reckoning with this racist history is giving rise to new initiatives excavating and retelling histories that have been erased or distorted, including a recent book on a *History of Arab Graphic Design*, as well as the long-awaited volume you are reading now!

This is not simply about "inclusion and diversity"—a liberal project that recognizes the design traditions of racialized groups. The issue is that the dominant approaches to technological design hide and perpetuate the violent frictions of our world. In *The Longing for Less*, Kyle Chayka argues that minimalism always obscures complexity: "The minimalist interface you use to order your takeout, for example, sits above a complex network of gig workers that make sure your ramen is still warm when it arrives. The simple presentation hides the complicated system just below the surface, whether that is the infrastructure for data collection or the multi-conglomerate corporation"[10]—or the labor violations upon which so much frictionless digital convenience rests.

But *less* friction for some humans means *more* friction for others, not inevitably, but predictably.[11] So now what?

In "Critical Race Theory for HCI,"[12] the authors offer a number of concrete steps for designers of all backgrounds. They note that while there is more race-conscious research that doesn't shy away from social frictions, most of this work still sees race as a characteristic of the researcher or the participant group that should be considered in design, rather than as a feature of our history and social systems. Indeed, many people still operate with a simplified understanding of race as a trait or property of individuals—you have a race and I have a race that we tick off on government forms—rather than as a founding political principle of modern life that justifies inequality. This principle operates differently in different parts of the world, such that the way people are racialized is shaped by class, caste, culture, religion, language, and other social fault lines, but that is all naturalized as an inherent characteristic of individuals.

Race, we might say, is all about minimalism. It is a technology for hiding complexity. And unless you are harmed by racist systems, it is hard to see beneath the slick branding of racial minimalism. But that is precisely what we must do. This point is often easier to grasp when we look to the past, as with this ad from a 1957 *Mechanix Illustrated* magazine:

> The robots are coming! And when they do, you'll command a host of push-button servants. In 1863 Abe Lincoln freed the slaves, but by 1965, slavery will be back! We'll all have personal slaves again. Don't be alarmed. We mean robot "slaves."

That one little word, again, lets us know who the imagined "users" of this technology are, certainly not those who are the descendants of people who were enslaved the first time. They are raced, classed, and gendered without race, class, or gender ever mentioned . . . these interlocking systems encoded again and again.[13]

At first blush, we may seem to have come a long way from "robot slaves" when, in 2021, the most popular Super Bowl ad featured the Black actor Michael B. Jordan as the embodiment of Amazon's Alexa. In the commercial, we see a Black woman shopping for an Alexa device and imagining Jordan as the sexy voice of her digital assistant. "Diversity," "inclusion," and "Black representation" are all rolled into one slick ad.

But at the very same time that Amazon gave us Sexy Black Alexa, February 2021, the company was trying to crush the unionization of mostly Black and Latinx workers in its Bessemer, Alabama warehouse. I wonder whether Michael B. Jordan as Alexa would top the list of what "inclusive" technology looks like, if we asked those who have to deal with oppressive algorithms governing how fast they must work, when they can take breaks, and whether they have enough time to shit or only pee. Too often, cosmetic representation—digital Blackface—stands in for substantive change to the real conditions of people's lives. So, how do we move toward the latter?

For starters, I invite you to listen carefully to the contributors to this volume, for they, like Lauren Olamina, are seeding new ways of thinking, imagining, and building a new world amid the rubble of the old.

NOTES

1. 'Abdu'l-Bahá. 1978. *Selections From the Writings of 'Abdu'l-Bahá*. Wilmette, IL: Baha'i Publishing, p. 161.
2. Butler, Octavia E. 1993. *Parable of the Sower*, p. 94.
3. Butler interview by Julie Dash, available here: https://www.youtube.com/watch?v=y4DHYK2y3zM
4. McKittrick, Katherine. 2015. *Sylvia Wynter: On Being as Praxis*. Duke University Press.
5. In "Eliciting Tech Futures Among Black Young Adults," Carrington and Dillahunt (2021) write, "When potential harm to Black and Brown communities is an afterthought HCI research is tasked to study how to alleviate harm or expand inclusion after system deployment, considering communities of color after development as opposed to them being considered architects of the initial innovation." https://dl.acm.org/doi/10.1145/3411764.3445723
6. Korsunskiy, Eugene. "Dismantling White Supremacy in Design Classrooms: My Conversation With Design Guru Cheryl D. Miller." *Medium*, Sept 1, 2020, available here: https://medium.com/future-of-design-in-higher-education/dismantling-white-supremacy-in-design-classrooms-my-conversation-with-design-guru-cheryl-d-miller-5dc9c48b15e4
7. Eglash, Ron, et al. 2004. *Appropriating Technology: Vernacular Science and Social Power*. University of Minnesota Press.
8. In Fuller's account, "the idealization of minimalism erases the vernacular of local cultures and the plurality of human experience—race, gender, class—reinforcing the myth that design decisions are neutral while creating aesthetic hierarchies of good and bad design. What started as a utopian ideal leading us into an egalitarian future, inevitably would become another system of oppression, pushing the tastes of the few onto the many." https://eyeondesign.aiga.org/graphic-designers-have-always-loved-minimalism-but-at-what-cost/
9. Shapin, Steven, and Simon Schaffer. 2017. *Leviathan and the Air Pump: Hobbes, Boyle, and Experimental Life*. Princeton University Press.

10. "Graphic Designers Have Always Loved Minimalism. But At What Cost?" available at https://ipassas.com/ graphic_design_and_typography/graphic-designers-have -always-loved-minimalism-but-at-what-cost/. See also, *The Longing for Less: Living with Minimalism* by Kyle Chayka (2020) Bloomsbury Publishing.

11. As the authors of "Who Gets to Future?" (2019) write, "As a discipline, HCI has taken steps to introduce policies and practices that remediate the effects of discrimination. Yet, rarely grappling with racism directly, this work raises questions of complicity within the field . . . To what extent do we, as designers, hide the workings of racism? To what degree do we learn to treat design techniques as portable without accounting for the legacies of racial struggle that surround them?"

12. Ogbonnaya-Ogburu, Ihudiya Finda, Angela D. R. Smith, Alexandra To, and Kentaro Toyama. "Critical Race Theory for HCI." In *Proceedings of the 2020 CHI Conference on Human Factors in Computing Systems*, pp. 1–16. 2020.

13. Benjamin, Ruha. 2019. *Race After Technology: Abolitionist Tools for the New Jim Code*. Polity. emphasis added.

WHY IS THIS BOOK NEEDED?
ANNE H. BERRY

You got to love it. This is flesh I'm talking about here. Flesh that needs to be loved. Feet that need to rest and to dance; backs that need support; shoulders that need arms, strong arms I'm telling you. And O my people, out yonder, hear me, they do not love your neck unnoosed and straight. So love your neck; put a hand on it, grace it, stroke it and hold it up. And all your inside parts that they'd just as soon slop for hogs, you got to love them. The dark, dark liver—love it, love it and the beat and beating heart, love that too. More than eyes or feet. More than lungs that have yet to draw free air. More than your life-holding womb and your life-giving private parts, hear me now, love your heart. For this is the prize. —Toni Morrison, Beloved

In the summer of 2020, the United States was on fire, both literally and figuratively. The *unprecedented* forest fires raging along the West Coast and the physical toll taken on the natural environment became a metaphor for the emotional impact on the country in the aftermath of the police killings of Ahmaud Arbery, Breonna Taylor, and George Floyd. The deaths of these Black Americans, along with countless others, served as the spark that gave rise to subsequent flames, igniting national protests born of frustration and anger at the lack of police accountability and the trivialization of Black lives. Across the country, as organizations and businesses publicly touted their support for the Black Lives Matter (BLM) movement and promoted Diversity, Equity, and Inclusion (DEI) initiatives in response to national BLM protests, the renewed and collective sense of urgency about America's racial reckoning seemed to take root.

Yet predictably, many months later, the signs of change—or, more charitably stated, commitments to change—are difficult to measure. As we speak, legislators are actively working to repress the voting rights of millions of Americans, disproportionately affecting communities of color; to bury American history centered in Black experiences and perspectives; and to ban Critical Race Theory (CRT) from being taught or even discussed in schools.

Consequently, the question of "Why is this book needed?" is both rhetorical and evergreen. Broadly speaking, this book is needed because documenting and preserving Black American history, a history that elected officials are attempting to erase before our eyes, in real-time, is of national and international consequence. Not unlike the Negro spirituals/slave songs that helped preserve the narratives of Black people in American, we must share, we must tell, we must document, and we must remember. The alternative is to trivialize the devastating impact of slavery and its aftermath, deny the value of immigration, erase the reality of who and what America is, and dishonor the memories of so many who suffered in order to hold the United States to its highest ideals.

On a narrower, design-focused level, this text is needed because published works by Black creatives about our own contributions are still too few and far between. This book is needed because Black creatives have been historically excluded and consistently represented through a white lens, our work and efforts co-opted and appropriated by predominantly white, mainstream culture. And perhaps most importantly, this book is needed to reaffirm that Black people, Indigenous people, and people of color, whether students or practitioners in creative fields, are part of a community where our gifts and talents are needed.

Additionally, the perspectives represented in this book are wide-ranging and varied, reflecting the diversity that exists within Black communities. In this sense, the very title is an intentional paradox. There is, in fact, no single Black experience. There is no single Black perspective. Nor is "The Black Experience" a concept that can be easily captured, branded, and packaged with a beautiful design bow. The essence of Blackness is simultaneously complex, deeply rooted, deeply felt, and above all else, human.

Beyond shared experiences that exist for Black people in the United States, what is Black in America is also inherently diasporic. In some ways, consequently, this book is as much a conversation about what it means to be Black as it is a book about design or a book about Black designers. And though many of the conversations and essays are situated within an American context, the contributions are also indicative of the cultures and influences that exist outside the United States. For us, that which is local is also global. There are, for example, a number of references to the concept of "sankofa," of looking back in order to inform the ways in which we move forward, as well as emphases on community and community-building across continents and cultures. So, whether our ancestors were brought to America as slaves in chains or emigrated, or whether we ourselves came to the United States from other countries, we are connected and bound, somewhat ironically, via the diaspora.

The threads of these global and local connections are woven together throughout each chapter, beginning with the late Sylvia Harris's seminal essay, "Searching for a Black Aesthetic in American Graphic Design." In addition to asking the question "How do we construct and document a Black design tradition?" she urges us to "contribute to [the existing] body of knowledge and support a generation of designers hungry to see their people and experience reflected in the mirror of our profession." *The Black Experience in Design* is our response to this call: by sharing our stories and highlighting our contributions—including new/innovative methods and models for teaching and research—we are painting an inclusive picture of the design world that also contributes to the larger establishment of a constructed and documented Black design tradition. As a postscript to Harris's essay, Steven Heller provides reflections about their collaborative work and his accounting for the larger, systemic problems regarding the lack of published texts by Black designers.

In *Design Practices*, we learn how Black creatives cultivate, hone, and master the skills necessary to develop and sustain their creative work and output. Artist, designer, and educator Dorothy Hayes provides a historical foundation by acknowledging the work of Black design trailblazers. Her essay for *Communication Arts* is followed by Darhil Crooks, Ian Spalter, and Dantley Davis, R. Vann Graves, Jon Key, Quinlin B. Messenger, and Annika Hansteen-Izora who identify the processes they've gone through in order to move past barriers and celebrate their successes. They emphasize the role of identity in shaping their respective modes of practice that are also free from psychological and institutional constraints.

Design Education subsequently captures the voices of Black design educators Maurice Woods, Colette Gaiter, Steve Jones, Terresa Moses, Chris Rudd, and Kaleena Sales. Reflecting on education, themselves, and how their own experiences as Black design students are manifested in their roles as educators, they lay bare the obstacles they continue to confront and offer the methods they employ for addressing these challenges.

Building on the previous chapters, the essays in *Design Scholarship* provide insights into the tools employed by Black scholars for critical approaches to design, including the interrogation of existing systems and structures—even the premise of "The Black Experience in

Design." Most important, Audrey G. Bennett, Nii Kommey Botchway, Cheryl D. Miller, Alicia Olushola Ajayi, and David Pilgrim each identify the experiences that inspired them to pursue their respective areas of research, building on existing scholarship to document the earliest roots of Black contributions to design.

Activism, Advocacy, and Community-Engaged Design calls attention to the sense of purpose that is a necessary part of the creative process for many Black creatives. From utilizing collective voices and modes of expression to embracing politics and advocacy and amplifying marginalized voices, Mugendi K. M'Rithaa, Jennifer White-Johnson, Sloan Leo, June A. Grant, Michele Y. Washington, Amos Kennedy, Liz Ogbu, and Raja Schaar make evident the extent to which design practice is synonymous with design activism. This chapter delves deeply into aspects of design that focus on serving communities in need and magnifies the voices of practitioners who partner with underrepresented and under-resourced communities. Though this design subfield is popular among designers looking to use their skills for social good, lack of experience with long-term relationship-building and cultural competencies—particularly when designers opt to work in communities outside of their own—have led to harmful systemic practices. Contributors to this chapter also speak about the various opportunities for healing that can be nurtured.

Though discussions about race in design often focus on the past or present, contributors to the chapter on *Afrofuturism in Design* demonstrate ways in which imagining and reimagining more inclusive technological futures can provide agency for Black designers. Lonny Avi Brooks, Woodrow W. Winchester III, Adah Parris, John Jennings, and Folayemi Wilson speak to the power of storytelling, challenging oppressive systems and notions of race, working within new and generative frameworks as a part of design practice, and celebrating Black imagination.

Journeys in Design highlights the diversity of career paths of Black designers and the routes their respective trajectories have taken, regardless of their traditional training or informal paths into design. Essays by Yocasta Lachapelle, Forest Young, and Schessa Garbutt prelude artifacts from recent design students that are represented through a single object accompanied by a single word. Michelle Joan Wilkinson, Sabine Maxine Lopez, and Aisha Richards bookend the chapter. Addressing topics from Black and Queer representation to navigating career shifts and evolutions across institutions, the authors identify barriers associated with developing professional networks and navigating professional careers as well as the importance of taking advantage of opportunities that present themselves.

In Design = Art ≠ Design, Nontsikelelo Mutiti, Cey Adams, Rick Griffith, Mimi Ọnụọha and Romi Morrison, and Rhea L. Combs provide wide-ranging perspectives on the relationship between art and design. The contexts in which they encounter or practice design differ, yet the distinctions in how the terms are defined, how Black designers and creatives position their work, and how Black identity and representation intersect within the space of art/design collectively speak to the necessary and symbiotic relationship between the two.

Lastly, in Collective, Radical, and Liberatory Spaces in Design, Lauren Williams, Terrence Moline, Maurice Cherry, Malene Barnett, Ari Melenciano, and adrienne maree brown talk about the necessity of building spaces specifically for Black self-preservation, emancipation, liberation, and celebration. From professional organizations, networking websites, social media groups, podcasts, design guilds, conferences, and tech camps, they share the models and methods they have developed to both foster community and help Black creatives thrive.

Given the extent to which these chapter areas over-lap, drawing distinctions might be somewhat of a contradiction. And yet, categorization, however imperfectly configured, provides a way for us to acknowledge and document the breadth and depth of contributions Black designers and creatives are making. We aim to emphasize the substantive nature and impact of the work being undertaken as a testament to our influence in shaping the field of design as well as American culture more broadly.

The Black Experience in Design is our collective effort to acknowledge, celebrate, and document the ways in which Black people generally and Black creatives specifically have been contributing to the very fabric of America and helping to define what it means to be American for centuries. We were here! We are here! We will continue to be here!

SEARCHING FOR A BLACK AESTHETIC IN AMERICAN GRAPHIC DESIGN: SYLVIA HARRIS

0.2

Editor's Note: In order to help frame the significance of The Black Experience in Design, we have republished Sylvia Harris's seminal essay, "Searching for a Black Aesthetic in American Graphic Design," and her call to broaden entry points into design and help students find rootedness in the design profession through cultural connections. Because the late Harris was so pivotal in bridging connections between design education, design practice, and design scholarship, we have also included some reflections by Steven Heller about her contributions and the larger questions around the lack of published writing by Black designers.

What influence have African Americans had on contemporary graphic design? Is there such a thing as an African American design aesthetic? These are questions that I have been asking designers and art historians for the last ten years. The answer I am usually given is, "I don't know." The relationship of ethnic minorities to the development of American graphic design is rarely discussed or documented by our profession because of the historic lack of racial diversity in the field. However, increasing numbers of African Americans entering the profession are calling for a fresh look at graphic design history in order to discover the aesthetic contributions of their people.

In 1971, when I entered design school, there was only one other Black student in attendance. Twenty-five years later, this situation has improved slightly. Today, I teach graphic design at the university level and have one or two Black students in my department each year. Those students often exhibit insecurities that negatively affect their performance. In fact, they experience a problem common to many Black design professionals: the feeling that they are not completely welcome in the profession. Lack of exposure to the prevailing aesthetic traditions also puts them at a disadvantage. This outsider posture leads many Black designers to compulsively imitate and assimilate mainstream aesthetic traditions in order to feel accepted and be successful. More often than not, Black designers and students are trapped in a strategy of imitation rather than innovation.

The graphic design profession is driven by visual innovation. The most visible and celebrated designers are those who are continuously innovating within, or in opposition to, the prevailing schools of design thought. Black designers are working at a disadvantage when they do not feel a kinship with existing design traditions and also have no evidence of an alternative African or African American design tradition upon which to base their work. In 1995, Claude Steele completed groundbreaking research on the links between performance and self-esteem, which indicated that self-confidence may be the single most important influence in the lives of successful African Americans. For instance, the spectacular success of Black musicians demonstrates the relationship between confidence, leadership, and success. Black musicians have been successful because they feel confident and secure about their work. They are secure because they are working within intimately known traditions built by others like themselves, and they are motivated by the thrill of adding to that successful body of work.

Is there a potential design tradition that can fuel Black designers in the same way that Black music traditions fuel Black musicians? By "Black tradition" I do not mean Black subject matter or imagery, but the styling and expressions common to people of African descent. I believe this tradition does exist, but Black contributions to America's rich graphic design history have been overlooked, so far, by design historians who have focused either on European influences or on the current phenomenon of cultural hybridity. Buried in libraries and design journals is evidence of Black graphic styles and influences stretching from the New Negro movement of the 1920s through the hip-hop aesthetics of the latest generation of designers. I believe that this material, if uncovered, has the potential to nurture a new generation of designers.

How do we construct and document a Black design tradition? There is already a small body of research on the lives of America's first Black designers. Chronicling the work of these pioneers is an important first step, but most of these brave people were so concerned with surviving within a hostile profession that their work expresses little that is uniquely African American. I believe that the building blocks of a Black design aesthetic are scattered across many disciplines and will be found in unlikely places. For instance, some of the best examples of the potential for a Black design vocabulary are found in the work of white designers who have been inspired by Black culture and take advantage of the market for Black expressive styles.

We must also look outside the design disciplines to the performing arts and to fine arts movements, such as the Afri-Cobra, which have based visual explorations on African and jazz rhythms. We can study these disciplines for characteristic Black expression (improvisation, distortion, polyrhythms, exaggeration, call-and-response) that can be translated into graphic form. Black design traditions must be pieced together from a variety of sources to make a complete canon of Black expression.

In discussion with design educators (both Black and white), many argue that to focus too much attention on Black aesthetics will limit the full creative expression of Black designers. They argue that Black designers have spent the last twenty years working to erase race and class bias in the profession; to them a focus on Blackness invites discrimination. I disagree. Black designers have access, training, and opportunity; what they lack is the drive that comes from innovation. And in order to thrive, innovation requires a tradition to either build on or oppose. It is up to us as historians and educators to research and teach in a way that addresses the unique cultural experience of all our students. Right now, Black design students would benefit greatly from a study of their design traditions. Otherwise, they may be doomed to a future of bad imitations.

The notes below are excerpts from my ongoing search for Black influences in American design.

1920S: THE NEW NEGRO MOVEMENT

In his first design history book, *A History of Graphic Design*, Philip Meggs stated that "a collision between cubist painting and futurist poetry spawned twentieth-century graphic design." Early twentieth-century cubist artists were obsessed with visualizing modern technological and social freedom. The style of the non-Western people of the world, particularly those who had perfected forms of abstraction and symbolism, were quickly drawn into the stylistic vortex created by this modernist revolution. In this way, Black graphic expressions made their debut in the Western world indirectly, through the works of cubist artists such as Georges Braque, Pablo Picasso, and Fernand Léger. All these artists later acknowledged the significant impact of African art on their work; however, most scholarly writing about cubism has obscured its African roots. Postmodern art scholarship, starting with William Rubin's book *"Primitivism" in Twentieth-Century Art: Affinity of the Tribal and the Modern*, has begun to record and study the role of African art in the invention of cubism and the success of the modernist movement.

By the 1920s, "jazz" became not only a musical term, but a stylistic one. European designers, who were influenced by the pioneering work of cubist painters, struggled to capture the spirit of modernism through the expression of jazz rhythms and motifs. The expression of jazz style in the design of popular communications in the 1920s represents the first appearance of what can clearly be considered a Black-inspired graphic design style. The jazz-era climate of relative freedom in the North created an environment for Blacks to publish and design their own publications. During this "renaissance," Alain Locke cited the emergence of the "New Negro" and declared that Black culture was the appropriate source of inspiration and content for African American artists. He argued that the art of Black people was a powerful inspiration to successful white artists, so why shouldn't Black artists also work with this powerful force? One of the first designers to give graphic expression to this call was a European modernist, Winold Reiss, who created African-inspired logotypes and titles for the book *The New Negro*. Young Black artists, most notably Aaron Douglas, were encouraged by Reiss and Locke to expand the emerging modernist trends and lead the emerging New Negro art and design movement.

The line between artist and designer was still blurred in the 1920s. Many artists were illustrators, and illustrators were often typographers. The best examples of the African aesthetic in the designs of the 1920s are seen in Black-owned journals. The designers of these publications were often Black artists, influenced by European cubist painters, who were, in turn, influenced by African art. Artists such as Aaron Douglas, one of the best of these artists/designers of the time, learned to recognize and resonate with the African in cubism. Douglas and other Black designers had a unique opportunity to express Black style in a world that was starved for fresh, anti-Victorian imagery. Douglas's covers for the quarterly magazine *Fire!!* show the emergence of a unique graphic design expression that combines the syntax of cubism with the forms of African art.

1930S: REVIVAL OF BLACK FOLK TRADITIONS AND THE ICONOGRAPHY OF BLACK LABOR

The prolific jazz-age production of Black art and design was cut short by the Depression of the 1930s. However, during the 1930s and early 1940s, a revival of Black folk traditions occurred, prompted by the direct observations of anthropologists and folklorists such as Zora Neale Hurston, Southern white writers such as DuBose Heyward, and interviewers for the Works Progress Administration's (WPA) oral history project on slavery. Artists supported by federal arts programs and socialist groups interpreted Black folk and labor themes in programs, posters, fliers, and other printed materials. It is not clear how much of this material was designed by Blacks; examples buried in archives await inspection, interpretation, and inclusion in the design history texts.

1940S TO 1950S: COMMERCIAL ART

Printing and publishing before and during World War II were significantly segregated. Unlike the fine arts professions, publishing institutions were restricted by racism and classism. Most printed publications and commercial art that circulated in Black communities were generated by white-owned presses and designers. However, we do know that some Black printers and photographers worked successfully in Black communities; their products, including letterpress posters for popular music performances, were based on vernacular traditions and contributed directly to a continuing Black graphic aesthetic.

1970S: THE AESTHETICS OF BLACK POWER

It is interesting to note that the bursts of Black graphic production in the twentieth century occurred during eras in which young people were preoccupied with concepts of freedom. It is no surprise that the 1960s saw a renewed interest in African American visual expression fueled by Black cultural nationalism. Some of the work of this period combined socialist protest-art forms with Black in-your-face bodaciousness to create a graphic design product that was uniquely African American. This decade of Black graphics reflects the aesthetics of resistance and Black power.

1980S TO 1990S: TRIBAL CHIC

Popular designers and illustrators such as Keith Haring and David Carson benefited from the lack of Black participation in the design profession during the late-1980s surge of interest in rebellious urban style. They shaped new styles and lucrative careers based on bold public vernacular expression such as graffiti and rap, class rebellions and Black rhythms, and tribal symbolism. At the first Organization of Black Designers conference, filmmaker Arthur Jaffa cited David Carson's *Ray Gun* magazine as offering the best example of a visual jazz aesthetic.

1990S: THE NEW NEW NEGRO MOVEMENT

There are a handful of Black designers who are designing for Black audiences and, in doing so, are continuing Black visual traditions into the next century. For instance, designers for new Black media, including the magazine *YSB*, give graphic form to contemporary Black culture. Like the artists of the original New Negro movement of the twenties, these designers use Black vernacular stylings and African expression to inform their aesthetic decisions. The designers of this new generation are not isolated. They are working within a long tradition that, though they may not be aware of it, stretches across the century.

These notes are presented as snapshots and pointers to the research waiting to be undertaken. It is my hope that American designers and scholars will contribute to this body of knowledge and support a generation of designers hungry to see their people and experience reflected in the mirror of our profession.

ON SYLVIA HARRIS: THE CONTRIBUTIONS OF BLACK DESIGNERS

0.3

Editor's Note: As an addendum to the reprint of Sylvia Harris's essay "Searching for a Black Aesthetic in American Graphic Design," which was published in *The Education of a Graphic Designer*, I spoke with author Steven Heller about the impact of Harris's contributions to design as well as the design industry's responsibility when it comes to challenging "subtle or benign white dominance" in the field.

ANNE H. BERRY: **What did you learn through the process of coediting the "Who Owns Cultural Imagery" *AIGA Journal of Graphic Design* issue with Sylvia Harris? What was significant or noteworthy about that collaboration?**

STEVEN HELLER: When I edited the magazine version of the *AIGA Journal* (this was 1996), I often invited coeditors to collaborate on themes dear to or burning in their hearts. Sylvia Harris Woodard was the perfect choice for this one. The overall number was called "The Property Issue" based on the fact that in 1995 Bill Gates had bought the Bettmann Archive, the largest licensing and rental repository of public domain and copyright protected visuals. The implications of such ownership were astounding then. Think of it now. Sylvia and I discussed the fact that even before this acquisition, widespread and injurious appropriation and "borrowing" of cultural images was status quo throughout the advertising and graphic design industries. I wrote in the editorial that Sylvia selected various writers, critics, historians, and designers "to explain the cultural, legal and ethical ramifications . . . issues that every designer should address about . . . the right of cultures to determine the use of their indigenous symbols and images."

In Sylvia's introduction to the theme, she wrote that the "losers . . . are often cultural minorities who have been systematically locked out of the American image making industries or silenced by a lack of capital and legal representation. Today that silence is being shattered as the protest against the misuse and commercialization of cultural imagery is directed not only at our clients, but at us: the image makers."

My memory is fixated on the cover showing one red and one Black plastic toy cowboy shooting at a Native American against a luminescent purple background. The issue title, "Who Owns Cultural Imagery" was set in typeface simulating East Asian characters. In other words, it is a visual cacophony of twisted clichés. We both loved that image.

Noteworthy about Sylvia's work is how she spoke with authority from cultural, historical, and legal perspectives. That she was able to leave emotion at the front door and enter the room with a firm grasp of what must be addressed and rectified. I gather that this issue made an impact on readers, but I'd be hard pressed to tell you we received many (or any) letters pro or con, but that was not unusual.

AHB: **Since that journal issue was published, there has continued to be a dearth of books, articles, and other published materials focused on the perspectives and contributions of Black designers. From your perspective, as someone who has published many books and articles, what are the root causes of these sustained disparities?**

SH: Until recently, designers could justify being above the fray, so to speak. I think there is a subtle (or not-so-subtle) form of benign neglect. So as not to look as though race really matters, racial concerns were marginalized. That said, certain designers and design scholars, including Michele Y. Washington and the late Victor Margolin, have made deep dives into the contemporary and historical practices of BIPOC designers, to compensate for that neglect and to discover designers lost or forgotten in the weeds. This investigation is not easy, because the root cause is simple: Most designers did not sign their work or take credit in the broader sense, in part because it took chutzpah to ask for or demand credit and many designers did not care as long as they had jobs. So agencies and studios took blanket credit. I believe that is changing now because the designer population is gradually changing. Women came first and BIPOC designers are beginning to teach and write more. That said, there are not as many outlets as there once were. This is a disappointment.

AHB: **What has made it particularly challenging for BIPOC designers to get their work or writing published? How has the design industry as a whole created "barriers to entry"?**

SH: There has been—and to an extent still is—a deep-seated but nevertheless demeaning undercurrent of "This is ostensibly a white profession" and only white writers can address critical complexities—in the same way that designers once claimed that non-designers (and even design educators) could not write critically about professional design practice (you may not recall but there was a schism between working professionals and full-time teachers). Of course, that's bullshit. One of the influential books on my own research and writing was by Eli Kince, a Black designer and Yale grad, who wrote *Visual Puns in Design: The Pun Used as a Communications Tool,* which opened my mind to how the lowest form of humor was the highest form of conceptual graphic problem-solving.

AHB: In 2004, Victor Margolin wrote about his epiphany regarding the lack of recognition given to Black designers and his own complicity in that lack of recognition. Would you say that you have had a similar experience or moment of revelation/awareness?

SH: Yes. I think it is the rule, not the exception. For me, it was, as stated before, benign neglect. I followed the historical trails that had been laid out by Eurocentric modernists and American traditionalists. The few Black designers I knew or knew about worked in a derivative Swiss or modern style—and sometimes in a generic manner. My epiphany came when Victor told me about his research. I began to realize that there was not a monolithic/white style.

            I also recall seeing a paper promotion that had portraits of some of the major design firms in the United States. Most of the principals in these group photos were of white males (some females, an Asian or two, and almost all in shirts, ties, and suspenders, looking like lawyers). Black design history is a more complex mélange in terms of its hierarchies of power and influence. Merit is not the only measure of significance. I think the advertising field caught on a little earlier than graphic design.

AHB: It's 2021. W. E. B. Du Bois's infographics are increasingly part of mainstream design history; Maurice Cherry has an award-winning podcast focused on the stories of Black designers; Polymode studio launched the BIPOC Design History lecture series which was well-attended and positively received; and a group of six Black designers is editing the kind of book that has not been previously published. What are your thoughts or reflections about how or why avenues of publishing and dissemination of content focused on Black, Indigenous, and people of color are opening up?

SH: I'd like to say, in the argot of the sixties "our *consciousness* was raised" but that's too facile. I loved the sixties film by Robert Downey Sr., *Putney Swope* about a New York ad agency, where a Black man, Putney Swope, was mistakenly elected the agency's president; he fired all the whites and fostered a Black Power revolution that brought Black culture to all the commercials. It was a great satire that predated the hip-hop ascendancy as a major aspect of global popular culture.

In truth, I think the time has come for subtle or benign white dominance in our field to be challenged. There is Black history in college, in film, in drama, in literature, in art, in music—why shouldn't there be the same in design? In fact, if design is treated as a consequence of social factors then it is inevitable that BIPOC design history is inevitable, needed, and wanted for many. (Nonetheless, some designers don't even give a damn about design history).

AHB: Technology obviously plays a role but what are the other factors? (Or, do we owe the majority of thanks to technological advancements?)

SH: Access to technology is a reason. So is a changing demographic. It is the rise of Black capitalism that civil rights leader Floyd McKissick proffered in the late sixties. Affirmative action, for all its naysayers, had something to do with it. Now more emphasis on Inclusion, Equity, and Diversity programs with professional actors taking a role in facilitation. A loosening but not altogether abandonment of the traditional caste system, too. There is the rise of design departments in art schools and universities (but not enough). All of this contributes to a new status and new status quo.

AHB: Is this evidence of a larger shift within the design industry or are there still a lot of barriers that BIPOCs will have to continue contending with?

SH: Change is always incremental. And there are always blocks that are viewed as new. We still need to redefine what best practices are and where cultural differences make a difference.

DESIGNING WITH COMPLEXITY: AN INTERSECTIONAL VIEW

0.4

PART I: INTERSECTIONAL US

Seventy writers, six editors, four continents. We are many ethnicities, genders, beliefs, languages, educational backgrounds, and professional practices. We are designers, artists, poets, writers, curators, futurists, activists, and critics. We are descendants of the great diaspora and ancestors for any who see themselves reflected in our stories. Our stories. They are a rich and honest tapestry of expressions that, even seventy strong, represent a modest fraction of the innumerable Black experiences in design. This anthology represents the many—though certainly not the all—of what it means to be a Black designer, educator, curator, or writer. It reflects many—though certainly not all—forms of Black expression, aesthetics, and perspectives on design.

We joyfully offer this book as an intersectional experience in which each essay is, in fact, much greater than any single practice, purpose, or point. While the essays are literally bound to a specific place inside of the physical object of this book, we invite you to read beyond that constraint. Their work and ideas are not containable only within the context of a narrow practice, which, of course, is the point.

Writers bound into chapters about community-centered practice intersect intimately with the makers of liberatory spaces, as well as those who are navigating the intersections of art and design. Our design scholarship essays might be read in the context of design practices or Afrofuturism. And the writers who share their journeys find themselves in dialogue with colleagues across all of these pages. These are all intersecting, cross-pollinating concerns that frame the range of discourses we are all initiating with one another and with our readers.

Intersections also abound in the multidisciplinary definitions of design: graphic, brand, product, UX, architecture, systems, and service design. As these essays reflect on the means, methods, and materials of design, the writers often propose pushing the boundaries of their salient disciplines. Architects consider the materiality of space while brand designers reflect on the wearability of identity. Industrial designers weave in and out of the physical and virtual while futurists transcend the very existence of time and space.

So here we all are in all of our complexities, intersection-alities, and multidimensionalities. There are no prescriptions to follow; no guidelines or tool kits to copy; no demands to align your particular, unique practices with ours. Just invitations to engage with the stories shared by these seventy unique souls who have agreed to share their particular Black experiences in design.

As we all embrace a range of intersectionalities that inform our identities and practices, we hope our readers see themselves reflected in this work, as well.

PART II: WHAT DO WE MEAN WHEN WE TALK ABOUT INTERSECTIONALITY?

First coined by the legal scholar Kimberlé Williams Crenshaw, now head of the African American Policy Forum (aapf.org), the term "intersectionality"[1] has transformed from a specific critique of legal and labor practices to become a more all-encompassing term referencing each of our multi-varied identities. It's worth noting that Crenshaw began her critique by invoking the term "multidimensionality," arguing that her critique will "center Black women in this analysis in order to contrast the multidimensionality of Black women's experience with the single-axis analysis that distorts these experiences."

The term "multidimensional" might serve us well here, as the term Intersectional is often misunderstood, distorted, or weaponized for political advantage. Crenshaw's terms—intersectional and multidimensional—frame the particular, dual oppressions Black women face, specifically in the workplace and in legal systems, because of historic discriminations against women (as a class) and African Americans (as a class). Intersectionality is, therefore, a temporal critique—a way of understanding how historical acts of disenfranchisement continue to materially impact Black women, in particular (but add to that Black lesbian women or Black trans women or Black disabled women or any other intersecting set of identities that have been historically marginalized by economic or social systems).

To be clear, intersectionality addresses systems of oppression that operate in ways that disadvantage particular identity groups, but it is not a critique of individual identities. Put more clearly, intersectionality as a critical framework is not antiwhite nor is it anti-male. It is a lens through which we can understand how built systems functionally disadvantage those who are *not* white and/or white males because those systems have historically advantaged three specific, intersecting classes of individuals—white people, white males, and males; and most systems continue to privilege those who hold those historically, culturally- and economically-dominant identities.

In one of the core cases Crenshaw cited in the original text—*DeGraffenreid v. General Motors*—she demonstrated that Black women were disproportionately impacted by company layoffs because they were hired later than either men or white women, both of whom had more seniority at the company as a result of historically discriminatory labor practices. In other words, the company had a history of employing white men, and only began hiring Black men in nonmanagement roles, and white women in discreet, gender-based roles. When the company started to allow Black workers to be hired, they only hired Black men, disallowing Black women from holding the types of jobs Black men held as well as the types of jobs white women held. When Black women were eventually permitted to hold (generally low-wage, low-skilled) jobs, they discovered that layoffs disproportionately removed them first from the payrolls because layoffs were based on how long workers had been employed, as well as how essential they were deemed, a judgment that was too easily made to favor white over Black workers.

Crenshaw's example was specific, but also broadly applicable. In companies around the country, hiring practices that favored white men first also established rules that centered the practices and proclivities of white men in their norms, standards, and cultures. As white women, Black men, and finally Black women gained entry into those spaces, the rules of white maleness had been fully established as *the* norms and thereby disadvantaged those who could not show up to suit. Among the clearest examples of the dual oppression against Black women can be seen in attitudes by white employers against Black women's hair. The demand for Black women to show up with straight, Europeanized hair has, for the better part of the last century, imposed both an emotional and financial tax on Black women in the workplace, and prevented many Black women from being hired for positions for which they were eminently qualified.

Replace hair with clothing choices, vernacular speech, and even given names to see how "corporate culture" has provided the means for marginalizing Black professionals who could not show up looking or sounding like their white counterparts. If you've heard it, you know it: The chosen word for this is "inappropriate." To be deemed inappropriate is to be told that your form of being in the world does not conform to the expectations and demands of the dominant culture. It is, in fact, a demand to shed personal culture in favor of dominant "universalism." To "fix" one's manner of speech, personal style, and moniker to the acceptability of the powerful. To speak appropriately is to sound "white" on the phone, to hide the diasporic dimensions of the body's curves, and to pretend that straight hair is somehow preferred. It's to be the right kind of Black in spaces where to be the Black friend is to assent to being a tool of progressive angst rather than accepted for the differences you carry. It's to hear a supervisor or colleague say, "Oh, I never think about the fact that she's Black." It's to be told by your white boss that class matters more than race in America, which she knows is true because her wealthy and successful Black friend told her.

In design firms, the pressures of cultural fit are an explicit element of studio culture based on the presumed benefit to collaborative work in which all parties speak the same basic cultural language.

Of course, the presumed benefits of cultural hegemony should be anathema to any design spaces that purport to be global, universal, or oriented toward social good. Yet, throughout the 1990s and 2000s, many creative workplaces adopted the standard of "cultural fit" in their hiring practices, arguing that colleagues could only effectively work together if they shared cultural experiences and expectations. The concern they expressed was that, in order for a creative business to work well, to thrive, the people in the company had to hold a general understanding of one another along cultural lines. Speak the same language, hold the same basic beliefs and values, understand the same references.

Reflecting back on my time at the AIGA (in the late 1990s) and later Pentagram (in the early to mid-2000s), I'm struck by how similar many of us were in physical type. No one is particularly fat or tall. The girls are all quite pretty. The men are all quite square. For the most part, if we all traded clothes, you might not blink an eye. As the only person of color on my team, I might stand out for my slightly darker skin and curly hair, but as a light-skinned woman, it's not a striking difference. It feels less like a choice than a preference, and so perfectly benign. But in fact, company culture is a tool for discriminating against difference in the name of unit cohesion. A culture of sameness becomes a culture of consent as everyone's anxiety to fit in prevents anyone from articulating dissent. In fact, I frequently voiced my concerns about the "default whiteness" of photographic images on corporate communications and was routinely shut down and quite overtly made to feel like the troublemaker. More than ten years later, in the shadow of the George Floyd protests, a former colleague reached out to me to acknowledge that she wished she had spoken up at the time. The pressure to conform had silenced her, even as an ally or advocate. What cultural hegemony breeds is not just collaboration but complicity, as our peers are taught not to honor their intersectional differences—their multidimensionality—but to prioritize fitting in. That's the damage of appropriateness. That's the harm of neutrality. That's the fallacy of cohesion.

In design spaces, the challenges of identity have manifested more insidiously, as a preference for an aesthetic defined by European Modernism—which draws as much from Afrikan, Black, and global diasporic cultures as it does from strictly European traditions. European Modernism came to define excellence in the field, and so to seek acceptance as a designer has required mirroring European Modernism and its disciples as closely as possible. If you were a Black designer making work that defied, challenged, or rejected the prevailing preference, your work was simply deemed wrong. Inferior, perhaps. Unprofessional, likely. Niche, if you were lucky. Aesthetics, somehow, could be cast as an objective judgment distinct from a judgment of the designer's personal presentation.

You're not *not* being hired because you're a Black designer but because your portfolio expresses your Blackness in a way that does not conform to the aesthetic ideal. Or in the flippant vernacular of a renowned design leader at a prestigious, East Coast graphic design agency, "It's crap."

Again, an intersectional lens in this context does not require that Black or POC designers reject European modernism in whole or in part. It is not an anti-Bauhaus, anti–Swiss Grid, or anti-minimalist stance. What it does allow us to identify is the way in which the design field privileges that aesthetic viewpoint and those who practice it to the exclusion and marginalization of all others. Zimbabwean, Guatemalan, Anishinaabe, Laotian, Maori, Pakistani, or Guyanese designers in the US are required to smooth the edges of cultural or aesthetic particularity for the false universal, translating them into European modernist terms in order to be seen as contemporary or relevant. A video tour of a Swiss Grid exhibition at Poster House posted on Vimeo in in 2020 (which has been removed from the platform and is no longer available for viewing), begins with design critic Paul Shaw referring to a pre-grid poster as "terrible" simply because it does not abide by the grid. The critique does not meet that work on its own terms but rather only in the context of the method that has come to be seen as preferable. While Shaw may indeed prefer the Swiss Grid posters, that preference should not render all other forms valueless.

So within the context of intersectionality, we are also seeing an argument between Pluriverse-ness and Cosmopolitanism, between the cultural positionalities-of-place in a globalized cultural and economic ecosystem and the fallacies of "universalism."

PART III. INTERSECTIONAL FUTURES

This anthology positions itself at the intersection of critique, discourse, manifesto, and invitation. It is also a celebration and exploration of many intersections we carry as Black and Black PoC designers, educators, scholars, curators, and writers. We hope that this book reflects some of the multidimensionality of its readers, and also that it creates space for us all to be whole in all the places we create, critique, teach, and learn design. We hope that it provides new languages and inspirations, new histories and futures, new data points and lyrical expressions for its readers' particular intersectionalities. Because design has always been that. At its best, design has always been multidimensional and complex; and it has also been small and particular.

In June 2021, as I began working on this essay, my beloved mother became an ancestor. In her passing, I've found myself going through her things—clothing, jewelry, papers, precious mementos; items she purchased and the many, many beautiful things she made with her own hands. My mother made lace, sewed clothes, embroidered everything from pillows to wall hangings. My mother—an Afro-Indigenous-Brazilian woman who was an immigrant to the United States—was never called a designer. Her identity card lists her profession as "dressmaker," but to many people she was a maid, a housekeeper, a domestic worker. She was undereducated and worked in what was deemed "unskilled labor." But she was also a designer. She utilized tools and materials to make things that gave joy to and had purpose for others. She wasn't constrained by the needs of mass production or cultural critique. She never scaled up or suffered over how to brand herself. What she made were expressions of the love she transmitted into the objects she designed and produced with care.

As I reflect on the future of design, and the future of Black experiences in design, I look to my own mother's past and ask, how did the act of making make her feel whole? How did her many forms of identity—her race, ethnicity, gender, beliefs, and concerns—intersect in the spaces where head, heart, and hand met the materials of making? And equally, how did structural systems disadvantage her capacities as a designer because they could never see her in that way; because she could not perform "designer" as would have been required of her? How can we ensure that our design spaces correct the marginalization and erasures of its too proximal past and make space for any and all of us? How are we all made whole in the spaces where our various forms of identity and creativity allow us to thrive with complexity, multidimensionality, and our most honest forms of self? The editors of this anthology hope that these stories join in the conversations designers are already negotiating wherever they are. We hope that all the voices that seek to be heard, all the hands that apply themselves to making, and all the ways in which design finds users, audiences, participants and critics—that all find some version of themselves reflected here.

NOTES

1. Kimberlé Crenshaw, *Demarginalizing the Intersection of Race and Sex: A Black Feminist Critique of Antidiscrimination Doctrine, Feminist Theory and Antiracist Politics* (University of Chicago Legal Forum, 1989).

DESIGN
PRACTICES

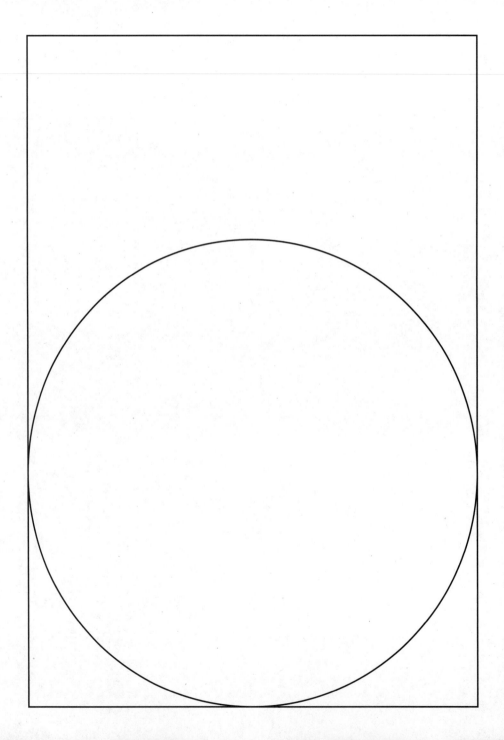

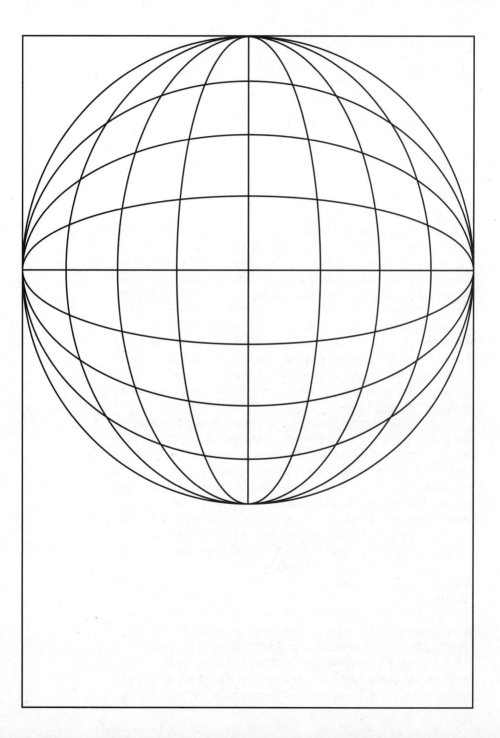

DESIGN PRACTICES

1.1

Chapter Introduction:
Kareem Collie

A design practice, a creative practice, it occurs to me, is something outside of how and what we are responding to as we wind down the clock of each workday—a set of reflexes developed over time to meet specific challenges on the job. Instead, practice should be understood as an intentional ongoing act of honing skills, methods, and techniques to move one's craft forward. It is a deepening of understanding about the subtle nuances of an area of knowledge, through trial and error, inspiring new insights that are then exercised. Practice is a conscious process of cultivating expertise; it is a journey toward the mastery of your craft. And, for the Black creative professional, this journey can be an obstacle course, a course filled with distraction, seemingly insurmountable barriers, land mines, and it is a journey often traveled alone.

Practice takes focus, awareness, support, and space, and professionally these characteristics may not be readily available for Black creative professionals as they seek to navigate majority-white spaces. Before the Black designer can set out to practice their craft, there is a need for them to practice being a creative professional within these spaces—a need to learn a new language, new reference points, and new ways of being in one's body. Early in my career, I remember being stopped while walking through the office by one of the leadership. They'd stopped me to ask why they never saw me smiling. It hadn't struck me that I didn't often smile as I moved throughout the workday. In fact, I considered myself a beacon of positivity around the office, both socially and productively. In reflecting on their question I realized that as a young man I'd actually practiced a type of stone-facedness in my East New York neighborhood. Walking around happy-go-luckily might not have gone over so well. Their question could be seen as a fairly innocuous query, but it had an impact. It's a subtle thing, remembering to put a smile on your face, but each time I knowingly curled my lips up was a reminder of my practice of being in that space, a space that felt "other." The aggregate of these subtle practices can add up to what Dr. Courtney Cogburn calls a *weathering* of the Black body in the *1000 Cut Journey*[1] of the life of that body—living, working, and being—in majority-white spaces.

And, in truth, it isn't always subtle. Sometimes, you are simply confronted with racism. Once, a project manager from a prominent beverage company (I would rather not equate them to the company on a whole), in an effort to rally my small design team for a project being conducted in West Africa, stated that they wanted to so thoroughly swarm the market that mothers would feed their babies this beverage instead of breast milk. They followed this statement with, "not really . . . but seriously . . . " The comment and the image it aroused hit viscerally. It took a certain practice to maintain my demeanor. At that moment I decided that my job on that project would be as a shield, an amplifier of that community, and as a leader on the project that's what I did.

Being in these spaces, often as one of less than a handful of other Black bodies, takes focus, awareness, support, and space . . . it takes practice. This section, "Design Practice," asks the following: What do we practice as Black folk to support and sustain us in our professional design practice? What must we master on our journey to master our craft?

Over the course of this section we will hear from design professionals who have found success on the road to mastering their craft and ask them what it is that they've practiced as Black folks to arrive where they are in their careers.

We introduce this chapter with a 1970 essay by design icon Dorothy Hayes, who curated an exhibition with a concurrent article for *Communication Arts* titled, "An Exhibition by Black Artists." Her prescient work set the stage for the design community to begin the long, difficult conversation about how Black designers are seen, though more often not acknowledged, by the profession. Much of what we know today as the question "where are the Black designers" begins with Hayes, who spoke not only of her own struggle but advocated fiercely for Black artists, illustrators, and designers.

In a conversation, Dantley Davis, Darhil Crooks, and Ian Spalter reflect on their careers—beginnings, hurdles, successes, drivers, and what it has been like to often be the only Black person in the room making decisions for some of the world's largest online and media platforms.

In "Another Brick in the Wall," R. Vann Graves shares wisdom he received from his parents early in his life that has had a great impact on his journey as a leader in the advertising world. He describes his practice of fortifying his acceptability in the predominantly white advertising industry.

In "The Four Pillars," Jon holds up his design practice with the four pillars that he has identified as fundamental to his identity as a Queer Black designer and educator. Quinlin B. Messenger and Jon Key both practice a celebration of intersectionality in their design work. In "To Be Just . . . Steward: Some Life Lyrics," Quin draws from experiences along three legacy vectors that construct his racial and cultural identity to form a model of design as a mode of stewardship.

And finally, Annika Hansteen-Izora discusses approaches to both navigating spaces and collaboratively creating spaces that nourish and facilitate connections as part of their design practice. She/they/he notes the importance of building new spaces that exist outside of structures already "informed by the academy, or hierarchy, or supremacy" and the necessity of actively making and sharing as a process for generating sources of joy, community, and a sense of personal authenticity.

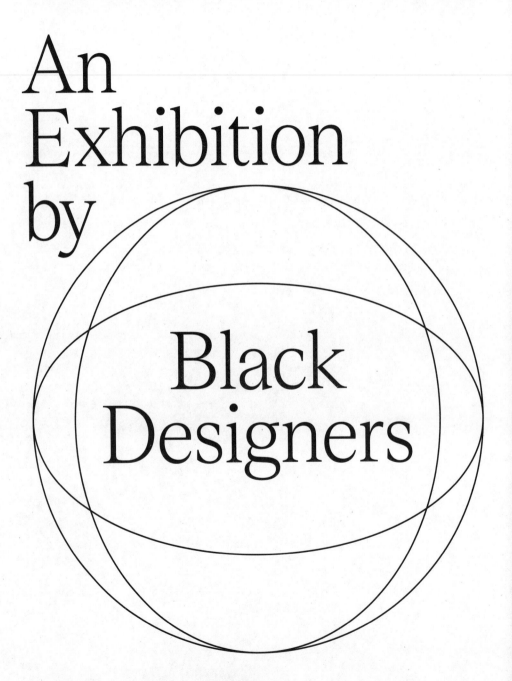

DESIGN PRACTICES

1.2

An Exhibition by Black Designers

DOROTHY HAYES

This essay is reprinted with permission from *Communication Arts* Magazine. When designer Dorothy Hayes first came to New York in 1957, she found few Blacks in the art and design professions. She vowed ". . . that if I made it I would never turn my back on any Black person who came to me for advice and information, and who really wanted to learn." This exhibition is part of her total effort in keeping that promise.

—Kareem Collie

Excerpted from the original published essay: A wide-ranging exhibition of graphic communication—including design, illustration, advertising, television commercials and film—is currently on a two-year tour of art schools and colleges. Originated, planned, selected and produced by Black artists, it presents the work of forty-nine Black men and women from the New York metropolitan area. Except for collections of fine arts assembled under museum auspices, it is believed to be the first exhibition in this country to present a representative showing of graphics by Black professional artists.

The exhibition was the joint idea of cochairmen Dorothy Hayes and Joyce Hopkins. Miss Hayes teaches advertising concept at the New York City Community College as well as operating her own design studio in New York. Joyce Hopkins is a designer with Harper & Row, book publishers. The selection committee was made up of Black artists and designers. In addition to Miss Hayes and Miss Hopkins, it included Seldon Dix, Jr., graphic designer; Alex Oliver, Carl Overr and Roy Lagrone, art directors; Reynold Ruffins, illustrator; and Mahler Ryder, illustrator and instructor in drawing at the Rhode Island School of Design. Georg Olden served as a consultant to the committee, as did Leo Fassler, vice-president and associate creative director at Benton & Bowles.

Lubalin, Smith, Carnase & Ferriter volunteered their resources to design and mount the exhibition which appeared first, early this year, at the Composing Room's Gallery 303 in New York.

DOROTHY HAYES

When designer Dorothy Hayes first came to New York in 1957, she found few Blacks in the art and design professions. She vowed ". . . that if I made it I would never turn my back on any Black person who came to me for advice and information, and who really wanted to learn." This exhibition is part of her total effort in keeping that promise.

An Exhibition by
BLACK ARTISTS

A wide-ranging exhibition of graphic communication — including design, illustration, advertising, television commercials and film — is currently on a two-year tour of art schools and colleges. Originated, planned, selected and produced by Black artists, it presents the work of 49 Black men and women from the New York metropolitan area. Except for collections of fine arts assembled under museum auspices, it is believed to be the first exhibition in this country to present a representative showing of graphics by Black professional artists.

The exhibition was the joint idea of co-chairmen Dorothy Hayes and Joyce Hopkins. Miss Hayes teaches advertising concept at the New York City Community College as well as operating her own design studio in New York. Joyce Hopkins is a designer with Harper & Row, book publishers.

The selection committee was made up of Black artists and designers. In addition to Miss Hayes and Miss Hopkins, it included Seldon Dix, Jr., graphic designer; Alex Oliver, Carl Overr and Roy Lagrone, art directors; Reynold Ruffins, illustrator; and Mahler Ryder, illustrator and instructor in drawing at the Rhode Island School of Design.

Georg Olden served as a consultant to the committee, as did Leo Fassler, vice-president and associate creative director at Benton & Bowles.

Lubalin, Smith, Carnase & Ferriter volunteered their resources to design and mount the exhibition which appeared first, early this year, at the Composing Room's Gallery 303 in New York.

Several films were shown as part of the exhibition. Poet, composer, painter, photographer and filmmaker Gordon Parks was represented with a 25-minute autobiographical film. Seventeen television commercials by Georg Olden were shown, as were commercials by producers Ted Shearer, Bill Mason, Alex Oliver, Dorothy Hayes and Tee Collins. An IBM sales recruiting film designed for use in recruiting sessions in Black schools was also presented. It was produced, directed and shot by Roy Inman.

A special music score to accompany the exhibition was written by Gene Casey.

*Illustration by
Tom Feelings for his
forthcoming book,
"A Black Artists Pilgrimage."*

The 49 artists
represented in the
*Black Artist
in Graphic Communication*
exhibition are:

Dorothy Akubuiro
Roosevelt Allison
Romare Bearden
Charles Boyd
Cecil Elombe Brath
Ronnie Brathwaite
Oraston Brooks-El
Wallace E. Caldwell
Elmore Theodore Collins
Donald Crews
Leo and Diane Dillon
Seldon Dix
Philip Draggan
Loring Eutemey
Tom Feelings
George Ford
Veronal Grant
Robert A. Gumbs
Donald Harper
Dorothy E. Hayes
Joyce Hopkins
Bill Howell
Roy Inman
Louise E. Jefferson
Jo Jones
Roy E. Lagrone
Vincent Lewis
Alexander Mapp
Andrea Marquez
Bill Mason
Don Miller
John Morning
Georg Olden
Alex Oliver
Carl Overr
Gordon Parks
Jerry Pinkney
George Robert Pruden
Samuel Reed
Reynold Ruffins
Mahler B. Ryder
Ahmad Sadig
Ted Shearer
John Steptoe
Otis D. Sullivan
Mozelle Wilmont Thompson, Jr.
Alex Walker
Bernadine Watson
Verona Witcher

*Symbol designed by George
Ford, Jr. for the New Lafayette
Theater. Originally designed
for a poster, it was adapted for
letterheads and envelopes,
and it was then cast as a
medallion to be worn by
the cast.*

Tom Feelings illustration

DOROTHY HAYES

BLACK ARTISTS

The art director for the Brentwood ad was Wallace Caldwell.

Alex Oliver art directed the two Gulf ads.

The poster below was designed by Andrea Marques, with the illustration by Romare Bearden.

Seldon Dix, Jr. designed the logo for Teletape Productions, as well as the USA logo for the Times News Tour of the U.S.A.

The cjd design is by Dorothy Hayes.

Using a motif from Uganda pottery, the African American Institute logo is by Louise Jefferson.

One section of the exhibition
is devoted to a retrospective
showing of the work of
Mozelle Thompson, whose career
was halted by his death a month
before the opening of the exhibition.
The illustration above appeared
in "The New York Times." At the
right are illustrations from
"Tuesday," the syndicated Sunday
newspaper supplement.

DOROTHY HAYES

BLACK ARTISTS

"Stevie" was written and illustrated by John Steptoe. His illustrations for this book earned him a Gold Medal from the Society of Illustrators.

Donald Crews wrote and illustrated "Ten Black Dots." He also designed the cover for "Across the Pacific" (below).

Josephine Jones was the designer for the other two book covers illustrated below.

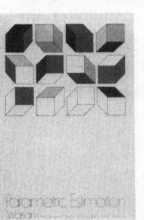

Four record album covers —

Left and below: Loring P. Eutemey, designer
Bottom left: Leo and Diane Dillon, designers
Bottom right: Oraston Brooks-El, illustrator

The illustration below is part of a series,
"The Great American Subway Rider,"
by Mahler B. Ryder.

DOROTHY HAYES

BLACK ARTISTS

Seldon Dix, Jr. created an
unfamiliar Statue of Liberty
by combing a Bourke-White photo
of the statue with a photo of
a Black woman's face by Gordon Parks.
Dix was also the designer for the
doll's face cover, and he was the
photographer for the other cover.

Philip Draggan was an associate designer
for the Seatrain Lines, Inc. annual report.

Oraston Brooks-El designed "No Exit."

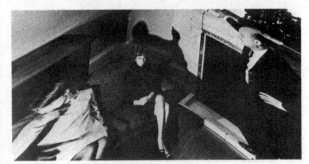

The woman's profile is a
Tom Feelings illustration.

Reynold Ruffins illustrated
"The Antkeeper" and
the "Harlem On My Mind" posters.

Romare Bearden was the illustrator
for the "Fortune" cover.

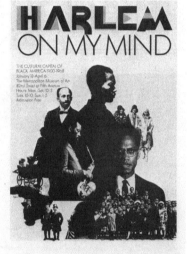

DOROTHY HAYES

BLACK ARTISTS

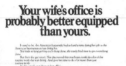

Facing page —

Bill Mason was the art director
for the IBM ad.

The Pan Am ad was art directed
by Ahmad Sadiq while he was
with J. Walter Thompson's
Pan American Division.

Sam Reed was the art director
for the unpublished AT&T ad.

Three children, an illustration
by Mahler B. Ryder.

"The Arts" cover was designed
by Dorothy Hayes.

Right: The Children of
Rio Bueno, Jamaica, by Don Miller.

Leo and Diane Dillon designed and
illustrated the Ground Zero poster.

THE CHILDREN OF RIO BUENO, JAMAICA

In Conversation:

Darhil Crooks, Ian Spalter & Dantley Davis

The following interview took place on June 17, 2021, via videoconference from Northern California and Tokyo, Japan. I facilitated the conversation between Dantley Davis, chief design officer at Twitter, Darhil Crooks, creative director at Apple, and Ian Spalter, head of Instagram Japan, about practicing design, holding space for others, mastering one's craft, and being the lone Black voice in the room. This conversation has been edited for length and clarity.

—Kareem Collie

KAREEM COLLIE:	**Let's start by talking about how you three have navigated creative spaces as Black men.**

DARHIL CROOKS: Beginning at *The Source* was probably the best thing that could have happened for me because you could be yourself, I wasn't going into an corporate office. We were a bunch of twenty-year-old kids that all loved hip-hop, partying together, hanging out together, and it was also our job. There are a lot of people who started out like that, working with people like Arem Duplessis and Wyatt Mitchell, who started at *Vibe* and *Blaze*. There was this moment in the late 90s, early 2000s, that I think was pivotal to a lot of early careers. Suddenly, we were the ones creating the content. I could be myself, have fun, have a job, and study this craft. That gave me the confidence to say I don't have to do the corporate thing. Yes, I've had to do it in some versions, I guess; there have been times where I've rocked the tie every day, just because I wanted to be the tie guy. We were figuring all this stuff out.

IAN SPALTER: I had a similar experience. I started at New York Online, which was founded by Omar Wasow, another Black tech luminary. I'd say he's definitely OG status, starting up in his Brooklyn apartment, a very entrepreneurial environment. It was a purely multicultural environment, not just Black and Brown, different types of people. I was in an internship, when the web was just getting started. I think as an environment, I didn't have to really think about my identity much. In fact, Omar was biracial in the same way I am—Black and Jewish. They'd actually filled all of their slots when I applied, but Jen Beckman, a white woman, checked out my website and they opened another slot for me. You know there is this element of—who's going to give you the opportunity to get your foot in the door? It's a blessing to have that. This first opportunity led to BlackPlanet and other things. It was tremendous for me. It's during this early phase that you are just trying to practice your craft, let alone master it. I had the opportunity to do that and be treated professionally. There's just so much to learn about the craft, let alone jumping straight into environments where you must figure out how to operate. Not just how do you be a designer, it's about "how do you eat?" There is a decade of that. Getting started in a space where we don't have to worry about the other stuff is tremendously valuable.

DANTLEY   Early in my career, I worked for a company called
DAVIS: Net Noir, which was a competitor of BlackPlanet.

IS: Not really a competitor. I mean . . . !

DD: You're right . . . It was nipping at the ankles of
               BlackPlanet. The founders were Black. And a few of
the production team were Black, but I didn't feel any form of camaraderie. One, I was the only Black person doing development work, the only
designer, and also the engineer. And the producers were all white. There
was a Black man who was a producer, who I confided in at times. But one
of my biggest challenges was the generational gap. I was nineteen and
they were all in their thirties or forties. Because of that generation gap, I
just felt awkward. I couldn't share music; my social scene was different.
I freaked out about everything that happened, and they were all cool
and collected. I did find solace that the subject matter that came up in
the office was not controversial. It was all culturally relevant. That was
a very stark difference from other start-ups I'd been at prior and then
with companies that I went to afterward. In these other spaces I could
not get any form of connection to what was happening in and around the
culture and zeitgeist of Black people.

       One thing that was odd to me was that even though the
company was cofounded by Black men, it wasn't supportive; I was made
to feel small, a lot. I was made to feel that I had a place in this environment.
And that place was on the production side. There was a chasm between
the folks who were on the business side, the Black cofounders. And then
there were the people who were basically tightening the bolts to make the
business operate. I remember one particular moment, in which I was wearing an Eddie Bauer jacket that I'd just bought, and the CEO came to me and

told me, "I paid for that." Here is someone who I respected because he's a successful Black man; he wore a suit every day. Something that I had not ever seen in my life. But he felt okay belittling me. I think that soured me in some way, moving forward working with companies that were about that type of culture, if they weren't about degrees of inclusion, beyond just race.

I've worked in other environments where I worked with very explicit racist people. But I knew that. And so, I knew where the line was. I knew where they stood on issues. Although it was isolating, I knew where the landmines were, versus being in a place where I let my guard down. And I stepped on a landmine.

IS: You know, there is usually a lot of trauma running through families, right. But in families you don't have to put your guard up or worry about a certain expected type of decorum. That's what I'm taking away from your anecdote, Dantley. I can imagine that surely this person was also made to feel subjugated. And now you're going to feel what I felt. It takes a certain evolved person to get past that and say, this is someone I can help lift.

DD: Yeah, I never thought about it that way. But in thinking back to some of the conversations we had and the way that he acted toward me he may have seen me like a kid brother.

IS: Reflecting on the beginning of this conversation. I definitely think there was a phase where I was thinking about trying to master my craft, and then figuring out where I need to go work to do that? I needed validation from companies that weren't particularly focused on our communities. There is definitely a trap that you can get into when working in spaces like the ones we started in. They're accepting and welcoming, but breaking out to other more mainstream companies can be difficult; they don't necessarily value the work that you're doing in those companies. As a young designer a lot of my career decisions were based on seeking work that was suited to a more mass audience to build my portfolio.

I managed to find environments that, while they weren't particularly less diverse, I wasn't the only one. Although, I felt the weight of being one of the few Black male designers there. I think that I definitely practiced being myself; I never got too dressed up, maybe for big presentations and things. But I've always dressed how I dress; I had locks for many years. I always felt physically comfortable showing up for work. However, I definitely felt I had to evolve my design practice, to be in spaces that were certainly more white and maybe a little more competitive.

Stepping into those environments certainly helped me to sharpen my skills. That said I feel as though in that phase of my career, I wasn't thinking enough about bringing more of us into those spaces. I remember interviewing this Black guy for an opening at the agency I was working for. I gave him the thumbs-up. But, I remember just grilling him. I knew he was talented, but I was very self-aware of how we reflect each other. In that environment any one of our failures would reflect on the other's failures. Later, after he got the job, I apologized to him. But looking back I feel like I went in there with some baggage that in hindsight wasn't about me. Before me, there was another Black designer that left a bad reputation at the agency who'd ended up being more talk than actual work. They'd grilled me coming in as well, reflecting this other person onto me. And I did the same . . . traumatic programming that plays out there. You chase that validation, and once you have it, you're trying to protect it. In a world where we're all reflecting on each other, you end up judging; you can potentially end up judging your own people more harshly as a result.

DC: That desire for validation is super real. I never wanted to feel like I'm a Black designer who only designs things that are related to the Black experience. As a designer, you want to be able to design everything. That meant working at *The Source* is cool, but I got to get to *GQ*, to *Esquire*, *New York Times*, these prestigious publications. I think that's the part of what has kept me going. And maybe part of what helped me get to where I am, as messed up as it might sound—this is cool, but I gotta get there.

I mentioned Rem and Wyatt earlier. In magazine and publishing these two were the only Black guys that were creative directors; there were women, no Black women, no Black people, except for these two out of all these magazines. Gail Anderson did amazing work at *Rolling Stone*, but she was out of the magazine industry at this point. For me it was "I got to get there!" Based on that idea of validation. It's messed up that we need that validation, because of these other properties, other magazines, etc. . . . If there's talent there, I'm sure everybody's saying, I gotta get to that next thing, this isn't good enough. And I think that's the problem with this industry, with the way we work as a society.

DD: I couldn't imagine my design practice without race; it helped me advance in so many ways. With it I see a-round corners that my peers can't see. As an example, when I was at PayPal, as a designer on the eBay account: I asked "how might small businesses get to leverage PayPal as a service in parts?" My mom is a Korean small business owner with a shop in K-Town. Seeing her struggle with trying to

68

set up a website and put our merchandise online—I was like there's no way she's gonna be able to manage this. What if buying from a small business owner's website were as easy as buying from eBay? So, I pitched the idea of having third-party cart integration for PayPal. I wouldn't have had that insight, I don't think, had it not been for race. When I was at Netflix, I looked at my work, my race, and my experience as a Black man and asked "How can we tell stories about what is happening in our community on this platform, in a way that is bespoke and differentiated to different types of people?" That was a core thesis when I was working on the Netflix UI. No one else was thinking about that idea. And I wouldn't have thought about that idea, either. Had it not been for my experiences of being a person of color on this planet.

IS: It's probably true for almost any designer—how do you differentiate? It's your personal experience, and the richer those experiences, the more interesting a designer you're going to be. I view my experience as a Black person as extremely empowering and differentiating, and as a multiracial person I am pretty comfortable with ambiguity, with being in between. I credit this to my identity. As a designer you have to differentiate yourself and know that your point of view is valuable. And, the further you go in your career, having a distinct point of view, is pretty critical. Coming from an identity on the edges, identity has to be a part of what's on the forefront of your mind. That can be a real differentiator; you can use it to your advantage.

DC: I work with a lot of photographers, and in thinking about what story you want to tell? How to tell it? And who tells it? Is something that I've always done subconsciously. Today, I'm . . . it has to be this way. I know these photographers are great, but I want the story to be told by this person. I wasn't always that forceful, and I wish I had been early in my career. In a lot of ways it wasn't possible. There were not a lot of Black voices, photographers, illustrators, getting that exposure back then. Shout out to Instagram! The floodgates are now open, there's no agency as the gatekeeper between them and this magazine or company, which has been crucial to the explosion of diversity—it's a beautiful thing.
             I won't say the name of the magazine in this example, there was a picture of a black male athlete posing on a pedestal flexing for a fashion shoot. The guy that I was working with says, "This is cool, right?" No, it's not cool. That's a terrible photo. Here's why. He looks like he is on display like a slave. Like he's being idolized for his body and nothing else. And he's like, "Oh, I hadn't even thought about it that way." And that's the

point, he didn't think about it. I'm always thinking about it—how does this make me feel as a Black person? This is why you need different voices in the room to say, "Hey guys, that's not a good idea." I think that there is some catching up happening.

IS: That's a big part for me—who gets to tell the story. The people being represented are the ones who actually make a difference.

DC: It made a difference when I was working on the cover for *The Case for Reparations* by Ta-Nehisi Coates, at the *Atlantic*—and I'm not throwing darts at anybody—but the immediate thing was to say let's get a photo of a slave and put it on the cover. Absolutely not! We got to move past this imagery. It allowed us to consider a bigger, better way to tell this story. Just go big and go type and just hit people in the face with it! What would that story have been in somebody else's hands? I don't know the answer. But I do think part of that solution I came up with was because I am Black, my reaction was like, no! We get hit with those images so often in our lives. Every Black History Month, it's jarring and traumatic. I am definitely more conscious of that today. I wasn't always. But now I'm actively looking for it.

IS: Dantley, I'm going to put this to you. I'd like you to talk about the practices that you've put in as a leader building more inclusive teams, which I think will have reverberations for years to come. And saving people from a lot of the wrongs you felt. I'm also curious about things that surprised you about your approach? Or how you've changed your approach? Because you probably went in saying "I'm gonna build this team my way this time." And you made progress there. But there's got to be some other things that are like, "Oh, shit, wait, I didn't think about this."

DD: This is a book of multiple chapters. One of the first things I did was to articulate why having diverse teams was important to business objectives. In particular Twitter, we're a global company. And we needed the perspective of diverse voices on our teams, if we were to make a product that was actually going to be meaningful for people around the world. And the design team just wasn't there in terms of that representation—it was behind company goals. Once I had alignment that the goal was something we should strive for, I made managers accountable for actually building diverse pipelines. When I joined, I made promotion, hiring, and firing criteria based on a manager's ability to attract diverse talent. And that motivated people, when people are going to get promoted, because they're being asked to spend more time building relationships, they'll do the work. And so I started to see a shift in our pipeline. I also took some industry lessons like adopting the Rooney Rule. When no one else at the company was doing it for women in leadership roles. And men went to our HR to complain about me. When I brought Black people to the company, based on relationships I'd built—qualified Black people—people went to HR and complained. I don't know what I would do differently, but I can tell you that it's not all sunshine and puppies.

I've been a vocal advocate for doing this work. For ensuring that tech companies in particular, and design teams specifically, prioritize hiring people of color and giving them a chance, promoting them, ensuring that there's equity from a product standpoint. And that invites vitriol. Last year I was the target of multiple death threats against me and my family, for the things I've said and done. I don't know if I would do things any differently. Maybe I would have seen the therapist sooner to maintain my own mental health.

It's important that if you have an opportunity to have this type of influence within an organization, for there to be clarity and transparency on the decisions you're making. One tactic I would do differently is to be more candid about why changes are happening, both in terms of people coming in and people going out. So there isn't a narrative that you have to fight against, in addition to trying to do the work to have a more inclusive workplace.

I think it's part of my responsibility to ensure, especially when putting out a global product, that is, that there is representation. And I don't buy into the notion that there is a pipeline problem. And I don't buy into any other excuses as to why you can't have talented people of color, and women on your team and not just entry-level roles, leadership roles. I've seen firsthand the benefits that a business has by having better representation: the ideas are better, the execution is better. And so, I put my foot on the accelerator in terms of making this happen.

DC: To echo what Dantley is saying, you just have to work a little bit harder to find folks. And, because of the democratization of information happening in both of your relative companies there's no excuse. They're out there. They're making noise. There's all these opportunities and channels that exist now that didn't exist, five, ten years ago. It's important to work on it.

KC: **All right, ya'll. We gotta do this more often! There's so many more people that can be a part of this con-**

versation. Talk soon and Happy Father's Day. What? Isn't that down the road? A week and a half? I'm just saying it now. In case we don't rap for whatever reason. All right, cool. Gentlemen. Thank you.

DESIGN
PRACTICES

1.4

Another Brick in the Wall

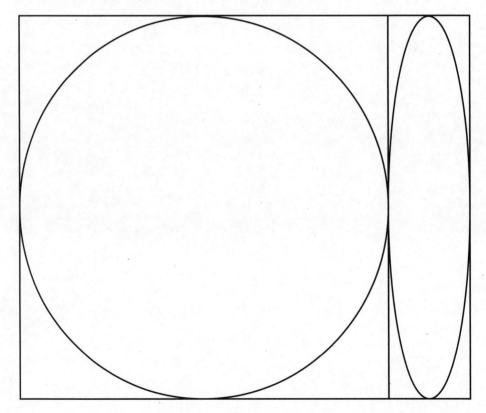

R. VANN GRAVES

Some people are born creatives. I don't believe I was gifted in this way; I aspired to be creative. To find success as a graphic designer, I needed to learn the craft. But I didn't take whether I had talent into consideration at the time. Rather, I built a framework of what I thought was needed to get to the goal I set my sights on. A major component of this framework was something my father referred to as "The Wall." The Wall was something I could lean on. People would always see my Blackness first, but if they looked past me, they would see The Wall. It was a backdrop, a fortification, supporting what was otherwise perceived as a deficit. The Wall behind me backed my legitimacy.

My parents were active in the civil rights movement. One of their first acts as a couple was to protest at the "white only" counter of Thalhimers department store in downtown Richmond, Virginia. They were fighting for the right to exist—to have full rights as United States citizens. My dad was arrested at that demonstration with thirty-three other Virginia Union University students who later became known as the Richmond 34. My parents' strife, of course, came with an expectation that I would take full advantage of those hard-earned rights.

My parents fought for and encouraged me to do or be anything. Well, almost anything—as long as it was a doctor, lawyer, teacher, or perhaps "businessman." That's what they fought for. That's what success looked like. The idea of me going to school for graphic design and art direction was firmly outside their frame of reference.

My parents didn't realize that they also fought for me to imagine greater possibilities. At Howard University, I pursued the best of both worlds: a business degree in marketing pieced together with graphic design. When I told them I wanted to study fine arts and graphic design, they could not fathom that such a course would lead to great things. I may as well have told them I wanted to study witchcraft.

The first thing I hung on The Wall was that Bachelor of Business Administration from Howard University, which was closely followed by a master's in Communication Design from Pratt Institute. A few years into my advertising career, I also added a master's from Harvard University to The Wall. Though that achievement was put on hold after September 11, 2001, when I enlisted in the Army. Anytime someone looked at my résumé, at The Wall behind me, they would see these achievements. I often reflect on how my achievements would be viewed differently if I were white. If I were white, many of the career and educational mile-stones—captain in the Army, a two-time CCO, a director, degrees from top institutions, including my latest pursuit of a doctoral degree from the University of Pennsylvania—would make me exceptional. In reality, I am following the only blueprint I was taught: as a Black man, you need the credentials. Because what may be considered exceptional for some only makes me acceptable to most.

I've built this Wall to be acceptable to the masses, especially in the advertising industry. These achievements merely level the playing field. But you still have to run the race better, faster, and stronger than the other guy. And you can't play to tie, you must play to win. A difficult task on a field where my white contemporaries have a cultural advantage.

My first experience in the industry was as an intern at *America's Most Wanted*. I sat in a meeting with producers and stakeholders as they discussed making an episode about Black-on-Black crime. I was one of the only, if not the only, Black person in the room and the conversation fired me up but, as a junior, I wasn't invited to sit at the table. Literally. Like the other juniors, I sat in a ring around the perimeter of the room. So while the twentysomethings can stand up and speak their truth easier nowadays, things were different back then; the juniors sat and listened.

The following day, I met with my Howard University marketing professor Vince Carter. I told him the story and about my subse-quent intentions—I wasn't going to stand for it. Next time, I would tell them how I felt, about how they were wrong. Professor Carter sat me down and firmly, but politely, said: "No, you're not." He told me that he was confident I had the talent and skill to be an important part of the advertising industry, and that was exactly why I needed to hold my tongue. If I opened my mouth now, I would never get a seat at the table. I'd be blocked, blackballed, before

I even had a chance to finish my first sentence of grievance. He informed me that I was destined to endure many frustrating points in my career but, provided I played my cards right, one day I would know when I could speak out and truly use my voice. At the time, I didn't understand what he meant, but because I had a lot of respect for him, I took his advice.

The first time I recall using "my voice" was during the early 2000s, or more specifically, what I refer to as the first awakening: when the advertising world began speaking about diversity and inclusion. I was working with a big client, but this time, I was sitting at the head of the table. I was driving the meeting and selling concepts as, once again, the only Black person in the room. At one point, the client looked at me and said: "We really want to make sure there's diversity and representation in the work we produce." I remember saying—and it felt so good—"I will ensure there's more diversity in this campaign than there is in this room." I was finally living the moment Professor Carter had foreseen for me.

Today, I am at a different vantage point and can clearly see what Professor Carter saw so many years ago. There are certain things (more things) that young Black creatives will have to do, as much as the world says it's woke. My advice: stay conscious of the fact that not everybody cares. They don't care about your Blackness, about your history, about this, or that. And when they say they do, it may be performative. That's where The Wall comes in. You must have whatever "The Wall" is for you in place. It can and should look different from mine. Nowadays, The Wall could be a thoughtfully curated Instagram feed or a massive TikTok following; maybe you've designed some great innovation. The Wall "decor" all have something in common, though: no one can take these achievements away from you. Ultimately, you still need proof points that show you have done well and have a reason to be in the room. You have to be in the room, and you have to be valued. You are not a token. It's about playing to win and waiting for your moment to speak your truth and make a difference.

In the end, it's just another brick in the wall.

DESIGN
PRACTICES

1.5

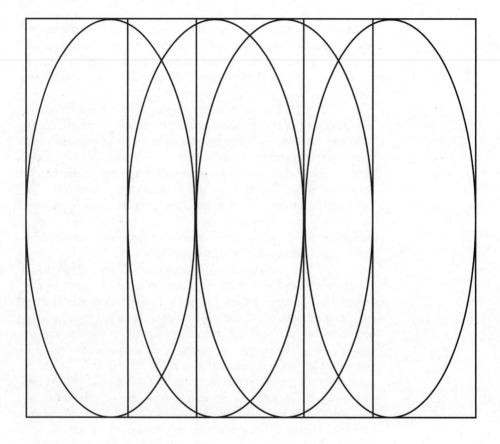

The Four Pillars

JON KEY

Graphic design is the catalyst between meaning, communication, and image. I am defining graphic design as a professional practice through the lens of and through "traditional design objects" i.e. branding, logo design, typography, poster making, book making, web design—in other words, visual design that serves a commercial function. Historically, in the design canon, Queer design objects and their modes of production have been rooted in and limited to protest, activism, and survival. Images of ACT UP poster campaigns, the reclaimed pink triangle, (white) power fist, lapel buttons, etc. come to mind.

Often the surviving artifacts, messages, photographs, and images prioritize white voices and are predominantly male (not unlike the design industry as a whole). This has prompted me to ask—What is the role of the modern Queer graphic designer of color? Is there a rejection of identity-centered responsibility in order to thrive in this capitalist-motivated economy? Or is there a desire to push forward the vulnerability of the self, revealing work that addresses the tension, anxiety, and love—the range of emotions and moods—of present-day representation and language of modern QTPOC life?

In an industry where Black and Brown folks are often under-hired, undervalued, and completely ignored, what community is there to comment on? Even more specifically, a Queer POC community? I have personally made it my mission to connect with as many designers of color and Queer designers throughout my years of working. We always discuss how they got into design . . . How many Black people were in their university program, what most excites them about design today . . . ? And every time the conversations always end with "I'm so happy we met! You know there are not a lot of us. We have to stick together." These interactions renew my spirit and belief in the work I do. Also, these conversations serve as a reminder that there are more QTPOC designers working than are immediately apparent. With social media, technology, and larger institutional archives developing, my own personal tête-à-têtes are indeed critical interpersonal starting points for my own investigation, but I am also beginning to realize the vast contributions and interpretations of queerness—as our narratives are being shared with the larger world.

In early 2020 (pre-pandemic), my graphic design studio Morcos Key, which I run with my husband Wael Morcos, shared our work in a lunch-style lecture series to Yale MFA students. Our practice, as a whole, focuses on art and cultural branding and editorial work with an emphasis on multicultural typography and amplifying underserved communities. Many of the projects we shared emphasized our role as a graphic design studio creating work authentic to the communities we represent. We shared a selection of editorial projects from the Tenth Magazine, a Black Queer fashion and lifestyle magazine, to a season campaign series for Heartbeat Opera's annual Queer drag extravaganza. In the end, Matthew Carter, a prominent and well-awarded white male type designer and professor at Yale, congratulated me on the studio and our work and offered, "but the work doesn't look very Queer to me."

I laughed and responded with a smile, "The context of the work is Queer. The narrative and the story being shared is what makes it Queer. I can't define the spectrum of queerness in a singular pattern or typeface . . ."

He smiled and added "I guess that would be too stereotypical and on the nose anyways." What makes graphic design Queer? How do these objects pass into art/institutional and gallery spaces? What are the codes, symbols, and messages that "outs" a designer's hand?

My childhood in Alabama established my unbreakable relationship with art and self-expression. My mother Linda would transform the kitchen table with a repurposed wax plastic Christmas tablecloth. Covered in faded green leaves and red holly berries with a worn felt underside, the tablecloth turned the table into a craft zone for my twin and me.

Encouraged by my mom and this space for play, I began a lifelong pursuit of art and making. From recorder classes to piano and trumpet performances, theater plays, and pageants, my time in grade school reinforced the power of art to be not just a tool of creativity but a catalyst for community and friendship-building. The pursuit of art and learning did not stop in elementary school. I continued my art education at the Rhode Island School of Design (RISD) for undergrad. There, in my design history lectures and critiques, I did not learn any stories that reflected my experience as a Queer Black designer. A gap existed in the curriculum—devoid of anyone who looked like me.

When I arrived at RISD in Providence, I was suddenly surrounded exclusively by artists—creative people who I thought would universally understand me and my work. I quickly realized this wasn't the case. Writing became a retreat from this dissonance, a tool to question why my work was misunderstood. Why were my white and Korean classmates silent when I presented graphic design projects that centered my personal identities? What did it mean to be a graphic designer? What did it mean to be a Black graphic designer? A Queer graphic designer? Someone from the South? Could my personal narratives be communicated through a poster or a book?

Through my writing reflections at RISD, I deconstructed my identity to reveal intersecting and legible fields for myself. Southernness, Blackness, Queerness, and Family emerged as my personal framework for navigating the world—to articulate, and therefore define who I am. These four pillars ground all of my work across disciplines and lay the foundation for my research and writing practice. This rubric helps me understand who I am and how I perform in the world.

I realized I had created survival mechanisms not only to grasp and take control of my performance in the world but also to dictate how my work was discussed and perceived.

In *Disidentifications: Queers of Color and the Performance of Politics*, José Esteban Muñoz articulates this strategy as Disidentification: Disidentification is the tool or "strategy" with which minoritarian, namely Queer people of color, navigate heteronormative society. Through legislative systems, the status quo, and/or outright violence, the public sphere excludes those who do not conform. And though the public sphere, or the majoritarian in most cases, is synonymized with white supremacy, in the case of queerness, communities of color become majoritarian themselves, within which queerness is prohibited as a natural trait—seen as the fringe. A body with multiple identities struggles within the interior and exterior, within the public and private, within performance when interacting and intersecting within a shared community.

The minoritarian includes people of color, Queer people, disabled people, women, and folks who inhabit multiple axes of these identities—Black women, women of color, Queer people of color, etc. Specifically Muñoz references Kimberlé Crenshaw's coining of "intersectionality," a term she introduced into legislation as a specific argument for the complex identities of Black women in the corporate and judiciary space. Through clarification, the term revolutionized the complexity of Black women's lived experience. Intersectionality is a convincing tool to think about the multiple identities comprised in my body, a Black Queer body as well.

Intersectionality insists that fragmented identities can be connected, shared, and transformed into a powerful defense for defining your place in the public. Experiences of disidentification and inter-sectionality can be shared between Queer people through history and time. And as a Black, Queer artist and designer, I mold these shared experiences into visual codes and messages.

All of my adult life working as an artist, designer, educa-tor, and writer, I have been searching for objects, stories, examples of Black, Queer narratives—containers that reflect me. Now, I live in New York City and I use my design and art making skills learned at that kitchen table to share with the world who I am—to build communities around individuals sharing their personal narratives through their work.

To Be Just . . . Steward:

Some Life Lyrics

QUINLIN B.
MESSENGER

The following are entries from my 2021 journal. As well as lyrics from my life.

I share these with you out of gratitude for my ancestors, and yours . . .

ENTRY 27 To be just is to steward.

Have we lost sight of this? . . . have empathy and honor been cast out of sight—a vision clouded by gain and greed? I f*cking hope not . . .

With roots in harmony, stewardship can have a compassionate musicality . . . being many notes, leading many movements. In a way, like music, stewardship can take many forms, meanings, and actions—as a practice of justice, stewardship can manifest . . .

> . . . by accepting the responsibility to shepherd, and safeguard the values of others.
> . . . by caring deeply.

> . . . by showing love and reverence for our Mother Earth . . .

Stewardship as a practice of justice can manifest . . .

> . . . by ethically embodying the responsible planning and management of resources.

... by honoring and respecting.
... by taking a moment to carefully and actively listen.
... by cultivating a seed into a mature plant.
... by sharing stories of our ancestors with
our children and grandchildren.
... by facilitating healing through acknowledging trauma.

... by remaining sensitive to our duty to serve equitably.
... by living a life of empathy.

... by justly designing ...

Design ...
so much of my life has been by design, a design that was not my own ... a design to disadvantage, suppress, and strike out. Some say the system is "broken"—my experience has shown me it was built this way on purpose. I stand at the crossroads of a multitude of cultural vectors ... a spectrum of experiences shaped by oppression, and liberated through legacies of cultural stewardship.

I am a son to a mother ... a mother who was daughter to an indigenous Mexican father—a mother that is daughter to a Jewish mother who was adopted into the Lakota tribe.

I am son to a father ... a father who was son to an African American father—a father that is son to a biracial mother whose Black mother was raped by her slave owner.

The experiences of my ancestors have shown me that the system can be rebuilt for a different purpose ... my ancestors imagined a future by a different design—with stewardship as a guiding light to heal and empower legacies founded in justice.

My design practice cannot exist without stewardship as the foundation .. . it's in my bones, in my blood, coded in my DNA. Stewardship is not just a common thread, but a foundational modality of justice within the Black, Native American, and Jewish legacies that I AM—

... I AM Black Legacy
continuing to steward through innovation, resiliency, and cultivation ...

*. . . I AM Native American Legacy
continuing to steward through reverence, compassion, and tradition . . .*

*. . . I AM Jewish Legacy
continuing to steward through service, integrity, and knowledge . . .*

Out of love for my future grandchildren, and respect for my elders, it is my duty to honor legacy through design . . .

. . . "honor legacy through design". . . this warrants questions . . .

Can legacy be designed into an experience?
Can legacy be experienced through design?

Can legacy be physically made and felt?
Can legacy be spatial?
Can legacy be place?

Legacy is family, and family is like home . . . hmm . . . "home" . . .

"home"

"home"

"home" may hold some answers? . . .

Lyric—Lynched Skies

*I awake from a dream—a vision of my father as
yours, being lynched in my bedroom
Bleeding, red skies paint everything light
Flashing, lightning was the spark
Raining, ash in day darkness*

Raging, fires are our fault
Crying, is our mother
Learn, to love her

Fig. 1

ENTRY 28   Home links us to legacy.

Have we lost sight of this? . . . have we forgotten to honor our elders through our actions—misplacing the truth that we all share this planet as our home? I f*cking hope not . . .

With roots in tradition, legacy emerges as ephemeral home, a series of nodes and portals carrying us back to our ancestors, back to our origins. In a way, like legacy, home can be many places, forms, and meanings—home can manifest as . . .

. . . a vessel for our experiences and memories.
. . . a house embodied—a space, whose aura
has been transformed into place.

. . . a collection of meanings—a curated assemblage of memories ephemerally captured in objects and items . . . a spirit

shaped through valuables . . . enabling us to value.

Home is an acknowledgement that we are all human, in that we all share a common pursuit for shelter.

. . . home transcends space, and walls, and occupies place.
. . . home can be a gateway to experiencing legacies.
. . . home can exist without walls.

. . . home is family . . .

Fig. 2

Family . . .

Grandma Judy told me, "'the takoja' is about the grandchildren, seven generation before and seven generation thereafter" . . . Takoja as a place is this for me, a place to experience legacy. The legacy of the two-hundred-year-old adobe cabin resounds in my space . . . the ancient time that each adobe brick is made from, soil that our ancestors walked on . . . the sound of countless newborns' cries resonating off the earthen walls and floor, the cabin was a midwifery centuries ago . . . the viga beams were cultivated and brought down from the Sangre De Cristo mountains to become the roof, the wisdom of the forest at arm's reach . . . the whole space vibrates through the legacy of its making, and invites you to experience it if you quiet yourself . . .

Fig. 3

Takoja is a place where I've felt closest to home . . . a place where I've experienced the legacies of the universe . . . the sweat lodge, like the adobe cabin, is a place that is purely earth legacy—made from hand-cut and bark-stripped willow branches near the creek upstream, fed by the snow melt of mountains overhead . . . the sacred geometry that guides the weaving of the structure, rendering a dome that honors the four directions and Father Sky . . . a marriage of the universal elements of water and fire heat the stones to create steam, purifying the spirit through sweat and song . . . the cowhide drum as the heartbeat of the earth, synchronizing us all in vibration . . . your bare hands on the cold earth and freshly handpicked sage from the century old brush, you're within the womb of the earth . . . this is the closest I've been to home . . .

> . . . being this close to the earth,
> you realize that you are always home—
> as long as
> you respect the planet,
> and compassionately care for her as you would your own mother . . .

. . . this is a just way to be,
and is just the way we should be.

By honoring home we homage our roots and steward what was into what can be. As designers we must steward with compassion so that our imagined solutions can shape actionable realities . . . realities that are open and available to all . . . available to people—available to animals—available to the ecosystems which make our lives possible.

This is the responsibility all designers have, to respect and honor our shared home—to respect and honor the legacy that is Mother Earth.

Many of those in power have lost sight of this . . . design practice for many, has become something else—an agent for power through the subjugation of others . . . hmmm . . . "power"

. . . "power"

. . . "power"

"power" has silenced so many, but why?

Lyric—Gas Camp

I'm immersed in breathwork—a vision of my hands
as yours, clawing at blood-filled mud
Embodied, within ancestral pain and anguish
Screaming, bone fingers on barbwire
Crack, baton on skull collapse to fall
Ripple, raindrops in red reflection
Confused, is our mother
Learn, to love her

Fig. 4

ENTRY 29

Power can be designed to disadvantage.

Have we been persuaded to accept this? . . . have ethics and value become so diluted that we can't show love to those we don't understand? I fucking hope not . . .

With roots in gain and ego, power can inflict immeasurable trauma . . .seeding metaphysical pain in many for a sense of security for few. The sickness and imbalance that Mother Earth is experiencing is a result of this—in many ways, this has happened . . .

. . . through capitalist economies shifting value sets to prioritize efficiency and return.

. . . through scales of operations moving from micro local to macro industrial.

. . . through the dissolution that empathy can serve us all better.

. . . through dishonor and injustice becoming widely accepted modalities of design practice and process.

. . . though a designer's lack of respect for the rights of the planet.

. . . through environmental racism.

. . . through slavery.

. . . through "purification."

. . . through genocide.

. . . through greed . . .

When led by greed and gain, the pursuit of power is placed over the WELL-BEING of people, communities, and the rights of Mother Earth. In this case, empathy is rarely a priority, or even a value at the outset of a design process—establishing the flow for an overall design approach, where shared and holistic wellness become an afterthought, embedding sickness in the larger ecosystem . . . we aren't well until all of us are well. Subjugation has become a wicked modality for gain, but can power serve something greater? . . .

. . . instead of subjugation through power, what if we empower through sovereignty!?

. . . what if we celebrate through liberation!?

. . . what if we design legacies through justice!?

. . . design can be, and should be so much more than subjugation.

. . . design can be a platform to heal.

When I was given my mantra, Grandma Judy told me, "everything has a vibration, grandchild . . . whether it be a person, a stream, a rock, a cloud, a bird, or a star—everything is made of atoms and molecules in constant vibration . . . linking us all as one . . . as you breathe, I breathe." We are all connected, whether we want to be or not—a universal vibration that is the song of life. As designers we must choose how we will calibrate the frequencies we write into the experiences of people's lives, and the impact these vibrations will have on our environment.

By holding a space to listen to the vibrations of place we can begin to hear the breath of its nature, and open ourselves to design new possibilities that can empower its meaning, and heal its traumas . . . hmmm . . . "heal"

"heal"

"heal"

. . . "healing" could be a powerful goal? . . .

Lyric—Vision Quest

I sit still in the landscape, a vision of ancient relics
as yours, destroyed and renewed
Shimmer, glass and stone vessels cradle life
Echo, voices fill earthen culture canyons
Refuge, our air is becoming our own
Reborn, harmony in balance

Breathing, is our mother
Learning, to love he.

ENTRY 30

Fig. 5

Stewardship as a practice of justice can heal through the empowerment of experiential legacies.

Can we gain sight of this? . . . striving to honor the history of a place by listening to the vibrations of its constituency—shaping opportunities to address inequities, and innovating through wellness? I fucking hope so . . .

With roots in healing, design practice can emerge as a conduit for empathy . . . by placing people closer in touch with experiential legacies, we can steward more just futures. This can be achieved . . .

. . . by integrating questions of stewardship into the design process itself:
. . . "what will the design process steward?"
. . . "how can my process be shaped to serve through stewardship?"
. . . "how can fully realized design solutions act as stewards themselves?"

. . . by honoring and seeking out the constituency of a place, and finding ways to serve them.

. . . by acknowledging that we as humans are a part of a larger ecosystem, and must respect our role in maintaining balance.

. . . by coauthoring with place
. . .by leading with listening . . .

Listening . . .

While the act of listening is auditory in nature, I feel it can also be a visual phenomenon, even metaphysical. Collage as a tool and process can reach at this—an ontological opportunity linking conceptual thought with graphical representation . . . a visual dialogue and conversation to understand connections between history, people, and place . . . the very process of collage is one of time, connections slowly evolving between content and emotion, drawing the experiential legacy of a place into image-based narratives.

. . . I think of the collage process for our Broad Art Museum proposal, where the notion of "potential energy" emerged as a founding concept—drawing inspiration from the tectonic vibrations of earthquakes, and from the vibrations of intention that people bring when they call Los Angeles home—a gateway to enrich their dreams and amplify their aspirations.

Fig. 6

Museums in their nature are founded in ideals of colonization and siege, evolving as exclusive experiences for the privileged, and perceived by many of the disadvantaged as a place foreign and uninviting. In tandem, museums are known to have enormous carbon footprints through their energy use in lighting, heating, and cooling. The Broad proposal strived to address these factors as a means to steward healing through . . .

. . . coauthoring with place.
. . . dissolving the notion of "museum as temple."
. . . prioritizing the creation of public space over the privilege of access.

. . . integrating strategies for passive heating and cooing through close relations with the earth.

. . . building from the earth itself.
. . . participating as a net producer of energy.
. . . rainwater capture, and greywater infrastructure.
. . . cultivating local flora, and culture.

We engaged in an architectural evocation through the observation of social behaviors and trajectories on the site, rendering a specific center, defined through social movement and the climatic elements of earth and water. As a groundswell of culture, the flow of these energies harken a sense of erosion, shaping pathways for circulation and program, while simultane-

Fig. 7

Fig. 8

ously embodying the realities of climate change as our coasts experience unprecedented sea-level rise and drought.

Speaking through earthen walls made from excavated soil from the site, fractures invite light to spill into gallery spaces below grade, passively cooled within the womb of the earth. Shaping meeting grounds for art and echo. The notion of museum as temple is dissolved through seamless integration of the architecture within the landscape, shaping new public spaces to support civic engagement and encourage pollination.

By merging function with the innate natures of place, and by employing strategies to address inequity, opportunities for healing can emerge where vibrations manifest through time and space to render legacy in experiential form. As designers, let us not lose sight of the fact that we've made our mother sick, so we must do our parts to restore her wellness, and be stewards for justice . . . hmmm . . . "justice" . . .

"just"

"just"

. . . the future can be just—design it.

Lyric—Hawk Talk

I am awake, a vision of two hawks as yours, delivering a message
Soar, healing magic is brought by the messengers
Call, from generation to generation to generation
Discern, the purpose in voice and echo
Hope, futures can be better
Joyous, is our mother
Love, to learn her

Fig. 9

IMAGE CREDITS

1. Mixed-media collage, Quinlin Messenger in
    collaboration with Ahshohn Casilan
2. Takoja Institute, Adobe workshop, Quinlin Messenger
    in collaboration with Andy Cisneros
3. Takoja Institute, Sweat Lodge
4. Mixed-media collage, Quinlin Messenger in
    collaboration with Ahshohn Casilan
5. Ibid.
6. Mixed-media collage, Quinlin Messenger
7. Ibid.
8. Mixed-media collage, Quinlin Messenger in
    collaboration with Ahshohn Casilan
9. Ibid.

In Conversation:

Annika Hansteen-Izora

ON IDENTITY,
COMMUNITY &
AUTHENTICITY

I interviewed Annika Hansteen-Izora by email in Spring 2020 to learn more about how identity, community, and the spirit of authenticity inform their work as a graphic and user experience (UX) designer. This conversation has been lightly edited for length and clarity.

—Jennifer Rittner

JENNIFER RITTNER: Is there anyone you'd like to call into this conversation with you?

ANNIKA HANSTEEN-IZORA: I want to call in my ancestors, who I wouldn't be here without. I also want to call in Black feminist thinkers and artists who have been a key part of grounding my relationship to my art: Toni Morrison, Octavia E. Butler, Toni Cade Bambara, June Jordan, among countless others.

JR: Who were some of the artists, designers, activists, role models, mentors, or loved ones that you looked to for inspiration when you started to identify as an artist and designer?

AHI: I come from a family of artists, and they've always been a flowing source of inspiration since I was a kid. My grandmother, Lakiba Pittman, is a singer, writer, and artist, and she always taught, and continues to teach me, that my voice is valuable, that it's worth sharing, that my creativity is something to nourish. Poets also teach me so much about creation, especially in design. I see design as storytelling, and poets capture story with verse and rhythm. Angel Nafis, Danez Smith, Morgan Parker, Harmony Holiday, Dionne Brand, Hanif Willis-Abdurraqib, Aja Monet, and countless others have done so much for my artistry.

JR: **When you started out, what were you making? To what extent do you think you used your design practices to comment on or express your personal, intersectional ideology (either intentionally or not)?**

AHI: When I first started designing—and I didn't understand it or name it, I should say, as "design"—was when I was in second grade and I was obsessed with 'zines. I was obsessed with magazines. I wanted to be a magazine editor. I loved the idea of being able to capture so many different types of stories, comics, interviews, columns in one space, and to be able to hand it to people and share it with people.

So, I started out with just clipping together pieces of paper and writing articles, and that ended up growing as I got older. And in middle school, I learned how to use my computer to look at Pages—the design application Pages—and create from there. And in high school, I ended up joining my school's paper. And all of this, I never set out to be a designer, but I've always been a multimodal creative. I've always been someone that uses various sources and art forms and mediums to express my creativity.

And so when I think about, to the extent that I've used, my design practices to comment or express on my ideology, I think it's to a great extent, to answer that very, very quickly. But to go a little deeper there, I think I've always been someone that is so . . . I'm very struck by the emotion of wonder. I'm very struck by the things that make people feel a sense of awe because I think those are emotions that allow us to access joy.

And through my personal identity, through my personal experiences with mental health with someone, as someone with depression and anxiety and ADHD, as someone that has varying relationships with power, as a Black and Queer person, accessing joy is a very important thing for me. It's a very important activity to me, an important source for me. And so design is another way that I'm able to tell a story. It's another way that I'm able to express myself. So it's a huge part of why I design and how I design.

JR: **Who is your work trying to speak to (past, present, and/or future)?**

AHI: I think my work is trying to speak to my childhood self. And I don't even care if that may be corny to some people to hear. But really, I think my childhood self was a G, is a G, is the source of my creative energy. And so I think, "Okay. Is this work speaking to them? Would this piece move them?" And I think speaking to my childhood self is an articulation of also my ancestors. It's also an articulation of my relationship with creativity, with artistry. I think in speaking to these shadows of myself, to these corners of myself, I'm also reaching those that may struggle with creativity, may struggle with seeing creative energy within themselves.

I think, a lot of the time, I'm trying to speak to anyone who doesn't think that their voice is valuable. Because for so much of my life, I felt that my voice was invaluable. And so really being able to hold space for anyone that wants to create because I think we live in a world, or in a society I should say, that makes it seem like you can't be an artist unless you've gone to said school, or read said book, or, you know, use said tools. And I want my work to be speaking to anyone that has heard those narratives, and has embodied those narratives, and wants to rid themselves of those narratives, anyone that wants a new creative energy. That's who I hope to speak to in my work.

JR: **How did you get involved with Salimatu Amabebe and the Black Feast project?**

Fig. 1

This is made
—FOR YOU

Welcome in

BLACK FEAST

A creation of Black narrative, an offering to Black lineage, Black Feast is a culinary event that celebrates Black artists and writers through food.

Founded and Directed by *Salimatu Amabebe*, Black Feast was created as a way to not only *make space* at the table for Black artists, but to design a whole new table *for us*.

At our table, guests participate in an experience that weaves together food and art, where Salimatu works with Black artists to create a four-course vegan, gluten-free, and cane sugar free gourmet meal based off of the artist's work. Black Feast events have featured artists across disciplines, such as Jamila Woods, Madison McFerrin, Jayy Dodd, Lukaza Branfman-Verissimo, Amenta Abioto, and others.

Supported with creative direction by *Annika Hansteen-Izora*, Black Feast is led by two queer, Black artists that believe in food and art as a site of possibility. Our dinner experiences are a space where food celebrates Black art, Black stories, Black love, Black movement, & Black voices.

We are based in Portland, Oregon, and host our dinners

AHI: I got connected with Salimatu miraculously and at the exact perfect time. It was a funny time for me because I had just graduated from college at Oberlin College, and I moved back home to Portland. And I should say that I moved back home to Portland because I had applied to over fifty, sixty jobs and internships to try and get into creative strategy, and I did not get accepted to a single one. And so I went home to figure things out. And at that time, none of my friends from high school lived in Portland anymore and my family had just moved to a new home in a new neighborhood in Portland.

And so it felt like a brand-new city to me in a way. And that's a very romantic way to also say that I felt very alone. I was very lonely. My college was where I was able to find a really strong Black and Queer community. And I went from that to Portland, Oregon, which if you may or may not know is one of the whitest metropolitan cities in the US. And so after cocooning for some months, after being depressed for some months, after really sitting with myself and what I wanted to do for a while, I ended up getting connected to some of the arts organizations in Portland, and some of them would host open mics.

And so there was a particular open mic and I decided I was going to read some poetry because I'm a poet. And when I got on stage, I said to the crowd, "Hi, my name's Annika and I'm an introvert that's looking for an extrovert to adopt me." And after I performed, I got off stage and Salimatu immediately walked up to me and was like, "Hi." And we were friends ever since. And I learned that Salimatu had this project called Black Feast, and Black Feast is a culinary and arts space. And we create culinary works that are based on Black artists' projects and pieces.

And so it was really this beautiful joining where I connected with someone that I so needed, that I'm pretty sure it was like, I definitely was meant to meet Salimatu for a reason, but we just started creating from there.

JR: **Which ancestors were you calling in with this work?**

AHI: Salimatu created one of the main lines. That really is a mantra for a Black Feast, which is that this work is made for you. And the "you" is meant to mean Black people. And that is very particular, because I think in the society that we're in, the default so much of the time is whiteness. When I look at advertisements or brands and they say, "This is made for everyone." Or, "This is made for . . ." Yeah. Whenever they say something that's along the lines of, "Well, this is made for everyone . . ." And I know what everyone they're talking about. That everyone is a white person. That person that is always being given directed attention, and care, and energy, and love is a white person, is whiteness. And so, "This meal is made for you," is meant to be a reclaiming and meant to be a centering of Black people.

And when I think of the ancestors that I'm calling in with this work, I come from a line of storytellers and I come from a line of artists. And so I feel like I am calling in the ancestors that specifically want their stories to be held, and want their stories to be told in a way that expresses gratitude, in a way that expresses love. Because in my spiritual practice, you can't just go and call in all of your ancestors, because some of your ancestors don't want you to have the best life, honestly. There are curses to be broken. There is pain that our ancestors hold. And so when I'm calling in the ancestors into this work specifically, it's the ancestors whose stories want to be held tenderly and gently, and with intentional care.

JR: **Can you talk about the visual language of this digital space, and how it carries over or reflects the physical (IRL) experience?**

AHI: The visual language of Black Feast is meant to be rooted in archives, in knowledge, in the wisdom of what came before us. And so I really use that message to hold the visual language of Black Feast. We use really dark and rich and full colors and imagery and text in order to capture attention. And I think that carries over in our physical and IRL experiences in the way that we want people to know that they're being held strongly and being held intentionally and also held in a way that makes us reflect back on the wisdom that came before us.

JR: **The relationship between food, poetry, design, and wellness feel central to your work.**

AHI: I feel like in each of these spaces and in every space that I move through, I'm thinking about, how can I access love here? And how can I help others access love within themselves? And how can I help us access the love and see the love within each other? And food and poetry and design and wellness are all tools by which I'm able to be in relationship with love.

Food has been a huge part of how I love and how I practice community with others. I remember being in my grandmother's kitchen and my grandfather's kitchen, it was one of the main activities that we held with one another. Writing down those recipes was an act of poetry, and it was also an act of design. And I think about all of the moments in my life that I feel that the academy wouldn't recognize as design. I think of Black hair, and I think of Black braids and how that is design. I think about records and how the liner notes that tell you who actually created the music, that is design. And I'm going a little off here, but I feel like each of these spaces is, again, really speaking to how can we see and how can we access love? And I also think that food and poetry and design and wellness helped me articulate the ways that power is constantly showing up in who we see as deserving of care and who we see as deserving of love.

JR: **The color palette for this work, like all of your work, is so striking. Can you talk about your relationship to color?**

AHI: I love color. I love vibrance. I love abundance. And I love lushness. And I love maximalism. I love the idea of really harnessing vibrance, and maybe not harnessing, but really sitting with and being completely in awe of vibrance and being in relation-

Fig. 2

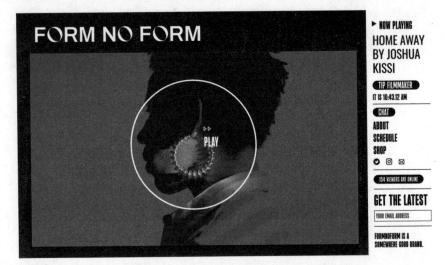

ship to vibrance. And I talk about my grandmother all the time, but she really is not only one of my best friends, but she also is one of my main inspirations. And I think about her home a lot because her home is just a trove and well of colors and arts and plants and books, and it all is sprawling everywhere. And it's just completely abundant and you can feel the love in that space there.

And I think that's really beautiful, because I think when I was introduced to design, and I think a lot of the popular narrative of what is good in design, at least what I've seen, is minimalism, is making things very clean, very clean-cut. And minimalism is interesting because I think about if minimalism is hoping to cut out that which isn't necessary and that which is messy, who decides what's messy exactly? Who decides what is good? Who decides what is clean? I'm suspicious of that. I'm suspicious of that in no shortness of words. But I want each of us to be able to access lushness and brightness and color. And that is why color is so much a part of my work. In a way it's a refusal to be quieted. It's a refusal to be clean. It's their refusal to be perfectly organizedly, even though that's not a word, but perfectly cut down. Color for me is just an announcement of joy, and that's why I lean so much into it.

JR: **Form No Form feels both direct and subversive, celebratory and serious, artful and intimate. You designed the site to literally center the artists' work, no frills, no extraneous UI. Can you talk about the act of centering others in your design work?**

AHI: Centering others, and I'll be specific here, centering Black artists' work in my design work is a privilege and it's an honor to be able to do so. Really, what I'm thinking about and what gets me excited in design, because there are infinite ways that someone can be in relationship to design. I believe that my relationship to design is informed by community and articulating what community actually means, because I feel that community often is just used as this very general term, without actually being specific about what it means to people and what it means to spaces, but being able to articulate what community means to me is a way that I'm in relationship to design.

And I also think about how the act of centering others in my design work is a part of being able to create tools and being able to create archives of knowledge that we can access. I think that archivists who are really finding the work of Black artists are just truly doing the work that we need in the world, because we need to know our stories. We need to know where we come from, and we also need to know that people have thought about similar ideas and similar concepts that we're thinking about. And so centering others in my design work gives me the ability to create new forms of digital archives, to be able to really center Black artists' work, and that is really just a gift to be able to be a part of.

JR: **Like so much of your work, this platform is intentionally designed as a For Us By Us space. As a career designer, can you talk about how you've made yourself available to this kind of work? How are you navigating opportunities to design within community and those that come from predominantly white, cis, het spaces?**

AHI: I've allowed the other ways that I'm creative to be and I've really taken time to nourish all those other creative parts of myself. A lot of the ways that I've been able to connect with people who are also interested and inspired to create these types of intentional platforms came from communities that were in no way related to design. A lot of the ways that I've connected to these folks is through my poetry communities, through writing communities, through dancing communities. So, I feel like just being able to really intentionally be connected to artists has made me available to this kind of work.

When it comes to navigating opportunities to design within community and those that come from predominantly white, cis, and het spaces: At this point in my design career, I want to make things that bring me and that bring others joy. And I think joy is often . . . How can I say? When I think of joy, I think of spaces that allow someone to be their most authentic self and I think when I understand joy, sadness and joy can happen at the same time. As someone who moves through mental health, as someone with a mental health journey . . . Trying to find a way to articulate that. It really was a liberatory feeling to understand that I can experience joy and sadness at the same time. And so, really when I think about who I want to work with I'm thinking about who is making those types of authentic spaces. Those are the spaces that I want to work in.

I'm really putting myself out there, really sharing what I am making. And sometimes what I'm making is strange. It's weird. I know not many people are going to like it but I know that somebody is going to like it and I know that that somebody, if they're into the weird shit that I'm making, then they're probably someone that I really want to be working with.

When I think about navigating opportunities with predominantly white and cis and het spaces, I mean I'll be real. Sometimes you just need to get your bag. Sometimes you just need to work with these spaces for whatever reason that may be. And if anything, what I can underscore is that when I navigate those types of opportunities, I'm really think-ing about, "Is my work being valued here? Is it being held here intentionally? Is it being respected here? Am I being respected here?" And if not, then leave. Or I should say, because sometimes that isn't actually available to all of us, but I want . . . When I navigate design opportunities I'm really thinking about, "Is this going to be nourishing to me? Am I going to make something that I'm proud of?"

And even if it's a situation where it's not something I'm the most proud of, because that happens . . . Sometimes as a designer you just have to make something for a client and you just have to get it out the door. At the very least, am I being respected? Am I being nourished? Am I being held . . . Does it feel like this is leading toward a creative journey that I want to be a part of? Is this important to me in some kind of way?

JR: **What would you say to young designers who are trying to make decisions about their own career trajectories?**

AHI: Make weird shit! Make things that inspire you. Make things that you want to see. Make things that your childhood or teenage self would look at and be like, "Yo, that is dope." Make things that excite you. I think if you're creating for someone else or creating for the academy or for creating an eye whose excitement is not your own, the inspiration and creativity and originality of that work can only go so far.

And so I love a weird side project. I love a weird like, "Hey, I just made this random website, and all you do is you press a button and fruit just pops up onto the screen." It doesn't really matter what it is. If the idea really makes you be like, "This is really fun," then I say, go to where that energy is in your designing. Because somebody will see it. And that's the other important thing is to not be so precious with your work that you don't share it. Somebody is out there looking for your eye. Somebody is out there who really would love to work with you. But if you make yourself hidden, nobody is ever going to know who you are. So I would say create your work, don't be precious with it, don't think about it too hard, and share it with the world in whatever way feels most nourishing to you because some really incredible things can happen from that.

JR: **Ethel's Club and Somewhere Good are both so playful and loving! How are you making room for yourself to be in community when you are designing projects for community?**

AHI: When it comes to making room for myself in community, when I'm designing a project for community, I am
so obsessed with making sure that I understand the story of a piece, both
Ethel's Club and both, well, both Ethel's Club and Somewhere Good, are
playful and loving because those were the stories behind them. Ethel's Club
came from Noge Austin, who's the CEO and founder, and as well as her
grandmother's home. And when I started that project, I started it with really
understanding why she made Ethel's Club. Where did the name Ethel's Club
come from? Who was she hoping to speak to with this project? And not a
shock to me about how her grandmother's home was this space of warmth
and this space of community, because people gathered in it.

     And with that story, I knew that the entire visual
language needed to be grounded in that. And so it is key for me to make room
for myself, to be in community when I'm designing a project for community,
because that actually makes the work authentic. I feel like as a designer,
you must know why you are designing. What is the intention behind your
work? What is your relationship to the people who this work is speaking
to? If it's inauthentic, then perhaps you should not be designing for that
particular project. But I really love to ground myself in the story of a project
because that really just makes it the most vibrant and abundant one.

JR: **What would you say to, let's say, cis/het/white designers who believe they can design anything for anyone?
Do you think someone who doesn't live within these communities could
design for us? Could "universal design principles" be applied to the projects you've worked on?**

AHI: This one made me laugh. I will say that universal design
principles do not exist. Universal design principles are
just an articulation of white supremacy and the ways that white supremacy pervades design. The idea that there is a universal way that something
should look, I mean, that just seems to be the most black-and-white look
at it. It's pretty much just like, that is white supremacy, the idea that your
way can be applied to the entire universe. I do not believe that a universal
design principle could have applied to the projects that I've worked on, I
think. But each of the projects that I've worked on, they obviously have
similarities. There are similar things and similar principles in their design
and in their visual system, but each of them required a different take and
they each required a different authenticity.

     I don't think that someone who doesn't have a relation-
ship with these communities could design for them. Well, let me go back.
You asked, do you think someone who doesn't live within these communi-

110

Fig. 3

Fig. 4

ties could design for us? Yeah, they could totally design for us, but it won't be that good. It won't be very authentic. It will not hit. And I think we've seen that in every design industry. We've seen it in fashion design. We have seen it in brand design. We have seen it in graphic design. Again and again and again and again, we see cis het white designers designing for communities that they have no relationship with, and the work is bad. When I say bad, I mean that it is not thoughtful and it is not intentional and it is not authentic.

I do believe that there is the possibility for someone who does not live within the community to design for the community, but that must be done with very careful intention and very careful care. And sometimes that means in that intention, letting go of the space that you're holding. So, yeah, I feel like the only thing they had to say about this question is just that if you've been taught that there are universal design principles or anything like that, there is a very good article called "Design Thinking is a Rebrand for White Supremacy," and I think you should definitely go read it.

JR: **I imagine you are continuing to grow as a designer, artist, poet, writer, and person. What does the future look like for you in this moment? Where are you finding joy, wellness, and inspiration for yourself? (If you would like to share that.)**

AHI: To me, the future looks well rested, and nursed, and brimming, and full of a lot of possibility. What I've been seeing is a lot of refusal to work with these systems and academies and hierarchies that institutes power. I feel like folks are over them. Or maybe not over them because there's still entanglements for sure, because those entanglements are deep. But what I am seeing is more movement to be curious and question these systems and these academies. And I think there is so much possibility in that questioning. And that is what I'm hopeful for. I'm hopeful for a future that really sharpens our attention against systems of power to really articulate how power moves through our relationship to love and community.

When I think about where I'm finding joy and wellness and inspiration, that has really been in rest and, in really taking my rest seriously. Because I think for most of my life, I don't believe that I am . . . I don't think I'm worthy of accessing rest until I've hit my breaking point. It's not until I have run myself into the ground that I'm like, "Okay. Maybe I should go lie down and maybe I should rest." I'm trying to move against that. I'm trying to get rest before the breaking point to get rest every day. And honestly, that has been a huge source of joy and wellness and creative inspiration. So I'm really hoping that everyone finds ways that can nourish their rest.

JR: **Final question: what advice would you give to design students who are trying to navigate their own intersectional identities and spaces?**

AHI: The advice I'd give to design students who are trying to navigate their own intersectional identities and spaces is, if the thing that you're looking for doesn't exist, to build your own tables. I think that's the biggest advice that I have is to build your own tables, to build your own spaces, your own journals, your own zines, your own sites, your own archives that can hold all the abundance that you are. To refuse to dilute yourself for organizations or academies or companies, whatever it may be. If there is a space that is asking you to dilute a part of who you are, I would move away from it and build your own table and build your own space.

There's so much power in building spaces that are truly nourishing for ourselves. And I think that power resides in the experience that, once the space is built, then you can connect to others and you can build with others. And that is so much of what is needed. And that is so much of a source of joy, is when we can connect with others and build from a new space, from a space that isn't informed by the academy, or hierarchy, or supremacy. So I would go to where joy is calling for you and build your own table so that you can access that joy.

IMAGE CREDITS
Figures 1-4: Courtesy of Annika Hansteen-Izora.

DESIGN
EDUCATION

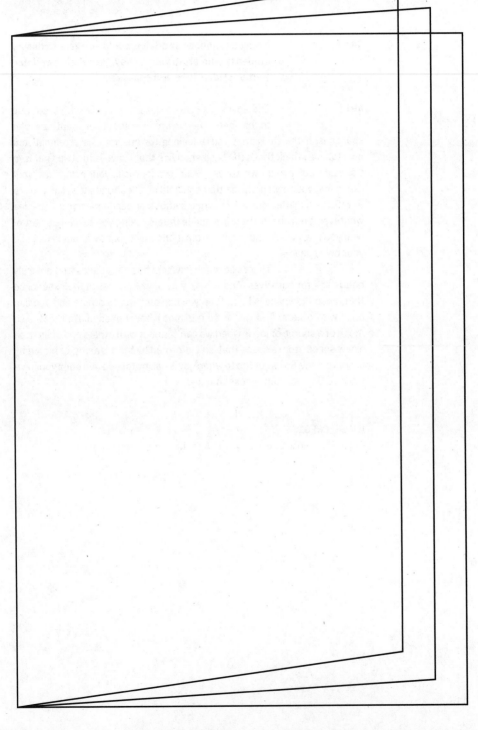

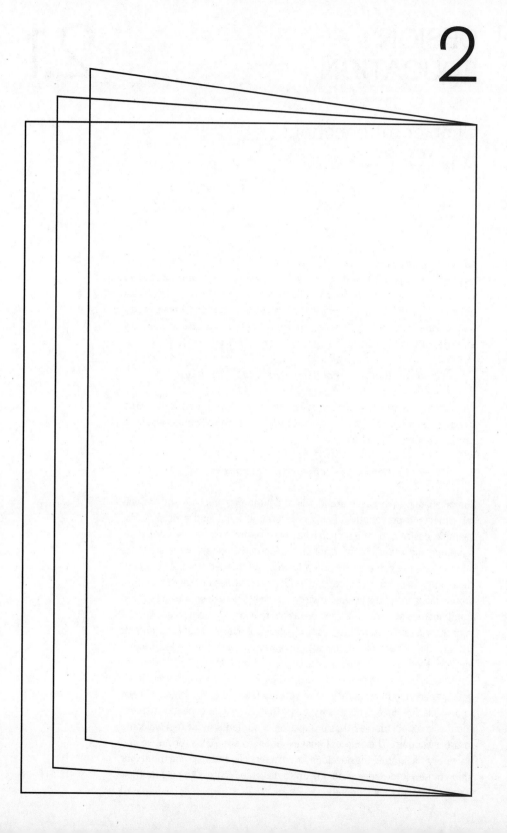

2

DESIGN EDUCATION

Chapter Introduction:
Anne H. Berry

As teachers, our role is to take our students on the adventure of critical thinking. Learning and talking together, we break with the notion that our experience of gaining knowledge is private, individualistic, and competitive. By choosing and fostering dialogue, we engage mutually in a learning partnership.

—bell hooks, *Teaching Critical Thinking*

The engaged voice must never be fixed and absolute but always changing, always evolving in dialogue with a world beyond itself.

—bell hooks, *Teaching to Transgress*

Too often, due to imposed standards or limitations, teaching and assessment become prescriptive. Being creatures of habit and efficiency, for example, design educators teach what we know from our own experiences, passing along the same information we learned when we were students and utilizing the same books and resources we learned from. As a result, the ubiquitous nature of European influence via Swiss design, the culture around design, and the language we collectively use to describe it results in traditional design curriculum and pedagogy that look the same regardless of institution, student demographics, or social, political, and cultural context. Despite the impact of technology, globalization, and the United States' increasingly diverse population, design education in the United States has not broadly evolved to reflect these realities. Rebuilding curricula and navigating academic bureaucracy can certainly take time. Yet, change is not impossible. It is, in fact, necessary. Apart from the skill sets needed to meet the design opportunities that are available, students must feel welcome in the classroom. Their educational experiences should be formative and liberatory, facilitating the development of new skills and inspiring the acquisition of new knowledge. And it is up to design educators to nurture their natural creativity and curiosity.

Though one's design education never truly ends, the contributions in this section collectively capture the breadth of a designer's educational trajectory, from being a student to becoming a career professional or academic. Most importantly, the contributors are also intensely mindful of what it's like to be a Black student in a predominantly white industry.

In my conversation with design practitioner and educator Maurice Woods, we discuss the Inneract Project, which he developed over 17 years ago to support historically excluded, primarily Black and Brown youth in the field of design. While a great deal of focus in design education circles is on diversifying classrooms and industry, Woods highlights an area that simultaneously plays a role in designers' career prospects: technological advancements and digital media. Learning skills in emerging technologies, such as user experience design (UX), user interface design (UI), human-assisted AI, augmented reality (AR), virtual reality (VR), and mixed reality open more opportunities for design students. However, portfolios solely focused on branding and print design make the accumulative opportunities for Black and Brown designers smaller. He also provides insights into the ways he and his staff are inspiring and engaging young designers.

In "The New Visual Abnormal," Colette Gaiter shares her perspectives on the harmful, systemic impact of "white as normal," in education as well as in society at large through the lens of publication design. She offers parallels between the 1970s—a period that heavily influenced her professionally—to the current societal and political crises in the United States. She also discusses her experience with "visual whiplash" and the power of visual media and the necessity of teaching diversity as normalcy at a foundational level in design education.

Steve Jones emphasizes the significance of one's cultural context in "Unvisible (What's the Scenario?)," contrasting his experiences with his advice for Black design students/design students of color. He describes scenarios that are painfully familiar, identifying common barriers within design education. But in acknowledging uncomfortable truths and the reality that educators and professionals may not appreciate the creative individuality students of color bring to their work, he also advocates the need to "embrace what you intimately know."

In "The Strong Black Woman: Using the Racism Untaught Framework to Contextualize the Design of Misogynoir," Terresa Moses discusses an educational framework she codeveloped to critically analyze "racialized" design and create anti-racist design approaches. She walks readers through an investigation into the first step of the Racism Untaught tool kit using the "strong Black woman" stereotype to examine how the trope has been designed within societal normalities.

In "A Reading List for Politics of Design," Chris Rudd deconstructs his Illinois Institute of Technology Institute of Design course Politics of Design. The syllabus and accompanying reading list reorient students' approach to and engagement with design, moving from a capitalist model to a model that is critical, curious, and anti-racist. As a result, students come to understand that there is no neutrality in design and, therefore, no neutrality in designers; our politics guide our work, and designers must interrogate their beliefs while in pursuit of becoming their best creative selves.

Lastly, in "Beyond the Universal: Positionality and Promise in an HBCU Classroom," Kaleena Sales provides a personal essay on her examination and reexamination of what it means to be a Black design educator working within a historically Black college/university (HBCU). Though operating within a context that she knows and understands, Sales shares some of the poignant revelations she makes along her own journey as an academic, including the challenges she navigates when considering the dynamics of teaching the traditional European design canon to mostly Black students whose connections to design are rooted in their own cultural communities.

In Conversation:

Maurice Woods &

Anne H. Berry

ON MEETING THE DEMANDS OF THE FUTURE

I spoke with designer and educator Maurice Woods to discuss the foundational roots of the Inneract Project, an organization he created to support historically excluded, primarily Black and Brown youth in the field of design, and his perspective on design education. This conversation has been edited for length and clarity.

—Anne H. Berry

ANNE H. BERRY:	What does outreach look like? How do you initiate conversations about design with the students you bring into your programs?

MAURICE WOODS: I start by understanding what kids are interested in and explain how design fits into that world. Over the years I've learned that our youth are much more likely to engage or become active learners if they are able to understand how design is infused into past or current experiences with products and services they are familiar with. We generally initiate conversation by asking and learning what students love to do, and we present students with short workshops that give them a hint of the type of work designers do to assess interest.

When I first originally started writing curriculum in 2004, honestly, I didn't know what I was doing. I was just trying to put together a class to teach some kids some things that I knew. Because I was working with middle school students the question was "How do I make courses engaging?" And I knew that teaching kids design—which is somewhat technical—would have to have some component of fun in order for them to stay actively engaged. So, along with setting context, a lot of the work I did early on was to figure out how to develop curriculum that had a lot of play. I would do a lot of Pictionary-like games and have them put together word puzzles. I'd have students working on projects inside and outside, such as taking photos and converting the images into black-and-white images. It was important to not make learning in my program feel like school. I wanted it to feel lighthearted and fun—I wanted students to look forward to taking classes on the weekend even if their parents forced them to be there.

Our educational focus and logic is based on three pillars of work: Skills + Awareness + Mentoring. This equation informs what programs we offer and how we measure success. It serves as a North Star for all of our educational offerings and supports our prioritization efforts. All programs and initiatives with students, whether ongoing engagement or first-timers, refer to these three areas of coverage, providing structure and benchmarks for skills our programs provide, preparing our students with the relevant training needed to be successful in the design industry.

AHB: **You've had a formal design education. What do you feel you are able to provide students, especially at an early age, that traditional design education doesn't have the scope to address?**

MW: Inneract Project provides context building, support for basic needs, and an emphasis on cultural acceptance. We have a focus on addressing systemic barriers that often restrict students and families from "seeing" the opportunities:

CONTEXT BUILDING

Before students can even know that they can take a college class for design, they must know it exists. All people are consciously or subconsciously connected to things that were designed for them, for a reason. This is where we use exposure and awareness to highlight and educate both students and parents about how design already impacts their world. By doing this, we build a bridge toward design that they can relate to and, therefore, see how design can be a formidable career that allows them to see themselves in context of their own world. This is a particularly fundamental piece in underrepresented communities, because much of what they see in design comes from white perspectives.

SUPPORT FOR BASIC NEEDS

Much like context building, Inneract Project also considers not just how underrepresented communities are exposed to design, but why they are not. Exploitation, marginalization, powerlessness, cultural dominance, and violence all present barriers for Black and Latinx families. We look at the barriers that impede underrepresented groups from "seeing" by providing basic needs such as free classes, paid opportunities

122

for students, free software and hardware, free lunches and, if needed, Wi-Fi to ensure that families are supported regardless of their socioeconomic status. We want students to feel unbound as they enter our classes so they can be empowered to learn.

EMPHASIS ON CULTURAL ACCEPTANCE

Cultural acceptance is by far one of the most critical areas of support we provide our students, the scope of which can be difficult for traditional design programs to cover. Cultural acceptance, or lack thereof, is a condition that has caused a great deal of generational and cultural damage to the psyche of underrepresented people of color. For hundreds of years, we have been dominated by European and American doctrines, which have made a number of our contributions to our world. Namely, making us feel less worthy or accomplished when in actuality, we have contributed significantly to American culture. One could even argue, moreover, that American culture has been built of the backs of the marginalized—from our food, dance, ideology, language (slang), inventions, sports and entertainment, to name a few, the impact of our influence is embedded in everyday, American life. At Inneract Project, we work to make sure students see these accomplishments by celebrating a variety of different cultures in the messaging and projects we support.

AHB: **And it seems to me that you're providing some of that context to help students get a sense of what they're going to be encountering, whether it's in the workplace or an educational setting.**

MW: Yeah, that's right. Some people think that we are only teaching. Obviously, we spend a great deal of time training, but teaching only represents a portion of the work we do. We look at how students are impacted in a variety of different ways—sometimes it is about hands-on teaching and explaining how to think, discover, and relay information creatively. For others, it is simple exposure or mentorships (this was the case for my own career trajectory). People tend to learn just as much or more outside the classroom as they do in the classroom, therefore, contextual learning is key. If you are more interested or familiar with a subject you tend to pay closer attention and process information more efficiently.

Over the years of work, what I have also experienced is that learning design doesn't just happen by putting curriculum in front of someone, especially young kids who don't have any understanding of what design is. It takes time for most. We try to surround students with a variety of different options to explore many facets of design, throughout the year—retention is something we strive for. We attribute our success to not only training students but building long-standing relationships with families and continually pressing upon communities to discover another profession they might not realize has the potential to be a fruitful career.

But, how do you teach someone design, who, you know, doesn't have money to eat? We try to be very mindful of that. And also we try to provide support through means beyond just education. For example, during the height of the pandemic, we had wellness check-ins, especially for students where they can come in and talk about things that matter to them. We had that for our volunteers, too. So we're really thinking about this from a broad standpoint, whether you're in middle school, high school, college, or working professionally. That's sometimes hard to explain to people outside of our organization because we have these portals or avenues where people can come in at various different stages throughout their lives and get connected and get supported in different ways.

AHB: **It's easy for students to fall through the cracks, especially if they're not feeling welcome in a classroom environment. Where do you think traditional design education has gone wrong when it comes to students of color?**

MW: The foremost concern I have, outside of students falling through the cracks, is the gap between traditional design education and where the professional design industry stands now, as a whole. I work at a large tech company and as a designer I've worked on AI and machine learning—and that's just the tip of the iceberg! New forms of media and content, such as human-assisted AI, augmented reality, virtual reality, and mixed reality are flooding the market, and it appears that the next generation of design students (regardless of race) are not getting the design experience necessary to be on par with the velocity of technological growth in these industry spaces. As I look at design portfolios I review, they are, in general, branding portfolios, which are still useful but limit the plethora of opportunities students might otherwise have to fill positions at companies or explore new ideas at the collegiate level that push the boundaries of these emerging technologies.

Now, coming back to Black and Latin students who are even less likely to be enrolled in a design school with deeper resources— this puts marginalized designers of color at even more of a risk of starting from behind.

Secondly, the fact is, nationally, educators in design schools are probably 80 percent white. If I was teaching a class [in higher ed] and I was teaching design to students of all races, I would focus time on history and the significant contributions many of our marginalized forebears have made to the design industry, including Aaron Douglas and other early Black and Latin innovators in graphic design. I'd also propose curricula on the various different creative movements, such as the Harlem Renaissance and the black art movements, and examine the way visual artists and graphic images have shaped and defined American culture while also representing the vibrancy of racial diversity and ethnic identity.

The goal is to break down any psychological associations derived from the notion that good design has primarily come at the hands of white/Eurocentric ideologies. Regardless of race, students should see and appreciate Black and Brown designers as significant contributors to the well-being of our world. For the marginalized, this acknowledgment creates a feeling of belonging and a sense of purpose which is also key to staying committed. Through the Inneract Project, we help designers, whether in middle school or professional careers, feel uplifted in their work, feel valued, and enjoy a safe place to be themselves and find their purpose as designers. I don't know of other traditional design schools that are set up to provide these types of experiences and support, though I imagine some are out there, following similar models, but I applaud this type of thinking and commitment.

AHB: **But it sounds as though these are concepts that you're talking about and intentionally instilling in your Inneract Project students . . .**

MW: Yeah, I mean we want to be able to provide opportunities for students to learn but we also want them to also understand that they have a place in design as well, and what their trajectory looks like.

AHB: **So when it comes to the programming and curriculum that you've developed, why have you focused on Black and Brown students? Why is the programming you are providing a necessity?**

MW: In this world we've been conditioned to accept the ideals of "oneness," one perspective. And that is a European or European American perspective. And products and services should obviously be designed for all people. But the makeup of this country is becoming more and more diverse. And the minorities are now the majority in this country. From the perspective of a business, it is going to be even more important that you're able to connect to this majority market. And in order to do that and get the right representation of that market, you need to have people that reflect that market. And you can't do that with "oneness."

Secondly, design should take into account how the messaging of "oneness" has affected marginalized people across the world. The meaning/associations behind the visual images we see permeate our world. These narratives often are controlled and transmitted by designers at some point. Without any "truth checking" these visual images lead to misassociations. You can see a sample of this playing out with police brutality and racism. People that don't live in or understand another's lived experiences develop prejudices and misconceptions based on what they perceive is true—from what they have seen and heard—which can often lead to tragedy or racist attitudes.

I want Black and Brown designers to be behind the wheel, because these associations also affect marginalized people. Our kids are looking at these conceptions of beauty and culture through the lens of "oneness" and are being influenced by it. So, all these messages that are being pushed out need to be diversified, and we need to have more designers of color serving as "guardians" of our culture.

The New Visual Abnormal

COLETTE GAITER

When I took a commercial art class in high school, I knew that I wanted to become a graphic designer and change the way people perceived the world. Yes, it was grandiose thinking, but it was the 1970s, and changing the world seemed not only possible but immediately urgent to a lot of teenagers at that time. In 1971 the United States was in its sixth year of involvement in the sixteen-year Vietnam War. Black people, LGBTQ people, women, disabled people, Hispanic people, poor people, Native Americans, and everyone else denied American power and prosperity claimed their rights while culture wars raged.

Fifty years later, we are back in crisis mode, confronting similar issues on a global scale that affect every life, plus a pandemic and climate disaster. We survived the seventies, and some conditions did improve. In the third decade of the twenty-first century, designers absolutely can take the lead in accelerating progress for the next fifty years by visualizing a just and equitable future now.

The urgently essential thing visual communicators can do in 2021 is stop normalizing and foregrounding whiteness. Former Black Panther artist Emory Douglas was not much older than a teenager when he started laying out, designing, and making illustrations and cartoons for the *Black Panther* newspaper. The visual world was changing fast. Just a few years after the Civil Rights Act passed in 1964, guaranteeing fundamental rights for African Americans, mainstream white-controlled media started featuring (although rarely) Black people in ads, on magazine covers, and on television. Previously if Black people were present in the media, we were almost exclusively in subservient roles, primarily as actual servants, especially in advertising. A few Black television characters in the 1950s and early 1960s usually reinforced negative stereotypes or existed solely as sidekicks to the main white characters. There were several firsts when Black female models appeared on the covers of magazines like *Glamour* and *Vogue* in the late 1960s. On November 25, 1967, *Rolling Stone*, an innovator in music journalism and culture, featured the now-iconic Tina Turner on its cover. New images and representations seemed possible.

Fig. 1

Magazines were a big part of my childhood and adolescence. *Ebony*, *Jet*, *Vogue*, at least one weekly newsmagazine like *Time* or *Newsweek*, the "big glossies" *LOOK* and *LIFE*, and others regularly arrived in the mail at our house. I loved looking at *Vogue*, with its glamorous full-bleed art-styled photography and spare layouts. The *Black Panther* (BP) newspaper occasionally came into my household in 1971 when my older sister brought issues home from Howard University. The BP paper's lead artist and designer, Emory Douglas, visualized Black people living in ghettos fighting slumlords, brutality from police officers (drawn as pigs), and the institutions that rigidly enforced racism. I had a range of publications to look at—from establishment-enforcing news magazines to the radically beautiful *Black Panther* newspaper.

VISUAL WHIPLASH On one end of magazine culture, in 1971, *Vogue* pictured virtually all white people in its photographs and ads. *Ebony* and *Jet* presented Black people almost as exclusively. The *Black Panther* was full-blown non-assimilationist and anti-capitalist, showing mostly Black people but included other global people of color who joined their fight against Western imperialism in politics and commerce. The Panthers also fought white Western dominance in the American cultural imagination. In the late 1960s, contrasting the Black people in *Ebony* and *Jet*, who were usually meticulously well-dressed and coiffed, with women wearing straightened hair (Afros emerged around 1968), the people Emory Douglas and the other *Black Panther* artists drew looked authentically Black. Some wore Afrocentric clothing, showing solidarity with Black people fighting colonialism in African countries. Images of people with full Black lips, broad noses, and dark-skinned bodies filled the *Black Panther*'s pages. Douglas said, "The people saw themselves in the artwork. They became the heroes. They could see their uncles in it. They could see their fathers or their brothers and sisters in the art."[1] Lighter skin and straighter hair were preferred on Black people in mainstream media, even in Black publications, and the ads reflected those aspirations. Douglas's drawings were astonishing in their time because they showed beautiful Black people who had little money and radiated dignity and determination. In Black Panther leader Huey Newton's article in the July 20, 1967, issue of the newspaper he claimed that "strategic revolutionary art," including pictures of people defending themselves against the police, showed "the correct handling of a revolution."[2] The drawings were cathartic as metaphors, encouraging people to arm themselves against internalizing white supremacy by imagining power and control over their lives. At the time, looking at these publications and their oppositional racial representations gave me visual whiplash from observing such a range of culture.

People of color practice cognitive dissonance every day while living in the United States. We know that the mass-mediated world rarely reflects our experiences and ideas. It is not a coincidence that the United States ranks fifteenth out of forty-four countries in effective media literacy education according to the nonprofit organization Media Literacy Now. U.S. diversity complicates finding consensus in education values.[4] The default solution is often to ignore issues that could be addressed by acknowledging difference. Our lack of homogeneity encourages forming myths like the "American Dream" and forcing the dominance of fictional ideals that only work for some segments of the population. In 2021 controversies rage over teaching Critical Race Theory[5] or the seminal 1619 Project (which explains the country's long and continuing relationship with the institution of slavery).[6] The denial fueling this pushback insists on ignoring the past, limiting progress for the United States on all social fronts. Visual literacy in this country would require focused attention on our relationship with race, past and present. We have not looked at or learned from the ways visual media, starting with early newspapers, deliberately planted images of white supremacy in the American imagination, making racism seem necessary and expected.

UBIQUITOUS IMAGES, BIG LIES　　For example, the nineteenth-century lithographers Currier and Ives called their company "The Grand Central Depot for Cheap and Popular Prints." At one time, they produced 95 percent of the engravings sold in the United States.[7] Their engravings included the Darktown series, with over a hundred prints created from the mid-1870s into the early 1890s, primarily by artist Thomas Worth. According to William Thompson, "The series reinforced the widely accepted pictorial stereotype of the African American as a kinky-haired, thick-lipped, wide-eyed, simian creature that could not even pretend to live like white Americans, despite emancipation and the best efforts of sympathetic Reconstructionists—the position to which most late nineteenth-century Americans were retreating."[8] Most of their prints displayed bucolic landscapes and white people who embodied idealized small-town "Americana." Today the racist Darktown series is usually left out of Currier and Ives exhibitions. Harry T. Peters, the most prominent collector of Currier and Ives prints and related materials, wrote decades ago: "Currier and Ives were businessmen and craftsmen. . . but primarily they [were] mirrors of the national taste, weather vanes of popular opinion, reflectors of American attitudes."[9] Those attitudes included racism and white supremacy. Images like these justified Reconstruction-era and Jim Crow legal discrimination, visualizing the idea in white minds that Black people did not know what to do with our freedom and did not deserve equality.

Emory Douglas's 1960s and 70s illustrations comprised a visual antithesis to images like Worth's that sought to reduce African Americans to archetypal caricatures. Worth mocked Black aspiration, making it seem ridiculous, while Douglas's drawings show poor people with their pride and dreams intact. Racist ideas were deliberately and regularly embedded. They can be excavated just as intentionally.

Fig. 2

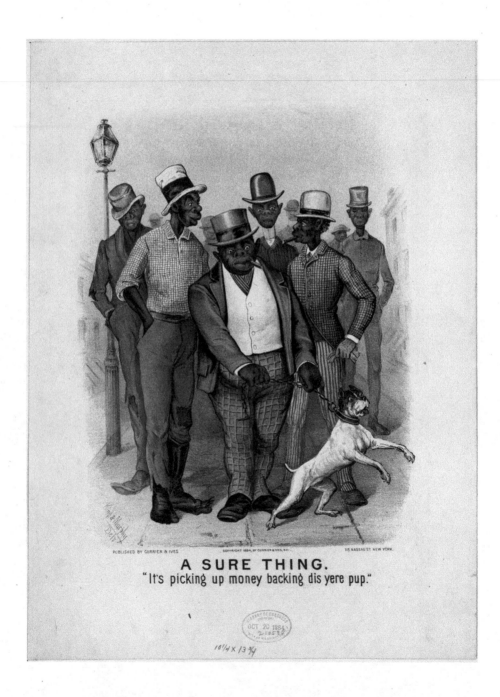

A SURE THING.

"It's picking up money backing dis yere pup."

Fig. 3

134

FILLING IN As a professor, I am still motivated by my high school
THE BLANKS revelation that visual media is ground zero for
influencing political and social world views. When I first
started teaching visual communication and graphic design, I found few
examples of non-white or even female designers and illustrators. In the
early 1990s, I assigned students a research project and included people like
the Harlem Renaissance artists Aaron Douglas and Miguel Covarrubias on
the list of potential subjects. I noticed that students (mostly white) always
chose the artists of color first. They were intrigued by images of lives that
were unfamiliar to them. I added other people of color to my list as I found
them, but there were never many because no one had written about them.
Later I located the former Black Panther artist Emory Douglas, whose work
I had admired in high school, and started interviewing him about his work. I
wrote explicitly about his visual work because it was only mentioned briefly
in books about the Black Panther Party. I realized that I had to contribute
to that incomplete body of texts.[10]

Most visual communications programs include courses
that specifically address semiotics and decoding visual media beyond the
obvious. I propose that college visual communications programs foreground identity in all learning experiences, requiring students to forget any
ideas they had of designing for "normal" or "average" people. Each student
is different, as is each audience. I developed and taught new courses
(open to all university students of any major) on the effects media, design,
and culture have on thinking and behavior. Students become aware that
racism, sexism, homophobia, transphobia, and ableism were intentionally
built into the mainstream visual media landscape to normalize them as
shared national values. Learning about the historical collective uncon-
scious reveals that images people have never personally seen continue to
influence contemporary culture through inherited memory and iterative
references. Too many people believe that the "isms" (racism, sexism, etc.)
are performed in the extreme by only "bad" people. These harmful and
antisocial ideas are so innocuously embedded into everyday language
and images that they continue unnoticed and even defended by those
who scream "political correctness!" at any suggestion that they might
be dangerous. Requiring all design and visual communications students
to examine their identities (inherited and acquired) and a range of backgrounds and experiences would be a huge step toward building an equitable
society. Most people cannot imagine equality because we have never seen
it. Visual communicators can lead by modeling behavior that moves toward
an elusive ideal. By 2045, when 2020s students influence visual culture
at the highest levels, most people in the United States will be of the global
majority, who are not white.[11] Design education can anticipate that change.

Despite demographic facts, Western white sensibilities dominate the worldwide popular culture landscape. It is imperative to show young people that biases are specifically taught in sometimes nefarious, but more often, seemingly natural ways. When I ask students to name some of their identities in private writing assignments, some write, "I'm just white," as if that is not an identity. Whiteness is an identity but persists as "default" or "normal" even though demographics tell a different story. "Whiteness-as-default" aggressively minimizes everyone's interior cultural life, especially for white people. Overrepresented people are usually the ones who believe in "racial color blindness." There is no such thing. Design students of color should never have to defend creating work that does not conform to media-generated ideas of universality. All students consciously and unconsciously bring individual identities into their work, overtly or subtly. Signs and symbols that are not part of the dominant white culture can be translated and learned the same way that young children absorb new words and pronounce them without self-consciousness or prejudice. These practices will expand our visual media literacy and challenge the entire concept of "normal."

THE NEW VISUAL ABNORMAL   The September 2020 issue of *Vogue*, the first after more than fifteen million people internationally protested George Floyd's murder by police, was full of global-majority people[12]—in ads and editorial pages. According to the *New York Times*, "employees at *Vogue*'s parent company, Condé Nast, were publicly calling out what they viewed as racism in their own workplace. At 316 pages, the issue, titled 'Hope,' featured a majority of Black artists, models, and photographers, a first for the magazine."[13] A painting of a Black woman by African American artist Kerry James Marshall was on the cover. *Vogue*'s editor Anna Wintour publicly acknowledged a history of omissions and mistakes. The public and the fashion industry received her words with both skepticism and appreciation. The important thing is that the pages displayed an adjusted view of the world from the magazine. As I turned pages, I imagined white people writing outraged letters and canceling their subscriptions after seeing the magazine showcase people of color. I also realized that the shift seemed normal and pleasing to my eyes and spirit. I look forward to inclusivity becoming the new visual abnormal.

NOTES

1. Marc Steiner and Emory Douglas. "The Life and Times
    of Emory Douglas, Minister of Culture in the Black
    Panther . . ." YouTube. *Real News Network*, November
    14, 2014. https://www.youtube.com/watch?v=hNy
    _S4z4vpw.

2. Huey P. Newton, *Huey P. Newton Reader*. Edited by
    David Hilliard and Donald Weise. New York: Seven
    Stories Press, 2002.

3. Joe Carr, "A New Index Shows That the US Scores Low
    on Media Literacy Education." Media Literacy Now |
    Advocating for Media Literacy Education, July 28,
    2021. https://medialiteracynow.org/a-new-index-shows
    -that-the-us-scores-low-on-media-literacy-education/.

4. Robert W. Kubey, "Why U.S. Media Education Lags
    Behind the Rest of the English-Speaking World."
    Television & New Media 4, no. 4 (November 2003):
    351-70. https://doi.org/10.1177/1527476403255808.

5. Cady Lang, "President Trump Has Attacked Critical
    Race Theory. Here's What to Know About the
    Intellectual Movement." *Time*, September 29, 2020.;
    Kimberlé Crenshaw, one of the founding scholars
    of CRT, defines it as "a practice—a way of seeing
    how the fiction of race has been transformed into
    concrete racial inequities." https://time
    .com/5891138/critical-race-theory-explained/.

6. Jake Silverstein, "Why We Published the 1619
    Project." *New York Times Magazine*. August 14, 2019.
    https://www.nytimes.com/interactive/2019/08/14/
    magazine/1619-america-slavery.html. The New York
    Times' 1619 Project, initiated by journalist Nikole
    Hannah Jones, "aims to reframe the country's history
    by placing the consequences of slavery and the
    contributions of black Americans at the very center
    of our national narrative." https://www.nytimes.com/
    interactive/2019/08/14/magazine/1619-america-slavery
    .html

7. "Amon Carter Museum Presents the America of Currier
    & Ives." Amon Carter Museum of American Art, July
    15, 2003. https://www.cartermuseum.org/press-release/
    carter-museum-presents-america-currier-ives.

8. William Fletcher Thompson, Jr. "Pictorial Images of
    the Negro During the Civil War." *Wisconsin Magazine of
    History* 48 (Summer 1965): 282-94. Quoted in Le Beau,
    B. F. (2000), "African Americans in Currier and Ives's
    America: The Darktown Series." *Journal of American &
    Comparative Cultures*, 23: 74. https://doi-org.udel
    .idm.oclc.org/10.1111/j.1537-4726.2000.2301_71.x

9. Harry T. Peters, *Currier & Ives: Printmakers to the
    American People*. Garden City, NY: Doubleday, 1942.
    Quoted in Le Beau, B.F. (2000), "African Americans
    in Currier and Ives's America: The Darktown Series."
    Journal of American & Comparative Cultures, 23: 71.
    https://doi-org.udel.idm.oclc.org/10.1111/j.1537-
    4726.2000.2301_71.x

10. Colette Gaiter, "What Revolution Looks Like: The
    Work of Black Panther Artist Emory Douglas." Essay.
    In *Black Panther: The Revolutionary Art of Emory
    Douglas*, edited by Sam Durant, 93-109. New York:
    Rizzoli, 2007.

11. William H. Frey, "The US Will Become 'Minority White'
    in 2045, Census Projects." *Brookings*. Brookings
    Institution, September 10, 2018. https://www
    .brookings.edu/blog/the-avenue/2018/03/14/the-us-will
    -become-minority-white-in-2045-census-projects/.

12. Daniel Lim, "I'm Embracing the Term 'People of the
    Global Majority.'" *Medium*, May 11, 2020. https://
    regenerative.medium.com/im-embracing-the-term-people
    -of-the-global-majority-abd1c1251241.

13. Edmund Lee, "The White Issue: Has Anna Wintour's
    Diversity Push Come Too Late?" *New York Times*
    (October 24, 2020), https://www.nytimes
    .com/2020/10/24/business/media/anna-wintour-vogue
    -race.html.

IMAGE CREDITS

1. © Copyright 1967 *Rolling Stone*, LLC. Tina Turner on
   the second cover of *Rolling Stone* magazine, November
   23, 1967.
2. ©2021 Emory Douglas / Licensed by AFNYLAW.com. *Black
   Panther* newspaper back cover. May 1, 1971.
3. Caricature issued as part of the "Darktown comics"
   series. Currier & Ives. Worth, Thomas, 1834-1917,
   artist. New York: published by Currier & Ives, c1884.

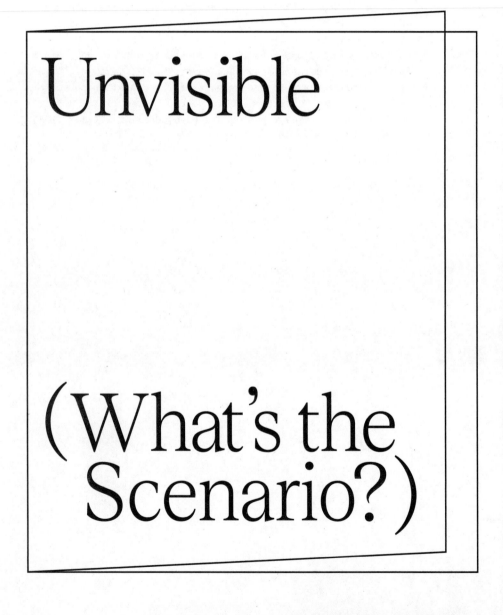

Unvisible

(What's the
Scenario?)

STEVE JONES

As a designer, I have come to terms with the fact that what and who design history has been interested in canonizing, up to this point, does not reflect me, my cultures, my values, and many of the tenets that make me a citizen, a designer, and a teacher. I don't see myself reflected in much of the narrative of design—not in the history, the theory, the practitioners or the outcomes.

—Ramon Tejada, professor, Rhode Island School of Design

Fig. 1

ATCQtownfan @atcqtownfan · 28m
I'm vexed, fumin', I've had it up to here
My days of payin' dues are over,
acknowledge me as in there #tribe

In the twenty-three years that I've been both a designer and design educator, I frequently wonder how different my design path would be if I didn't have the additional obstacles to overcome, obstacles that my white counterparts did not have to endure. Even today, the consistent theme of my design pedagogy is how to discuss and reflect on the topics and history I wish were taught to me as a design student. In the past year there have been too-many-to-count discussions around decolonization and DEI (diversity, equity, and inclusion). While the country and world (again) reckon with the issues of race; and as art schools and institutions of higher learning address (again) the issues of systemic racism, I often look back on my design education, and ask: *"Knowing what I know now, were there pivotal, often racialized, scenarios that shaped and impacted my path as a design student?"* Here is what I would impart to the young Black designer starting their design education journey.

SCENARIO 1

If I am not what you say I am, then you are
not who you think you are.

—James Baldwin

When the time comes—as is ubiquitous in every design program—you will have an assignment in which the creative brief calls for you to design something that explores your identity. The final outcome will be a document that reduces your selfhood into the form of a poster, book, or some similar artifact. If you approach this endeavor naïvely, you will make the mistake of actually doing an assignment—staying true to its parameters—and complete something that honestly, or theoretically, explores and represents who you are. For the Black American designer, this assignment is a slippery slope—and even more of a trap for Black designers from the West Indies, Africa, and outside the Black American diaspora. Be ready for the rude awakening during the final critique, when your white professor—and it will most always be a white instructor—is dismissive of and/or indifferent to your final comp.

Your professor will make it clear, in not so many words, that your self-portrait isn't sufficiently good, because your biography, your lived experience, is too foreign to him; something he cannot relate to. The language, artifacts, and confessions that comprise your work is something that he has never encountered, and therefore it does not meet whatever (familiar) "criteria" he envisioned a work on self-identity should be. You'll think to yourself: *"My identity is central to who I am and how I see the world. How can a professor diminish a project on self-identity, because he's not familiar with it?"*

I found form and theory in my fists—
Maybe they don't get the gist!
Ain't I got no art?[1]

As you fruitlessly try to argue your case, if you're (un)lucky, one of your more "enlightened" white classmates will step in and co-sign for you. Your classmate will testify on your behalf to your instructor that, in fact, the self-portrait you presented is valid. This white advocacy is usually enough for your professor to hesitantly concede, and in the end your project will pass with a marginal grade. (It should be noted this will not be the first time that a white classmate or so-called ally will come to your defense and guarantee the authenticity of your work to a white instructor.)

This experience, the marginal acceptance of your individual voice will be forever etched in your memory. From that moment forward, with every project, you will make an unspoken agreement with yourself: *That your true authentic voice will need to be neutered in order for it to pass muster with your white professors.* This will be a recurring performance that you play out throughout the rest of your design education.

SCENARIO 2

The glove has to be pulled inside out.
—Toni Morrison

You will begin design school, (hopefully) comfortable and fluent in your own design vernacular. A visual language that (although unschooled) serves you well. However, you'll soon realize that your (pro)active voice has no place in design school. You'll need to adapt quickly—sink or swim. You will learn to contort your graphic vocabulary in uncomfortable ways to fashion something that communicates in a way that you think is acceptable to your white professors and classmates. The inevitable problem with creating in this ill-fitting parlance—your lack of design elocution will reveal itself. It will expose itself in the lack of depth in your work—evidence of someone not well versed in a second tongue. Predictably, the work will be relentlessly dismantled during the final critique—and you won't possess the adopted vocabulary to defend yourself. The irony is that, if you had stayed true to your instincts and proceeded bravely, you would've produced something that you could be proud of—while at the same time educating some of the less enlightened among your peers, and in particular your instructor.

As Black folk, when we create work to appease the "white gaze," we will inevitably fall short; we will be unable to create something, in any logical manner, that feels truthful and comfortable. Instead, embrace what you intimately know. You will be hesitant at first, and rightfully so, because it goes against the very real, constant dynamic of what it means to traverse the brutal, racialized American landscape as a Black person. But it is not your burden to bring your instructors up to speed on the racial dynamics of this country. Remind yourself that your history *is* American history, not some remote concept.

You'll realize, by now, that it is so clearly a double standard that one can be effective, respected, even seen as an intellectual, while having a knowledge base that is so weighted on one side of the fence. There is no requirement, or even expectation, for your white instructors to know about the Black experience or our creative history. Imagine, if the inverse were true—could a Black professor be taken seriously if he did not know Paul Rand, de Kooning, Saul Bass, Phillip Johnson, Vignelli, and so on? You will hear of the importance of diversity in design education, but you'll be lucky to have even one Black design instructor.

What is asked of you, and patently unfair, is for you to be well-versed in the oppressor's graphic language, but never is the converse true. The oppressor stays comfortable in the sphere of their graphic ignorance, without ever losing any currency, without ever being required to leave that sphere to learn or familiarize themselves with your graphic vernacular.

SCENARIO 3

I'm a Black designer, not a designer who happens to be Black.

—Steve Jones

You will have teachers that question or challenge your identity. Your pure, Black identity represents one of fear, of otherness. Your white instructors will try to diminish your Blackness in order to find a space in which to see your humanity. They will ever so subtly, or overtly, steer you in creative directions that placate their guilt and/or lead you to situations where the rules are fashioned to your disadvantage. This will lead to outcomes that are flat and unrecognizable. Do not let this happen.

Fig. 2

ATCQtownfan @atcqtownfan · 22m

Sit back, relax, and let yourself go
Don't sweat what you heard, but act like you know #tribe

You must create work that exudes and posits your Blackness as a fully articulated construct. But understand that if your Blackness is only defined in opposition to whiteness, then you have failed. Your history, heritage, and culture are exquisite; they are sublime, and they are wonderful. Blackness is its own rich and fully formed narrative; and it can stand on its own. You will have instructors who are guilty of the "white gaze"—they will ask, implicitly or explicitly, for your work to be deemed valid: *"Where is the white voice? Where is whiteness in the solution?"* But know that your work has meaning. You owe nothing to the "white gaze." You do not need to explain, justify, or validate yourself to, or for, a white audience. Design in your own language, your first language—our (creative) language is the beauty of our survival and our treasure. Of course, it is wonderful and an advantage that creatively you are bilingual—you possess, as all Black folk do, a "double consciousness"—but even so, your native tongue is the one that expresses you best—not your adopted, forced-upon language. It's not a language that you're fully conversant in anyway. And that's okay.

Fig. 3

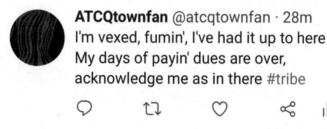

> **ATCQtownfan** @atcqtownfan · 28m ⋮
> I'm vexed, fumin', I've had it up to here
> My days of payin' dues are over,
> acknowledge me as in there #tribe

          In closing, be ready for these scenarios as you go forth in your design odyssey. I know it all seems exhausting, but what will it mean when you graduate, with your design degree—with all your technical skills, your (Eurocentric) design history, and theory—if in the end, you cannot tell your story? If you cannot design for or communicate with folks who look like you? This is very much the dilemma of what it means to be a Black designer. But I suggest that you embrace what is yours—this is the only beneficial alternative—the only way to be *unvisible.* The studio is lauded as the de facto space of creation (even in your classes, your workspace is called the studio). But recognize that the *kitchen* is just as authentic a space to create and draw inspiration from, as is the so-called studio. The kitchen is the Third World, it is our roots, our ancestors—it is a proud, fertile space, and it is yours.

NOTES

1. Carl Hancock Rux, "Save the Animals," in *Aloud: Voices from the Nuyorican Poets Café*, ed. Miguel Algarín and Bob Holman (Henry Holt, 1st edition, 1994), 130-32.

IMAGE CREDITS

All images retrieved November 9, 2021, https://twitter.com/atcqtownfan

The Strong Black Woman

TERRESA MOSES

Racism Untaught [1] is an educational framework (see Figure 1) developed to critically analyze "racialized" design and create anti-racist design approaches. The framework has been crafted into a tool kit that uses an intentionally revised design research model to investigate the design of societal oppression. The tool kit not only investigates elements of racism, but has now been expanded to examine elements of sexism and ableism, with the goal to offer more elements of oppression for critical analysis. This article investigates the first step of the Racism Untaught tool kit using the "strong Black woman" stereotype as the design challenge. I critically analyze how the trope has been designed within our societal normalities. I argue that this intersectional stereotype hinders Black women from contributing to society in a healthy and productive way due to the stress and pressure caused by this externally and internally racialized and misogynistic trope.

INTRO   The intersectionality [2] of oppression Black women face within our society is a barrier to not only the community of Black educators, but the overall success of our institutions of higher learning. This oppression not only affects the number of Black women represented in design faculty positions, but directly affects the learning experiences for students within educational institutions. Research shows [3] that Black women are set up to fail as a result of the undue amount of labor placed on their shoulders; they are expected to bear the weight of responsibility for equity and justice in design education due to the lack of representation and the lack of anti-racist policies and practices within the institution. The commitment among institutions who are *actually* willing to drastically shift their policies to create anti-oppressive actions

Fig. 1

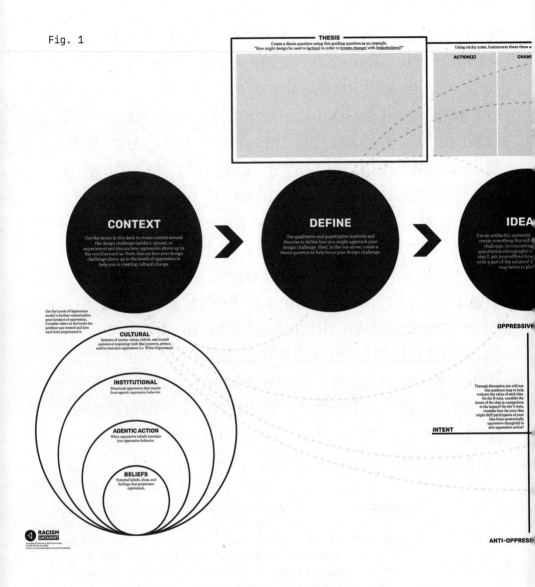

THESIS
Create a thesis question using this guiding question as an example.
"How might design be used to [action] in order to [create change] with [stakeholders]?"

Using sticky notes, brainstorm these three a

ACTION(S)   CHANG

CONTEXT
Use the terms in this deck to create context around the design challenge (artifact, system, or experience) and discuss how oppression shows up in the world around us. Next, discuss how your design challenge shows up in the levels of oppression to help you in creating cultural change.

DEFINE
Use qualitative and quantitative methods and theories to define how you might approach your design challenge. Next, in the box above, create a thesis question to help focus your design challenge.

IDEA
Use an artifact(s), system(s), create something that will challenge. Incorporating quantitative ethnographic step 2, ask yourself(ves) how or be a part of the solution? map below to plo

Use the Levels of Oppression model to further contextualize your instance of oppression. Consider where in the levels the problem was created and how each level perpetuated it.

OPPRESSIV

CULTURAL
Systems of norms, values, beliefs, and trusted systems of acquiring truth that preserve, protect, and/or maintain oppression (i.e. White Supremacy).

INSTITUTIONAL
Structural oppression that results from agentic oppressive behavior.

Through discussion you will use this quadrant map to help evaluate the value of each idea. On the X-Axis, consider the intent of the idea in comparison to the impact? On the Y-Axis, consider how far your idea might shift participants of your idea from systemically oppressive thought(s) to anti-oppressive action?

AGENTIC ACTION
When oppressive beliefs translate into oppressive behavior.

INTENT

BELIEFS
Personal beliefs, ideas, and feelings that perpetuate oppression.

RACISM
UNTAUGHT

ANTI-OPPRESS

eas to assist your thesis question process.

E(S)   STAKEHOLDER(S)

TE

nd/or experience(s) to
elp solve your design
the qualitative and
search methods from
you can affect change
stly, use the quadrant
your ideas.

THOUGHT

> **PROTOTYPE**

Fidelity refers to the function of your artifact,
system, or experience. A low-fidelity prototype is
non-functioning and is initially presented to
communicate your idea. A mid-fidelity prototype is
limited in functionality and a high-fidelity prototype
has minimal modifications needed for final deliverable.

> **IMPACT**

Academic: The participants will define a rubric
that demonstrates both a mastery in the
determined deliverable and the ability to
incorporate the methods and processes at an
advanced level of understanding.

Organization: Individuals will use the card deck to
measure their design impact on the
implementation of their ideas.

Use this academic rubric to
evaluate the project. Move the
workboard cards to the associated
areas or write the content of the
workboard cards to note how the
project will be graded.

UNDERSTANDING (30%)

Incorporating research methods that provide empathy for the user and a
reframing or definition of the challenge. Including but not limited to
brainstorming, thesis question, annotated bibliography, benchmark analysis,
heuristic analysis, and/or literature review.

APPLICATION (15%) ─ CRITICAL THINKING (15%) ─ JUSTIFICATION (15%) ─

The ability to develop a low fidelity
prototype(s), articulate learned
concepts in a non-functioning
design solution(s), and test the
initial ideals with users. Develop a
list of key factors asking the
questions: what worked, what needs
to be improved, are there new ideas,
and do you have new questions?

Apply key factors gleaned from low-fidelity
prototype(s) to your mid fidelity prototype(s),
developing a second set of key factors based off
of user testing. Ask the same or similar
questions to: what worked, what needs to be
improved, are there new ideas, and do you have
new questions?

The development of a high fidelity
prototype(s) providing a proof of
concept that addresses real user needs
based off of research acquired through
low and mid fidelity prototype(s).

CREATE DELIVERABLE (25%)

Final artifact(s) as well as a compelling story of the design process. Evidence of:
• Aesthetics: demonstrate effective visual communication
• Critique: the ability to give and receive effective feedback
• Justification: ability to effectively articulate design choices
• Organization: research, prototypes, and process
• Usability: the overall functioning of the design solution
• Skills: execution of final deliverable based on initial goals for project

IMPACT

E ACTIONS

is unsustainable and has a history of being financially unsupported. The lack of urgency and priority continues to perpetuate the Eurocentric design education canon. And while there are a few Black women sprinkled throughout the field of design education, increasing this number depends on the ability of the institution in question to recognize how the lack of representation is not a reflection of our communities and subsequently setting their programs up for failure. There are few Black women faculty because once hired, the institution believes they have reached their diversity goal and fail to provide support for the Black women they have hired. Instead of providing the support Black women need to be successful, oftentimes Black women faculty are given diversity-related roles and are taxed to answer questions about racism for their white colleagues, on top of the work they are already required to do as a faculty member. There is a culture within institutions that allows this practice to continue, stopping progress and creating a hostile work environment for Black women. Burnout becomes inevitable. Whether implied or explicitly stated, there is an ideology that Black women are strong enough to handle "it" and thus do not receive the support and representation needed to be successful with the academy.

CONTEXT To create context around this racist and sexist design challenge, which I have titled the "strong Black woman," I have pulled the following terms from the elements of racism and sexism to help better understand the issues, and hopefully lead to a gaining of empathy from participants.

Fig. 2

RACISM   Within the first deck of Racism Untaught cards (see Figure 2), racialized elements, found in the tool kit, the terms associated with the "Strong Black woman" stereotype are; 1) Anti-Black Racism: elements of racism directed toward and experienced by Black people, 2) Cultural Taxation: a unique burden placed on Black, Indigenous, and people of color to carry out responsibility and service as the only represented minority within an organization, 3) Gene Weathering: the genetic erosion on the mental and physical health of Black women caused by elements of racism, often leading to extreme stress and shorter life expectancy, 4) Post Traumatic Slave Syndrome: a term coined by Dr. Joy DeGruy described as the multigenerational trauma and injustices experienced by Black people from the dawn of slavery to the recent deaths of Black citizens at the hands of police, and 5) Tokenism: making a symbolic effort to recruit a small number of people from underrepresented groups in order to give the appearance of equality. These elements of racism speak to the expectations placed on Black women within society.

SEXISM   Recently, my colleague Lisa Mercer and I have begun to explore terms that relate to sexism and misogyny. When analyzing the "strong Black woman" trope, terms that relate are 1) Gender Role Expectations: an assumed social role encompassing a range of behaviors and attitudes that are normalized and considered acceptable, appropriate, or desirable for a person based on that person's biological or perceived sex (i.e. secretarial roles, cooking, cleaning), 2) Glass Ceiling: an unofficially acknowledged barrier to advancement in a profession, especially affecting women and members of underinvested communities, 3) Misogynoir: a term that was coined by Moya Bailey referring to misogyny directed toward Black women, an emphasis on the intersectionality of bias, and 4) Victim Blaming: when the victim of a crime or any wrongful act is held entirely or partially at fault for the harm that befell them, also known as Victim Shaming (i.e. blaming sexual assault on a woman because of the clothes she was wearing). These elements of sexism speak to the barriers Black women face and how the normalization of the "Strong Black woman" perpetuates unrealistic expectations that ultimately set Black women up to fail.

INTERSEC-
TIONALITY   In looking at both the elements of racism and sexism, we recognize the intersectionality of oppression. This convergence of discrimination describes how race, class, gender, and other social identities from historically marginalized and under-invested communities "intersect" with one another causing a multilayered oppression. When Kimberlé Crenshaw first coined this term, she was referring

to Black lower class women. " . . . Black women are subsumed within the traditional boundaries of race or gender discrimination these boundaries are currently understood, and that the intersection of racism and sexism factors into Black women's lives in ways that can captured wholly by looking at the race or gender dimensions of those experiences separately." Intersectionality goes beyond just identities that intersect and instead focuses on the identities that tend to be oppressed due to social normalcy.

> *As both a conceptual and analytic tool, intersectionality situates Black women in an autonomous social position and motivates understanding of their experiences from what Collins calls a "distinctive angle of vision," where Black women are at once gendered and racialized.*[5]

LEVELS OF OPPRESSION   After exploring the elements of racism and sexism that make up the design challenge, we have designed a sub-step to gain further context of the oppressive elements that help us understand how deep oppression runs within our society. We use the *Levels of Oppression* model (See Figure 3) to further contextualize the instance of oppression, considering where in the levels the problem was created and how each level perpetuated it. There are four levels that I explore below critically analyzing the "strong Black woman" trope.

BELIEFS   We have defined *beliefs* as an ideology that an individual holds: Personal beliefs, ideas, and feelings that perpetuate oppression. In the intersectional design challenge of the "strong Black woman" many individuals within and outside the Black community hold this belief. Even in understanding that Black women have had to endure much trauma[6] to make this stereotype hold fast, the continuation of harm on the lives of Black women will continue to perpetuate this belief.

> *You may write me down in history,*
> *With your bitter, twisted lies,*
> *You may trod me in the very dirt.*
> *But still, like dust, I'll rise.*

—*Maya Angelou, excerpt from "Still I Rise"*

Fig. 3

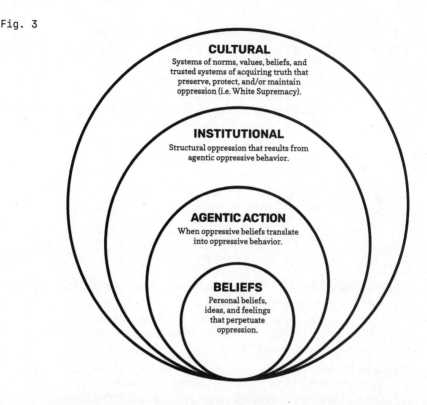

CULTURAL
Systems of norms, values, beliefs, and
trusted systems of acquiring truth that
preserve, protect, and/or maintain
oppression (i.e. White Supremacy).

INSTITUTIONAL
Structural oppression that results from
agentic oppressive behavior.

AGENTIC ACTION
When oppressive beliefs translate
into oppressive behavior.

BELIEFS
Personal beliefs,
ideas, and feelings
that perpetuate
oppression.

AGENTIC ACTION   We have defined agentic action as the practice of personal ideologies: When oppressive beliefs translate into oppressive behavior. Here is where we begin to see the practice of the personal belief that Black women are inherently strong. While this belief is supported outside the Black community, we see actions that support the intersectional trope within the Black community. In the expectation of duty from Black community members to have Black women show up on the front line of the protest, speak out on the Black communities' behalf, console those affected by white supremist violence, while simultaneously rearing children, getting an education, working a full-time job, and keeping their households in order. This is not only an expectation from Black men, but an internalized expectation and pressure due to the socialization of Black women to take on these duties from their mothers, grandmothers, great grandmothers, and so on. This perfectionist doer and self-sacrificing mentality is a trauma response from slavery[7] meant to keep us from revolutionary rest and from reaching our full potential.

The superwoman schema also reflects
gendered racial socialization that
African American women receive early
in life and throughout their life
course, [. . .] By identifying the
protective versus risky dimensions, we
also hope to figure out the type of
messages that should be conveyed to
African American women and girls.

—Vijie Wang, assistant professor
in the Department of Human
Development and Family Studies
at Michigan State University

INSTITUTIONAL We have defined institutional as systems created to support the dominant culture: Structural oppression results from agentic oppressive behavior. We see this in the cultural taxation that Black women face in predominantly white institutions. Black women are often expected to carry the weight of a regular employee while also teaching colleagues about diversity and anti-racism. Moreover, Black women are expected to shoulder these responsibilities while the continuation of anti-Black racism and misogynoir persists in their organizations which prevent them from seeing the same opportunities and promotions their white and/or male counterparts are presented with.[8] Black women are the most educated group of individuals in the United States,[9] however, they make up the smallest number of those in executive-level positions.

What they [Black women] were really
describing was this idea of being strong
Black women and feeling the need to
prepare for the racial discrimination
they expect on a daily basis; and that
preparation and anticipation adds to
their overall stress burden.

—Amani M. Allen, associate professor
of community health sciences and
epidemiology at the University
of California, Berkeley

CULTURAL   We have defined cultural as the widely accepted ideologies of society: Systems of norms, values, beliefs, and
trusted systems of acquiring truth that preserve, protect, and/or maintain
oppression (i.e. White Supremacy). Culture perpetuates the idea of the
Black superwoman trope throughout society, film, and even product design.
Black women that make it to the political realm are over-scrutinized and
pressured to show up in ways that make white people comfortable. For
example, according to the mass media, Michelle Obama is often referred to
as aggressive, masculine, and does "terrorist fist jabs."[10] As with any First
Lady of the United States, she would be subject to critique, but as the first
Black First Lady, the media descriptors are a reflection of the overall misogyny within the broader culture of this nation. This over-critique of these
women no doubt influences their decision-making on a daily (and political)
basis. Movies such as *The Color Purple* and *Queen & Slim* tell the narrative
of the suffering Black woman—an expected stereotype in our society. Even
advertising and product design frame the Black woman's role as a happy,
subservient being whose only joy is in serving our white superiors, i.e. Aunt
Jemima and Mrs. Butterworth. Our society is culturally inundated with imagery and narratives that perpetuate this idea that Black women can handle
the oppressions of life that are thrown at them, and will do so happily.

CONCLUSION   Using the first step in the Racism Untaught framework helps in critically analyzing how elements of
racism and sexism present themselves in the "strong Black woman"
trope. The next step in the framework is define, which uses qualitative
and quantitative methods and critical theories to define how you might
approach this design challenge. Participants then define a thesis
question that will guide their focus using the following template: "How
might design be used to [action] in order to [create change] with
[stakeholders]?" The question I might pose using this template is:
How might design be used to remove challenges and provide equitable opportunities to Black women without cultural taxation in order
to change the perception and expectation of Black women to both
themselves and the broader culture with institutions of higher learning? Within the ideation and prototype phases of the framework, ideas
such as campaigns, policy changes, and even ways to share personal
narratives might be used to help solve the design challenge. I believe
there is room to change this narrative and remove the pressures this
trope places on the identities of Black women. How might design be
used to reframe the expected societal roles of Black women in order to

change the unnecessary pressures the "strong Black woman" trope has within and outside the Black community?

While I do not yet have the answers to the questions posed above, I remain hopeful that Black women in higher education understand the oppression they face is not of their own doing. There are systems setting us up to fail, to give up. Find a community of like-minded individuals to encourage, provide tactics, and empower you to reach your full potential, regardless of the harm that these systems can do to our communities. *To learn more about the Racism Untaught tool kit, visit racismuntaught.com.*

NOTES

1. Moses, Terresa A, and Lisa E Mercer. *Racism Untaught*, 2018. http://www.racismuntaught.com.
2. Crenshaw, Kimberle. "Mapping the Margins: Intersectionality, Identity Politics, and Violence Against Women of Color." *Stan. L. Rev.* 43 (1990): 1241.
3. Hirshfield, Laura E., and Tiffany D. Joseph. "'We need a woman, we need a black woman': Gender, Race, and Identity Taxation in the Academy." *Gender and Education* 24, no. 2 (2012): 213-227.
4. Ibid.
5. Allen, Amani M., Yijie Wang, David H. Chae, Melisa M. Price, Wizdom Powell, Teneka C. Steed, Angela Rose Black, Firdaus S. Dhabhar, Leticia Marquez-Magaña, and Cheryl L. Woods-Giscombe. "Racial Discrimination, the Superwoman Schema, and Allostatic Load: Exploring an Integrative Stress-Coping Model among African American Women." *Annals of the New York Academy of Sciences* 1457, no. 1 (2019): 104.
6. Ibid.
7. Degruy-Leary, Joy. *Post-Traumatic Slave Syndrome: America's Legacy of Enduring Injury*. Portland, OR: Joy DeGruy Publications Inc, 2017.
8. Rockquemore, Kerry, and Tracey A. Laszloffy. *The Black Academic's Guide to Winning Tenure—Without Losing Your Soul*. Boulder, CO: Lynne Rienner Publishers, 2008.

9. "Fast Facts: Degrees Conferred by Race and Sex,"
   National Center for Education Statistics (NCES) Home
   Page, a part of the US Department of Education, 2016,
   https://nces.ed.gov/FastFacts/display.asp?id=72.
10. Roberts, Diane. "Michelle Obama Endures Public
   Scrutiny," *NPR* (NPR, June 22, 2008), https://www.npr
   .org/templates/story/story.php?storyId=91779977.

IMAGE CREDITS

1. Racism Untaught workboard, shown in black and white.
2. Close-up image of the first step on the first
   workboard tool kit prototype used at the AIGA
   Decipher Conference in September 2018.
3. The Levels of Oppression diagram as shown under the
   first step of the Racism Untaught tool kit, in black
   and white

A Reading List for the

Politics of Design

CHRIS RUDD

The Genesis of the Politics of Design

The class began from a conversation between myself and Jessica Jacobs, a PhD student at Illinois Institute of Technology's Institute of Design (ID). She and I are on the same wavelength; we believe that design, as an apolitical activity at large, cannot continue the way that it's been going; and that we can help inject the political into the practice by working with students to figure out how.

The idea is to be extremely explicit—design is a political act. Every designer, and therefore design, has a worldview, a world outlook. This is politics and it informs everything.

I tell students all the time that design is from my perspective, my subjective lens. This is especially true when you think about human-centered design. You have a user who is subjective, and we are trying to understand their experience. We then interpret that experience, which is subjective; we go through a process that's supposed to be objective, using ethnographic research, which ultimately has to be interpreted and synthesized into a point of view. All of this is subjective! It is subjectivity, on top of subjectivity, with the goal of creating an objective outcome—*here is an objective thing that we have created based on the design process*. This class makes visible the political nature of this nested subjectivity, by drawing out the students' worldview and giving them tools to interrogate their personal position and the positions that they take as designers

An example that I often give references the criminal justice system: Two million folks are in prison, one million of them Black. As an anti-racist, I look at that data and say, "Damn, the criminal justice system is racist as *hell*." Alternatively, someone with a different worldview might look at that same data point and say, "Damn, them Black folks are the worst criminals." Nothing changes except the perspective of the person looking at it. And that perspective is based on your politics, your worldview.

We have created a curriculum for designers that reveals that nothing we do is neutral. And, most importantly, if we're looking to design a just world, we can't be neutral—*we have to be extremely biased toward justice.* What do you believe in? What do you stand for? How is your worldview informed? And based on that, can you intentionally create for that world? We don't tell them what world that is. That's their job to figure out. I have not come across a student yet who doesn't believe that this world should be just. But if a student has alternative motives, let's not sugarcoat or hide the intention. Be clear about your intentions.

LEARNING OUTCOMES
» Understanding your individual politics and how that intersects or interacts with systems.
» Exploring and recognizing other ideologies, politics, and economies.
» Investigating epistemology: How do you know what you know? And what do we know? How is that influenced by the systems that have been built?
» Developing an understanding of how design enables oppression and exploitation. Looking at the design processes through the lens of power and shifting power.
» Evaluating and challenging how design enables oppression, exploitation, and destruction.
» Designing new methods to challenge exploitation and increase equity within current systems and structures.

WEEK ONE: DESIGN (AS POLITIC)
» Camacho, Jorge. "How Design Is Politics," *Medium*, January 9, 2018.
» Winner, Langdon. "Do Artifacts Have Politics?" *Daedalus* 109, no. 1 (1980): 121–136. jstor.org/stable/20024652.

The first two readings are short essays. "How Design Is Politics" really gets into helping students understand the role of politics as power, resources, resource flows, and the contribution of these mechanisms to equity. "Do Artifacts Have Politics?" is a great place to start exploring these ideas by looking at the intentionality behind some iconic and historic designs.

In "Do Artifacts Have Politics," Winner looks at the design of Robert Moses's bridges in New York City, which were intentionally designed to keep poor, and particularly Black and Latin people, out of majority-white communities on Long Island. What I find most fascinating is his research on industrial designers in the late 1800s and early 1900s in Chicago, at the McCormick Reaper factory. McCormick Reaper Works was the impetus for the historic May Day movement, the birth of the international labor holiday. The workers at that McCormick Reaper factory went on strike in 1886 and shut it down. Workers were beaten and shot for organizing and fighting back. In that article, Moses points out that the head of McCormick Reaper Works commissioned industrial designers to create a new machine to automate the production line to eliminate a specific position within the factory. They built the machine and used it for about three years. It cost the company more than they invested in it. If we think about it from a viability lens, it was a horrible machine. The only reason the company commissioned the design and production was that the job that the machine eliminated was the most powerful section of the union. This meant that the machine was built to break the workers' power, not to make a profit—profit was set aside. It's a potent example of how design can be utilized to oppress and to further situate power within a section of society.

Assignment: Mapping Power in a Design Process
Question(s): Where is power situated in the design process? Who has it? What enables them to have this power?

WEEK TWO: POWER (AS OPPRESSION)

» Lenin, V. I. *The State and Revolution: The Marxist Theory of the State and the Tasks of the Proletariat in the Revolution.* CreateSpace Independent Publishing Platform, 2017.
» Williams, Lauren. "The Co-Constitutive Nature of Neoliberalism, Design, and Racism," *Design and Culture* 11, no. 3 (2019): 301–321.
» Racial Equity Tools. "Racial Equity Tools Glossary." racialequity tools.org/glossary.

Once we begin to understand that we, designers, are not neutral actors in society, it is important to understand who it is that we are in service to. *The State and Revolution* is the best document I've ever read for understanding the current organization of society. It sheds light on the fact that it is not just government and it is not just business; these are not siloed things. They work together in service of a larger outcome. And so, what is that? How does it work? Why does it exist? In the first three chapters of the book, Lenin outlines why the state was designed, what group of people it serves, and the components of the apparatus. Understanding the interconnection of these entities and what they are in service to is important for designers to be able to design in a way that disincentivizes oppression and exploitation.

In "The Co-Constitutive Nature of Neoliberalism, Design, and Racism," Williams digs into the design thinking process. One case study explores an app called Money Think, which teaches poor kids financial literacy. Williams discusses how, if you develop empathy for poor kids of color, based on the design thinking process, you can end up wanting to help them figure out how to save their money better. However, she explains, when you don't have money, there isn't any money to save. Why are we not getting to that? What is the root cause creating these conditions for the users we are attempting to empathize with?

Paired together these two texts really help the students expand their thinking. Design's role in perpetuating the current socio-ecnomic system becomes clear. In this scenario, it's not just one person or the government that's bad. It's not just the businesses that are bad. In fact, it's not even about bad or good. It's about purpose and what's driving that purpose.

Assignment: Diagram of the State
Question(s): What are we in service to? Where is power situated in society? What is the worldview you hold? And therefore, what are you designing toward?

WEEK THREE: RACE (AS TECHNOLOGY)

» Coleman, Beth. "Race as Technology." *Camera obscura: feminism, culture, and media studies* 24, no. 1 (2009): 177–207.
» Bennett Jr., Lerone. "The Road Not Taken." In *The Shaping of Black America,* 61–82. Chicago: Johnson Publishing Co., 1975.

Lerone Bennett Jr. is probably one of the most brilliant brothers to walk the planet. "The Road Not Taken" is the seminal text in my journey to understanding racism as a designed system. Designers did not create racism, yet it is a designed thing, meaning it serves a user and adapts as conditions change. In "The Road Not Taken," Lerone brilliantly lays out across twenty pages how race and racism developed as infrastructure in the United States. "Race as technology" means race and racism are extensions of human ability. Lerone explains that the state is an amalgamation of government, business, military, schools, and healthcare, and that each of these components works in service of capital. He outlines how capital manifests itself in the technology of race and racism from the church to the newsroom. He then documents how this technology is impeded at the core of laws and policies driving our system of government.

Beth Coleman helps frame this technology as a tool. It is not a state of being innate in us; it was created by a group of people. If we can understand that, then as we're thinking about anti-racism, we must act against those components. The students must then take this understanding and make an object anti-racist.

Assignment: Anti-Racist Object
Question(s): What makes an object anti-racist? What are the affordances held within such an object that allow it to be anti-racist for the user?

WEEK FOUR: RACE (AS TECHNOLOGY)

» Benjamin, Ruha. *Race After Technology: Abolitionist tools for the new Jim Code*. Cambridge: Polity, 2019.
» Roberts, Dorothy. *Fatal Invention*. New Press, 2012.
» Kendi, Ibram X. *How to Be an Antiracist*. New York: One World, 2019.
» Young, Iris Marion. "Five Faces of Oppression." In *Justice and the Politics of Difference*, 39–65. Princeton University Press, 1990.

Exploring "race as technology" began as a one-week assignment, but I saw that students were struggling with the concept, so I shifted it to a two-week assignment and introduced some new readings to pick it apart. We've been indoctrinated with racism so long that it's hard to conceive of anti-racism as a technology that can be embedded into an object. In week two, we continue with Ruha Benjamin's *Race After Technology*, a brilliant book describing how technology enables racism. As designers introduce data and new technologies into their work, we must interrogate how racism is embedded within them and identify ways of deprogramming them.

We follow up with *Fatal Invention* by Dorothy Roberts, a sociologist from Chicago, my hometown. Her first two chapters illustrate how race has been embedded into American society. One of the key infrastructures that she cites is the US Census, which began in 1790 with five identities being accounted for—free white males above the age of sixteen, free white males under the age of sixteen, free white Females, all other free persons, and slaves. After twenty-four permutations, today a person can choose close to three hundred combinations of racial and ethnic identities on the census reifying the notion of race.

The main reason I use that book is that Roberts talks about how science and technology promote racism in the twenty-first century. Here she identifies one of the main culprits as 23andMe, a company founded on the idea that you can take your blood and parse out percentages of your racial identity, which she disproves. Companies like 23andMe utilize design to promote, package, and sell the notion of racial categorization. I bring in job postings from 23andMe—lead designer, product designer, package designer—and show how we make racism, this technology, palatable.

Assignment: Anti-Racist Object Two
Question(s): What makes an object anti-racist? What are the affordances held within such an object that allow it to be anti-racist for users?

WEEK FIVE: GENDER (AS CONSTRUCT)

» Bardzell, Shaowen. "Feminist HCI: taking stock and outlining an agenda for design." In *Proceedings of the SIGCHI conference on human factors in computing systems*, 1301–1310. 2010.

» Costanza-Chock, Sasha. "Design Justice: Towards an intersectional feminist framework for design theory and practice." In *Proceedings of the Design Research Society*. 2018.

» Whitely, Nigel. "Feminist Perspectives (Design for Society)." In *Social Design Reader,* edited by Elizabeth Resnick. Bloomsbury, 2019.

» Martins, Luiza Prado de O. "Privilege and Oppression: Towards a Feminist Speculative Design," in Lim, Y., Niedderer, K., Redström, J., Stolterman, E. and Valtonen, A. (eds.), *Design's Big Debates*, DRS International Conference 2014, 16–19 June, Umeå, Sweden. https://dl.designresearchsociety.org/drs-conference-papers/drs2014/researchpapers/75

"Feminist HCI" provides great examples of how design enables and perpetuates sexist notions of gender—gender as construct—a similar technology to racism. It offers tools to critically think about how design perpetuates notions of gender and gender inferiority. "Feminist HCI" gives a great example of the perpetuation of gender through everyday designed objects like the female Bic pen and women's razors (because you know, women need more comfort than men).

Interestingly, in the past two semesters, I feel like I've had more female students coming out of the gaming world and game design, and I have learned a lot about problematic culture. These students talk deeply about having to create inappropriate female characters for children's games—with sexy, voluptuous bodies who always play the victim or who need to be saved, perpetuating horrific notions of womanhood to young women.

However, gaming shows us that it goes beyond imagery and storytelling. The culture of gaming demonstrates what is enabled through these new socio-technical systems that support massive amounts of sexism in the online gaming world. If a person playing a shooter game is perceived to have a feminine voice, they are subjected to an onslaught of derogatory sexist language. If we build anti-sexist technologies—anti-sexist video games—we can have a positive effect on the culture and cut a player off, cancel them. We can no longer be neutral. We must take a strong stance.

Additional essays from *The Social Design Reader* complement the first two articles and help shape a framework of design through a feminist perspective. Personally, these readings forced me to think critically about myself and my practice. What I love about these readings is that the objects are visual and tangible—not abstract ideas. They have helped refine my practice to not be so heady.

Assignment: Visualization showing how anti-sexism benefits everyone
Question: How can we show a future free from sexism? How would men benefit from this new future?

WEEK SIX: CLASS (AS EXPLOITATION)

» Wright, Erik Olin. "A General Framework for the Analysis of Class Structure." *Politics & Society* 13, no. 4 (1984): 383–423. DOI 10.1177/003232928401300402.
» Jojola, Theodore. "The People Are Beautiful Already: The Indigenous Design and Planning" In *By the People: Designing a Better America*, edited by Cynthia E. Smith. Cooper Hewitt, Smithsonian Design Museum, 2016.
» Ansari, Ahmed. "What a Decolonisation of Design Involves: Two Programmes for Emancipation." *Decolonizing Design.* https://decolonisingdesign.com/actions-and-interventions/publications/2018/what-a-decolonisation-of-design-involves-by-ahmed-ansari/.

We often hear classism used in conversation as if it is a type of oppression. It's not. Class is the key to capitalism, a segmenting of social order. What class is at the root, what it allows, is for dominant segments of that social order to exploit other segments of that social order. That is the history of exploitation in class societies. As designers, we need to know *what class society actually means; what exploitation means.* It is not simply an identity, it is also a technology. Once learning that, students have said, "If I'm getting paid, then I might not mind the exploitation that much." It is still exploitation, whether you feel good about it or not. The reality is that we live in a society that allows groups of people to exploit other groups of people. This point is core to the entire class—the entire political project—and it's the point of all the readings and assignments up to that moment. Class as a technology of exploitation thrives on divisions of gender and race. It thrives on racism.

We have learned from a very particular perspective; we complicate that perspective by introducing Indigenous practices and Indigenous design that goes way beyond the Bauhaus tradition to the thousands of years of design practices and philosophies before the twentieth century. We reference beautiful community-centered indigenous design, planning, and spiritual practices from the Southwestern Native American cultures. As a chief in an Indigenous culture, you are also a steward of the land that you're on. The notion of stewardship is not core within the leadership of the US government. American democracy is focused on the governance of a body of people. What does it look like when we consider the natural world, community, nonhuman-centric interests in our design principles? How might we honor different perspectives and different experiences as designers?

Assignment: Visualization showing how anti-sexism benefits everyone
Question: What is the worldview you hold? And therefore, what are you designing toward?

THE FINAL ASSIGNMENT

The final assignment is to consider and offer new methods, frameworks, and practices for designers, *specifically* for designers that will enable us to create anti-oppressive, anti-exploitative outcomes. It's a very open-ended project that drives students to reflect upon the power within the process and prompts them to figure out ways to intervene. My goal for this class is to have students think dramatically differently about what they are doing and why. There is a quote that I love by Lerone Bennett, Jr.: "An educator in a system of oppression is either a revolutionary or an oppressor."

Design didn't destroy the world, and it won't save it. The people who will save the world from all the oppressions and indignities that we are confronted with are not designers; those people will be the folks in the street marching, causing a ruckus, giving voice to the issues. Change always occurs through the actions of social movements. I want these students to think about themselves beyond their professional title, beyond their nine-to-five jobs, to where the changes will be made. I want them, hopefully, to commit themselves to always asking, "What am I doing?" Because when these students get into the real world, they're going to be asked to do things they may not agree with. I want them to know how and where they are empowered to say yes or no, and to have the fortitude to say no.

If there were only three questions that the students stepped away from this course having considered, I would want them to be: (1) Are you a strong enough designer to say no to things that are wrong? (2) Who are you outside of your design world? (3) How are you using your abilities to push or support the social movements working to create change in the world?

As designers we have an important role to play professionally. But it's not our only role.

Beyond the Universal:

Positionality & Promise in an HBCU Classroom

KALEENA SALES

Historically Black Colleges and Universities (HBCUs) were established after the Civil War to provide access to higher education for Black students who were excluded from studying at white institutions. Uniquely American, these institutions of higher learning responded to an education system built on racism, exclusion, and white supremacy. Prior to desegregation, almost every Black person with a college degree attended an HBCU.

According to the US Department of Education, Howard University and Meharry Medical College are responsible for educating over 80 percent of today's Black dentists and doctors.[1] Today, HBCUs continue to offer affordable tuition, a quality education, and a cultural safe space for Black students. Many acclaimed Black artists have studied or taught at HBCUs over the years, including Aaron Douglas of Fisk University and David Driskell of Howard University. While HBCUs have educated successful Black fine artists over the years, design students from these institutions are often overlooked, with the industry setting its sights on the few Black graduates of elite design schools instead. Even while the design industry laments the lack of diversity, and HBCU classrooms are filled with young talent, these students often don't find the same level of mainstream success as their peers from White institutions. In my experience as both an HBCU graduate and associate professor at an HBCU, the primary contributor to this disparity is an industry unsure of how to respond to cultural differences that might show up in HBCU design portfolios. Additionally, educators are so indoctrinated in Swiss design—a grid-based, typographic system originating in Switzerland in the 1940s/1950s heavily influencing modern design education and practice—that we don't properly cultivate the talent of Black designers.

There is no monolithic Black experience, nor should there be an expectation that all Black designers will share a specific aesthetic. However, certain styles, trends, vernacular, and experiences are specific to Black American culture. This is proven by how easily we recognize it when it's appropriated by those within the mainstream. Many of the shared cultural roots can be attributed to a common socioeconomic experience."[2] When we consider these points, we understand that some Black people can have a discernibly different lived experience than a white person in this country. Relatedly, evidence suggests that our aesthetic preferences are impacted by the repetition of our visual environments. According to the research of scholar Robert Zajonc, a phenomenon known as the mere-exposure effect explains why people develop a preference for things they are familiar with. When we think about how this relates to design and education, we see how extended exposure to a specific cultural experience will impact one's preference for imagery and styles that reflect that same culture.

Teaching design at an HBCU forced me to confront the concept of the Black aesthetic and its contentious relationship with European graphic design. Historically, several Black visual artists have been celebrated for their ability to represent the experiences of their community using culture-specific imagery and symbolic style choices. Renowned visual artist Romare Bearden, for example, famously used photomontage techniques to depict the lives of Black Americans. The torn paper and fragmented images drew comparisons to their lived experiences. Similarly, Basquiat incorporated graffiti-style lettering and symbolism to help tell the story of urban life in New York City. However, unlike fine artists, design students aren't always encouraged to explore culture-specific style choices and learn instead to revere the neutrality offered by movements like International Typographic Style. Design educators often teach Swiss design as a solution to complex design problems because it appeals to our desire to be unbiased and objective. In some ways, the simplicity of a sans-serif typeface or the clean lines of a modular grid seem to legitimize the discipline of design, making the work less personal and more focused on clear communication. Yet, when we focus on communication as the end goal, we must recognize the ways in which people from different social and cultural groups interpret visual language, and how stylistic elements and ornamentation can sometimes make messages clearer—a concept at odds with Swiss design ideology. An HBCU homecoming flyer designed in Helvetica, for example, serves the industry's elitist ideologies over the community for which it's intended.

Perhaps what makes HBCU design students different from students who attend predominantly white institutions (PWIs) is that they are so immersed in Black culture that their work instinctually centers the Black experience. This act of centering Blackness is so counter to what is considered "the norm" that we may feel the need to rectify it, especially when preparing students to enter the design industry. In my most honest moments and purest reflection, I know that as a Black professor to mostly Black students, what motivated me in my early teaching years was that my students' work be accepted by a largely white design industry. In an effort to have their work judged equally alongside students at predominately white institutions, I encouraged a neutrality in their design styles. These efforts veiled student identities and reduced their work to mere imitations of what has come before—often from designers without their unique cultural insights and perspectives. At the time, I believed that wearing this mask was the only way to enter white-dominant spaces and make them less of a target for potential bias. In *The Assimilation of Afro-Americans,* author Alphonso Pinkney writes, "Throughout history Black Americans have repeatedly attempted to liberate themselves by becoming assimilated into the larger society."[3] Pinkney later writes, "Failure to assimilate meant that the individuals involved met discrimination or some other form of persecution."[4] Historically, many Black Americans with ambitions to work in white-dominant settings have understood the social and economic benefits of being able to blend in or "pass."

As these historical truths took root in the subconscious of my mind, my instinct was to retool my students' aesthetic preferences in favor of styles that blended into design "norms." That retooling involved preaching modernist principles and teaching Swiss design with a rigid devotion. Unfortunately, in teaching the canon, I, like so many other well-intentioned design educators, failed to acknowledge power structures or how Black and non-Western designers were systematically excluded from certain tools, training, and opportunities needed to gain mainstream success. Today, much has changed. Progressive ideologies in teaching pedagogy and research have reshaped what design education can look like. Many design educators now understand that the insights and cultural experiences of young designers from marginalized communities should not only be recognized but celebrated. This striving to belong, and struggle to feel safe in our differences, has plagued Black scholars, authors, and artisans for years. In his 1926 essay, "The Negro Artist and the Racial Mountain," Harlem Renaissance poet Langston Hughes once wrote: "To my mind, it is the duty of the younger Negro artist, if he accepts any duties at all from outsiders, to change through the force of his art that old whispering 'I want to be white,' hidden in the aspirations of his people, to 'Why should I want to be white? I am a Negro—and beautiful!'"[5]

Beyond teaching broader concepts of what defines "good" design, more work can be done to support the advancement of HBCU design students. Creative directors and employers who are interested in increasing diversity within the industry can help in a number of ways.

» **Become a Mentor.** Reach out to an HBCU Art/Design department and offer to be a mentor to students. If you run a local ad agency or design firm, get your entire team involved. Offer your contact information to design educators as a resource.

» **Show Up!** *Literally.* When local HBCU programs are having senior exhibitions or student shows that are open to the public, show up! Talk to the faculty and get to know the students in the program.

» **Expand Your Network.** Make a connection with design faculty members at HBCUs, and when it's time to hire for an open position, reach out to extend an invitation for recent graduates to apply. So many times, industry practitioners rely on existing networks to fill these positions. Doing so excludes a large pool of potential hires and reinforces a homogenous work environment.

» **Offer Paid Internships.** If you're able to do so, create a paid internship program for diverse candidates. Paying interns is a critical step toward equitable hiring. Many first-generation college students work part-time while in school and use the summer to take on full-time employment. If an internship is unpaid, despite interest, some students will be less likely to participate.

Educators have a responsibility to expand and reshape the canon to include work that honors diverse experiences and audiences. If we continue to indoctrinate new generations of designers into the industry by making them believe there's something inherently wrong with the way they see the world, we risk crushing their confidence and making them lose interest in an industry that desperately needs their voice.

NOTES

1. "Historically Black Colleges and Universities and
   Higher Education Desegregation," U.S. Department of
   Education, last modified January 10, 2020, https://
   www2.ed.gov/about/offices/list/ocr/docs/hq9511.html.
2. "The Case for Fair Housing: 2017 Fair Housing Trends
   Report," National Fair Housing Alliance, last
   modified 2017, https://nationalfairhousing.org/wp
   -content/uploads/2017/07/TRENDS-REPORT-2017-FINAL.pdf.
3. Pinkney, Alphonso. "The Assimilation of Afro-
   Americans."
4. *The Black Scholar* 1, no. 2 (1969): 36-46.
5. Ibid.
6. Hughes, Langston. *The Negro Artist and the Racial
   Mountain*, Duke University Press, 1994.

DESIGN
SCHOLARSHIP

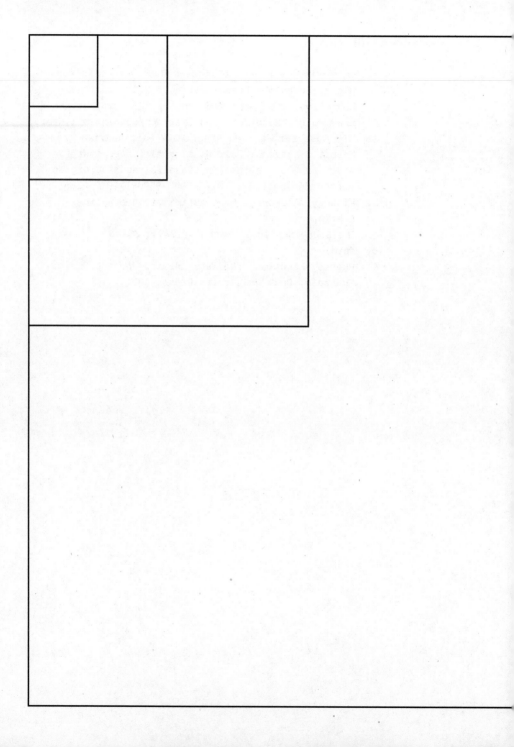

3

DESIGN SCHOLARSHIP

Chapter Introduction:
Lesley Ann-Noel

What is scholarship? What is design scholarship and what is this to a Black designer or educator?

For this section, we invited five designers to share their scholarly work or reflections in response to the theme "Design Scholarship." The five have very different academic and scholarship profiles. Audrey G. Bennett is a graphic design scholar who studies cross-cultural and transdisciplinary design that makes use of images that permeate global culture and impact the way we think and behave. Cheryl D. Miller is an award-winning communication designer and new media strategist, theologian and clergywoman, writer, author, and lecturer. She is recognized as a national leader of minority rights and advocacy in graphic design. Ghanaian-born, Nii Kommey Botchway is a design educator in South Africa. He is the chair of the graphic design program at Nelson Mandela University. Alicia Olushola Ajayi is an architect, researcher, and writer. She was a member of the design team for the groundbreaking Memorial to Peace and Justice in Montgomery, Alabama, a site dedicated to the racial terror and lynching throughout US history. David Pilgrim is a sociologist, author, public speaker, and a leading expert on issues relating to multiculturalism, diversity, and race relations.

In her essay, Audrey G. Bennett debunks the Greek origin myth of the golden ratio. She draws on the fields of anthropology, architecture, and mathematics to respond to well-known works in art and design by Samara, Bringhurst, and Elam that ignore the contribution of Africa and Africans to graphic design history. She demonstrates that the golden ratio has had a presence in traditional African architecture that predates its presence in Greek artifacts and sites. To make her case, she presents two historical examples from Africa, the first a chief's palace in Cameroon, the second a temple from ancient Egypt. Both examples provide evidence that early Africans use mathematically related organizing principles related to the golden rectangle. Bennet advocates for the more intentional use of math terminology in design, to create a cross-cultural aesthetic, by incorporating more shared terms between the disciplines of communication design and mathematics that are used to describe the fractals that the golden ratio creates—like translation, rotation, repetition, and scale.

In his piece, Ghanaian-South African design educator Nii Kommey Botchway rejects the framing of "the Black experience in design," challenging both the notions of Blackness and design, reminding the reader of the many ways that people of the African continent and diaspora might self-identify. Though he responded to the invitation to this publication as a Black designer, he opens his piece saying he is Afrikan, not Black. As an Afrikan from the continent, Botchway can be more specific about his identity than many from the diaspora. His design philosophy is rooted in place, people, culture, and heritage. Botchway points out that the education that Afrikans receive, even today, was not designed for them and does not liberate its recipients from the impacts of colonialism. He is critical of the field of design, and wonders if we should actually be trying to prop up this field that was never designed for us, or rather if we should aim to create something new that is relevant to Afrikan people and the Afrikan way of life. His spiritual consciousness as an Afrikan who designs makes him seek new role models and forms of practice rooted in West Afrikan ideologies, as a model for Afrikan designers today.

Author and communication designer Cheryl D. Miller's 1987 master's thesis, "Transcending the Problems of the Black Graphic Designer to Success in the Market Place" was turned into a *Print* article, "Black Designers: Missing in Action." In that article, Miller concluded that Black designers existed, but were missing from view. This put her on a thirty-plus-year-long journey around equity and inclusion in design education and design history. That graduate thesis from Pratt Institute and the *Print* article started a movement to research and to promote diversity in design. Miller was recently awarded an honorary doctorate by Vermont College of Fine Arts in recognition of her life's work around diversity in design. She shared her acceptance speech with us for this section.

Alicia Olushola Ajayi makes a case about how designed artifacts can have control over us. She writes about Free Negro Bonds, which the formerly enslaved needed to travel. The expression "free paper bun up" is a common one in the Caribbean, where I am from. It means something like "oops no more chances." In reading this article, it was fascinating to read the impetus of this expression, and sad to think how we have become so casual about this paper that guaranteed our freedom. Ajayi writes "For those in bondage, it was a precious artifact that ensured ones passage way to the Promised Land of the North or out West." These precious documents were the only legal route to freedom until the end of the Civil War. While reading this article, I found myself wondering where are the "free papers" of today? Is it birth certificates, visas, passports, and credit cards? What are the instruments of bondage in today's society that one hundred years from now will be referred to playfully in spoken language but with their original meaning forgotten? What could be our role as designers of society in redesigning these instruments of freedom?

Finally, in his essay, David Pilgrim describes the power of racist objects from America's Jim Crow period to teach social justice. While looking at racist objects, some viewers might fondly remember the past, and others will see vestiges of enslavement and segregation. He created the Jim Crow museum as a space where people who see the world in very different ways are safe to share their beliefs. He shares how the museum uses object-based learning to promote community transformation.

The Blackness of these five scholars manifests itself in different ways. They all challenge existing systems and structures. Bennett takes down revered texts, destroying popular theories about the Golden ratio. Miller walked into *Print* magazine to say "I know where the Black designers are even if you don't." Botchway says "I'm done! Your system is dead, I'm making a new one." Ajayi examines the papers that guaranteed our freedom. Pilgrim uses racist objects in ways they were not intended to be used. In their own way, each of these scholars rejects the status quo that has been presented to them, carving out space for new forms of design scholarship and practice that is relevant to the Black experience in design.

Follow the Golden Ratio from Africa to the Bauhaus

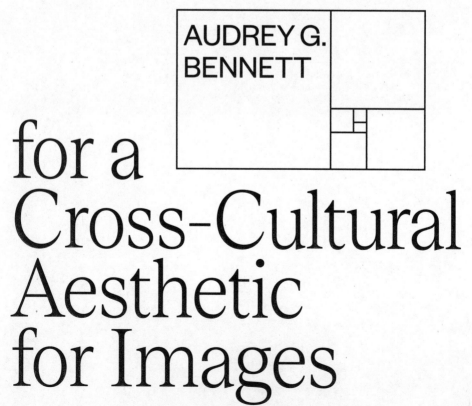

AUDREY G. BENNETT

for a Cross-Cultural Aesthetic for Images

EDITOR'S NOTE:

A version of this article was originally published as "Follow the Golden Ratio from Africa to the Bauhaus for a Cross-Cultural Aesthetic for Images" in *Critical Interventions* Volume 6, Issue 1, 2012: 11-23.

The golden ratio, a mathematical relation that often arises in fractals and other scaling geometries, is known for its ability to affect visual beauty.[1] As a result, communication designers have used it throughout history to compute a plethora of visual compositions.

For instance, many designers use the golden rectangle, a popular compositional grid derived from the golden ratio, to organize verbal and visual information into eye-catching images. However, within the discipline's literature, our European predecessors, primarily in ancient Greece, receive most of the recognition for being the sole contributors of the golden ratio to interdisciplinary discourse. Very few references in the discipline's literature acknowledge Africa as the one of the primary contributors of knowledge about the golden ratio. In this essay, I challenge the assumption that the golden rectangle originated solely in ancient Europe and examine existing evidence within broader interdisciplinary discourse that the golden rectangle is more of an outcome of interaction between African and European civilizations.

Herein I respond to Robert Bringhurst's *The Elements of Typographic Style*, Kimberly Elam's *Geometry of Design*, and Tim Samara's *Making and Breaking the Grid: A Graphic Design Layout Workshop* by noting that the African contributions are conspicuously absent in their accounts. My aim is to weave into the discourse other perspectives from anthropology, architecture, and mathematics that suggest that Africa's golden ratio exemplars predate the instances that create the current origin story. Specifically, I introduce perspectives that suggest that the structures derived from the golden ratio that organize typographic compositions and even structure living spaces also has presence in traditional African architecture, and that this presence extends further back than sites and artifacts in Greece. Two important examples derive from the analysis in Eglash.[2] The first is the chief's palace in Logone-Birni, Cameroon. This historical architectural site has a golden ratio scaling pattern embedded in its spatial design. The second is a similar scaling pattern in the Temple of Karnak from ancient Egypt.

These additions of African design in the story of the golden ratio need not be limited to merely correcting an incomplete history. We can use it to broaden perspectives on how the golden ratio can be used; to encourage its incorporation in the design of images that resonate cross-culturally. From existing cultural artifacts and spatial designs that reflect the golden ratio and other patterns, they can extract cultural grids—a phrase I introduce to explain the phenomenon of grids found in cultural artifacts and man-made and natural spaces that can apply to communication design practice, particularly to the printed or digital page—to yield cross-cultural resonance during the interpretation of images in the communication process.

THE PROBLEM WITH CULTURAL AESTHETICS AND A CROSS-CULTURAL SOLUTION

We are symbol-using animals.[3] As such we make symbols to share information with each other. These symbols communicate meaning that includes our cultural values and identities like social class, professional affiliation, educational achievement, religion, and gender, among other things. An amalgamation of symbols forms a cultural aesthetic that is recognizable and interpretable because it reflects shared cultural values between the communicator and his/her target user. That is, a symbol or set of symbols communicates meaning only to those who understand the cultural cues embedded in the visual form.

Since the time that humans originated—which some geneticists argue occurred some 150,000 years ago in Africa ("We are all African now")—we have self-organized into different cultural groups based on religion, ethnicity, age, gender, geography, linguistics, political affiliation, nationality, and impairment, among other categories. And each cultural group has its own set of values and ways of expressing them aesthetically. However it was probably not until relatively late in human existence that unique verbal expressions emerged in interdisciplinary discourse to represent the general phenomena of culture and aesthetics; what Niklas Luhmann would call a second-order observation.[4] Used in early Greece to mean multisensory sensation, the word aesthetics acquired its contemporary meaning of "sense of beauty" in 1750 due to German philosopher Alexander Gottlieb Baumgarten in his publication *Aesthetica*. By 1871 another culmination of second-order observations gave us the contemporary sense of "culture": anthropologist Edward B. Tylor defined it as "that complex whole which includes knowledge, belief, art, law, morals, custom, and any other capabilities and habits acquired by man as a member of society."[5] If we put those words together, we get the phrase cultural aesthetics, which this essay defines as a sense of beauty determined by cultural values, or sensory treatments that reflect culture and epitomize sensory beauty. Cultural aesthetics reflect the values of a specific cultural group or individual within that group. A basic example of this is the repeated use of a symbolic motif; for example, the cross appears in Christian images ranging from architectural forms to textiles. These geometric forms would be much less frequent in Jewish designs, where the Star of David would be far more likely. One can also experience and observe cultural aesthetics aurally in the ways that nations around the world speak different languages, or even through the tastes of food. Collective values can often be symbolized in the patterns and symbols of national flags. No two countries have the same pattern and/or symbol, though they may share similar colors and political ideals.

Cultural aesthetics carry important meaning in our everyday lives—on an individual basis and collectively in our communities. For instance, they can define our identity in relation to the cultural groups to which we belong. They also communicate meaning on an individual basis; and that meaning may be determined by the collective values of a larger cultural group to which they belong. Thus, cultural aesthetics can provide us with a sense of belonging to a community of people that share the same values.

Cultural aesthetics also bring meaning to our individual lives through their presence in our spatial interactions. For instance, African art historian Suzanne Preston Blier notes that dwellings of kings and queens (in general) are "impressive palaces marked by [visual] beauty and labor-intensive construction."[6] But an African palace created from clay and straw may seem completely alien to European ideas of labor-intensive construction. Thus it is the cultural group—Africans in this case—that determines the way that "beauty and labor intensive construction" are manifested aesthetically—which typically includes design complexity as depicted in the examples analyzed later in the essay. Thus, royal dwellings from different cultures around the world may have substantive differences in their designs since their aesthetics are derived from the culturally specific values of the group.

African American cultural critic bell hooks writes in *The Aesthetics of Blackness: Strange and Oppositional:*

> One of my five sisters want to know
> how it is I come to think about . . .
> space . . . She remembers [Baba's] house
> as an ugly place, crowded with objects

> *. . . She listens in astonishment as I*
> *describe the shadows in Baba's house and*
> *what they meant to me . . .*[7]

In contrast to her sister, hooks finds significant meaning in the childhood space of her family's house. Through its cultural aesthetics—that is, the way that Baba situated the objects in relation to each other and other components of that physical space (e.g. the window and doorway, decorations, etc.)—hooks extracts lifelong meaning. Baba created a variety of experiences for members of the family, the primary users of the space, through the way she inhabited their home. And although hooks and her sister are members of the same cultural group—Baba's family—they have different responses to the cultural aesthetics of their home because they have other cultural differences like age. Like Baba we all use aesthetics to communicate to others within our respective cultural groups or communities in the way that we dress, speak, and practice religion, among other ways by which we live out our lives. When we socialize and interact with people from different cultural groups, we learn about their values and observe the aesthetics they use to communicate their culture. In some cases, their culture fuses with ours—like when we adopt words from other languages into our own native tongue. Sometimes when we try to communicate aesthetically about people from different cultures from our own, particularly when we imitate their cultural aesthetics, the consequences can range from cultural stereotyping to violence. Examples of the latter occur frequently between religious cultural groups where cultural boundaries are more definitive. In religion, the perceived misuse of another religions' cultural aesthetic has led to acts of violence like those committed as a result of caricatures of an Islamic religious symbol of the Prophet Muhammad appearing in publications in the West ("Arson and Death Threats as Muhammad Caricature Controversy Escalates").[8] Whereas, the former impact of stereotyping occurs frequently between ethnic cultural groups where the boundaries are more blurred and less definitive.

Consider universities—institutions comprised of individuals from different cultures in terms of ethnicity, age, geography, gender, impairment, etc. These universities adopt mascots or nicknames to represent collectively their sports teams. Some universities in the United States, like Dartmouth College, have used a symbol of a Native American as a mascot to represent team spirit. In the case of Dartmouth, its student life webpage describes how the college acquired a Native American mascot around 1920 from Boston journalists. However, after decades of protest by various organizations about the use of Native Americans as university mascots,[9] many universities have retired those harmful representations

186

for more culturally appropriate mascots. It wasn't until five decades later that Dartmouth College's Board of Trustees called an end to its use of its Native American mascot for Big Green; today the college even denies ever having an official Native American mascot.[10]

Further evidence of cultural stereotyping that can occur from the misuse of cultural aesthetics can be seen in many infamous and perennial representations of African Americans in mainstream media. Coon, mammy, and Sambo are a few of many negative representations of African American culture created by non–African Americans around the time of slavery that have saturated media throughout history and made an imprint on the public's memory—generation after generation. An Art Directors Club Call for Entries published in 2005 for the 2006 awards season continued this tradition in an image of an African American man with a red afro in a Ronald McDonald costume standing under the title "Pimp My Brand"—a cross-cultural blunder that design critic Steve Heller called "a 14-karat tactlessness."[11]

Coexisting with the aforementioned cross-cultural blunders are more apropos representations of African American culture created by African Americans themselves. Their contributions to either critiquing or reinventing representations of African American culture can be found broadly in the traditional arts, film, literature, and even communication design. For instance, in his film *Bamboozled*, African American filmmaker Spike Lee intentionally re-presents numerous stereotypes of African Americans as a cultural critique of mainstream society's historical representations of his culture. Cultural critics such as Spike Lee, film producer Tyler Perry, and artist Robert Colescott, among others, seek to determine and understand the nature of aesthetics for their own culture through re-presentation of the stereotypes.

There is a dire need for more culturally appropriate representations of African American culture; and, in response to this lacuna, the late African American communication designer Sylvia Harris[12] encouraged African American students entering the profession of communication design to translate cultural resources such as the AFRICOBRA art collective, or even musical rhythms from African-influenced music such as jazz, into culturally specific designs. She also suggested that they seek creative inspiration from the work of Caucasian artists and designers whose work shows the influence of African American culture.[13] Since art influences communication design, it is no surprise to find discourse in communication design that encourages students to look at the work of African American artists like Aaron Douglas—one of the leaders of the New Negro art movement of the 1920s—for artistic techniques and strategies to translate into visual language.[14]

Though these suggestions are viable in providing creative inspiration to novice African American designers, the question my previous work[15] answers was: Is there an autochthonous aesthetic for African American culture, defined by African American communication designers? In response to this question, I posit that mathematics could be an unexpected pathway by which African Americans could develop cultural aesthetics for communication design. Specifically, I argue for the use of African fractals[16] as a resource for the visual semantics of the communication designer's canvas—a printed or digital composition that diverse users access for information and/or an aesthetic or cultural experience. With the emergence of Ron Eglash's observation of fractal geometry in African settlement architecture, art, hairstyles, and other indigenous cultural artifacts, and the rise of ethnomathematics and cultural design as schools of thought, an untapped opportunity has surfaced, offering a new path from African art and design history to a culturally specific aesthetic for present African American communication designers. Some of my own efforts in this area have been through a collaboration with Ron Eglash to develop

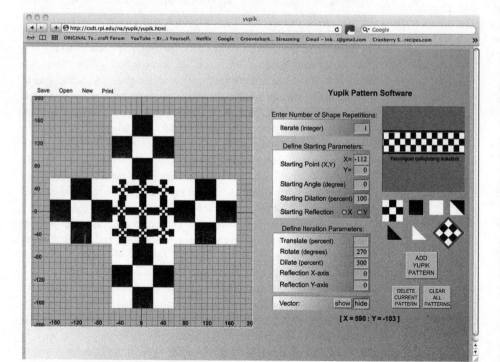

Fig. 1

Culturally Situated Design Tools (CSDTs), a suite of web applets that allow underrepresented ethnic youth to simulate African artifacts (like African art) and practices (like cornrow braiding) by using indigenous mathematical concepts and algorithms. However, these tools are not restricted to only African designs; in Figure 1 we see an artistic pattern created by one of the children in our workshop, based on a Native American design practice. It is particularly interesting since the original Native American practice is not fractal, but this student added a fractal character to their design: perhaps an influence from their previous exposure to the African fractals software.

However, the use of these mathematical principles to convey cultural aesthetics has not been explored collectively by African American designers, perhaps because of the growing accessibility to diverse cultures in communication processes. The leveling of the world[17] through technological development has had a profound impact on the communication of images in society. Since the publication of Friedman's book, internet usage in Africa, the Middle East, and Latin America has increased dramatically in all three regions. We are now living in a post-globalization age with increased and open access to most cultures around the world through the World Wide Web and other communication technologies that can virtually extend across geographic boundaries. The continuous emergence of technologies in our post-globalization age, engineered with Web 2.0 coding, continues to create unprecedented opportunities for global interaction in the consumption of images. As a result of the world flattening, cross-cultural communication is now the norm; and, there is a dire need for aesthetics that communicate across cultures. When communicating visually via media networks, cross-cultural resonance is paramount for attaining communicative effectiveness.[18] The integration of fractal patterns, for instance, in the construction of design grids and the positioning and treatment of elements within a composition can be the thread that weaves a cultural aesthetic that communicates African American heritage and culture and those of other ethnic groups as well.
Thus a new appreciation for the African geometric heritage need not be parochial; it can contribute to the development of aesthetics that communicate across different cultures. I posit that the cultural aesthetic of space can lead to a cross-cultural visual aesthetic through the use of cultural grids—that are, more specifically, an organizational network of horizontal, vertical, diagonal, and curvilinear lines and shapes found in cultural artifacts and spaces that can apply to communication design practice—particularly to the printed or digital page—to yield cross-cultural resonance during the design and interpretation of images in the communication process. In fact, if we return to hook's description

of Baba's house from the essay *An Aesthetic of Blackness*, she defines aesthetic as a "way of inhabiting space."[19] By space here she means domestic space and the way that Baba inhabited her house with objects. Thus, the previous definitions of cultural aesthetics could be combined and broadened to say that cultural aesthetics are the interaction of sensory treatments including spatial organization based on cultural values that creates a sense of beauty. In this essay, I purport that the golden rectangle is a cultural grid that has the potential to yield cross-cultural aesthetics that provide aesthetic appeal to users.

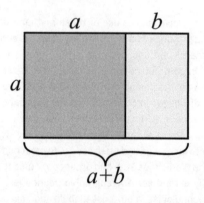

Fig. 2

DESIGNING CROSS-CULTURAL AESTHETICS WITH THE GOLDEN RATIO

The golden rectangle depicted in Figure 2 is a visual manifestation of the golden ratio (1:phi). That is, its sides reflect a golden ratio. The ratio of a to b is the same as the ratio of a plus b to a. Delineating a square on one side of the golden rectangle creates another golden rectangle. If we repeat the delineation of a square in each new golden rectangle that forms, in the same direction (clockwise or counterclockwise), we obtain a golden spiral.

Within the discipline of communication design practice, the golden rectangle is a tool that professional designers use to render aesthetically pleasing images and experiences. Livio supports this assertion when he states that "numerous authors have claimed that the golden rectangle is the most aesthetically-pleasing of all rectangles."[20] Indeed, generation after generation of communication designers use the golden rectangle to organize information visually and guide users to meaning. They regard the golden rectangle as a mathematical grid that yields visually appealing aesthetics—particularly in regard to typographic harmony in book design grids. The golden rectangle could be considered a "multicultural grid," in that it is a grid that corresponds to an organizational structure shared by many different cultural groups, and when applied to the layout of information has the potential to yield an outcome that resonates cross-culturally with many different cultural groups. Yet, when considering its cultural origin, the golden rectangle is usually associated with only one culture—the ancient Greeks with a line of more general European descent that runs through Leonardo da Vinci right up to the Bauhaus.

Because of the usefulness of golden rectangle grids to organize and structure information on printed and digital pages throughout history, the question of where the golden rectangle originates has relevance to its use for yielding cross-cultural aesthetics. However, communication designers probably did not invent the myth of a Greek origin for the golden rectangle; they may be merely repeating the claims made elsewhere. For instance, according to communication designer Kimberly Elam,[21] the golden section rectangle originates in early Greek civilization. Even when designers consider grids more broadly, Africa is usually left out, as in this quotation from communication designer Tim Samara:

> The Chinese, the Japanese, the Greeks
> and Romans, the Inca—all of these
> cultures have pursued structural ideas
> in laying out their towns, conduct-
> ing warfare, and arranging images.[22]

The exclusion of Africa from historical accounts of the origin of the golden rectangle is worthy of scrutiny. Contrary to most accounts, there is no mention of the golden rectangle in any Greek written sources, and the example most prominently used, the Parthenon, also fails:

> Certainly, the oft repeated assertion
> that the Parthenon in Athens is based
> on the golden ratio is not supported
> by actual measurements. In fact, the
> entire story about the Greeks and golden
> ratio seems to be without foundation.[23]

However, if the Greeks did not contribute the golden rect-angle, who did? Typographer Robert Bringhurst provides a hint in his account:

> If we look for a numerical approximation
> to this ratio, 1 : phi, we will find
> it in something called the Fibonacci
> series, named for the thirteenth-cen-

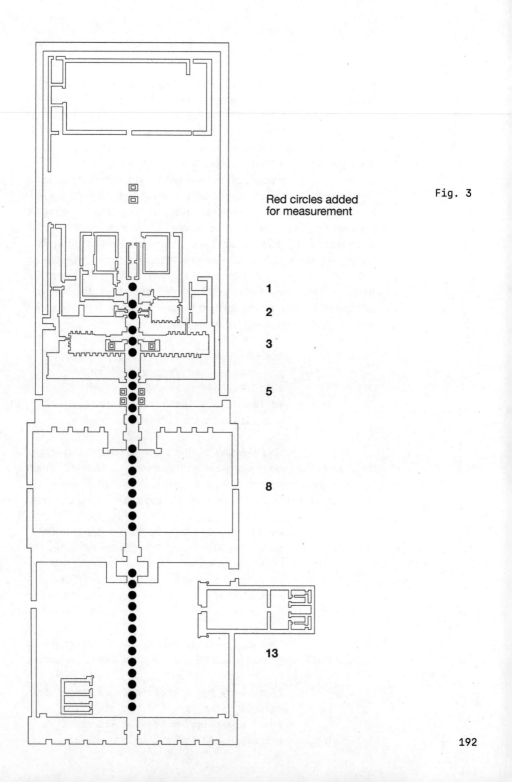

Red circles added
for measurement

Fig. 3

1
2

3

5

8

13

*tury mathematician Leonardo Fibonacci.
Though he died two centuries before
Gutenberg, Fibonacci is important in
the history of European typography as
well as mathematics. He was born in Pisa
but studied in North Africa . . .*[24]

As Eglash notes,[25] there is no evidence that ancient Greek mathematicians knew of the Fibonacci series. However Badaway[26] found a use of the Fibonacci series (1, 1, 2, 3, 5, 8, 13 . . .) in the layout of temples in Ancient Egypt.

Greek mathematician Euclid did describe dividing a line such that it created a golden ratio, but never discussed constructing a two-dimensional figure with that ratio. The most famous representative of Greek architecture, Vitruvius, worked exclusively with proportions that can be expressed in whole numbers, rather than irrational proportions that the golden ratio would require. This was in keeping with the ancient Greek distaste for irrational numbers and the infinite series, which clashed with Platonic notions of mathematics as static perfection existing in an eternal, unchanging "realm of the Forms." African designs, on the other hand, deliberately make use of such iterative sequences, since they fit well with the African cultural emphasis on fecundity, fertility, and cyclic aspects of life. One can hear this dynamicism in African polyrhythmic music and see it in iterative architectural designs such as Karnak and Logone-Birni.

The Temple of Karnak from ancient Egypt shows successive chambers with lengths determined by iterations of the Fibonacci series. The altar in the temple of Karnak depicted in Figure 3 creates the initial value for the generation of its form, just as we see for altars in other cases of self-generating architectural forms in sub-Saharan Africa. Since archaeological evidence shows that Egyptian civilization was founded when groups traveled down the Nilotic valley, it is no surprise that these traditions of recursive form were continued in Egypt. In the original sub-Saharan architectures the structures are not largely determined by quantitative formula; the Egyptian version thus provides a more formal version of the sub-Saharan recursive tradition. It is not unreasonable to speculate that Fibonacci brought the sequence from North Africa, where it was used in the weights of a scale balance as well as architecturally.

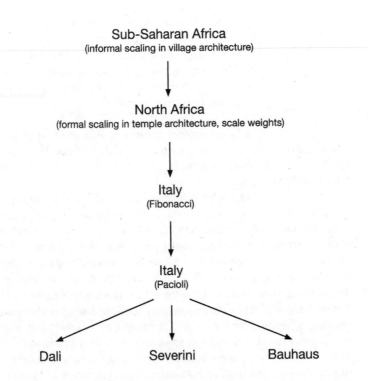

Fig. 4

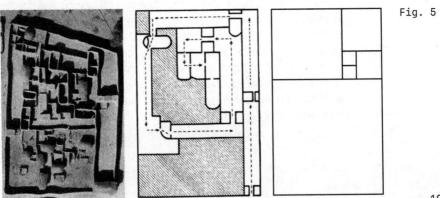

Fig. 5

As shown in Figure 4, we can postulate then that the golden ratio originated in sub-Saharan Africa, migrated north possibly to Egypt, and then traveled to Italy and onward around the rest of the world.

Another example of iterative sequences in African architecture can be seen in the palace of the Chief in Logone-Birni, Cameroon (Figure 5). This structure epitomizes culturally defined visual beauty and labor-intensive construction through its complex spatial design. The palace is relevant to the discussion on the evolving need for cross cultural aesthetics because of the mathematical concept embedded in its architectural design. It uses a fractal grid characterized by the repetition of similar shapes at ever diminishing scales.[27]

> *The real passage as a whole is a*
> *rectangular spiral. Each time you*
> *enter a smaller scale, you are*
> *required to behave more politely. By*
> *the time you arrive at the throne*
> *you are shoeless and speak with*
> *a very cultured formality.*[28]

As Eglash notes, the path that one takes to navigate the palace's space approximates a "golden spiral."[29] In other words, the iterative construction of the palace—from tiny rectangles to larger and larger rectangles—naturally lends itself to the golden rectangle construction for the overall form, even though the match along any one wall is far from perfect.

Logone-Birni and Karnak are evidence that early Africans used mathematically related organizing principles, such as the recursively generated ratios related to the golden rectangle, in their architecture and settlement design. These examples predate the use of such designs in Europe; and quite possibly contributed to their European utilization through travelers such as Fibonacci. Other routes by which this knowledge may have entered Europe could include Rosicrucians, alchemists, and other mystics interested in ancient Egypt, as well as the group of mathematicians and artists sent to Egypt under Napoleon in 1799. My previous work (Bennett 2003) notes that these recursive traditions of Africa offer a new basis for thinking about Black cultural influences in communication design. Here I've extended that argument, noting how the golden rectangle and its related iterative constructions add additional insight into what can constitute a cross-cultural aesthetic in communication design.

CONSCIOUS USE OF MATH PRINCIPLES IN THE
COMMUNICATION DESIGN PROCESS

The question that remains is: how might communication designers graphically translate mathematical principles like the golden ratio and grids derived from its formula into a visual aesthetic that communicates cross-culturally? A good place to start might be with the terms shared between the disciplines of communication design and mathematics and used to describe the fractals that the golden ratio creates—such as translation, rotation, repetition, and scale. The way that mathematicians define translation is similar to the way that communication designers define it in relation to the positioning of elements within a compositional space. Communication designers subconsciously use translation to create a variety of visual effects that include making elements look related. Scaling is particularly important in its use for contrast in size in communication design; and, contrast is a key to creating visual hierarchy. That is, change in size brings attention to particular elements in a given composition while smaller elements recede to the background and are barely visible. Communication designers frequently use repetition to unify a composition and make it less predictable during interpretation in order to attract the attention of users and make them linger for more information.

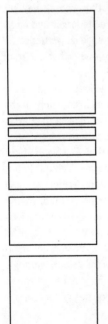

Fig. 6

The Temple of Karnak in Egypt provides a unique golden ratio grid (that is, successive members of the Fibonacci sequence converge to phi). Figure 6 shows how this architecture could be used to develop modular, scaling units for a visual layout. The palace of the chief in Logone-Birni, Cameroon, provides two more useful architectural structures that can translate seamlessly into compositional grids. The first grid is from the aerial photo in Figure 3 that shows the compartmentalization of a physical space, that is, how rooms are situated in relation to each other. When translated into the compositional grid in Figure 7, the designer can use it to compose a layout of verbal and visual elements that convey African American cultural heritage and Western values.

Fig. 7

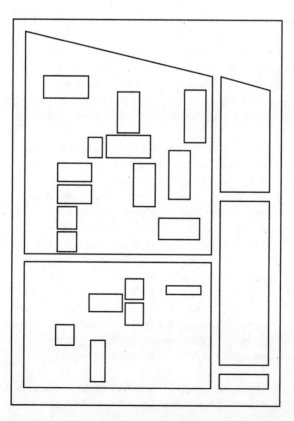

A second architectural grid associated with the palace of the chief in Logone-Birni is of the path through its space. The grid in Figure 8 generalizes the golden spiral path through the palace's space.

This grid is commonly known as a golden rectangle within the design community. On a practical level, it has been used prolifically as a tool to render aesthetically pleasing graphics and experiences. Thus we can reinterpret the golden ratio's role in design as having a new dimension in its cultural connotations; one that includes African culture among other cultures; an interaction between Africa and the West. The application of the golden ratio to the architecture of information is thus limitless for communication designers: it can move between the universal and the local; between a sense of beauty tied to histories and places, and a sense of beauty that transcends those boundaries. Further research and practice along these lines could be valuable not only in better understanding visual culture trans-nationally, but also in helping designers of all nations better utilize these geometric illuminations from the "dark continent."

CONCLUSION The two historical African sites discussed in this paper are significant because of the well-known mathematical concept embedded in both of their spatial designs—a phenomenon that has relevance to the history of communication design and African American design identity. The following excerpt from a prominent national organization's website supports the need for the inclusion of African contributions to Western communication design history and theory:

> According to the 2000 census, by 2025 what are currently considered minority populations is predicted to be 40 percent of the US population. By 2050, more than half of Americans are expected to be members of current minorities. In contrast, a recent survey of AIGA members finds that [communication] designers who responded, 2 percent are [African American], 4 percent Hispanic/ Latino, 6 percent Asian/Pacific Islander and 2 percent other. The design profession is still overwhelmingly homogenous in its racial composition.[30]

The low percentage of members from underrepresented ethnic groups—particularly African Americans—in the AIGA community

Fig. 8

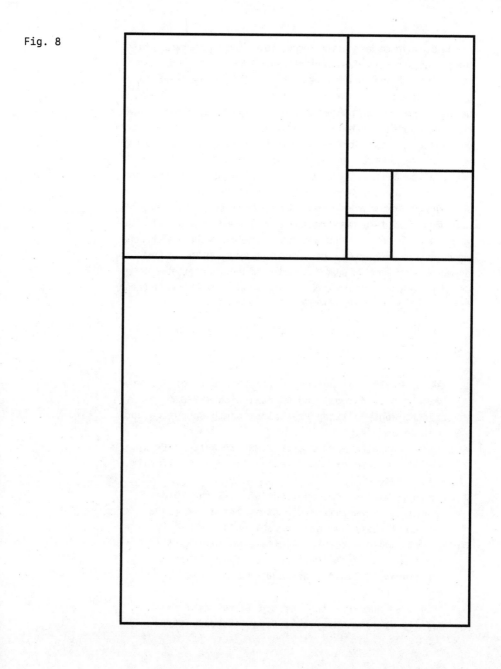

may be due to those designers or prospective designers not being able to see themselves reflected in the rhetoric of the discipline—in its symbolic visual codes passed down from one generation to another through the discourse. Designers from these underrepresented ethnic groups may feel a need to belong or a greater sense of belonging to professional design communities like AIGA, the professional organization for design, if they are able to see their culture reflected in the discipline's discourse on what constitutes good design. However, if the golden ratio concept was present in historical Africa or actually originates from there, then Africans and their African American descendants play a role in the development of good design standards in the West. No longer should African American designers feel left out of the discipline. All along they have been included—from the Bauhaus to the present. Thus, the use of the golden ratio as a tool for generating cultural aesthetics should have additional significance to the ongoing engenderment of agency in African American designers and a sense of shared ownership of the communication design discipline—a factor that could be used to attract more African American designers in order to at least diversify the discipline.

NOTES

1. Livio, Mario. *The Golden Ratio: The Story of Phi, the World's Most Astonishing Number*. Crown, 2008.
2. Eglash, Ron. "African Fractals: Modern Computing and Indigenous Design." 1999.
3. Burke, Kenneth. *Language as Symbolic Action: Essays on Life, Literature, and Method*. Univ of California Press, 1966.
4. Luhmann, Niklas. "Deconstruction as Second-Order Observing." *New Literary History* 24, no. 4 (1993): 763–82. https://doi.org/10.2307/469391.
5. Tylor, Edward Burnett. *Primitive Culture: Researches into the Development of Mythology, Philosophy, Religion, Art and Custom*. Vol. 2. J. Murray, 1871.
6. Blier, Suzanne Preston. *African Royal Art: The Majesty of Form*. New York: Prentice Hall, 1998.

7. hooks, bell. "An Aesthetic of Blackness: Strange
    and Oppositional." *Lenox Avenue: A Journal of
    Interarts Inquiry* 1 (1995): 65-72. https://doi.org
    /10.2307/4177045.
8. "Arson and Death Threats as Muhammad Caricature
    Controversy Escalates". *Spiegel Online International*.
    4 February 2006.
9. National Congress of American Indians "Ending the Era
    of Harmful 'Indian' Mascots," https://www.ncai.org/
    proudtobe (accessed October 16, 2021).
10. Brown, Thomas. "Moose, Wolves, Pine Trees and Kegs:
    A Look into Mascot Adoption Efforts." The Dartmouth,
    Oct 30, 2020 (accessed Sept 27, 2021).
11. Heller, Steven. "Exploiting Stereotypes: When Bad
    is Not Good." AIGA, Dec 13, 2005 (accessed Sept 27,
    2021).
12. Harris, Sylvia. "Searching for the Black Aesthetic
    in American Graphic Design" In *The Education of a
    Graphic Designer*, edited by Heller, Steven, 125-29
    New York: Allworth Press [in association with the]
    School of Visual Arts, 1998.
13. Ibid.
14. Ibid.
15. Bennett, Audrey. "Towards an Autochthonic Black
    Aesthetic for Graphic Design Pedagogy." *Journal of
    Design Research* 3, no. 2 (2003): 61-70.
16. Raymond Lutzky (2012) African Fractals and Culturally
    Situated Design Tools: Mathematics Education Through
    Self-Empowering Technology, Critical Interventions,
    6:1, 143-158, DOI: 10.1080/19301944.2012.10781421.
17. Friedman, Thomas L. *The World Is Flat: A Brief
    History of the Twenty-First Century*. Farrar, Straus
    and Giroux, 2005
18. Bennett, Audrey G. "Teaching Image Standards in a
    Post-Globalization Age." *Teaching and Training for
    Global Engineering: Perspectives on Culture and
    Professional Communication Practices* (2016): 47-68.
19. hooks, bell. "An Aesthetic of Blackness: Strange and
    Oppositional." Lenox Avenue: A *Journal of Interarts
    Inquiry* Vol. 1 (1995), pp. 65-72

20. Livio, Golden Ratio.
21. Elam, Kimberly, *Geometry of Design: Studies in Proportion and Composition.* New York: Princeton Architectural Press, 2001.
22. Samara, Timothy. *Making and Breaking the Grid: A Graphic Design Layout Workshop.* Rockport Publishers, 2002
23. Devlin, Keith. *The Math Instinct: Why You're a Mathematical Genius (along with Lobsters, Birds, Cats, and Dogs).* New York: Thunder's Mouth Press, 2005
24. Bringhurst, Robert. *The Elements of Typographic Style.* Vancouver: Hartley & Marks, 1992.
25. Eglash, "African Fractals," 1999.
26. Badawy, Alexander. *Ancient Egyptian Architectural Design: A Study of the Harmonic System.* Berkeley: University of California Press, 1965.
27. Eglash, "African Fractals," 1999.
28. Ibid.
29. Ibid.
30. AIGA Atlanta on Diversity: Color Blind Online. https://aigaatlantatalks.blogspot.com/, February 4, 2007. (accessed October 16, 2021).

IMAGE CREDITS

1. In this example, high school youth used math and computing principles to create artistic simulations from cultural artifacts like this striking one based on Native American Yupik pattern bits from Culturally Situated Design Tools. Image rights: Audrey G. Bennett

2. Visualization of golden rectangle Image rights: public domain

3. The Temple of Karnak shows successive chambers with lengths determined by iterations of the Fibonacci series. Image rights: Public domain

4. Migration of golden ratio from Africa to other parts of the world. Image rights: Audrey G. Bennett

5. From left to right: aerial photo of the palace
   of Chief in Logone-Birni, path through palace,
   visualization of golden rectangle spiral.
6. Compositional grid derived from the architectural
   plan of the Temple of Karnak in Egypt. Image rights:
   Audrey G. Bennett
7. Compositional grid based on aerial grid of palace of
   Chief in Logone-Birni, Cameroon. Image rights: Audrey
   G. Bennett
8. Visualization of golden rectangle spiral. Image
   rights: Audrey G. Bennett

The Pause:

Reflecting on a Righteous Consciousness that Informs Our Design as Afrikans

NII KOMMEY BOTCHWAY

I confess I have been pretty reticent about writing about this. My general feeling on the subject matter of this book could be summed up in one sentence:

The Black experience in design is death.

There. That's my piece written.

I'm not interested in talking about my "Black" experience in design. Because that very categorization situates me in a global design paradigm not of my, nor of my people's, making. And as I will show: it is death.

I don't identify as "Black."
I am a Ga. I belong to the GaDangme ethnic group; I am Afrikan. This is the design that ties me to a place, people, culture, and heritage.

In the words of Robert L Peters:

> Design creates culture.
> Culture shapes values.
> Values determine the future.

Fig. 1

AKPAKI

Hence the point of me asking, questioning, and seeking what consciousness or spirit creates a design.

The "design" that categorizes me and my people as "Black" does everything to disconnect me from my (our) culture, my (our) heritage, and my (our) future. It is a dead spirit. It is death. So having the spiritual (higher) understanding, why would I want to be defined by something that is death to my being and my people?

Framing "the Black Experience in Design" for me is a dead framing about the so-called "Black" experience in the Western world. I'm tired of talking and writing these things. We keep saying, talking, and writing about these things as so-called "Black" people . . . our experiences in a dead system. In a lifeless design. The system that we are in was not designed by or for us.

Writing in 1979 about the influence and impact of the English and French education system on their former colonies in Afrika, Saër Dione said:

> The differences are crystal-clear but, generally speaking, they have been exaggerated. What is most certain, however, is that neither system was designed to produce an African who would be proud of being African.

Writing forty years later in 2019, Chika Ezeanya-Esiobu states:

> In an independent Africa, the outcome of colonial education still makes the African identify with foreign concepts, knowledge, so-called foreign experts and consultants, and devalue the indigenous, home grown knowledge and more qualified experts on the continent.
>
> Several decades after the end of colonialism, sub-Saharan Africa has not made much progress in liberating the education process from the clutches of imperialism and dependency.

Thus, two publications separated by forty years are basically saying the same thing. That the education Afrikans are receiving is not designed for them. Far less to make them successful. And yet we refuse to hear and continue in the dysfunctional designs we find ourselves in.

As the past twelve months since the emergence of COVID-19 has demonstrated: the design we are in (as so-called "Blacks" and in fact as humanity) is dead. This is my focus today.

It has been a long journey. It has taken about twenty years to get to this point in my life and my growth as a designer, as an individual, as a teacher. That growth has not just been from an intellectual or academic perspective; it has also been from a spiritual point of view. I don't think we can do the work that we do, the work we are called to do—especially as creators— if we don't have a form of spiritual grounding or understanding.

Everything that we do has a spiritual grounding to it, which we tend to forget because we always operate through this Western materialist capitalist modality where everything is put into silos and boxes. So the spirit is null and void. Even though it's there. Trust me, it's there, even if we are not aware (conscious) it's there. Let me give you an example:

You know when someone says "let's follow the spirit of the law," what do you think they are telling or showing you? That even in the spaces that we're told are "rational" and "non-spiritual," sometimes people do acknowledge the spirit and its presence. But we are made to think that the spirit doesn't exist in this Western, rational, capitalist world that we live in, but the spirit is there. Because, as I stated, we are in it. We are in a design that is a manifestation of a spirit, a mindset. A consciousness.

More eloquent people have surmised as such—as evidenced here in this statement written by Arundhati Roy from her piece "The Pandemic is a Portal":

> Historically, pandemics have forced
> humans to break with the past and
> imagine their world anew. This one is
> no different. It is a portal, a gate-
> way between one world and the next.
>
> We can choose to walk through it, drag-
> ging the carcasses of our prejudice
> and hatred, our avarice, our data
> banks and dead ideas, our dead rivers
> and smoky skies behind us. Or we can
> walk through lightly, with little
> luggage, ready to imagine another
> world. And ready to fight for it.

When I think of the "Black experience in design," my (design) intention is not to keep anyone in this system. I don't want to prop up a system that was not built for us. Spiritually, we are just changing deck chairs on the *Titanic* if we keep grounding the work in the same ways of thinking. Therefore I want to push people to new places.

What is the actual design that we have to live as so-called "Black" people? I don't want to talk about the sinking ship that we are all on and finding new theoretical frameworks etc. The *Titanic* that we are all on has hit the iceberg, and we're all going down. I'm much more interested in building a raft to get off the doomed vessel with my people and anyone else who wants to get off. That is a lived thing, not a theoretical thing. I know what needs to be done.

Now it's about doing it and talking about it. You can't talk about what you haven't done, and what you haven't lived. The process now is about finding out who one is, and what one's purpose is and to live and be the manifestation of that design, that consciousness that one talks about.

The biggest problem with our people is that we talk about things that we don't actually make manifest. We talk about sustainability but our lives are not. We talk about non-gender-based violence, and then someone goes home and beats their wife. We talk about humanizing pedagogy, following the examples of Paulo Freire, but some of the same people who use these references have no ounce of humanity in their pedagogy and the way they treat other people. Let everyone live and be who they are. Your actions, your words, these are who you are. So from my point of view, I'm saying let me be who I am seeking to be and do. That higher self. My actions will speak. Not "theoretical frameworks" from a dead system.

I have a new spiritual (conscious) insight as I continue my personal journey in life as an Afrikan who designs. If I had been asked to write this essay five years ago I would have been running to respond in a different way. In the dead "theoretical frameworks" of the design that defined me as a "Black" person.

So, what am I to manifest via my design consciousness? What are we supposed to do?

Fig. 2

ASRAFOI

ASRAFOI: STRATEGIC THINKING HELPS TO BRIDGE BETWEEN WHERE YOU ARE AND WHERE YOU WANT TO BE.

I admire the work of Leah Perlman—the Afrikan American farmer in upstate New York. As a farmer, she is reclaiming the Afrikan connection to the land. This ties to my own belief about the land and spirituality. As elder Renard Turner, another Afrikan American farmer, states: "We cannot have culture without agriculture."

That's the foundation for what we have to do. Leah Perlman has a very spiritual basis to what she does and who she is, as a farmer. It is based in West Afrikan ideologies. It is where she traces her ancestry. I say all of this to say that what we tend to do and what we are in these spaces doesn't bring through our spirituality and who we are as Afrikan people. I think for me fundamentally writing this piece made me realize that I can't share what I want to share unless I bring in that spiritual aspect of who we are and who our people are.

Unless we challenge the underlying design of the world around us and the systems we operate in, we will be forever running around in circles operating in the mechanizations and schemes of others. We are all, because the West rules everything around us, operating in a wicked design that someone put into place. It's not "by accident." This system is doing exactly what it was designed to do.

Until you look at this thing from the perspective of a design/intent you will be forever chasing your tails looking for "solutions." Which is what so-called "Black" people are very good at doing—talking and looking for the system (that has been designed to keep them where they are) to somehow magically "save them."

And in my humble opinion there is no "saving" what we see around us. This system is done. In fact, I am not interested in saving something that was conceived in wickedness. We cannot waste our time in and on these systems. Let's build something that makes the existing reality obsolete (paraphrasing Buckminster Fuller).

This can only be done by a righteous conscious intention. Let us be part of the building of a new system. But truth be told, it's not a "new" system. What we need to do is return to our original design in which we were made by our Creator. By following that original design (intent), we return to our purpose as human beings on this planet. What is that design?

We were created in the image of:

LOVE
TRUTH
JUSTICE
RIGHTEOUSNESS
PERFECTION

And if we were truly operating in that design, we would see the results (fruits) around us. But because we are operating in another design currently, we can be of no doubt to its true intentions and the intentions of those who created it. After all its fruits are there for all to see.

Ultimately we have not been given the spirit of fear but that of love. If you are operating in fear you will fail. And this system is failing because it's designed out of fear, not love.

So I think that my journey over the past two decades has culminated with that understanding. The spiritual aspect of things, the why-things-happen, the why things-are-the-way-they-are. The spiritual is just the higher questioning and understand of why things are the way they are. And now once that I've gotten that insight, I can no longer continue to work as I did before, using the playbook that I was given. Operating in a redundant, obsolete dead design, moving the deck chairs on the sinking *Titanic*. I am moving away from a dead system and toward life-giving and spiritual design as an Afrikan designer.

Fig. 3

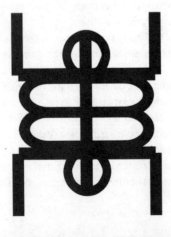

AKPOKPLONTO

AKPOKPLONTO: True progress is slow but sure.

Allow me to refer to something I watched very early last year as the pandemic took hold. It's called "The Warning." I decided to call this essay "The Pause," because I greatly believe that is what the past twelve months have been. A pause. Time for us all on this planet to pause, to reflect, to take time out, and to ponder on what we are being shown off the design we all find ourselves in. And we are being given a choice. To remain on the *Titanic* or to get off. To choose life or to choose death.

Because ultimately we all get what we design. I leave you with the words written in 1963 by the South African designer Selby Mvusi:

> *We do not therefore design for society or for that matter design in order to design society. We design because society and ourselves are in fact design.*
>
> *We do not design for living.*
> *We design to live.*

NOTES

1. Nii prefers to spell Afrika with a "k" as a way of honoring the continent. In traditional Afrikan languages, "c" is nonexistent as a phonetic of its own.

2. GaDangme have their own symbols. These are known as SAMAI and are used to teach values, motivate, educate, advise, and, when necessary, chastise. They form the basis of much of our oratorial as well as royal totem culture. These symbols are part of the cultural heritage of the GaDangme people found on the west coast of Afrika. They are similar to the Akan Adinkra symbols, which are not "owned" by anyone but belong to the society and culture from whence they originate. For more background: https://thegadangme.com/ga-samai/.

3. Dione, Saër. "The African Educational Pattern: Present Needs and Future Opportunities." *Présence africaine* 109 (1979): 50-64.

4. Ezeanya-Esiobu, Chika. "Indigenous Knowledge and Education in Africa.". *Nature*, 2019.
5. Roy, Arundhati. "The Pandemic Is a Portal." *Financial Times* 3, no. 4 (2020).
6. Turner, Farmer Renard. This Black Farmer Changed My Life! - First Time I Saw Farmer Turner Speak (Black Farmer Series): https://www.youtube.com/watch?v=B2-9zSLnn1M, YouTube. (14:46), Oct 17, 2018.
7. RootsTV Nigeria. "The Warning." YouTube video, 3:55, March 11, 2020. https://www.youtube.com/watch?v=C5gVRE9qNbQ.
8. Magaziner, Daniel. "Designing Knowledge in Postcolonial Africa: A South African Abroad." *Kronos* 41, no. 1 (2015): 265-286.

IMAGE CREDITS

1. AKPAKI, Signs are always there, we just choose to ignore them
2. ASRAFOI, Strategic thinking helps to bridge between where you are and where you want to be.
3. AKPOKPLNTO, True progress is slow but sure.

Finding Anthony:

Establishing a Research

Trajectory

CHERYL D. MILLER

I've been running for my life, my cause, my purpose, my advocacy, since I was young. I was a little Black girl of many colors, many ethnicities, and many cultures and came to discover that I was more than an artist—I was an activist. And I was running to free myself from oppression, prejudice, discrimination, white supremacy, institutional racism, and systemic racist practices that sought to thwart my every attempt to draw and paint beautiful visions inspired by the diversity in my background.

With a machete in one hand and a T-square in the other, I cut pathways for myself so that I could run the race away from my mid-century oppressors. I started praying, too, reiterating like a mantra, "I want to change. I want to see the change."

Along my journey, I discovered a love of footnotes and scholarship. I went all around the archives, back to Africa, W. E. B. Du Bois's sociological research and the data on the Negro Artisan, and to vintage books such as *The Other Slaves*. Moreover, something deep from my heritage told me the first Black graphic designer was the African with his images, his culture, and his techniques, who had traveled through the transatlantic slave trade to Providence, Rhode Island, and Virginia and other ports of entry along the northeast corridor where the African was sold.

I put in hours of research in my quest to answer the question I began asking fifty years ago: "Where are the black designers?" And then I found Anthony, the slave artist who was the woodcut artisan of the runaway slave ads.

I finally began to understand what happened and what I was missing. Footnote after footnote, proof upon proof, I found Anthony. He too, was running away from oppression and hatred, as documented in *The History of Advertising from Earliest Times*.

And he became my favorite footnote. A twenty-five-dollar reward for a slave:

Ran away from Raleigh, a month or two
ago, a mulatto man, named Anthony, well
known in Raleigh, and many parts of

the State, as having been, for several
years, the body servant of General
Jones, and mine lately as a pressman and
news-carrier in the Star office. Anthony
is about twenty-five or twenty-six years
of age, five feet eight or ten inches
high, is a mongrel white, has a toler-
ably large aquiline nose, bushy hair,
a scar on one of his cheeks; when in
good humour has a pleasing countenance.

The ad continues to describe Anthony, stating that he "is an excellent pressman, indifferent at distributing types, a tolerable carpenter and joiner, a plain painter, an excellent manager of horses, drives well and rides elegantly, having been accustomed to race riding . . ." The description then ends with, "He is an artful fellow, and if taken up will tell a most plausible story, and possibly show a forged pass."

W. E. B. du Bois confirms the existence of the likes of Anthony in several sociological essays documented in *The Negro Artisan*. Among other revelations, he notes the threat slave artisans pose to their white counterparts. In some cases, the fear of Negro competition among certain groups of white workmen in the North was so strong that they opposed emancipation. In Pennsylvania, for example, the legislature was urged to reenact laws permitting Negro slavery on the very eve of the Civil War in 1860. My favorite footnote tells me that what was done to the slave artisan in various attempts to kill his voice is an echo of what I have experienced as oppressive systems have repeatedly tried to silence me and keep me quiet.

Irony has a funny way of laughing at us. In the process of undertaking many years of independent research, the footnotes yielded the evidence I had been searching for: the first Black graphic designer may have been a slave artisan; the answer to my lifelong question has been right in front of me, right before my very eyes. The spirit of Anthony is also present in the preservation of the Williamsburg print shop—the physical space it holds—and in its advertisements, website, posters, and brochures. Consequently, I have come to love footnotes. I am on the hunt, daily, because I have the highest regard for the detailed information that can be found, buried in the margins. There is no "fake news" with proof, and footnotes become the foundation for building a design scholarship agenda.

But I must also give credit to Union Theological Seminary, which helped me master footnotes and grow as a scholar. In addition to learning about systematic theology, Black liberation theology, and womanist theology, guided by luminaries such as Cornel West, Dolores Williams, and the late James Cone, it was the place where I became an activist. And through a combination of theology, art, and design, I learned to demand justice, to set captives free, and to stand up for Anthony, the runaway slave.

From Booker T. Washington's *Up From Slavery* I have learned that success is to be measured not so much by the position that one has reached in life as by the obstacles which he or she has overcome while trying to succeed. Looked at from this standpoint, I almost reached the conclusion that often the Negro boy's/girl's birth and connection with an unpopular race is an advantage so far as real life is concerned. With few exceptions, the Negro youth must work harder and must perform his/ her task even better than a white youth in order to assure recognition.

But out of the hard and unusual struggle through which he or she is compelled to pass, he or she gets the confidence that one misses whose pathway is comparatively smooth by reason of birth and race.

NOTES

1. Sampson, Henry. *The History of Advertising from Earliest Times*. London: Chatto and Windus Piccadilly,1874, pg. 572.
2. Ibid.
3. Du Bois, W. E. B., *The Negro Artisan*. Atlanta: Atlanta University Press, 1902.
4. Du Bois, W. E. B., James E. Newton, and Ronald L. Lewis. "The Ante-Bellum Negro Artisan," *The Other Slaves: Mechanics, Artisans, and Craftsmen*. (1978): 178-180.
5. Spero, Sterling D., and Abram L. Harris. "The Slave Regime: Competition Between Negro and White Labor," *The Other Slaves: Mechanics, Artisans, and Craftsmen*. (DuBois etal. eds) (1978): 178-180.
6. Washington, Booker T. *Up from Slavery*. Simon & Schuster, 2013.

Bondage by Paper:

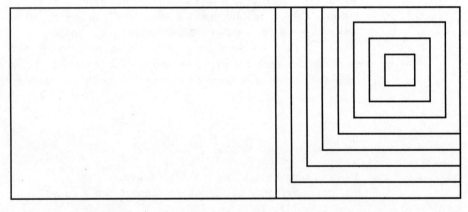

Devices of Slaveholding Ingenuity

ALICIA OLUSHOLA AJAYI

This device of slaveholding ingenuity, like other devices of wickedness, in some measure defeated itself . . .

—Frederick Douglass

INTRODUCTION In 1872, nearly thirty-five years before Frederick Douglass became the first Black man nominated for vice president of the United States,[1] he escaped slavery.

The prominent abolitionist vividly narrated his escape to New York in his first memoir, *The Life and Times of Frederick Douglass*.[2] Twenty-year-old Douglass had been enslaved near the city of Baltimore, Maryland—which boasted one of the nation's first major seaports when, disguised in a sailor's uniform, he boarded a train heading to New York. Though Maryland was a slave state, it was not unusual to see free Black sailors due to the volume of seamen the port received from around the world. While all sailors had to carry Seamen Protection Papers to move freely from country to country,[3] Black sailors were required to carry a second legal document—Free Negro Bonds—to prove their status as free men in the United States.[4] Borrowing Seaman papers from a friend, Douglass passed easily as a free Black sailor, having served as a deckhand on riverboats during his years in bondage. The ruse was a viable covert operation. Once on the train, Douglass was approached by a ticket conductor who was collecting fares and checking papers, a scene he describes as "a critical moment in the drama."[5] Already assuming the role of a freed man, he performed the retrieval of the document from the deep pocket of his friend's sailor uniform and presented it to the official. Douglass recounted:

> The merest glance at the paper satisfied him, and he took my fare and went on about his business.[6]

Douglas assumes the role of a freed man by performing the retrieval of the document; and based on the success of his perform-ance alone, grasps freedom. Indeed, in less than twenty-four hours Douglass arrived in New York and began his life on free soil, but not in accordance with the law. He lived in constant fear of being recaptured by slave hunters until he was able to obtain his freedom legally in 1846, a year after his first memoir was published, with his own papers: the Free Negro Bond or as Douglass referred to them, "devices of slavehold-ing ingenuity."[7] Without further scrutiny of the moment on the train, the success of the secret mission could be attributed, as Douglass suggests, to his confident performance, the carelessness of the train conductor, or even to luck. However, Douglass's critique of the system of Free Negro Bonds is worth further reflection.

BOUND BY DESIGN

Free Negro Bonds, dating back as early as the seventeenth century, were produced concurrently with the foundations of the American legal system.[8] The history of these bonds and America's beginnings as a country suggest an interdependent and symbiotic relationship between the legal documents and the legal institution that created them. In other words, the materialization of the institution (chattel slavery), based on ideology (racial subjugation), became concretized when it produced physical artifacts (in this case, free papers). Douglass's narrative on the train draws a compelling illustration of how artifacts can hold immense power to sustain the abstract idea of the institution. Once artifacts are produced by an institution, they reify that institution's purpose and power. The authority represented as material is so strong that the train conductor trusts the mere presence of the artifact. The bonds concretized the idea that Blackness, a construction implemented by racial subjugation toward those of the Africa diaspora, could be defined, contained, and contracted. Rather than a device of freedom, the existence of an object called a Free Negro Bond (or freedom papers) instantiated enslavement as a valid bureaucratic process. It masquerades as a bureaucratic formality, an ordinary transaction—one in which a human being passes from a state of bondage to one of freedom by virtue of owning a sheet of elegantly-written, formally signed and stamped paper. The papers instrumentalized the notion that freedom was an aspirational state that could be withheld, requested, earned, or lost.

W. E. B. Du Bois in *The Souls of Black Folk* draws out this striking duality of the Black experience in America as the double consciousness or "two-ness," which he explains as an internal struggle to be Black and American. A system that produces Free Negro Bonds extracts that internal struggle into an external reality. Blacks needed a piece of paper to exercise one of the most revered birthrights of the American people, which was to have one's own free will.

To have to ask for freedom contradicts one's existence as free. Even for those who were able to procure a bond and become "free," it was conditional and with limitations on what freedom meant. Freed Blacks still could not exercise free will or the free rights white citizens were afforded such as to vote, own property, buy homes, attend school, or participate in political life until the Reconstruction Era (1865–1877) and later. Material artifacts like the Free Negro Bond made that consciousness palpable for both Blacks and whites, who could—and often did—demand to see proof of a Black citizen's status at will (a phenomenon that has continued into the twenty-first century in the form of demanding birth certificates from prominent Black political figures and voting ID papers at the polls) as a way of proving (to themselves) their own status as empirically free.

Free Negro Bonds as institutional artifacts of slavery
objectified freedom for the one in pursuit of it while perpetuating the
dominance for those who had the power to grant it. As such, they were
a false promise of freedom, codified within an ideology, and ratified by
a legal system and a paper object. The ideology, institution, and artifact
provide an invisible infrastructure of relationships that are dependent
on and strengthen one other to maintain the morally corrupt system of
slavery. Each part in the system was designed to simplify, standardize, and
render efficient ideologies and acts of brutality that were the essential
foundations of a system whose explicit goal was to keep Blacks as an
inferior class—physically, psychologically, socially, economically, intellectually, and culturally. Scholars like legal theorist Luka Burazin[9] and political
theorist Langdon Winner[10] have reflected on the artefactual nature of law.
Beyond the legal representation of law, artifacts serve as political devices

Fig. 1

of oppressive systems, a phenomenon not relegated to the distant past: in the design of land deeds and eviction notices, birth certificates and green cards, federally recognized voter identification cards and COVID-19 vaccine passports. These artifacts establish what access to freedom looks like and who has the power to confer one's status of freedom. By examining the theoretical concept of paper as power, we can more clearly consider the underlying social ills of racism that still exist—remnants of a legal system that defined Blackness as property—which are best understood through the context of the artifact. Contemporary forms of Free Negro Bonds remain an overlooked but crucial element in the perpetuation of this unjust history.

A NOTE ON TERMINOLOGY   In antebellum America, legal documents that manumitted a slave on American soil were legally referred to as bonds or deeds. Used somewhat interchangeably as the conveyance of property or interests, these terms are still in effect in the twenty-first century. Today the most common type of deed is tied to "real property" transactions (i.e. ownership of land, possessions, and interests), and the familiar bond is the "bail bond," a conditional formal agreement that provides an "incentive to fulfill an obligation" which can be legally enforced.[11]

The many terms used for Free Negro Bonds pose a significant challenge to this research. There is a vast array of colloquial and legal terminology used to refer to this type of contracted freedom and the frequent conflation of language reflects the dual nature of the bonds—as devices of both bondage and (perfunctory) liberation. Popular and oral narratives often use the terms "freedom papers" or "free papers" as evident in Black narratives such as Frederick Douglass's or Solomon Solomon Northup's (1808-?), the latter of which was adapted to the screen in 2013 as Steven McQueen's remarkable *12 Years a Slave*. Consulting the bonds themselves, the terms "Certificates of Freedom" or the even more formal "Deeds of Manumission" reflect the bureaucratic, even transactional nature of the system, obscuring the particular evils they represent.[12] The euphemistic language obscures the humanity of the individuals being transacted upon, even as they convey that even in freedom, Blacks were required always to prove their status as human, document in hand, to be shown on demand. To that end, the term Free "Negro Bonds" embodies the negotiation of institutional artifacts to legally contract one's right to "bond" other humans.

FREE NEGRO BONDS AS INSTITUTIONAL ARTIFACT

By nature, an artifact is a remnant of the past, making it passive after a certain point in time. One may learn from studying an artifact but the artifact itself is rendered functionally useless. Political theorists suggest that artifacts created by institutions play a more active and significant role by cementing the role (and power) of the institution beyond the lifespan of the artifact. Ideological and institutional structures that manifest objects are so powerfully compelling they become undetectable by the individual and dismissed as customs and traditions.[13] In order to understand the lasting power in the relationship between institution and artifact, and in this case the American legal system and the Free Negro Bond, there must be an acknowledgement of the "artifactual character of law."[14]

Laws are created to legitimize legal systems. While laws are abstract and immaterial, they do share similarities of a material artifact such as authorship, intention, and function. Luka Burazin states that laws stem from the underlying intention to push forward the "authors' mental state and concepts."[15] The legal system, authored by white, materially-wealthy men with philosophical ties to English, Dutch, and French doctrine, establishes a set of ideals that are intended to govern how a nation-state functions. The legal system of slavery in America produced artifacts that were both intangible (ideological) and physical (artefactual). The most powerful artifacts came in the form of legal documents that were not always directly related to slavery. In fact, before 1865, the Constitution does not directly mention the word slavery, which historian Sean Wilentz argues was a deliberate attempt by the federal government to curb the growing power of the Southern states in their advocacy for slavery.[16] Importantly, as Burazin notes, the artifact authors ideology beyond the legal bureaucracy, and expands its authority to the general public if it is collectively accepted and observed at large.

Paper provides proof of the state's power. It is the tool of enforcement, utilized (or weaponized) by those deputized as enforcers of the system. For the paper to have power, everyone in the system—the enforcers and the enforced—must believe in its essential truth. During the eighteenth and nineteenth centuries, that truth was held, in part, by Free Negro Bond papers, which articulated freedom as an attainable transaction by those determined to have been born without the inherent right to it.

DESIGN OF AN INSTITUTION As illustrated by Frederick Douglass's story, some of the first free Blacks on US soil were sailors who, as early as the 1600s were required to carry "Seamen's Protection Certificates" or "protection papers" as they went from port to port on international seas.[17] While Congress abolished US participation in the international slave trade in 1808, this did nothing to eliminate the selling of enslaved Black in the United States. With the absence of large shipments of Blacks coming into the country, many Black men took to the sea to achieve freedom. Black sailors were so commonplace at the turn of the nineteenth century in cities with major ports like New York, Philadelphia, and Baltimore, that "about 18 percent of the one hundred thousand Americans at sea were African Americans."[18] Seamen Protection Papers became a powerful document and were often accepted as proof of one's free status without the bond.[19]

Plantation owners thought that the presence of free Blacks was bad for business and did not want their property (slaves) being infected with a desire to be liberated. State governments established and enforced Black Codes, with the main objective to restrict migration statutes for free Blacks. Often, free Blacks were given a certain amount of time before they had to vacate the state, which meant they would be separated from their family if they could not free them all, which was often the case. While this was not federally enforced, Black Codes were well-established in many Southern and Northern states.

To maintain the system of Black Codes, and more essentially the institution of slavery, the Free Negro Bonds were a crucial strategy. They enforced the norm by which Blacks were required to request the right to be perceived as free equals. The system within which the Free Negro Bonds operated had to be complex enough to be perceived as legally valid. To that end, there were several players involved: in order for an enslaved person to obtain Free Negro Bonds, they had to have a white guarantor or a white ally to vouch for their "good behavior," and this process had to be endorsed by a legal secretary and county commissioners. The templates for the Bond were presumably prepared by a calligrapher, with the courts filling in the name of the applicant, then signed and stamped by witnesses. The entire process of designing the Bonds begat an industry, much as contemporary voter identification cards or vaccine passports in 2021.

DESIGN OF For those who had achieved legal freedom, I speculate
AN OBJECT that these precious artifacts became an extension
of one's body, cemented into one's DNA. Bonds created
a spatial consciousness of the body that allowed for Blacks to assume the
act of place-making. The free Black body is hyperaware of the where of their
freedom at all times—where they reside and where their papers reside on
them. Free Negro Bonds—the paper itself, often handled with care and
close to the body so as to have easy access to it all the time—became a
part of one's identity, marking one's transference from being property to
having property.

The case of Priscilla Baltimore is instructive here. On
April 18, 1861, she secured her legal freedom for five hundred dollars at
the St. Louis county court. Having spent the first fifty-six years of her life
in legal bondage, the biracial child of a white slaveowner and an enslaved
woman, Baltimore had long cast her eye on freedom. In 1829, more than
thirty years before she had received her government-issued papers at that
country court, she had taken the remarkable step of founding a freedom
village on the eastern banks of the Mississippi River, just across from her
previous home in St. Louis, before she herself was deemed legally free by
the state.

Delicately creased in three distinct folds like a letter
stored in an envelope, the piece of paper that held Baltimore's freedom is
still pristine today, only lightly stained by the passing of time. On the bottom
are handwritten notes that would have described physical attributes of
Baltimore, a habit developed after paranoia spread that Blacks were using
others' papers to subvert the system. But importantly, the paper reifies for
the state what was already evidenced by the person: Mother Baltimore was
free by virtue of having built a village. The legal document was evidence of
the state's claims of control, the conceit of having the right to arbitrate
the legal status of citizens, but it was hardly a reflection of the individual's
value.

DESIGN OF Ultimately, the intention for creating the freedom paper
IDEOLOGY system was to regulate the movement of Black bodies.
Of course, in the turbulent days of legally owning Black
bodies there were times when carrying your freedom papers did not matter,
no matter how close one kept them. Solomon Northup had been born into
freedom in the early 1800s in Saratoga, New York, but after being tricked,
drugged, and kidnapped, was sold into slavery and spent the next twelve
years in physical bondage on a Louisiana plantation. He would eventually
be freed, but only reluctantly and as a result of the committed advocacy
by a white, Canadian man who acknowledged his identity. Northup's story

Fig. 2

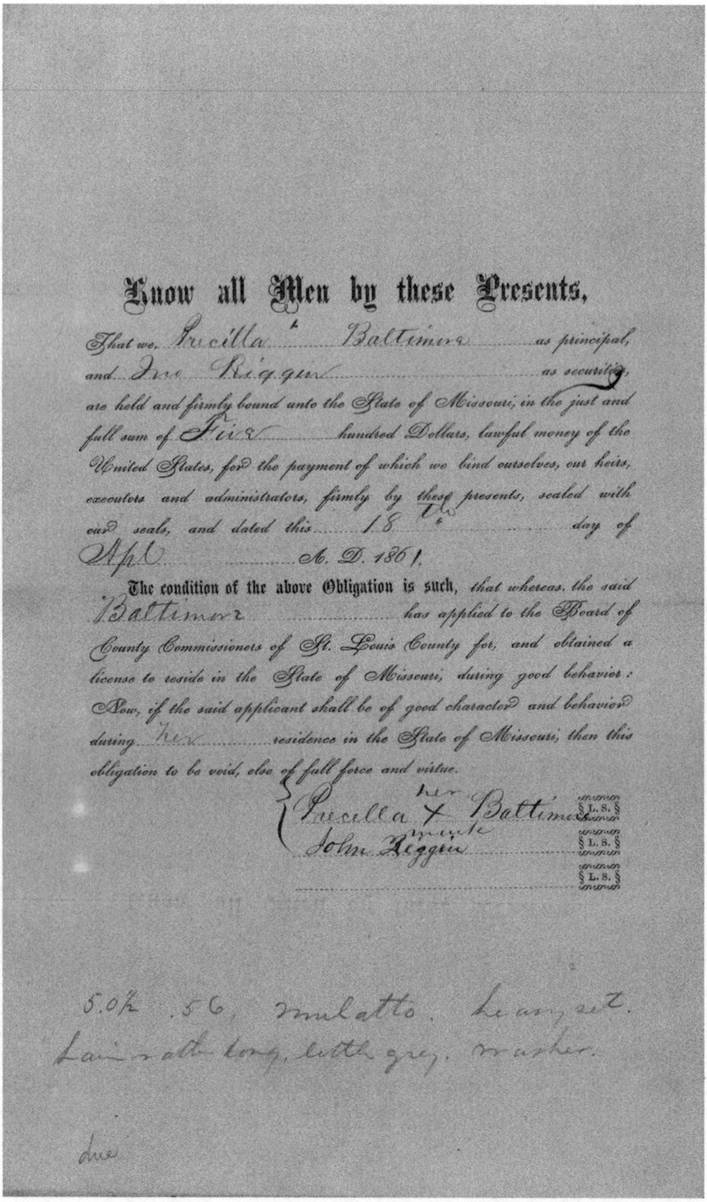

Fig. 2

Know all Men by these Presents,

That we, Precilla Baltimore *as principal, and* Jno Riggin *as security, are held and firmly bound unto the State of Missouri, in the just and full sum of* Five *hundred Dollars, lawful money of the United States, for the payment of which we bind ourselves, our heirs, executors and administrators, firmly by these presents, sealed with our seals, and dated this* 18th *day of* Apl *A. D. 1861.*

The condition of the above Obligation is such, *that whereas, the said* Baltimore *has applied to the Board of County Commissioners of St. Louis County for, and obtained a license to reside in the State of Missouri, during good behavior: Now, if the said applicant shall be of good character and behavior during* her *residence in the State of Missouri, then this obligation to be void, else of full force and virtue.*

Precilla her mark Baltimore [L. S.]
John Riggin [L. S.]
[L. S.]

5.0½ .56, mulatto. heavy set. hair rather long, little grey. washer.

due

was later published in his memoir *12 Years a Slave*. In his memoir, which served as the basis for the already mentioned film, Northrup recalls his last memory as a free man:

> I listened intently for some sign or
> sound of life, but nothing broke the
> oppressive silence, save the clink-
> ing of my chains, whenever I chanced
> to move. I spoke aloud, but the sound
> of my voice startled me. I felt of
> my pockets, so far as the fetters
> would allow- far enough, indeed, to
> ascertain that I had not only been
> robbed of liberty, but that my money
> and free papers were also gone.[20]

Northup's story would become a familiar tale. The theft of his free body was a reminder that the state-issued documents were limited in their power and adjudicated by the good will of those with legal powers.

OUR ONCE AND FUTURE BONDAGE

The prospect of freedom and the materialization of that promise on paper have a long history of presenting falsehoods for Black lives:

1860s: Special Field Orders No. 15, the federal policy commonly known as "forty acres and a mule" promised land deeds to recently freed Blacks following the Civil War; the orders were essentially meaningless as President Andrew Johnson repatriated the land to white landowners in exchange for their (conditional) loyalty to the union.

1960s: Redlining policies were instantiated by the design of maps indicating where Blacks were entitled to receive home loans; these policies intentionally and disproportionately discriminated against Black folks and led to decades of neglect, blight, environmental injustice, health crises, climate-related crises, and ongoing housing instability in neighborhoods throughout the United States.

2000s: Predatory lending policies were abetted by the issuance of value-less paper mortgages that led to a housing boom and bust during which Black families were disproportionately rendered homeless or forced to sell their homes at lower value.[21]

One's first recorded moment and, in a sense one's identity, is summed up on the birth certificate. The documents of one's birth remain a tool for determining the extent to which an individual can move freely in this world. It is a device of privilege, a weapon, or a form of bondage—depending on who holds it—preserved on paper and submitted as evidence of one's inherent worth. Today, in 2021, a federally recognized birth certificate is not even sufficient evidence of every citizen's right to participate in democracy. A request for federally acknowledged voter identification cards will establish a new classification of citizen with the right to participate in democracy versus those who will be declared second-class. That right will be written into law, but it will be manifested by design and by designers who put technical skills to work to establish the visual, tactile reality of our freedom. What then do we ask of our designers? It may be the request to consider how our legal rights to freedom continue to be defined and constrained by artifacts, often paper artifacts, though certainly also increasingly digital ones. To be Black or Brown in the United States is to remain bound by the demand to provide evidence of one's right to be free.

NOTES

1. Douglas was nominated without his approval as suffragette Victoria Woodhull's running mate. "Frederick Douglass, Convention Presidential Nominations, and Kentucky," *Notable Kentucky African Americans Database*, accessed May 8, 2020, http://nkaa.uky.edu/nkaa/items/show/2950.
2. Douglass, Frederick. *The Life and Times of Frederick Douglass: From 1817–1882*. Christian Age Office, 1882.
3. White, G. Edward. *Law in American History: Volume 1: From the Colonial Years Through the Civil War*. Oxford University Press, 2012.
4. Douglass, *Life*, 1882.
5. Ibid.
6. Ibid.
7. Ibid.
8. Wilson, Theodore Brautner. *The Black Codes of the South*. Ann Arbor, MI: University Microfilms

International, 1982.

9. Burazin, Luka. "Can There Be an Artifact Theory of Law?" *Ratio Juris* 29, no. 3 (2016): 385-401.

10. Winner, Langdon. "Do Artifacts Have Politics?" Daedalus (1980): 121-136.

11. "Bond," *Encyclopedia Britannica.* Encyclopedia Britannica, Inc., August 01, 2020.

12. A century after the legal end of slavery in the United States, Hannah Arendt would refer to this as the "banality of evil" in her essay. Arendt, Hannah, and Jens Kroh. *Eichmann in Jerusalem.* New York: Viking Press, 1964.

13. Althusser, Louis. "Ideology and ideological state apparatuses (notes towards an investigation)." *The anthropology of the state: A reader* 9, no. 1 (2006): 86-98.

14. Burazin, Luka, Kenneth Einar Himma, and Corrado Roversi, eds. *Law as an Artifact.* Oxford University Press, 2018.

15. Burazin, Law, 2018.

16. Wilentz, Sean. *No Property in Man.* Harvard University Press, 2018.

17. Sometimes protection papers without freedom papers were sufficient enough for some ports and Black sailors would only carry one or the other. G. Edward White, Law in American History (Oxford: Oxford University Press, 2012), 305.

18. Bolster, W. Jeffrey. "To Feel Like a Man: Black Seamen in the Northern States, 1800-1860." *The Journal of American History* 76, no. 4 (1990): 1173-199, doi:10.2307/2936594.

19. White, 2012, 305.

20. Northup, Solomon. *12 Years a Slave: A True Story of Betrayal, Kidnap and Slavery.* London: Hesperus Press, 2013.

21. 21. Chenjerai Kumanyika and Jack Hitt, "The Deed: Uncivil," *Gimlet* (Gimlet, April 15, 2019), Richard Rothstein, "Racial Zoning," in *The Color of Law* (Paw Prints, 2010), pp. 39-58.

IMAGE CREDITS

1. Freedom papers and handmade tin carrying box
   belonging to Joseph Trammel. Image credit: Collection
   of the Smithsonian National Museum of African
   American History and Culture, Gift of Elaine E.
   Thompson, in memory of Joseph Trammell, on behalf of
   his direct descendants
2. Precilla (sic) Baltimore Free Negro Bond. Image
   credit: Missouri Historical Society

DESIGN
SCHOLARSHIP

3.6

At the Jim Crow Museum, We Use Racist Objects to Engage Hearts

& Heads in Social Justice

DAVID PILGRIM

EDITOR'S NOTE:

This article examines the power of racist objects from America's Jim Crow period to teach social justice. For some people, certain images in the article may be disturbing. Yet, the presentation of these images is important. Many Black people lived in cultural contexts where they could not avoid the explicit and implicit imagery of white privilege. Tragically, many still do. As the author suggests, the achievement of social justice will require us to move beyond "happy history" to honest history.

Fig. 1

At a time when many Americans are destroying racist objects, I am taking a different approach. I have spent more than four decades collecting Ku Klux Klan robes, segregation signs, and thousands of everyday objects that portray African Americans as dutiful servants, childlike buffoons, exotic savages, hypersexual deviants, and most disturbingly, menacing predators who must be punished.

I collected these items because I believed—then later, knew—that objects, even hateful ones, can be used as teaching tools. In the mid-1990s, I donated the artifacts to Ferris State University in Big Rapids, Michigan, where I was a sociology professor. Later, I used the collection to create the Jim Crow Museum. Today the museum, housed at the university, is the largest collection of publicly accessible racist objects in the United States. Our tagline doubles as our vision: "using objects of intolerance to teach tolerance and promote social justice." The museum is my life's work.

Fig. 2

We know what we know because of what we have experienced. I was born in Harlem but raised in Mobile, Alabama, and Prichard, a city four miles north of there. It was the late 1950s, and both were Jim Crow towns. The neighborhoods were rigidly segregated. The schools were either all-white or all-Black. The churches were as segregated as the schools. Black people could not visit the local libraries. Whites owned all the big money and most of the good jobs. There were Black preachers, teachers, and owners of small shops—on the Black side of town—but most Black people had low-status jobs with poverty wages. "Whites Only" signs hung in the windows of downtown stores. The businesses that did accept Black customers did so under the terms of Jim Crow—a Black person, for example, could not try on clothes in a retail shop. The police departments, all white, had reputations for beating Black people. It is not hyperbolic to say that skin color was the primary determinant of one's place in those cities as late as the mid-1960s.

My ancestors from the past four generations include people from Africa, Venezuela, Spain, Barbados, and people indigenous to this country. I was a multiracial kid growing up in the deepest, Blackest South at a time when Jim Crow, though dying, was still alive. So, from my beginning, I thought about race a lot. When I was twelve or thirteen, I bought my first racist object, probably a mammy saltshaker, at a hybrid carnival/flea market in Mobile. I do not remember much about that day, but I do know that I threw the figurine to the ground. It broke. It was not a philosophical act. I simply did not like it. That was the last racist object that I purchased to break.

I attended Jarvis Christian College, a Black Disciples of Christ school in rural Texas. The school was poor, but my education was top drawer. Benton Adams made us polished public speakers. Roy Uyechi tried to make historians of us. John H. Morgan, a theologian and sociologist, demanded that we think in ways that were nuanced and defensible. We learned our share of what is called General Education, but, equally important, we were taught about the daily heroism of the maids, butlers, and sharecroppers who risked their jobs, and sometimes their lives, to protest Jim Crow segregation. O. C. Nix, who taught political science and history, used the Socratic method to test our understanding, arguments, and patience. He also showed us the power of objects as teaching tools.

Fig. 3

One day he brought a chauffeur's hat to class. He set it down, then asked about its relationship to the Jim Crow period. The obvious answer was that Black people who lived during Jim Crow were restricted by a race-segregated job economy; chauffeuring was one of the few jobs open to them. But that was not the answer Nix wanted. The first answer was too obvious. He talked to us about the small Black middle class that existed in the 1940s in rural Texas who wanted the material things that white people wanted: good-quality clothes, a nice house, expensive furniture, and maybe a shiny brand-new car. But they needed to be careful. A Black person, even a professional, who drove a new car violated the Jim Crow social script. The hat, an inanimate object, spoke for and protected them. I am a chauffeur; this car does not belong to me. People like me do not desire or deserve new cars. I am not uppity. I am not a threat to you. I know my place. You do not need to hurt me. Please let me go on my way.

I remember that story so vividly. No object holds any meaning other than what we assign to it, but this was a powerful meaning to assign to an object that, on the surface, had little to do with racism. It was during my time as a student at Jarvis Christian College when I first had the idea of building a large collection of racist objects. If Nix could use the cap to teach a compelling lesson about Black life under Jim Crow, I reasoned, it should be easy for me to use the objects in my collection as teaching tools.

Long before I became acquainted with what pedagogical specialists call object-based learning, I used racist objects as tools to facilitate learning in my sociology classes. I introduced objects—typically everyday items that caricatured Black people—and then asked questions. *What is it that you see?* What else do you see? This was not simply an icebreaker to get students to talk about race; it was an early step on the road to viewing the objects and what they represent in deeper, more layered ways. *Have you always seen it that way? Have your experiences shaped what you see? How do others see this object?*

At the museum, we recreated a kitchen displaying hundreds of objects: Gold Dust Washing Powder, Aunt Dinah Molasses jars, Fun-to-Wash boxes, and cans of Luzianne Coffee and Chicory. We also display dozens of signs: Topsy Chocolate Honey Drink, Aunt Sally's Cake Flour, Famous Black Nancy Coal, Smoky Jim's Sweet Potatoes, and Aunt Jemima dolls, cookbooks, ceramic figures, and boxes on which she appeared for more than a century.

While some visitors wistfully remember the past, others of us look at the same items and see vestiges of enslavement and segregation. So, the museum is a space where people who see the world in very different ways are safe to share their beliefs. It may sound trite—and a little dangerous these days—to say that we still believe in dialogue.

Fig. 4

Fig. 5

Fig. 6

The past is what happened; history is a narrative of what happened. The Jim Crow Museum uses objects to help us understand the past, even when examining the past is painful and what we find contradicts historical accounts. Americans like happy history—narratives that make us look smart, brave, and exceptional yet ignore our mistreatment of the weak and disfavored. This approach to history is neither honest nor mature. A lynching tree sits in the center of the museum as a visual reminder, for example, that more than four thousand Black people were lynched in this country during the Jim Crow period.

There are many stories told in the Jim Crow Museum, but none are as chilling as the accounts of white people using the skin of Black people as human leather. Our research found newspaper stories, from the period of Reconstruction to the mid-1920s, where the skin of Black people was sewn into purses, shoes, belts, and other products. This ghoulish practice is, of course, disgusting to contemporary Americans; however, there was a time—not so long ago—when the debasement of Black Americans was so ordinary that one could read about the skin of a Black person being tanned in the same newspaper that reported the previous day's baseball box scores.

The majority of the eight thousand–plus objects on display at the museum are racially caricatured everyday objects and segregation memorabilia. But some objects document the efforts of African American artists to deconstruct racist imagery.

For example, we have a copy of Jon Lockard's 1967 painting No More, showing a Black woman on an Aunt Jemima box. Her bandana bears the colors of the Pan-African flag: red, Black, and green. Her face is stern, eyebrows raised, her fist bursting through the box and serves as a not-so-subtle refutation of the smiling "mammy" whose greatest fulfillment came from serving her white "family." Lockard's painting and the Aunt Jemima iconography it attempts to deconstruct serve as fruitful tools for discussion.

Artists like Lockhard used their work to push back against Jim Crow, but these are not the only objects at the museum that serve as starting points for discussing the efforts of individuals and groups who worked to undermine white supremacy. In one exhibit, you will find a blanket from the Brotherhood of Sleeping Car Porters, the first labor organization led by African Americans chartered by the American Federation of Labor. The organization's first two presidents, A. Philip Randolph and C. L. Dellums, became leaders in the civil rights movement.

The Jim Crow Museum also houses several portraits of African Americans who came to Michigan's Ferris Institute (an early incarnation of Ferris State University) from Virginia's Hampton Institute, now known as Hampton University. From 1910 to the mid-1920s, more than a dozen of these students came north to take college preparatory courses and escape the daily indignities of Jim Crow. They distinguished themselves in their chosen professions and became civil rights leaders.

Long before it was normative, Ferris State University founder Woodbridge Nathan Ferris created an institution for all students, irrespective of their backgrounds. And for many years, the university's mission was "to make the world better." Woodbridge Ferris's legacy has become our mandate and we continue to grow. From the mid-1990s to 2011, we were housed in a five-hundred-foot-square room. In 2012, we moved to a larger facility to give us the space necessary to tell the stories we believed should be told. We have subsequently outgrown that space and envision a stand-alone facility, with state-of-the-art archives, storage, and technology that will allow us to display ten thousand additional objects.

Wherever we are, we remain committed to the triumph of dialogue. When hearts and heads meet through honest discourse, especially about difficult, painful topics, the possibilities for lasting change emerge. The Jim Crow Museum uses objects to stir passionate feelings and incite deep thinking in visitors. As famed twentieth-century African American anthropologist and educator Zora Neale Hurston understood, "show-and-tell" can be a pathway to significant personal edification and communal transformation. She once wrote, "Tell me, and then again, show me, so I can know."

Year after year at the Jim Crow Museum, we tell people, and then we show them aspects of our problematic past so that we may know better ways to create a more positive present and a more hopeful future.

IMAGE CREDITS

1. Founder David Pilgrim sits with items donated. The museum receives thousands of object donations. Photo courtesy of the Jim Crow Museum
2. In the early 1800s, minstrel performer T. D. Rice popularized the term "Jim Crow" as a pejorative term for African Americans with his hit song "Jump Jim Crow."
3. This object was used in the mid 1900s as an ashtray and incense burner. Photo courtesy of the Jim Crow Museum
4. A Ferris State University student examines the Mammy showcase. Photo Courtesy of the Jim Crow Museum

ACTIVISM, ADVOCACY & COMMUNITY-ENGAGED DESIGN

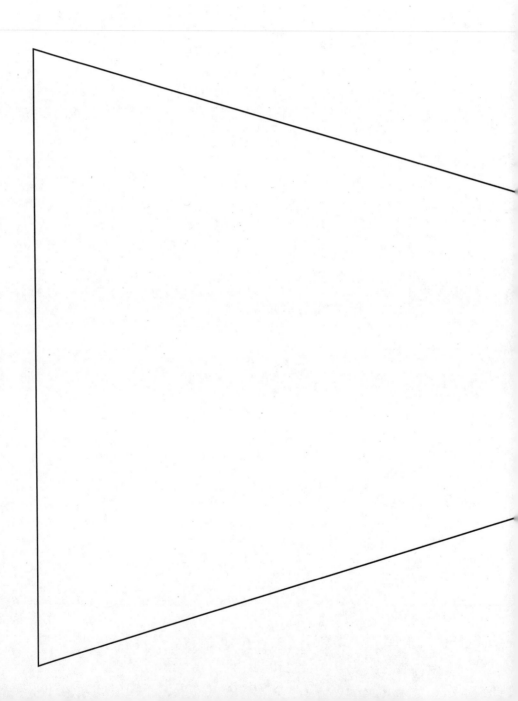

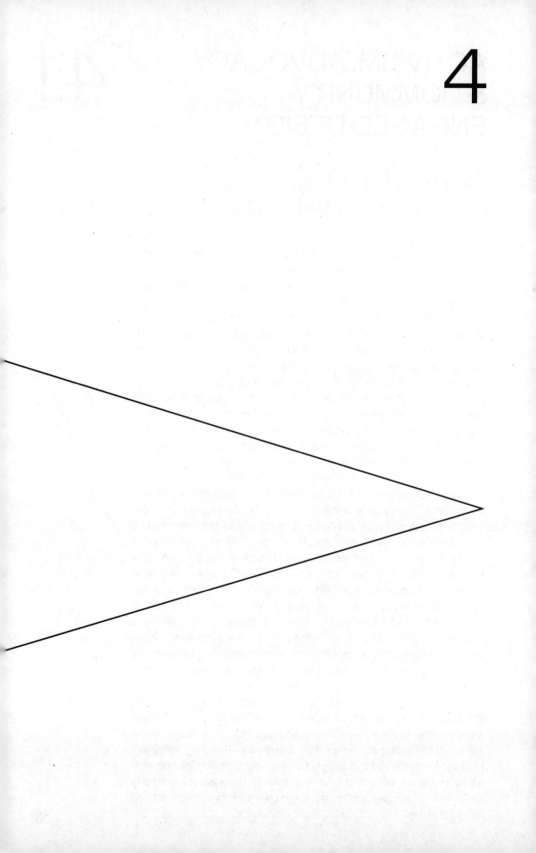

4

ACTIVISM, ADVOCACY & COMMUNITY-ENGAGED DESIGN

4.1

Chapter Introduction:
Kareem Collie & Penina Laker

Community-engaged design involves design practitioners working in close partnership with people from underrepresented and under-resourced communities to develop ideas that address their most pressing issues. This work is complex. Humans are complex beings. And the challenges facing these populations are rooted in harmful systemic policies and practices. All this to say, if not approached with the utmost care, attention, and intention, there are intended and unintended consequences that are bound to emerge and, furthermore, perpetuate the very issues that were already causing harm to the community you are working with.

The seven contributors in this chapter share both personal reflections and critical perspectives on various aspects of community-engaged design and practice from four different lenses. They're all drawing from their experiences working within communities they belong/ work closely with in the United States and on the African continent.

Our first contribution is an article by Prof. Mugendi K. M'Rithaa, "Participatory and Emancipatory Aspirations in Afrika." Mugendi interrogates the relevance of popularized community-engaged practices such as human-centered and design thinking against the emancipatory sustainable design agenda for the Afrikan context and other "majority developing world" contexts. He leaves the reader with this question, "How can we develop contextually responsive curricula?" Mugendi calls upon design practitioners and design educators working to broaden the scope of community-engaged design pedagogy to not only include culturally relevant practices prominent on the Afrikan continent, but also challenges them to make a habit out of recognizing design champions from Afrikan contexts who have spear-headed these processes in addition to prioritizing a transdisciplinary approach that allows for various disciplines and schools of thought.

In "From the Black Anti-Ableist Diary: A Tribute to My Black Disabled Son from a Black Disabled Mother," Jennifer White-Johnson shares with us her joys, fears, and insights as a mother holding space for her son "to celebrate and embrace his differences." This story will inspire, reminding us of the power of imagination, play, and the boundless nature of a child's mind and spirit. White-Johnson draws on these lessons to amplify the voices of disabled and marginalized communities through art and design activism.

In their essay "The Infrastructure of Care: Community Design, Healing, and Organizational Post-Traumatic Growth," Sloan Leo unpacks and shares practical strategies—adapted from community engaged design—that organizations can leverage and institute within their cultures to inspire sustained healing. How can organizations working in the social sector prioritize healing by dismantling harmful power structures at the root cause of organizational trauma? And furthermore, how can they cultivate a culture where critical shifts are made to distill power to ensure sustained healing?

June A. Grant and Michele Y. Washington reimagine space and intimacy in communities of color. Grant presents an argument for re-centering the focus of urban development away from "political pressure bonded solely to economic-models" to that of creating healthy communities in "The Centering in the Margins: Locating Intimacy in Multi-Communities," arguing for moving away from "multiunit" to "multi-community" development.

In "BioPhilia Patterns in Black and Brown Spaces," Washington walks us through a student project in which her design class cocreates with a community to reimagine their connection with nature. We spoke with printmaker Amos Kennedy about advocating for a world in which designers can take their time and honor their own best humanity.

Building upon a similar thread, in her essay "The Preconditions to Healing," Liz Ogbu reflects on how designers might focus on collective healing practices to lay the foundation toward healing the wounds caused by spatial injustice. She writes about her journey, which she stresses is currently concerned with "taking down the structures of harm (white supremacy, capitalism, patriarchy) and replacing them with structures of healing." Liz details the type of cultural leadership needed in this time —an approach that acknowledges the depth of pain caused by unjust systems, normalizes vulnerability, and prioritizes care and healing in order for cultural change to occur.

We wrap up this chapter with a conversation between Raja Schaar and Jennifer Rittner. Raja and Jennifer have a "delightfully far-reaching and unbounded" conversation about hair, navigating the importance (albeit complexity) of our racial and gender identities, and navigating how the way Raja self-identifies and expresses herself intersects and informs her work as a designer, educator, and a "nerdy global climate change activist."

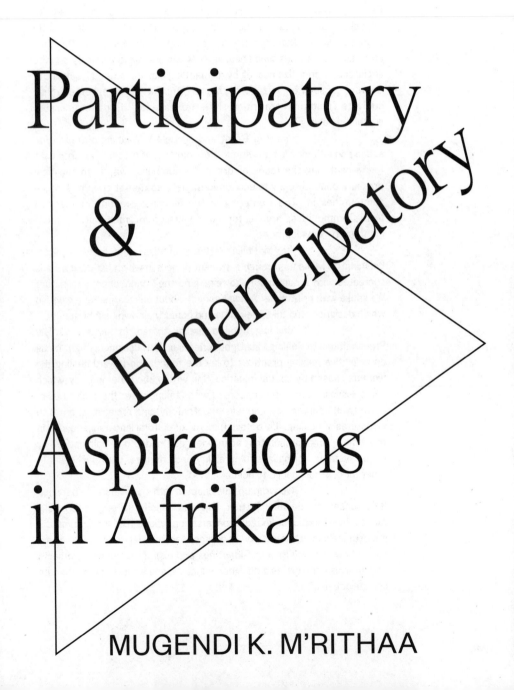

Participatory

&

Emancipatory

Aspirations
in Afrika

MUGENDI K. M'RITHAA

Afrika is known for many things—among them the rich cultural heritage and vast reserves of natural resources that are critical to sustained sociotechnical and socioeconomic development. Scant attention, however, has been paid to the value of social capital associated with participative processes of cocreation and co-production on the continent, particularly within creative industries on the continent.

Additionally, the endurance and resilience of collective efficiency modes of engagement that have served to advance the aspirations of myriad communities deserves some recognition, particularly within postcolonial and transdisciplinary discourse. This chapter explores the relevance of human-centered design (HCD)—and by extension, Design Thinking—in advancing a community-engaged ethos that encourages participation and holds promise for a potentially emancipatory agenda for sustainable development in Afrika.

Keywords: Afrika; Community-Engaged Design; Design Activism; Human-Centered Design; Participatory Design; Social Innovation; Sustainability; Transdisciplinary

1.0   IF THE RHYTHM OF THE DRUMBEAT CHANGES, THE DANCE STEPS MUST ADAPT KENYAN PROVERB

Change is a constant, and the disruption occasioned by the COVID-19 global pandemic has reinforced this reality of life. Afrika has had its fair share of disruptions and upheavals ever since time immemorial. Traditionally, such disruptions emanated from natural phenomena such as drought, flooding, and sporadic internecine conflict over pasture and farming land. The greatest disruption to Afrika's progress, however, came about when imperialist agendas emanating from Europe and the Americas fundamentally altered the geopolitical landscape of the continent. Subsequent colonial hegemony subverted and subjugated Afrikan aspirations and disrupted the social fabric of the continent's denizens with devastating consequences. The consequences and negatory effects of the colonial project continue to plague Afrika to date. Notwithstanding such collective traumatic experiences, Afrikan communities have been able to weather these vicissitudes by harnessing their accumulated transgenerational social capital.

It is heartening to note, though, that despite the tumultuous upheavals impacting the Afrikan people, certain practices stemming from traditional societies on the continent have endured and adapted to our present circumstances as context-specific homegrown communitarian expressions of ubuntu. Ubuntu (which is an isiZulu word) is also known as utu in kiSwahili (spoken in Central and Eastern Africa), unhu in chiShona and botho in both seTswana and seSotho (all spoken in Southern Africa). Ubuntu is evident through various forms of self-reliance and mutual assistance such as bataka kwegaita (communal solidarity) among the Banyakore people of Uganda, boipelogo (self-reliance) in Botswana, haramee (pulling together) in Kenya, and ujamaa (familyhood) in Tanzania.

Similarly, in Ghana, n'nobua (reciprocal assistance) is an invitation to family, friends, or neighbors to join in the activity of plowing the host's farm in the knowledge that should any of the participants require assistance in future, the host would answer the call to action accordingly. Fortuitously, these values are still alive on the continent and in the diaspora wherever an authentic African presence is detectable. In Bhengu's words, ubuntu is "a way of life that contributes positively towards the well-being of a people, community or society." The communitarian ubuntu ethos contrasts significantly with the pervasive Cartesian logic and allied Western philosophical traditions with their resultant hyper-individualism. As Desmond Tutu elaborates:

> Ubuntu is very difficult to render into
> a Western language. It speaks to the
> very essence of being human. When you
> want to give high praise to someone
> we say, "Yu, u nobuntu"; he or she has
> ubuntu. This means that they are gener-
> ous, hospitable, friendly, caring and
> compassionate. They share what they have.
> It also means that my humanity is caught
> up, is inextricably bound up, in theirs.
> We belong in a bundle of life. We say,
> "a person is a person through other
> people". [. . .] I am human because
> I belong, I participate, I share.

248

2.0   **UNTIL LIONS HAVE THEIR OWN HISTORIANS, TALES OF THE HUNT WILL ALWAYS GLORIFY THE HUNTER**

—NIGERIAN PROVERB

Afrika is home to fifty-five countries speaking some 2,200 languages. With just over 1.3 billion people (roughly the same as India's), Afrika accounts for 16 percent of the global population. Additionally, Afrika has the world's youngest population and is home to some of the fastest-growing economies globally. Indeed, a number of economic projections have raised the possibility of the twenty-first century as "the African Century" and fueled the "Africa Rising" narrative. Additionally, the African Union (AU) Agenda 2063 articulates a bold and progressive set of aspirations as "Africa's blueprint and master plan for transforming Africa into the global powerhouse of the future."

Simultaneously, an emergent homegrown epistemology known as Afrikology is gaining credence, particularly within intellectual, scholarly and professional discourse. Afrikology challenges prevailing stereotypes about the continent and offers a refreshing alternative view of the continent through an authentic endogenous lens of creativity, empathy, inclusion, participation, cocreation,, and consensus building. Similar voices were raised by pioneer literary giants like Ngugi wa Thiong'o, Chinua Achebe, Wole Soyinka, Okot p'Bitek, and Taban Lo Liyong and more recently through the prose and satirical works of Ben Okri, Binyavanga Wainanina and Chimamanda Ngozi Adichie's 2009 TED Talk titled "The Danger of a Single Story." Additionally, Ron Eglash's "The Fractals at the Heart of African Designs" highlighted the efficacy of Afrikan ethno-mathematical and computational indigenous knowledge systems. Likewise, within the domain of graphic design and typography, Saki Mafundikwa documented the visual richness, sophistication, and diversity of Afrikan alphabets and writing system.

3.0   **A SINGLE BRACELET DOES NOT JINGLE**

—CONGOLESE PROVERB

As discussed herein, Ubuntu is a participative, empathic, and inclusive ethos. For the vast majority of Afrikans, participation is a means—not an end in itself. Stated succinctly, "I participate, therefore I am." In his somewhat prophetic views, Ivan Illich warned against the role of industry in disrupting socially constructed tools for conviviality. Illich argued for limits to industrial growth, particularly where there is demonstrable tension with convivial aspirations of community members.

The role of design in promoting social innovation and sustainability has also been extensively documented by Ezio Manzini (2015)—such promising cases are showcased on the Design for Social Innovation and Sustainability (DESIS) network website. Carla Cipolla further argues for recognition of the value of interpersonal relationships in enhancing conviviality. The socioeconomic phenomenon of relational services is also noted in particular in Brazil, Afrika, and other majority world contexts.

Human-Centered Design (HCD) and the related Design Thinking methodologies lend themselves elegantly in unlocking creativity and promoting collaboration and cocreation within the Afrikan context. Consequently, the Human-Centered Design Africa Toolkit (inspired by the highly influential IDEO HCD tool kit) was developed by a team of Afrikan Design Thinking practitioners in 2016 in response to the latent need for a context-responsive and community-engaged design tool kit.

The author has had the privilege of working on a number of community-engaged design projects in Afrika. These projects have all benefited from an interpretivist (qualitative) research paradigm that deployed appreciative inquiry as an empathic mode of engagement. The following examples highlight some of the key characteristics and insights garnered through such cocreative engagement:

3.1 Genadendal is a historic town in the Western Cape province of South Africa that was established by the Moravian Mission from Germany in 1737 some 137 kilometers from Cape Town. Genedendal (which means "valley of mercy" in Afrikaans) is situated near Greyton, which is a popular tourist destination and boasts a number of pioneering initiatives in South Africa, including inter alia: the oldest kindergarten; the first printing press; the first teachers' training college; the first chemist; and the unique Genadendal chair. Notwithstanding, Genadendal had experienced "significant social discontinuity [. . . and] social disenfranchisement [. . .] occasioned by religious and [Apartheid] political practices in the past, and more recently by structural economic policies." M'Rithaa et al. The community engaged project that was initiated therein adopted Design for Sustainability (DfS) and situated development lenses to cocreate novel community-based tourism opportunities (incorporating its natural attractions, the rich material culture, and unique indigenous honeybush tea; indigenous knowledge in architecture, furniture, and knife making; and long-standing Khoi heritage. The resultant cocreated solutions deployed directed storytelling and multi-actor dialogue to contribute toward greater social equity and cohesion in the community, as well as a focused intervention on engaging the youth in the social reengineering and redefinition of their historic town.

3.2   Enkanini (which means "taken by force" in isiXhosa) is an informal settlement (or slum) in Kayamandi township which came into existence in 2006 within the wine-producing region of Stellenbosch—one of Afrika's wealthiest regions per capita. The project explored means by which the quality of life for residents could be improved via radical incrementalism and transdisciplinarity. In particular, access to electricity and sanitation were identified by the community as priorities for design intervention—these were effected by enhancing public-private and quadruple-helix partnerships for the benefit of the community members. The resultant prototypes for dry sanitation and solar lighting have been rolled out for adoption at a subsidized fee for participating residents and have become an essential benchmark for similar "bottom of the pyramid" and allied robust products designed for extreme affordability.

3.3   Doornbach is an informal settlement in the Dunoon ward within the greater City of Cape Town. Doornbach was a 130,000-square-meter dairy farm prior to a spontaneous invasion by squatters in 1994 when South Africa became a democracy. That land was acquired for eventually purchase by the City of Cape Town in 2015, paving way for the provision of municipal services—including grid electricity, water, and sanitation. Following the designation of Cape Town as the World Design Capital 2014, Doornbach was selected by the executive mayor for a pilot project titled "Design Strategies for enhancing service delivery in Solid Waste Management." The project resulted in a renewed sense of identity as the community adopted the aspirational name Sibabalwe (meaning "we are blessed" in isiXhosa) to identify with their new home. Additionally, community-engaged sustainable livelihood projects as well as cocreated sanitation, housing, and solid waste management solutions were developed, prototyped, tested, and implemented in typical HCD fashion.

3.4   Grabouw is the commercial center of the largest single export fruit producing area in Southern Africa and was established in 1856 by a German settler. Notwithstanding the agricultural richness of Grabouw and the outlying areas, myriad social challenges were identified in this multiethnic town, including low levels of formal literacy, and high levels of poverty and drug abuse, as well as a high child mortality rate and related maternal and healthcare challenges. The service design intervention sought to ameliorate the aforementioned challenges by engaging women in the cocreation of novel Afrika-centric visual communication systems and strategies, as well as a targeted intervention to improve quality of life and general well-being for community members.

3.5 Machakos is situated some sixty kilometers to the southeast of Nairobi, Kenya, as well as being East and Central Africa's largest metropolis. A leading producer of synthetic hair extension products sought design intervention in mitigating the ecological impact of their discarded products upon reaching the end of their usable life cycle. This resulted in a community-engaged design project that has been documented in a video titled "UNWASTED: A Human-Centered Approach to Solid Waste Solid Waste Management of Synthetic Hair Extensions." The participating community members (the majority of who were women, as well as persons with disabilities) utilized their basket-weaving and brick-making expertise in cocreating a range of durable upcycled baskets and eco-friendly sun-dried and oven-baked clay bricks with embedded recycled synthetic hair fibers. These solutions not only provided entrepreneurial and vocational opportunities for community members, but also contributed toward the realization of specific United Nations Sustainable Development Goals (UN SDGs) and targets.

> **IF YOU WANT TO RUN FAST, RUN ALONE; IF YOU WANT TO RUN FAR, RUN TOGETHER**
> **—AFRIKAN PROVERB**

Whereas there are a number of similarities in the community-engaged design interventions listed above, each project was unique in scope, scale, and sophistication from a design point of view. Every single project in the South African cases forced the collaborating design teams to confront issues of race, identity, poverty, and social (in)justice exacerbated by the traumatic history of oppression and systematic exclusion from mainstream socioeconomic opportunities. This form of directed design activism holds promise of more aspirational, participatory, and emancipatory outcomes for community-engaged design interventions on the continent. Additionally, whereas design activism focuses on very specific microcosmic and acupunctural interventions, socially conscious designers should never lose sight of the macro-level implications for future design pedagogy through their interactions with diverse social, industrial, and geopolitical actors.

In conclusion, a number of considerations for design practitioners and design educators are recommended:

» An urgent need to interrogate the relevance of current offerings of design pedagogy with an aim toward re-curriculating the same for greater cultural relevance, and social impact should inform community-engaged design endeavors. This is deemed germane to the current discourse on post-colonialism and the decolonization of education in general;

» Concerted effort is required in identifying and honoring the creative
and cultural champions, heroes, and positive role models already doing
inspirational work among various Afrikan communities—their cumu-
lative knowledge and institutional memory should be documented for
posterity. Examples include the indefatigable traditional Ndebele artist
Esther Nikwambi Mahlangu, who is one of the best-known creative and
artistic ambassadors from our continent;

» Greater opportunities for networking, mentorship, scholarship,
apprenticeships, and exchanges should be provided for in a competen-
cy-based mode of education for the creative industries. Myriad design
platforms such as the virtual Pan-Afrikan Design Institute (PADI) are
emerging on the continent that the diaspora can join in a dialogic and
cocreative spirit for the advancement of knowledge of the rich traditions in Afrika; and

» Appropriate and context-responsive curricula should be prioritized with emphasis on humility, respect, curiosity, openness,

NOTES

1. An endogenous perspective of the continent as seen
   from "the inside out."
2. M'Rithaa, Mugendi K. Embracing Sustainability:
   Revisiting the Authenticity of 'Event' Time . . .
   Proceedings of the *2nd International Symposium on
   Sustainable Design* (ISSD), 5-6 November 2009. Sao
   Paolo.
3. Ibid.
4. Bhengu, M. J. *Ubuntu: The Essence of Democracy*. Cape
   Town: Novalis Press, 1996.
5. Tutu, Desmond. *No Future Without Forgiveness*. London:
   Rider, 1999.
6. African Union. Agenda 2063: The Africa We Want,
   https://au.int/en/agenda2063/overview (retrieved on
   October 4, 2021)
7. Nabudere, D. W. 2011. *Afrikology, Philosophy and
   Wholeness: an epistemology*. Pretoria: Africa
   Institute of South Africa.
8. M'Rithaa, M. K. 2020. "The Afrikan Maker: Hacking
   Our Way into a Hybrid Future. . . " pp. 21-30 in S.
   O'Hara, V. Bradburry, and J. Newin (eds), *Art Hack*

Practice: Critical Intersections of Art, Innovation and the Maker Movement. London: Routledge.

9. Wainaina, B. 2008. *How to Write About Africa*. Nairobi: Kwani Trust.

10. Adichie, Chimamanda Ngozi. *The Danger of a Single Story*. TEDGlobal, 18:33, July 2009. https://www.ted .com/talks/chimamanda_ngozi_adichie_the_danger_of_a _single_story

11. Eglash, Ron. "African Fractals: Modern Computing and Indigenous Design." 1999.

12. Eglash, Ron. *The Fractals at the Heart of African Designs*. TEDGlobal 2007. https://www.ted.com/talks/ ron_eglash_the_fractals_at_the_heart_of_african _designs?language=en retrieved on October 16, 2021

13. Mafundikwa, Saki. *Afrikan Alphabets: The Story of Writing*. Brooklyn: Mark Batty Publisher, 2006.

14. M'Rithaa, Mugendi. K. "Embracing Sustainability: Revisiting the Authenticity of 'Event' Time." Proceedings of the *2nd International Symposium on Sustainable Design* (ISSD), 5-6 November 2009. Sao Paolo.

15. Ibid.

16. Illich, Ivan. *Tools for Conviviality*. New York: Harper & Row, 1973.

17. Ibid.

18. Manzini, Ezio. *Design, When Everybody Designs: An Introduction to Design for Social Innovation*. MIT Press, 2015.

19. Design for Social Innovation and Sustainability, https://www.desisnetwork.org/ (accessed October 4, 2021)

20. Cipolla, Carla, and Ezio Manzini. "Relational Services." *Knowledge, Technology & Policy* 22, no. 1 (2009): 45-50.

21. Regions where 90% of the world's population live.

22. Manzini, E., and M. K. M'Rithaa. 2017. Distributed Systems and Cosmopolitan Localism: An Emerging Design Scenario for Resilient Societies. pp. 29-37 in: A. Skjerven and J. B. Reitan (eds), *Design for a Sustainable Culture: Perspectives, Practices and Education*. London: Earthscan (Routledge).

23. Human Centered Design Africa Toolkit. https://www
.fsdkenya.org/wp-content/uploads/2021/aws/Archive%20
data%20FSD/HCD-Africa-Toolkit-FINAL.pdf?_t=1611135593
(accessed October 4, 2021).

24. M'Rithaa, M. K., B. Qually, and L. Sprong. 2012.
Design for Dialogue: Community-Based Tourism as
a Catalyst for Social Redefinition. pp. 139-153
in: R. Bartholo and C. Cipolla (eds), *Inovação
social e sustentabilidade: Desenvolvimento local,
empreendedorismo e design / Social innovation and
sustainability: Local development, entrepreneurship
and design*. Rio de Janeiro: INOVABR.

25. Joubert, E., M. E. Joubert, C. Bester, D. De Beer,
and J. Honeybush De Lange. "Honeybush (Cyclopia
spp.): From Local Cottage Industry to Global Markets—
The Catalytic and Supporting Role of Research." *South
African Journal of Botany* 77, no. 4 (2011): 887-907.

26. Ambole, L. A., M. Swilling, and M. K. M'Rithaa. 2016.
"Designing for Informal Contexts: A Case Study of
Enkanini Sanitation Intervention." *International
Journal of Design*, 10 (3):75-84.

27. World Design Organization. https://
wdo.org/programmes/wdc/past-cities/
wdccapetown2014/#:~:text=Cape%20Town%20was%20
officially%20designated,city%20has%20earned%20the%20
title. (accessed October 16, 2021).

28. City of Cape Town. PILOT PROJECT: DESIGN STRATEGIES
FOR ENHANCING SERVICE DELIVERY IN SOLID WASTE
MANAGEMENT AT DOORNBACH, CAPE TOWN (PDF). February
6, 2017. http://andreacouvert.co.za/wp-content/
uploads/2020/05/5_Testing-prototypes-phase.pdf"http://
andreacouvert.co.za/wp-content/uploads/2020/05/5_
Testing-prototypes-phase.pdf (accessed October 17,
2021).

29. City of Cape Town. City collaborates to (b)innovate
in Doornbach informal settlement. YouTube (1:36),
July 13, 2021. youtube.com/watch?v=ZwzixKrXgOs.

30. Debrah, Ralitsa D., Retha De la Harpe, and Mugendi K.
M'Rithaa. "Design probes and toolkits for healthcare:
Identifying information needs in African communities
through service design." *The Design Journal* 20, no.
sup1 (2017): S2120-S2134.

31. Holos Creative Solutions. Unwasted: A Human-Centered Approach to Solid Waste Management of Synthetic Hair Extensions. https://hcs-afrika.com/2020/04/06/unwasted-a-human-centred-approach-to-solid-waste-management-of-synthetic-hair-extensions/ (accessed October 3, 2021).
32. United Nations Department of Economic and Social Affairs, Sustainable Development. https://sdgs.un.org/goals. (accessed October 16, 2021).
33. Fuad-Luke, Alastair. *Design Activism: Beautiful Strangeness for a Sustainable World*. Routledge, 2013.
34. Illich, Ivan. *Deschooling Society*. New York: Harper & Row, 1972.
35. South African History Online. https://www.sahistory.org.za/people/esther-mahlangu. (accessed October 16, 2021).
36. Pan-African Design Institute. https://thepadi.org/. (accessed October 16, 2021).

From the Black Anti-Ableist Diary:

A Tribute to My Black Disabled Son from a Black Disabled Mother

JENNIFER
WHITE-JOHNSON

So let me tell you about my favorite human. His name is Knox; he's eight—he's got a cool Afro, one of his favorite shows is *My Little Pony: Friendship Is Magic*—and he's my son. From preschool to kindergarten, all you heard in our house was *My Little Pony*, even his seventh-birthday party had a *My Little Pony* theme.

We've watched all five seasons at least twice, and Knox has embodied all the dialogue and the character traits; one episode we've watched at least a hundred times is called "Sonic Rainboom."

In the episode, Knox's favorite character Rainbow Dash, a Pegasi Pony who has wings, who's known for her bravery, loyalty, and for being the fastest pony in the land. During the episode she aims to defy the odds and her insecurities to win the Best Flyer race. She wants to join the ranks of a top pony racing team. Before and during the race Rainbow Dash gets bullied, and her bullies convince her that she can't pull off the epic, rare Sonic Rainboom speed she needs to win the race. And while she begins to doubt her skills, her friend, Earth Pony Rarity, joins the race with a fake pair of wings. Rarity, known for her vanity, gets caught up in the extravagance of her wings, and when she flies too high during the race her delicate wings burn to ashes due to the sun's rays. As she begins to plummet to the ground, Rainbow Dash flies to save her from danger and pulls off her Sonic Rainboom! Rainbow Dash catches Rarity just before they hit the ground. It's pretty intense, and Knox gets a kick out of seeing Rainbow Dash's Sonic Rainboom speed. We're not a family of runners, so he definitely gets his need for speed from Rainbow Dash. He dashes around the house—always leaving his own trails of rainbows behind him.

Knox relates to Rainbow Dash the way he does in no small part because, when he was three, he received his Autism diagnosis. After we got the diagnosis, the doctors told us we were supposed to get therapy to modify his behaviors to help Knox be more "normal." Like so many other neurodiverse families, I started to feel isolated and pressured, figuring out if Knox should mask his disabilities while I compared him to other kids.

Before I became a mother I was teaching and advocating for kids in the community, and I knew forcing my son to conform couldn't be a part of that message. I try not to live by those oppressive standards, and I want Knox to feel free and to feel liberated to be himself—he's pretty amazing—he's got this infectious smile and belly laugh—he's hard not to love and he even looks like an old man when he cries—it goes against his code to cry—he hates it when I cry! So we amplify lots of Autistic Joy in our home. And we try to find ways to bring some of that joy outside of our home too.

When Knox was about five years old we went to a neighborhood community center for the first time to get him out of the house. And when we got inside we stumbled upon this huge track in the gym. Instantly, I knew what he wanted to do! I knew as soon as he saw that track he was going to want to race, but I was hoping he wouldn't ask me to race him! Let me tell you something about this kid; he was born at two pounds and fifteen ounces and two months premature; he's not even supposed to be here. But he's fast and active; I don't know where he gets his speed—definitely not from me!

So I told Knox I wouldn't race him. There were, however, these other kids there (tough-looking kids like they came outta the womb with a football or basketball in their hands) that were much bigger than him! He actually asked them to race! I wasn't so sure how they would respond—at first they seemed like bullies, doubting his abilities to race. I feel like when we're at home we can be ourselves, and that sometimes the actual world isn't always welcoming. I've spent so much time preaching acceptance and advocacy and asking the world to appreciate my kid's joy, but in this moment, I was tempted to shield and shelter him. But in the end, I knew I had to follow his lead and let him go.

The race begins, and while the bigger kids dash past him, he keeps racing. His goal wasn't to win or to compete, or to get caught up in the fame or accolades like Rarity—it was simply to finish. He wanted to prove the haters wrong, so when all odds were against him, his Sonic Rainboom took over when he wanted to show me he could do it! He showed me he's just fine dashing at his own speed. Knox showed me that if I let him dash, I don't have to get caught up in the competition while comparing him to the bigger kids. Knox continues to help me come to grips with greater realizations of myself. This narrative has become the heartbeat of my disability advocacy and creative practice, as it's rooted in a joyous strength and not oppressive ableism.

Using motherhood as an act of resistance—using it as a vehicle for my creativity—allows me to stay focused on the truly important things. I don't have to plummet; I can soar—and I can be saved just like Rainbow Dash saves Rarity.

Fig. 1

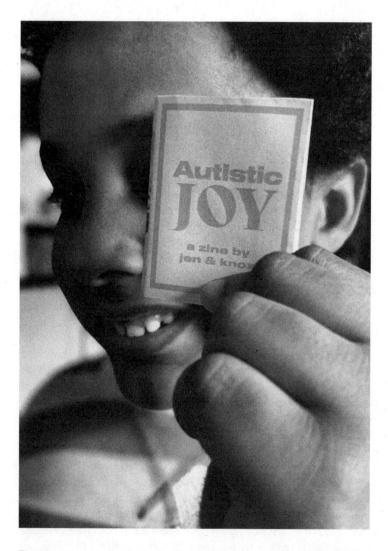

There's a reason why this story is so important—being a Black disabled parent to a Black and autistic son, I worry that my Knox's identities aren't always uplifted as being acceptable. I worry that others aim to fix what appears broken, but really isn't broken but a masterpiece. I look at my son every day, wanting to be just like him, and he encourages me to take flight— to get my Sonic Rainboom on.

This story teaches me to challenge what care-work in Art & Design spaces within academia and within our communities can be. In tribute to celebrating my openness in identifying as an ADHD Black parent, artist, and educator, my focus continues to amplify collective academic liberation while deconstructing the pedagogy that our academic institutions are holding our students back out of fear. If we let our students thrive, what might we discover? What might they teach us about prioritizing wellness and accessibility? It's our collective responsibility to plant seeds, cultivating a culture of acceptance and access in creative spaces and beyond, making sure that the disability community's perspective isn't ignored or spoken over. As art and design thinkers and educators, our work should be rooted in shifting culture, co-conspiring with our disabled comrades, helping to build anti-ableist spaces, and eliminating the cultural constructs of oppression that pathologize certain bodies and minds for being different.

How are we encouraging our disabled faculty and students to hold space for their vulnerabilities and trauma? How are we unlearning and creating inclusivity by valuing all bodies in different ways? How are we letting their lived experiences embolden their creative thinking and process? How do we discourage a culture of masking (being forced to hide one's disabilities) in fear of being misunderstood. How do we encourage a culture of freedom as a creative practice? How do we dismantle the desire for normalizing oneself to achieve a sense of belonging?

My work within the disability community in and outside of academia has allowed me to lead access-centered zine-making and photo workshops where intersectional storytelling centering the participants, lived experience is paramount. The freedom to create stories in an uninhibited space that celebrates their disability and differences encourages them to create visuals uplifting wellness and normalizing need. The workshops and projects have proven to be essential in destigmatizing how they've been taught to view themselves.

I hold space for my son to celebrate and embrace his differences. I give him room to run; giving him opportunities to showcase his strengths. Freedom cannot live or thrive in fear.

The spaces where we engage our families and students should be anti-ableist safe spaces for disabled bodies and minds to engage in full artistic autonomy, holding space for their true authentic selves. Our job as care workers and educators is in cultivating liberatory cultures. And, the act of collective liberation cannot be done in our silos of fear. If our children, family, and friends want to run, aiming to find their own artistic paths, that's a form of self-advocacy we should honor.

My definition of Mothering as an act of Resistance means to redesign ableist visual culture. The sole intention is to empower and activate change—encouraging families and communities to engage in conversations about acceptance, rooted in how Black neurodivergent children are treated, valued, and seen.

I am inspired by the revolutionary mothering and Black activism of Fannie Lou Hamer, a radical feminist, a true mother of political and carework activism. She said it best: "When I liberate myself, I liberate others."

IMAGE CREDIT

1. Kids Solidarity Zine Fest my son held during the coronavirus pandemic lockdown in Summer 2020. Photo credit: Jennifer White-Johnson

The Infrastructure of Care: Community Design, Healing & Organizational Post-Traumatic Growth

SLOAN LEO

This essay interrogates the relationship between power, decision-making, and organizational healing. It asserts that community design as a practice offers a theoretical framework for organizational dynamic healing that structurally enables those harmed to set the pace and nature of resolution and repair.

Consider a hierarchical organization of which you are a part. What is your role in the organization? How do your contributions shape the experiences of others in the group? And what would it look like if the needs of everyone in the group were met through a process of participatory decision-making at every level of the organization? These are the questions that the community design methodology seeks to answer through applied theory and a radical dismantling of harmful power structures.

Recent evolutions of community design have brought the forty-year-old concept out of its historical roots in urban planning and into new arenas. Innovative contemporary practitioners have applied the values, beliefs, and tools within the context of social justice-informed work, to grassroots-led initiatives and community-based projects. However, the application of community design as a practice for organizational development is novel and emergent. Community Design as an organizational practice explores, interrogates, and invites creative action-oriented strategies to relocate power and decision-making. Ultimately, community design is a pragmatic strategy for social sector reform.

The summer of 2020 catalyzed an inflection moment in organizational development. The events of last summer, the murder of George Floyd and the subsequent protests, as well as the pandemic, have forced most organizations to reflect and rethink their approach to relationships, strategy, and work generally. For many Black folks working in every industry, the issues of equity, inclusion, and justice could no longer be a future priority. However, in the social sector, the urgency burns even brighter. The traumatic dissonance of expressed commitments to equity being so deeply out of alignment with the experience of marginalized team members requires rapid response and remedy.

Black feminist theorist bell hooks, in her lecture "Moving from Pain to Power," states that that imperialist white supremacist cis hetero-patriarchal structures rely upon an internalized "voice of judgement," which positions oppressed peoples as needing external validation to catalyze their power, credibility, and legitimacy. She asks—what is it that is truly needed for self-actualization? What does it take to move from pain to power and from power to joy and healing?

Organizational Self-Actualization is the alignment of organizational development, strategy, structure, and culture with the original intent of progressive social sector organizations—to be sites of collective action, healing, and care.

SPECIFICALLY, HOW DO ORGANIZATIONS MOVE FORWARD—AND HEAL—FROM ORGANIZATIONAL TRAUMA?

In order to see sustained progress and organizational growth, community practice needs to be centered around healing and care. Healing happens as a non-linear process. There is no direct path from A to B, and progress can often feel slow and unnecessarily incremental. Sustained healing is an ongoing practice, not a response to an individual moment. The practice of sustained healing is just that, a practice. It requires bravery, accountability, resilience, and the ability to sit in the tension of discomfort. Healing should be a conscious practice, with care at the center of the work. How we show up for ourselves and others will determine the foundation for healing practice.

It's worth noting that healing in the absence of political analysis is not healing, it's placating. Healing as an organizational political practice that seeks to address harm requires several critical shifts in the way organizations approach and distill power. True, sustainable healing is about finding justice in organizational decision making and power sharing.

Organizational healing is about finding justice in organizational decision making, culture building, and power sharing. To accomplish this several critical shifts are necessary:

Understanding that nonprofits exist in our capitalist ecosystem—and as such, they are marginalized organizations that often intentionally and inadvertently assimilate into capitalist structures.

Accepting that organizations are one of the many ways that state and institutional governments are built, so their foundation within white supremacy cannot be structurally decolonized

A commitment to practice decolonizing relational infrastructure in organizations.

Community Design as an organizational development practice offers a theoretical framework and actionable approaches for organizational development that structurally enables those who have experienced harm to set the pace and nature of resolution and repair.

PRINCIPLES OF COMMUNITY DESIGN FOR ORGANIZATIONAL DEVELOPMENT

Design with People—Leaders need to meet teams where they are, focus on designing solutions together, and prioritize building new capacities.

Build on Existing Assets—Rather than framing through a deficit lens, focus on building based on what's working. From this place of strength, support organizational communities to build the momentum they need for the changes they seek.

Hold a Facilitator Mindset—Use collaborative methods to create with people rather than for them. Responding to real needs identified through iterative and inclusive conversations.

Aim for Engagement—Resist abstraction through direct engagement with groups and individuals during workshops, consultations, and cocreation activities. Cocreate using specifics, real opinions, and life experiences.

Design-Infused Process—Infused multidisciplinary processes with valuable design competencies like facilitation, visualization, and modeling, offer a path to more meaningful and durable progress.

IN PRACTICE HOW DOES/CAN THIS LOOK?

Organizational care and healing can take many forms:

» Cocreating equitable norms and holding each other accountable
» Recognizing the inherent value within each of us
» Acknowledging the validity of each other's lived experience
» Care infrastructure in organizations creates ease

Ultimately, post-traumatic organizational growth is possible when we channel the stress of trauma and harm into working toward specific progressive outcomes. It's about how we relate to ourselves and each other. Building trust in relationships is foundational to overcoming the harm caused by trauma. Growth depends on addressing the trauma, while also holding onto the things that make an organization strong and identifying what's worth fighting for.

How we show up for ourselves and others will determine the foundation for healing practices.

Systematizing and building these theories into practice requires acknowledgment as the first step. Organizational leaders should spend time exploring their own organizational structures to get a sense of where to start dismantling harmful practices. When leaders take this approach, they are able to build back radically supportive organizational structures that allow people to bring their full selves into community. Only then can there be full congruence between the values that the organization hopes to hold, and the ones that are put into practice. While this work is challenging, it is worth the outcome of developing a strong community with healthier, more fulfilled community members.

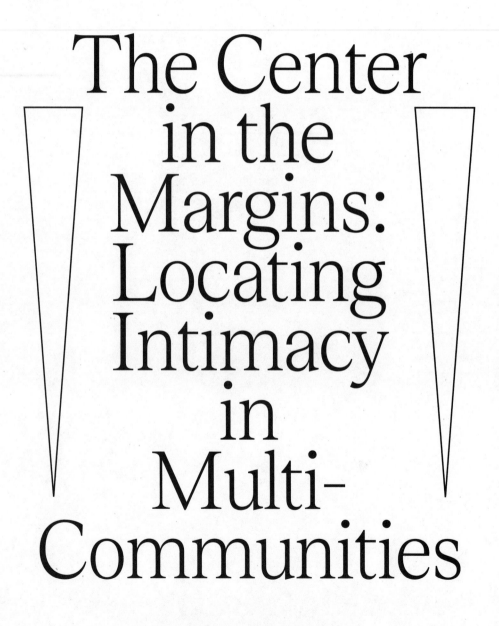

The Center in the Margins: Locating Intimacy in Multi-Communities

JUNE A. GRANT

"Do not confuse that beneath every Black architect is a desire to design a white architecture."[1] We are a pluralistic group of individuals with a multi-dimensional history, who have chosen to practice in the field of design—the creation of what is yet to exist—which is our interest. As a Black architect, my passion in design revolves around the rigorous unraveling and seeing beyond to make room for a self-envisioned future. I seek to make the invisible visible.

Fig. 1

Through the use of language as a barrier, Hispanic and Asian communities have marked land and urban zones as culturally owned. Many of these cultural communities are the result of coalescing around a shared language, history, and journey. Deemed as exotic entertainment and, on a whole, culturally unthreatening, these communities appear to be allowed peaceful existence—spatial presence adjacent to the psychological urban "center." In contrast, Black Space is seen as a cultural and psychological threat.

Nowhere on the American urban landscape is the deliberate delamination and spatial cleansing of the Black experience more persistent than in the domestic realm—i.e., housing.

The record of housing resolutions based on function is reductive, dehumanizing, and has repeatedly resulted in the creation of systems for social failure. Housing design is littered with superstar actors[2] rushing in with star-architect design solutions for Black people and Black communities in crisis.

When compared against the successes of Langston Terrace, Washington, DC (designed in 1938 by architect Hillyard Robinson) and Leimert Park Station, under construction in Los Angeles, for which the design process was led by Perkins Will Architects, the conclusion that design based on programmatic dictates oversimplifies the complexity of relationships and places a singular aesthetic onto spatial organization which ultimately leads to lack of communal acceptance and ultimately decay. The history of city planning is characterized by decisions based on the primacy of economic development, sanctioned, and administered by city staff that is paid with public dollars. Beyond city staff being defacto publicly funded private real estate agents, the creation of a closed city-planning system denies civic ownership and cultural expression while enrichinga select group.

For cities such as Oakland, Minnesota, Baltimore, Indianapolis, Los Angeles, and other cities with large ethnically diverse populations, it is instrumental to ask at what point did economic development supersede neighborhood planning? Are we at the point of unaffordability where it is appropriate to switch from the economic dictates of the "multiunit" and investigate the "multi-community?" The point where we should divorce policy from Planned Unit Development to one that is grounded less in mathematical units and instead in the relationships of human beings? Can we return to the idea of designing as both qualitative and quantitative interactions that define communities?

HOUSING THE UNITS

If Black lives do matter and figure in Saarinen's[3] description of the role of architecture, then the architecture of housing design has been the directional opposite when applied against the experiences of the Black community. Prior to the COVID-19 pandemic, cities with large Black populations prioritized market-rate housing. The arrival of the pandemic has shone a light on not only the economic fragility of African American communities but also the economic vulnerability of all Americans.

As in the past, there is a clarion cry for speedy resolution; speed to production and speed to construction. But in building fast, it is critical that designers take into account how things fell apart in the past. If we stay on the path of multi-unit, we are destined to repeat the outcomes of St. Louis' Pruitt-Igoe housing complex.

Political pressure bonded solely to economic models are once again yielding support of mass-produced housing. The production

Fig. 2

method is not the critique. The critique is what are the items included in the Balance Sheet? Past densified housing models failed due to the absence of cultural input, social amenities, and a sense of civic ownership. Black Lives Did Not Matter!

Instead of housing unit production, the pandemic reveals the crisis requires a deeper and wider perspective. If we track the history of urban densification, a constant has been a persistent primacy of the optimization of production "units" and the decline of individuality.

Fast-factory production and speed-to-construction methods, supported by trusted experienced real estate developers is not unique. What is also consistent in each historic housing cycle is the reduction in family-focused design advocacy, reduction in family-focused amenities and support systems, and the consistent pursuit of reduced cost.

Micro-units and cohousing solutions being promoted are shelter-solutions, but what about the social and community outcomes when living together has not been the American way. Simply plastering a Scandinavian social model upon a multicultural society where race relations are as distrusting as they have ever been is, at best, a social experiment and at worse, Pruitt-Igoe V2.0.[4]

The rush to build multiunit housing by harnessing the predictability of science and technology has a well-trodden history with Russia's hundred-year track-record of mass production being the most indicative of the future of US multiunit affordable housing design. All signs indicate housing design in America leaning toward Russia's *Khrushchyovka*[5] more than Switzerland's *Regenerative Communities*—the micro-unit apartments with minimum footprint versus community-focused supportive amenities targeting individual wellness.

Political spatial urgency's intended/unintended consequence of reinforcing racial and ethnic segregation is not new. South
African Apartheid and Nazi concentration camps were rationalized, sanctioned, and operationalized through official government proceedings: a
re-grounding conservation of one group's right to space and the right to
dictate space use and presence of others.

These efforts to organize human life based on prioritized capital outcomes and production efficiency deny the existence and
role of cultural patterns and systems inherent in our multicultural society.

The time has come to cannibalize exclusionary housing
policy delivery methods, but instead, look to our social and cultural patterns
as a way to design for the multicultural, healthy citizen. What if our cities
were designed based on a relational approach rather than discrete housing
units?

CENTERING IN THE MARGIN

One surprising outcome of the COVID-19 pandemic has
been to disrupt and up-end Kevin Lynch's observation of the city as one
that focuses on economic production but denies the existence of racial
considerations in the spatial planning of cities.[6] As the *New York Times*
study revealed,[7] neighbor districts and communities fare better than downtown. Forced to stay at home, residents were forced to rely on informal and
formal systems to meet their daily needs.

As an African American designer, I believe I have an
obligation to recognize the tensions inherent in communities of color—
between hope and despair; between past and present racism; and to exercise design as a platform to record, witness, and engage through a level of
citizenship in celebration of Black spirit.

As a Black designer working in Black Space, housing
presents a personal opportunity to confront the history of denial defining
the Black experience as contributory, general ignorance of Black designers,
and denial of Black spatial organizing systems.

With no clear path to correcting income inequalities,
groups have energized to coalesce, imagine, and invent new forms of organizational structures; a new spatial organization that recognizes social
germination processes as a priori and primary physical mechanisms.

What I am proposing is not an attempt to pull the margin
to the center. In opposition to Kevin Lynch's functional city,[8] I propose that
our societal future depends on centering the margin.

What we know from those who live in the margins—
those who are denied fair and open presence in the predominant public—is

survival is dependent on a network of trusted relationships, a social infra-structure that provides information, food, social and psychological safety.

The richness of systems, experiments, and experiences of the margin are appearing in the arts. As Black artists are always in dialogue; it is essential that architects and designers be in dialogue through our work. A call-and-response through our creations will be a means to create a conversational line of inquiry, through architecture, into knowing our communities as we are.

Centering in the margin requires new questions, grap-pling with suppressed expressions and an ethnobotanical approach in order to arrive at a coalesced form. Centering in the margin means shifting from the design of Lynch's "what" to the "who."

However, it is not the majority of people who make the shift. It is not the superstar who will deliver. Instead, the solutions will be created by those who are close enough to the ground to see the lived networks of survival who will design the shift.

As architects and designers during this time of pause, it is critical that we lead by articulating where we as designers of spatial structures fell short. But also we need to articulate the signs and signals that point toward a more variegated solution that solves not only the imme-diate need for housing but the need to re-knit communities.

DESIGN THE MANY WE IN THE VARIED-CITY
#WeBeintheMultiCity

The time is now to face the philosophical question, the perennial question of what it means to be human.

A major focus of my architectural practice has been to celebrate a segment of humanity that has been cast off and made invisible. Through architecture, an ambiguous profession dedicated to the transfor-mation of space, I've created a platform to bring what has been erased or denied back into the public gaze.

Cultural erasure is most persistent in the design of urban structures for domestic living; where standardization prevents individuality, and where multi-unit housing structures have overtones and undertones beyond the satisfaction of shelter from the weather. Residential structures across the United States reflect the four-hundred-plus-year history of design in the United States as a continuous reaffirmation of a supremacy of singular aesthetic history and the denial of all others; i.e. the perpetual rebranding of enlightened European values.

Black condition, Black consciousness, and even the future of US democracy have shown to rely on Black people. If we can't embrace differences, we can't celebrate similarities. I propose that architects and urban planners reintroduce the experiences of the human in the terms we use in order to design for the varied city that exists today—to let go of the multi-unit and embrace the multi-community.

As designers, we must shift our position in order to perceive the city of the "who," not the city of the "what." The switch from multi-unit to multi-community is the first step to reinjection of the space of difference. This is not an arbitrary proposition but one that takes into account that both the unhoused and those who are wealthy or housed share a reliance on social infrastructure as the structural underpinning of formal and informal relationships. This is even further demonstrated by the *New York Times* study of the five boroughs during the COVID-19 pandemic—community stability is dependent on multiple adaptable social and cultural networks.

As designers and organizers of space, Black designers of spaces of self-fulfillment and congregation, we must imagine new structures and infrastructures as social forces for good. Instead of housing unit production, the pandemic reveals clearly the crisis requires a deeper and wider perspective.

What will it take to shift from economic principles of ordering space to humanitarian principles? These are the deeper fundamental questions.

We have to shift from the economics of probability to the human expression of possibility; the allowance of intertextual multiple readings and the breaking away from popular tropes to open and invite what we cannot control. As Black designers, we are mandated to task the ancient, modern, and contemporary ideologies to become more, much more, than they have been.

The level of openness required in densified housing design options is a call for a system of cultural openness[9] that allows encounters and collisions. Romantically, I believe what I am seeking to express is the right to spatial intimacy. The poet Juliana Spahr offers another view through the lens of a poet; that as writers they are trying to create new models of intimacy that are full of acquaintances and Publix. For architecture, and architects, it is at the point at which we allow for intimacy that we will begin to house communities.

NOTES

1. Paraphrased from a lecture given by filmmaker Arthur Jafa.
2. Whoriskey, Peter. "What Happened When Brad Pitt and His Architects Came to Rebuild New Orleans" *Washington Post*, August 28, 2015.
3. "Architecture is more than space and shelter . . . it enhances man's time on earth." Rosen, Peter (Director). "Eero Saarinen: The Architect Who Saw the Future," PBS: *American Masters* (1:08:52), 2016.
4. U.S. Department of Housing and Urban Development, "Why did Pruitt-Igoe Fail," PD&R EDGE, www.huduser.gov/portal/pdredge/pdr_edge_featd_article_110314.html (undated)
5. Early Krushchyoykas were low-cost, five-story structures characterized by living units of no more than 650 square feet and shared bathrooms.
6. Hong, Nicole. "Is Brooklyn Leading New York City Out of the Pandemic?" *New York Times*, September 1, 2021. nytimes.com/2021/09/01/nyregion/nyc-brooklyn-pandemic.html
7. Ibid.
8. *Image of the City*, by Kevin Lynch is his theoretical exercise in observation of the city that focuses on the movement of capital, production, and domestic spatial designations are the primary contributors in the evolution of the city.
9. Eco, Umberto. *The Open Work*. Harvard University Press, 1989.

IMAGE CREDITS

1. Black Cultural Zone, Courtesy June A. Grant, Blink!LAB Architecture
2. Pruitt-Igoe, United States Geological Survey, from their website, Public Domain, https://commons.wikimedia.org/w/index.php?curid=5584780.

Biophilia Patterns in

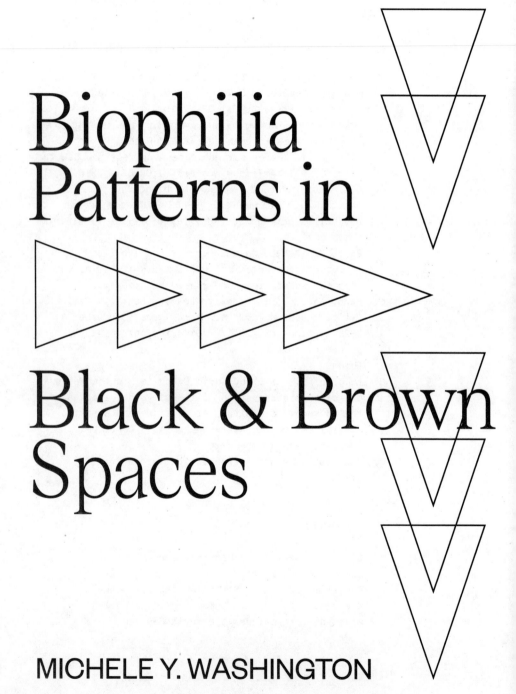

Black & Brown Spaces

MICHELE Y. WASHINGTON

We need nature in a deep and fundamental fashion, but we have often designed our cities and suburbs in ways that both degrade the environment and alienate us from nature.

—Tamarack Media[1]

As daily life becomes increasingly impacted by severe climate and environmental disasters—hotter summers leading to expansive droughts and uncontrollable wildfires; Atlantic hurricanes continuing an accelerating trend of annual landfalls; and flood events causing disastrous property damage and loss of life—there is a vital need for artists, designers, urban planners, architects, scientists, community activists, and residents to operate through a more transdisciplinary model of environmental activism that situates design as an essentially biophilic practice. The following reflections on my own journey toward embracing biophilia serve as an invitation for my peers to likewise consider modeling a biophilic vision, one that particularly uplifts Black and Brown communities that have been most harmed by segregationist and class-driven urban planning practices of the last century.

BIOPHILIA AS A DESIGN PRACTICE

Biophilia expresses the human tendency to interact or be closely associated with other forms of life in nature; that is, a desire or tendency to commune with nature. The term was coined by Harvard naturalist Dr. Edward O. Wilson to describe what he saw as humanity's "innate tendency to focus on life and lifelike processes"[2] and to be drawn toward nature, "to feel an affinity for it, a love, a craving."[3] If human beings have within us an inherent sense of connection to other forms of life, can this natural feeling, this "biophilia," both enhance our respect for ourselves and reinforce our sense of obligation to treat other forms of life with loving care? From the Black perspective biophilia can serve as a reparative and restorative practice, not only for niche or speculative design but as a deeply transdisciplinary, collaborative model activated by and within communities of color who provide the mandate to design teams: design as a radically humanist act. Proclaiming a consciously Black urban planning practices, biophilia serves as the underlying philosophy for reclaiming connection and the restoring communities that were intentionally built in harm's way.

Of the many overtly anti-biophilic designs in U.S. cities, a model case can be found in the South Bronx, NY. Block by block, the pattern of scarification-by-expressway meets the looming shadows of housing projects. Where biophilic patterns build on the concept of balance, including creating access to natural spaces, the South Bronx seem intended to remove residents from any connection to nature. This is no accident. Historically, the design of Black-centered spaces—neighborhoods, communities, homes—neglected or intentionally disrupted connections with nature. Spaces of concrete and stone—built high and close with limited access to natural sunlight or soil, and situated almost pathologically near waste sites—they have long been sites of environmental insult. Not only in cities but in Black and brown suburbs and rural communities, as well, neglect is the point; disconnection is the point; disruption is the point. Biophilia is, therefore, not a luxury but a political mandate that acknowledges the punishing tendencies of Black-, immigrant-, and poverty-centered design.

A BIOPHILIC BLUEPRINT FOR HUMANIST DESIGN

To consider a biophilic practice, we might turn to *Biophilic Design*,[4] the text by Stephen Kellert, Judith Heerwagen, and Martin Mador that defines six essential features of biophilia. Their model is useful in assessing the failures of existing structures and spaces in Black communities, and serves as a blueprint for future development. The six interrelated elements they identify are:

» Environmental features—access to the natural world
» Natural shapes and forms—organicism in the built environment
» Restorative patterns and processes—designing for all of the senses, including that of the psyche and soul
» Light and space—constantly reaffirming our connections to the circadian rhythms within our bodies and the physical world
» Place-based relationships—an emphasis on geography, ecology, and culture
» Evolved human-nature relationship—rebuilding our fluency with nature

Building a biophilic practice radically rejects the architect's centrality and instead centers the community and its relationship to that of the natural world. As a Black practice, it is a clear investment in repair of the psyches and souls of residents who have suffered too long from the dehumanization of their communities by city planners, as well as an investment in diasporic cultural representation. "Place-based relationships" in fact situates biophilic design as a form of aesthetic activism, leveraging local artists and designers, and building capacities within the community to create the neighborhoods they desire.

The biophilic patterns of neighborhoods, then, are defined by the specific geographies, ecologies, and cultures expressed there: not the designer's vision, or the architect's vision, or the city's vision, but the community's vision. To build a biophilic practice requires an investment in the local activists and advocacy groups and the many community programs that have been building in communities for genera-tions. Importantly, a biophilic practice is radically interdisciplinary, and asks practitioners to work with one another across various fields of study in order to successfully fulfill the interconnected needs of a vision inspired by and based on the natural world.

WORKING WITH CITY AS A LIVING LABORATORY (CALL)

Developing a biophilic lens for my own practice as a design researcher and educator brought me, during the spring of 2020, into a collaboration with City as a Living Laboratory (CALL).[5] Founded by artist and designer Mary Miss, CALL employs art as a form of community engagement to tackle environmental inequities, in this case on the Daylighting Tibbetts Brook[6] project in Van Cortlandt Park,[7] a 1,146 acre public greenspace in the Bronx, in collaboration with local community groups and leaders, New York City's Department of Environmental Protection (DEP), and the Van Cortland Park Alliance. The plan for the Alliance was to restore both the natural site (Tibbetts Brook, the last remaining fresh water marsh in New York State, and historic fishing and farming lands of Munsee and Lenape peoples), as well as the community (specifically the Marble Hill Housing Projects, which houses as many as 9,000 residents).

PAST IS PRESENT IN THE BRONX

Much of the disruption in this sector of the Bronx is a by-product of former city builder Robert Moses's interventions in the borough throughout the 1930s, 40s, and 50s. His fervent highway-build-ing was instrumental in destroying communities throughout the Bronx, in particular by extending a section of the Major Deegan Expressway (constructed from 1935 to 1956) and building the Cross Bronx Expressway (constructed from 1948 to 1972). As a six-lane highway, the Major Deegan (named for an Irish-born American architect and a major in the Army Corps of Engineers who advocated for the rights of Black veterans) runs along the western border of the Bronx at the Harlem River until it reaches Marble Hill, where it then cuts right through several previously vibrant neighborhoods on its route north to Westchester. The six-lane Cross Bronx services the east-west route and similarly scars neighborhoods on its journey through the Bronx. Both highways increase noise and pollution levels, and result in frequent flooding in the neighborhoods they abut.

Those highways are symbols of neglect, as disruptive building in the Bronx served the development of wealthy, intentionally white (by law), ostentatiously green suburban communities that surround NYC, including on Long Island to the east, Westchester County just over the border to the north, and northern New Jersey across the Hudson River. Moses clearly prioritized building transit routes for suburban residents over stewarding local, city communities, particularly those populated by Black and Brown residents. His contributions to the cultural erasure of those communities, as well as the high rates of health-related problems that have plagued residents for multiple generations, are the legacy that contemporary designers must confront.

Numerous U.S. cities have begun to rethink these problematic highway systems that cut through Black communities, and designers and activists have begun advocating for replacing or supplementing them with greener interventions—nascent biophilic spaces that rehumanize those environments. Importantly, Black designers, activists, and community member observing the biophilic blueprint, must fervently advocate for the conscientious attention to all of what biophilia engages— not just nods to greenery, but contact with soil, water, and light; emphasis on natural forms and textures; and honoring local aesthetics ecologies that stimulate all of the senses and foster closer relationships with nature.[9]

DEVELOPING A PEDAGOGY FOR BIOPHILIA AS COMMUNITY ACTIVISM

I am activating an emergent perspective on biophilic design in my studio practice and in my pedagogy. During the 2020–2021 school semester at the Fashion Institute of Technology, my students— representing a range of skills including architecture, interior architecture, product design, and curation—had an opportunity to collaborate with CALL and the Marble Hill Houses to develop a set of speculative, biophilic design proposals. Together we conducted field research, met with community members, and studied the core readings in biophilia patterns. Their research as well as their imaginings created space for them to conceive of their own biophilic vision, and tapped into research methods that connected would-be fantasy to reality.

Fig. 1

Traveling to the Bronx meant riding my bike from my home in Central Harlem along the Harlem River bike path—a scenic vista through a lush, green, park esplanade—before hitting a dreary stretch of streets that lead to Broadway in upper Manhattan, and finally crossing the 225th Street Bridge overpass into the Marble Hill section of the Bronx.

Fig. 2

During my ride and throughout the site visits, I documented the neighborhood with photos and short videos, including during my walks through the Marble Hill Housing complex and Van Cortland Park. It was on those visits that I first learned about the Outer Seed Shadow Project (OSS), a public green space that incorporates urban farming, arts, and public programming, founded by Jacki Fisher (a local resident) and Juanli Carrion (an artist and New School professor).

I see this as the beginning of a teaching and professional practice that radically shifts the conversation about what type of design is possible in historically Black spaces (not only possible—not optional—but mandatory) and how we can teach the next generation of students to take up the mantle of change. Teaching about biophilia, I am hoping we can impart to emerging designers and architects the demand for humanism in both the process and the products of their making. Biophilia is the future of our cities because it is a way out of harm and a path toward healing. It honors our ancestral practices of growing things in and for our communities, and it reclaims our bodies, minds, and spirits, which is where community happens. Our Black spaces deserve nothing less.

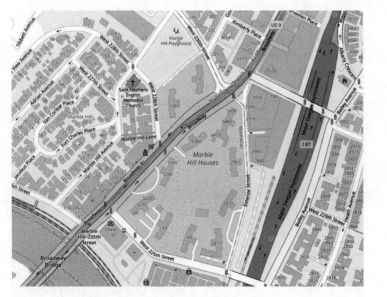

Fig. 3

In both boroughs, Broadway is a major thoroughfare shadowed by the elevated Number 1 train; and in the Bronx, it bifurcates the Marble Hill neighborhood, which is further shadowed by the Major Deegan, a North-South highway that borders the neighborhood's eastern edge.

Fig. 4

Fig. 5

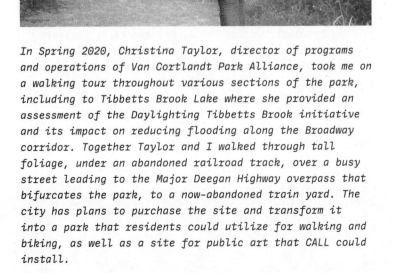

*In Spring 2020, Christina Taylor, director of programs
and operations of Van Cortlandt Park Alliance, took me on
a walking tour throughout various sections of the park,
including to Tibbetts Brook Lake where she provided an
assessment of the Daylighting Tibbetts Brook initiative
and its impact on reducing flooding along the Broadway
corridor. Together Taylor and I walked through tall
foliage, under an abandoned railroad track, over a busy
street leading to the Major Deegan Highway overpass that
bifurcates the park, to a now-abandoned train yard. The
city has plans to purchase the site and transform it
into a park that residents could utilize for walking and
biking, as well as a site for public art that CALL could
install.*

NOTES

1. *Biophilia Design: The Architecture of Life*, by Tamarack Media, 2016.
2. Wilson, Edward. O. (1984). *Biophilia*. Cambridge, Mass: Harvard University Press.
3. Angier, Natalie. "Managing Planet Earth: Adoring Nature, Till It Bites Us In the Back," *The New York Times*, August 20, 2002.
4. Kellert, Stephen R., Judith Heerwagen, and Martin Mador. 2008. *Biophilic Design: The Theory, Science, and Practice of Bringing Buildings to Life*. Hoboken, N.J.: Wiley.
5. City as a Living Laboratory (CALL), https://www.cityaslivinglab.org/.(accessed October 5, 2021).
6. For more about the Daylighting Tibbetts Brook, visit the Van Cortland Alliance, https://vancortlandt.org/programs-overview/daylighting-tibbetts-brook/ (accessed October 5, 2021).
7. The park was named after a Dutch colonial family that claimed ownership over thousands of acres of historic Munsee and Lenape lands. In the Unami language, the Lenape-populated area was known as Keskeskick.
8. Outer Seed Shadow Urban Garden, https://outerseedshadow.org/ (accessed October 5, 2021).
9. Plan to Transform the Cross Bronx Expressway Gains Momentum (April 27, 2021),https://www.publichealth.columbia.edu/public-health-now/news/plan-transform-cross-bronx-expressway-gains-momentum. In 2018, researchers at Columbia University proposed a speculative plan to build a greenway on the site of the Cross Bronx Expressway in the South Bronx.

IMAGE CREDITS

In Conversation:

Amos Kennedy &

Kareem Collie

ON ADVOCATING FOR HUMANITY

I spoke with designer and printmaker Amos Kennedy to learn how being a human being with a printing press brings humanity to design. This conversation has been edited for length and clarity.

—Kareem Collie

KAREEM COLLIE: How do you define yourself as a designer?

AMOS KENNEDY: Well, I don't define myself as a designer. I don't define myself, I just find myself as a lost human being. I am very fortunate that the forces of the universe provide. I know people who are designers, they work hard at it, and they study it to develop a philosophy. I just kind of mess around. I have a printing press. I have some type, I just mess around all day.

KC: In describing yourself as a lost human being, how would you say you found yourself here?

AK: When I say a lost human being, I mean, this civilization wants you to have this profound definition and meaning in your life and purpose, but all this really centers around the capitalistic system that we operate in. They're not interested in you finding your relationship with the world, your relationship with the planet. I'm attempting to minimize the impact that I have upon this planet, and maximize the impact that the planet has upon me. Once you become aware of what the planet is doing to you, you can attempt to be in sync with it, because ultimately the planet is not here to serve me. I am here to serve it. It will be here long after I'm gone.

KC: What sparked your interest in printmaking? When did you decide to become a printer?

AK: It was the first piece I did and that connection of the process. When the first impression was pulled, it was like, this is where I want to be. The woman who taught me how to print had been teaching for a number of years. And she said that over the years she'd learned that there are certain students that when they pull that first print there is this expression that shows that they experience was so profound that she can just say, "oh, it's over for them" this is what they are going to do.

Other people find this doing other things, but it was printing for me. It is a way for me to express my humanity.

KC: **What kind of work are you making and creating right now?**

AK: Well, am I making and creating? Or am I just transforming? You know, when I think of making, I think of creating something that never existed. I am not creating something; I am taking things that already exist and I'm just rearranging them.

KC: **What then would you say your intention is for the person ultimately engaging with the result of your rearranging?**

AK: The goal is that people in some way identify with what I have said. And that they are in alliance with me. That's the outcome I want. People imagine a world they want to manifest. Artists and designers, through our work, are broadcasting the world we want to live in.

For example, a painter who painted a landscape that is very peaceful and quiet and gentle. In some way they're saying this is the type of world that they want. That's what I'm doing as a designer.

It's very minimal what I do. The equipment I use should have been in a landfill by now. Most of the letterpress equipment has ended up in landfills or scrapped and just trashed because it's no longer needed. We have new technologies that are faster and can produce more. I have an old letterpress machine that's almost a hundred years old. This is better for the planet than me going out and buying a new machine. All the metal that was used. It was made for a purpose and that steel, that metal, was transformed for the purpose of humanity, and humanity is still using it for the reason it was transformed today—all the energy that went into to making that machine.

We humans are constantly changing and adding, we call it improving when we just toss stuff aside. As if we have an endless supply of resources that we can just continue to dip into, but we don't. Why does somebody now need a printer that can do ten thousand impressions in an hour? You know, most of the printed material is going to be thrown away.

KC: **Why do you think people are drawn to the work that you produce? Why do you think you have found success doing this work?**

AK: I believe that people are drawn to the work because of the text. I did a proverb from the African continent—"Children of the same mother don't always agree." Everybody relates to that who has a sibling. It's the text.

KC: **Is there a certain type of environment or mindset that you create for yourself while you're working?**

AK: You know that that's a really interesting thing to look at. We've been presented throughout our lives through education through the entertainment, all these things that there is this way that things can be done, like you hear people say, I can only write between 5 and 7 a.m. in the morning because that's just right. I have to do it this way or that way. I believe that the way you do, it is not as important as you're doing it. And if you do it, that will define the way that you do it.

So, if you say, I have to clean my press before I print, that is because this is the way that you did it before and so you want to do it again. You can print without the press being clean, but you want to do this in order to do the next thing. You want to have some sort of protocol. But it is doing that thing that really ignites in you. It connects you to something that is greater.

KC: **Would you say that one of your main drivers is advocating a more aligned engagement with the world as humans?**

AK: Well, here's the thing. Every human being is an advocate. The question is what do you advocate? The person who works for GM designing the ad is advocating consumerism. Not anything special.

We like to think advocacy is someone involved in social justice, right? What about the person who's trying to sell you an iPhone? They are advocating for consumers, for the continued exploitation of the planet, for no reason. Everyone's an advocate. The question is "what kind of advocate are you?"

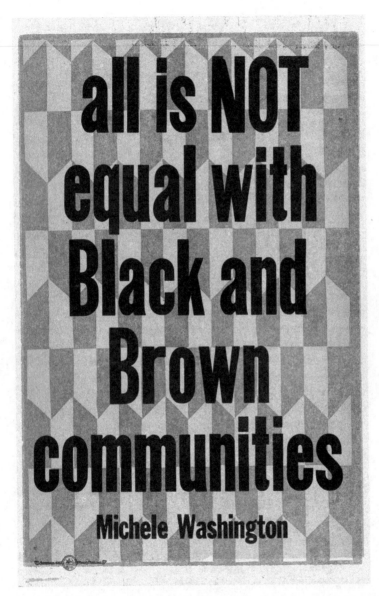

Fig. 1

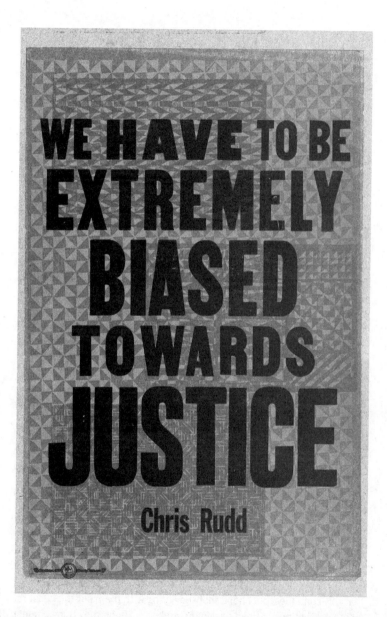

Fig. 2

I am advocating for a world where people relate more with all facets of the world. I would like to see a world where people are more in touch with the forces of the universe, the rhythm of the planet. I would like a place where people can see sitting in the grass as not unusual; where walking in the rain is a pleasure, not something that we try to avoid; where we celebrate every day, not just the sunny days, because we know we need the rain. Yeah, there's certain rains that you want to protect yourself from, but there's certain rains that you should be out and enjoying.

KC: **We feel so honored that you designed five posters for the book. What was your process in creating them?**

AK: Process. One of the problems with Western civilization I think is that we overthink everything. We just think all the time, we are just busy little thinkers. You know, there is some thought that goes into what I do, but primarily that thought occurs in the moment that I'm making something. I do not make sketches. Today, a lot of letterpress printers are actually doing the design work on computers, but I don't go about it that way. I look at it this way, each mockup is valid. There is no perfect mockup. Each time you do a mockup, you are changed by that mockup. You learn from that mockup so the next one can be better. If you did ten mockups the validity of the first one is just as great as the validity of the last one. And just as important, the person who made the first mockup no longer exists, because they've made nine more, that person is no longer here. They've gone.

KC: **As a Black designer and artist, what possibility would you say this moment holds for you, and for other Black designers?**

AK: What I am attempting to do as a part of humanity is to get us to create a civilization where all human beings reached their maximum potential; and that potential has a very light existence upon the planet, taking only what we need from the planet to live.

I am delighted to see more Blacks in design. I am hoping that this continues, but I hope that they bring with them not the quest for greatness that has defined design up until now. I hope they bring a quest to help humanity. As they rise, I hope that they will lift humanity as a whole and that they will design a better world. Not a better pair of Nike, or a better car for GM, but a better way of living. This is what I hope that they design. This is what I hope the Black experience is: looking at humanity and saying, "How can I design a better way for humans to exist?"

Fig. 3

IMAGE CREDITS

1-3. Courtesy Amos Kennedy

The Preconditions to Healing

LIZ OGBU

EDITOR'S NOTE:

A version of this essay was originally published in *On Topic*, the Minneapolis College of Art and Design's digital publication, in fall 2020.

"Before there can be political change, there must be cultural change." Said by the artist activist Favianna Rodriguez in 2016 shortly after Donald Trump's election, this comment comes to mind often, especially now. As I write this in the summer of 2020, it has been nearly three weeks since the murder of George Floyd and the attempted murder of Christian Cooper. Nine weeks since the murder of Breonna Taylor. Twelve weeks since the murder of Ahmaud Arbery. And sadly, the list goes on . . . It has felt like the ground has shifted more in the past three weeks than it has in three decades. There are daily protests in streets not only around the country, but also around the world. Heads are rolling, figuratively at corporations and literally from statues. Books about antiracism and white fragility have gone from the special interest section to required reading for the [white] mainstream populace. And for those of us whose work is interwoven with the fight for racial justice, this head spinning moment is often filled with hope, exhaustion, and wariness.

Hope is for the daring belief that this inflection point is different, and that the cracks in the system of white supremacy are breaking open in ways we've not seen before and that might meaningfully help the communities that we serve and partner with. Exhaustion is for the labor that often falls on those who have been in the fight long before the change was big enough to be visceral and visible. And the wariness is from the knowledge that the inspired action that comes with the urgency of now often gives way to the enduring stuckness that accompanies the complacency of later. I can't help but wonder where we will be by the time you read this: urgency, complacency, or some third state that has yet to be defined.

As an architect and spatial justice activist, I have come to realize that my work is, in part, to support that third state. For some time, I've been diving deeply into explorations around this. And while I haven't figured out every step of that journey, there are some thoughts that I can share.

First and foremost, this journey is ultimately about taking down the structures of harm (white supremacy, capitalism, patriarchy) and replacing them with structures of healing. Healing is something that I focus a lot on in my work. To work on spatial justice means acknowledging that justice has a geography, and that in countless cities across the country, we have far too many examples that show differences in which communities get good housing, transport, parks, etc. and which don't. For the neighborhoods that are on the losing end, the physical impacts of these differences are like visceral wounds on the land. And when we layer demographics over this geography, we find that Black, Brown, Indigenous, and poor communities have disproportionately been harmed. This has been no accident. The wounds of spatial injustice aren't just physical; they're also emotional. This means that healing won't come about just through building more housing, establishing new bus routes, or even repurposing funds from a police budget into a new community center. It requires more; it requires holding space for the complexity that created and has sustained these wounds as well as doing the work to close the wounds in such a way that they can never reopen. In other words, continuing to drive cultural change forward also requires embracing the preconditions to healing.

Before we can heal, we have to acknowledge the wounds: their existence, their depth, and their pain. And while this has been a feature in my work for years, perhaps what is making this moment feel so different is that it feels like in the space that is being made for the cries of the protestors, the more public accounting of and within non-Black communities, and the reaction to images and statistics documenting the disproportionate impacts of COVID-19 on communities of color, that the acknowledgment of the wounds caused by the structures of harm finally feels broad and collective. Holding space for acknowledging these wounds is critical and hard, but it is also not the only precondition we must embrace. To move toward healing also requires that we grieve.

Grieving means leaning into the discomfort and uncertainty of sitting with that acknowledgment. It is about being willing to stay vulnerable and brave long enough to ask hard questions of ourselves and others, listen to and be in dialogue around the answers, and make peace with where those conversations take us. It is not something that many of us know how to do well, if at all, but it is a necessary step for healing.

Grieving, like cultural change, doesn't just happen. It relies on a collection of healers whose work is to tend to the wounds. As I think about who those healers might be, I find myself recalling the words of curator Ashara Ekundayo, who talks about "artists as first responders," essential workers to cultural change. In the liminal space between urgency and complacency, I'm reflecting on what it would mean to use my skills and resources to support and increase our individual and collective capacities to grieve. And I can't help but wonder what healing and change could ultimately be unleashed if every artist, designer, and cultural worker also committed to that purpose.

In Conversation: Raja Schaar

& Jennifer Rittner

ON SUSTAINABILITY
AS A HISTORICALLY
BLACK PRACTICE

My conversation with Raja Schaar was delightfully far-reaching and unbounded. Over three hours, we covered everything from the heritage of our hair to gender normativity to sustainability as an inherently Black form of community activism. This conversation has been lightly edited for length and clarity.

—Jennifer Rittner

HAIR AND FAMILY LINEAGE

JENNIFER RITTNER: **Raja, let's start by acknowledging how you are showing up in spaces right now because, for one thing, I am in love with your hair color.**

RAJA SCHAAR: I always play with my hair. It was white before. It's platinum blonde every few weeks. I was trying to match the color of the poster for Lesley-Ann Noel's *Design Thinking Breakfast* (March 26, 2021),[1] and I'm like, I have so much hair dye. I have short hair now because I just cut it off. I'm like, hair is hair. Do whatever you want with it.

I have students who are rethinking the cold cap. I was like, what if you let your hair fall out and they're like, "How dare you? This is people's crowning glory!" There's so much tied into hair and identity. But, *so what* if you start all over; and maybe you have a different texture—straight hair instead of curly, or gray where it was a different color?

JR: **My mom and I have had a lot of tension around how we treat our hair. Whereas I'm like, "Mom, go natural. Let your hair be natural." She's like, "I can't do that." So much of her life she had received the message that her natural hair wasn't acceptable or good enough. In the last few weeks of her life she let it go natural and I loved looking at her looking at herself that way. It felt so liberating, like she was seeing her childhood self again.**

RS: My mom is the one who always is sad [when I do new things to my hair] because she loves my hair. It's her hair. My mom's mom is biracial. And my son has my mom's mom's hair. So she sees the family through our hair. Whenever it's the same she's like, "Oh, we look alike."

DEFINING THE SELF IN SELF-PRESENTATION

JR: **The thing I've noticed with my child is how they're navigating racial identity, because they're very white-appearing, but identify as mixed. So they're trying to figure out where they fit in the race conversation, because nobody's going to look at them and not think they're a white kid. They're trying to figure out the distinctions among experiences versus presentations versus perceptions of race.**

RS: That was me as a kid because my mom was very light-skinned. And so, I mean, I'd already seen a range of hues as a kid growing up. So when I heard the term Black and white, or like in school, when it really hit me and I was like, but no one's skin is actually white and no one's actually Black. And there were some really light-skinned Black people. What makes someone Black? Because it wasn't about your skin tone. Is it hair texture? I had Indian and East Asian friends who were very dark and had different hair texture. As a kid I was trying to piece it out. My dad was like, well, they don't have our lips. And I was like, "Oh, what are her lips like?" But then my uncle has small lips. So is he not . . .? You know, it's so confusing! My great grandmother's nose was very straight and she had straight hair. If you had no understanding of what race was or what ethnicity was, and you were trying to figure it out, the only thing you can do is look at features and even the features don't match.

Siblings from the same parents can look so different that you can't even tell if they are actually siblings. How can we look at a skeleton and decide its ethnic or racial makeup?

When my kids are checking boxes on standardized test forms, which [demographic options] are they going to pick? They always pick Black, which is interesting to me. But at the same time, like, yeah, you could pick white. Why don't you? You're actually more white than you are Black. You can pick whatever you want. And they're like, "Nope, this is fine."

REJECTING RACE & GENDER NORMATIVITY

JR: **How we navigate the importance of race relative to anything we're doing in a given moment is complex, isn't it? It's a looming presence.**

RS: That's a distraction, right? International students [to American colleges and universities] who come from majority or very homogenous countries have almost no concept of race. For them the more salient distinction is socioeconomic class, maybe gender, or ethnicity. They are often so naive to that conversation [about race in the US] until they come here. So they're learning it from scratch.

I hear people say they want to get beyond race. Get beyond gender. I appreciate that, and more power to them. Everybody should have the option to do that. But for me, as a Black woman, what I'm trying to do is acknowledge that that is the way that I'm perceived by the rest of the world. And that is how I will be treated. That is also how others who look and present like me have been treated. And if I want to try to learn from the experiences of those who have succeeded and those who have failed in their striving, I can look to see how presenting in this way means that you show up in the world or what you've been able to accomplish in spite of or because of that. The historical connection to that experience is something that I need to acknowledge and carry forward.

For many years, when I was a kid, I didn't want to be called a girl because girls get treated shitty. I had no knowledge of what gender identity was. I only knew that if someone said, "Hey, I need some guys to help me move a table," I would think, "Well I can help move a table! Just treat me like a guy." It was like, I just need for you to treat me like a person who can do things and has abilities.

Categorizing our bodies as "boy" or "girl" wasn't useful for things like moving heavy objects around, or determining who was faster and slower. I was always the biggest and strongest and fastest, so I knew I should just be over there [with the boys].

JR: **The nuances of gender in 2021 feel more liberating than when we were coming of age. It was entirely binary: you're either this or that.**

RS: My friend H, who is 6' 3", big lambchop side-burns—he made himself a denim skirt in high school. It was the grunge era so people would wear whatever, like pajamas to school. I remember the shit he got for making and wearing the skirt. JNCO jeans were all the rage, and then the big, wide skateboard jeans. So he had those, and then he had skirts that he would wear. And he was like, "I just like the way they feel. I'm going to wear whatever I want." This is a kid growing up in South Georgia, and people lost their ever-loving minds. They were like, "What does it mean?" Well, it means that he made a skirt.

Gender presentation or dress is a matter of self-expression: "What do I want to wear today?" I would never have worn what Prince wore because I was like, "Who wants to wear lace all the time? That just gets in the way and that's too much. And who has time to do their hair and makeup?"[2] To me, that's all too fussy. But not because they were men. I just can't be bothered.

The amount of self-assuredness and confidence that you have to exhibit in the world requires a rebellion to peer pressure. I feel like, because of my identity I just was like, "Eh, you're gonna make fun of me anyway." And that was my attitude all along. I know that some people are very sensitive to other people's opinions of them, but I decided that everybody was stupid when I was about four.

Now, as I watch kids and even my own kids, I'm worrying about how they might conform to the ideals of others or do they feel strong enough in themselves and whatever it is that they like? One of my sons is very much into what's not cool. First of all, who's deciding what's cool?

BLERD GIRL WORLD

JR: **You are navigating several intersectionalities that inform your work as a designer and educator. Can you talk about some of the places you draw inspiration from?**

RS: A lot of my work is inspired by how I have learned to imagine possibilities, especially through science fiction. I've always been like, "Ooooh, what could we do?" I've always identified as a nerd, a geek, a Blerd, a Bleek. I feel very at-home in the nerd and pop culture community because whenever I go to conventions and things, it's people who are seen as outliers in the world in some way, including people who are neurodiverse—I'm ADHD. You see a high percentage of people with noticeable, physical disabilities. You see people of all different skin tones, language, abilities. Some are traditionally cool or hot appearing. Some are, you know, "Oh, you got made fun of in school."

It's always this beautiful gathering of outliers. And I think that part of the reason I am attracted to that is I like looking at people who are embracing their outlier status and now using it in the same way that we were promised. "The nerds are going to rule the world!" They are the ones driving what is considered cool, culturally. Look at all the hype around the Zack Snyder release of *Justice League*, right? Like, nerds are able to have a direct influence by making their voices heard.[3] So, one identity for me is around connecting as a nerd and outlier from a point of resilience— being okay with not fitting into a bucket.

On the Black woman side of things, I saw a lot of really strong representation in my community growing up, of women in charge. It just never occurred to me to see women as anything other than strong and capable. Whenever I heard theories about "women are less than," I was like, "Who is telling you that?" Because look at all these people like my mom and my aunt, and the woman who owns this business and the woman who owns that business, and the superintendent of the school here. I have always been surrounded by very strong, vocal Black women who were in charge of things. I identify with women who speak their minds and speak their truth. That whole "lift as you rise," has always been about furthering the movement around Black women, their position in the world, because we are very competent.

GLOBAL CLIMATE ACTIVISM AND CIVIL RIGHTS

RS: And then the other part of it . . . I think about my vulner-
                abilities as a Black person and what I was privileged
enough to have access to, but by the skin of my teeth. My existence growing up in South Georgia in a very diverse, Muslim community, near an Air
Force Base, afforded me friendships with people who had been all over the
world. That is not a common experience across the Southern United States;
or even anywhere else. A lot of other people in my school had different
experiences as Black students. From middle school and older, I realized that
there was a lot that I knew about the world that other people weren't paying
attention to.

I understood things about how racism can affect people,
not just because you come from enslaved people, but because there are
constructs of race, or stratas of society, based in caste systems. I had a
friend who had one Japanese parent and one Chinese parent. I learned
early on that there was a lot of friction in his parents' relationship rooted
in the history of those two countries, specifically around the Rape of
Nanking in 1937. How could you understand that as a kid growing up in the
US unless you studied it in college? Or you learned about the skirmishes
that happened in the Eastern part of Asia for hundreds of years. There's a
deep history there, similar to the politics of the Middle East. So from that
standpoint, I've always been thinking about, "where are my vulnerabilities

as a person," but also, "how do I use what I understand [about history, social caste, and historical violence]?"

Climate change was a space for thinking about how we need to preserve society. I started looking to see who was being impacted, even in my own community. Trying to understand what I now know was historical redlining, where our neighborhoods were always next to the factories. Then looking at the impacts of natural disasters like hurricanes and seeing that the pancaked houses are so often trailer parks, in poor Black and Brown communities.

I started to pay attention to those things, and looking for nerdy Black women who are climate activists. I get jazzed when I find them because the conversation around the environment and society has always been part of the conversation around civil rights. But that hasn't gotten the traction that white climate rights activists have gotten. The white narrative around sustainability is very one-sided and consumer focused. What can the consumer do to make their lives more sustainable? They can recycle and sort. We don't talk about it from the standpoint of trees and whales. We talk about it from the standpoint of houses, people, poverty, and health. And people don't equate that to sustainability. But that is sustainability!

Black climate activists are teaching about the connections between extreme weather, design, the environment, and architecture. Some folks are working on issues of water and climate justice, and doing community-based activism around watershed management and pollution in Flint, Michigan.

JR: Do you think that the mythologies around sustainability as a white-intellectual endeavor or as a space for white intellectualism has prevented more Black scholars from entering or being recognized in that space?

RS: Octavia Butler was an environmentalist. Her *Parable Books*[4] are all about rebuilding community; and climate change was at the root of it, right? She wrote, "The world is on fire." When I read her work, and I read people who studied her work, like adrienne maree brown,[5] they don't talk about it exclusively as sustainability. Because whenever I say the word sustainability, people think, "Oh, you mean like reduce, reuse, recycle" or "Oh, you mean circular economy as a business model." And I'm like, yeah, but also if you think about the fact that we used to reduce reuse, recycle a hundred years ago, literally everything.

Being efficient and being economic in our use of food materials was how we survived because there was scarcity, because we didn't have economic access to be able to hire someone to make things for us. There was also scarcity of time.

When industrial processes made that more efficient, easier, and more democratic, it contributed to a culture of waste. Cheap, disposable goods started flooding our communities. Our communities are littered because of it. Neighborhoods prioritized for infrastructure had organized trash collection, **and** they also didn't need cheap, disposable things because they could have white tablecloths and silverware, as opposed to plastic forks and Styrofoam containers. The whole infrastructure of cities was built to cut off poor, Black neighborhoods from access.

Women were largely the caretakers of the home and thought about economic uses of things: mending clothes, caring for things, and doing repairs, making sure to use every scrap of food. These are things that people the world over did until it was convenient to **not** do it.

JR: **The sustainability argument predicates itself on an assumption that consumerism and modernity are inextricably linked. That "modern people" are essentially consumers— of products, of information, of resources. Indigenous, female-centered, and Black economies are perhaps presumed to inhabit a space outside of "consumerist modernity," in that they are historically aligned with practices and philosophies of stewardship, communalism, and conservation.**

RS: Poor people and people of color often maintain sustainability culture. If you look at people who wear old tattered clothes and repair them, society's perception of them is they must be poor. They can't afford new clothes. There is no value in maintaining something and having something that shows visible signs of wear or tear or repair, because what it looks like from an American lens is you must not be able to afford the good version. Right?

The Black community has fallen into this white supremacist view that new and shiny means wealthy. We had been fed this line that if we do these things, then we will get ahead, and we are actually doing those things to our detriment. We are killing ourselves to buy the best of and have something new, even if we can't afford it, because society gives us more status where we have none. With skin tone and hair like mine, what can I present to the world? My car, my material goods, my clothing, my hair. You buy hair, you buy nails, right? We buy these things to show people that we can afford these things, that we have economic power.

Whereas if we maintain a culture of repair and keeping up with old things, that would be better economically. It would be better environmentally. It would be better for our health—personal health, public health.

That's environmentalism; that's sustainability. It's not just showing pictures of turtles with straws up the nose. It's showing how people who are making our goods are polluting our waterways with clothing dye, and now communities don't have access to clean, potable water. They have higher incidences of cancer and asthma; higher rates of morbidity and mortality.

Dr. Ayanna Elizabeth Johnson,[6] a climate activist, talks about the fact that all things are designed. The built environment is design. Anything outside of policy is a physical thing someone had to make.

A former student, Jasmine K. Burton, who earned a master's in global health talks and founded *Wish for Wash*,[7] talks about her intersectional practice as an Afro-Indigenous woman. Her identity gives her some currency and privilege as she moves and works in the global sector, because she resembles the communities she enters; and so she's able to engage in much more authentic conversations. She also has the cultural sensitivity to not assume a lot of things; doesn't see her work as a designer as reinforcing her beliefs on a group; and is therefore a much better listener. In terms of designing for sanitation, she is committed to reducing cholera in communities that are suffering, but she's also sensitive to cultural nuances. Pooping in public is not taboo in some societies. So she's designed a way for them to do that while reducing the incidence of cholera. As an undergrad, she developed and prototyped a compostable toilet system that launched her entire career.[8]

That sanitation work overlaps with women's health, which overlaps with epidemiology, which overlaps with communities of color, race, pollution, all those things. So she had a very intersectional approach to design.

JR: I wanted to make sure we circled back to the element of trust and the fact of her being visibly multiethnic, which allows her to blend into spaces and perhaps forge connections with others through *her* otherness.

RS: It's about building trust with community, which I think everyone wants a strategy for. In design, you can do these seventeen steps or you can just come from that community. You know what I mean? Like there's all these things that you can maybe do to make yourself more authentic and take a care-informed sort of approach, or you can have some lived experience that connects automatically.

JR: I think part of what we're saying is that we actually don't want white designers to copy the practices of Black or Indigenous designers like Jasmine Burton. We need more

people like her, like us—Black, brown, Indigenous, people of color, immigrants—doing this work. Our identities are a part of how we are making connection. Not because of how we look—it's not a Rachel Dolezal thing about "looking Black" and therefore being able to blend into intersectional spaces. It's having an intersectional experience, which brings insight into the nuances of cultural difference and cultural expression.

RS: Yes. People want to know how to put it on, which, I get because, you know, is the choice to leave the profession and not do the work at all? No, there are definitely people that you do connect with. There's a whole globe, right? It's just that there are conversations that you are not going to be able to have at the same level unless something in the way you grew up, the way that you identify, the way you're treated, where you lived, your regional, ethnic, racial, religious, gender experience informs how you live in this world. You cannot replace the overlaps and experiences.

You also have to know that there is no monolithic experience. As a Black woman, I know that other Black women don't experience the same things as I do. Other people see Black women as a model with the group. And when they're designing for Black women, it's for all Black women. Whereas I know if I was designing for a Black woman, I'm going to be talking with my very specific point of view. And if you don't have any experience with that at all, then it's impossible for you to truly develop that empathy.

Empathy is not compassion. You can care for someone, but you may not ever really feel what they feel. Right. In some design spaces, especially in the design for disability or accessibility space, people have developed tools to simulate experiences. But if you're born blind, you have figured out how to be blind for, like, the last thirty years. Designers walking around simulating blindness—they're terrible at being blind. That blind person is really good at it. That lived experience over years—the treatment, the education, the social stigma—that's part of the experience, as well. So maybe simulating the physical experience gets you to ask better questions and listen more, but you cannot call that empathy. That might be understanding. You can talk about people who use a wheelchair, and maybe you can relate to it in terms of a temporary injury, which anyone might have, right? Maybe you were skateboarding and BAM, what happened? "Oh, I got hit by a car and broke my leg." Suddenly, "Oh, now I see, because when I was faking it, I really didn't get it." But so many other things came up once they were actually living through it.

JR: In a way there's a temporal lens you're applying to this, which is that putting on an identity temporarily is a
limitation to anyone's capacity for true empathy. There's a significant

difference between masquerading as a character and living through a life, day by day by day by day. When we talk about micro aggressions, for example, I wonder if people who don't experience them just can't fathom what it's like to be asked hundreds of times over a lifetime, "What are you?," "No, where are you really from?," or told, "You're so articulate."

RS: Yes. One of my mentees, Danielle C., who was a grad-
             uate student of mine, was very vocal on bias and race
in design. She's Chinese, been here for eight years. She said that coming from a majority country, she just really felt the need to assimilate. But here in the US, she was othered pretty quickly and that experience led to her finding friendships with other "othered" students—like Muslim or other Asian American students. It eventually opened her eyes to the racial experience in the United States. At the same time, she almost felt like she could not talk about her own othering, because she didn't really understand that there was a racial stigma around being Asian unless you're foreign. She thought it was a foreign thing. Like, if you're from China and you have an accent. So the response is, "I'm going to have to get an American accent." Or the name. "I'm going to change my name. I'm going to do these things so that I can assimilate." But that difference feels tied to foreignness.

             Recently she admitted to me that when she was work-
ing on my "Black Girl S.T.E.A.M. Through Dance" project, she initially didn't understand the significance of it from an identity standpoint. Why was it so important for my research team to reflect the girls who were participating in it? When she had the opportunity to talk to someone as a mentor and help them navigate something, she realized that that connection with people, it wasn't just about caring for someone and just wanting to help, but that working closely with someone who reflects some part of our identity is going to be a connection. It's deeper. And part of that was forming a community out of being othered.

             That also requires people to admit their vulnerabilities
and get to know one another.

JR: You saying that makes me wonder the extent to which
             so many of us are living in a state of constant anxiety
and or trauma—for so many different reasons—and how we're not actu-ally hearing each other in our individual traumas.

RS: There are so many hidden things about people that you
             just can't tell.

JR: As professionals, though, we're also taught to be neutral or objective, to not get personal. Leadership is framed as a way of performing empathy while sitting above everyone else. Maybe we need to rethink that model. From a climate justice and design perspective, shouldn't we all take that deeply personally?

TIME IN THE PROCESS

JR: I'd like to go back to something you said early about sustainability being taught in an essentialist or reductive way—like, "reduce reuse recycle" or "save the polar bears." We strip away complexity in order to brand it, and for the sake of efficiency. Like calorie counting, which reduces eating to data consumption—decentering health or joy in and with one's body.

Education does this when it preferences the consumption of knowledge and the efficiencies of time (a unit, a semester, a graduation date) over all else. So even in art and design school, we're often churning students through without giving them time or space to sink deep into the complexities of their curiosities. Maybe we need more open-ended curricula that embrace the messiness of learning more honestly.

I keep encountering this weird interpersonal efficiency in design spaces that have become performatively empathetic; where we're asked to introduce ourselves with invitations to talk about our identities (which is almost always, as my friends Liz Jackson and Alex Haagaard refer to it as "Oppression Olympics"). We've mechanized getting to know one another because we've built interpersonal scarcity into the process. When you're focused on knowing quickly, making efficiently, presenting slickly, how can you get to know people, including yourself? By building efficiency into the process of being human with each other, we're only able to deal with the surface aspects of our identities and experiences. And if you're from an historically marginalized community, that often looks like becoming a representative for everyone in your identity group. You've got to be the woman on a project because you're the only woman in the room; and therefore you're the stand-in for what all women need, want, and do. You're the only Black person so you have to stand in for all things that are Black. It's a wickedly essentialist view.

RS: I think that that's the crux of it, but also that means that people who *are* living through multiple intersections of identity are probably just going to be better designers to begin with. Or better educators. Because you're not going to dismiss when you're confronted with those things, that's what I've seen.

What makes me the maddest is how dismissive people can be about other people's experiences. When confronted with information that makes people uncomfortable, they dismiss that as, "Why should I care about that?" But that dismissiveness goes in multiple directions.

An old classmate of mine from Georgia Tech, when Trump won in 2016 and everybody got on Facebook because they couldn't stand talking to people, I had this one guy who was always the devil's advocate, in the middle, independent. Since when we were President Scholars at Georgia Tech—and we were a small group of us, and he was the Aaron Burr of the group, never wanted to pick a side, saying, "There are nuances." So he was trying to explain through these posts on Facebook, that he totally saw Trump winning because he saw that everybody is so stuck in their own communities. He said, "Black people don't live in most of America. They literally don't give a shit about you or know about you or not even hate you or not hate you. They form no opinion. There are people who are suffering and are very, very poor who are in the middle of America. And Donald Trump said that he was going to save them the same way that you were looking for someone to save you. And even though the majority of the wealth is held by white people, majority of white people are poor." And our reaction was, "Stop making us be empathetic! Fuck those people. They voted for a racist." And he was like, "I'm trying to explain to you that they don't see themselves as racist. They don't know you. They have never had to see or interact with you. You'd never been in their grocery stores. You're not in their neighborhoods. But they don't have their lights on. They're also on welfare. They also are losing their jobs." At the time I didn't want to hear him tell me to be empathetic to people who I see as having privilege. They saw the conversations of privilege as erasing their experiences. They looked at data and did not see themselves reflected in it.

And so I remember, I was like, "Oh, I am being dismissive of the experiences of people who are vulnerable." Because if they were in my community, they would have more privilege than me. If I was in their community, I would be subjected to harm. But that's not the reality. Look, when we said they're uneducated, we'd say they're backward. We say, they're racist. We say all these things. And he's like, you don't really know them. And I was like, you're right. We don't know them.

But I also don't think it's my job based on my position in society as a Black woman to use my emotional energy to try to get to know the plights of poor white people. Privileged and middle-class white people need to go deal with those people and try to educate them, because I'm not going out to befriend the Ku Klux Klan, like the guy who's getting posted over and over again. I'm like, no, no, no, not interested. I'm fine over here.

RACE IN THE ACADEMIC WORKPLACE

JR: **Can you train the racism out of people? The idea of diversity training is another smokescreen to make institutions feel like they're doing something. But actually they're using the least effective conduit for change, which is to say words. Saying the things that you hope will lead to change versus actually examining and dismantling structural inequities. It's not about the individual who feels one way or the other who sees one way or the other; it's the larger structures that allow their feelings to actually do harm to people.**

RS: Whenever I work with DEI people—like HR or the officers that do trainings around campus—they always talk about this idea of thinking about your own privilege and thinking about other people and trying to be empathetic. And I was like, this is a Black woman you're talking to. Why do I have to be empathetic with a racist? I don't want to be nice to a racist. I'm out. I don't want to do this exercise with them. I don't want to play the other side. You can talk to all these white faculty members about this, or at least all these white men. Talk to **them**.

They want me to try to get in the mindset of a white guy. But I've been in their mindset my entire life through every piece of media in history, academic texts, and everything that I've ever seen my entire life. I don't care to put any more energy and to try and understand their perspective. They need to do work. "Can I go back to work now? Because I don't need to be in this meeting."

And I would get triggered by questions like, "What are microaggressions? How can all these things be microaggressions?" I was like, I'm not here for this. It's like, I **am** the diversity equity inclusion. I do not need to sit through this training.

JR: **The work you're doing with your students, regardless of where they're coming from, these individual interactions are the spaces where the relationships, not the words, are affecting some kind of change.**

RS: Bake it into everything. It should not be special. When I teach professional practice, I'll intentionally invite women as the guest speakers. It's like, how many women of color can I get? I won't point it out to the students. I let the students figure it out. And I don't ask the guests to talk about being women or women of color. The truth is they always bring up identity at some level, and how it's affected their career path or their practice.

It's about centering the work of a diverse group of people with diverse perspectives; as opposed to inviting them to share their work, and then pointing out, "this is special." It should not be a special time of month. That should not be a special time of year.

I'll bring in men to talk during women's history month. We have conversations about sustainability, beyond Earth Day. If you distribute these conversations across as wide a swath of time, in as many different classes as you can, it doesn't become about the students signing up for Black history class or a Black art history class or Black design class. We can have an African art design class, but you should also be talking about African art or artists and designers anyway. I shouldn't blink that I see Japanese or Iranian on the curriculum because who cares where they came from, if that's something that you wish to bond to aesthetically.

CONSIDERING AN ANTI-HEGEMONIC CURRICULUM

JR: **I hear you saying that if you are intentional and anti-hegemonic about the prompts, you can get people to see things beyond the canon.**

RS: Industrial design doesn't really have a strong canon, unless you want to say Dieter Rams but I didn't find out who he was until I was in my thirties. I'll be honest with you. I was like, "Oh, I've seen that record player before. Not my style. But oh, is that why all the Apple products looked like that?"

I think that that's a benefit to my profession is we're terrible at writing anything about it. There's not a lot to compete against.

IDEO's definition of design thinking as it has been disseminated and distilled and made digestible for the masses is probably one of the more harmful things.[9] As the hallmark approach to how you do design, packaged up in a way, it's not true. [Before the human-centered design method was developed], it was the Wild West. Designers were open to all sorts of methods. They would just make up on the fly. Like, "I'm going to go work at a hospital and get more experience doing that." So that's what you'd go and do. But now it's all dictated and packaged, and there are prompts and frameworks that people rely on. And then they only look at a certain lens of them as opposed to looking at the diversity of ones that are most appropriate for the context of the community that you're designing for that. That may be more harmful than any canon because it is the loudest voice in the room. And it's been exported globally, so if I think about how design is sort of colonizing the practices of everyone else, it is through "Design Thinking."

It does work for some folks. But there's also a lot of harm and trauma in that. There needs to be a range and diversity of approaches. Why do we have to name them [as branded methodologies]? We have this need to name and label people and processes and things. As a result, there's less trust in the messiness of exploring, learning, doing the research, trying an entirely different approach. As an educator, I have a process. I have to do these five things to make sure that I'm doing it right. But that's my particular process; I can't foist it on everyone else.

For example, I have a student who wants to understand people's reactions to morbidity and death, because she wanted to rethink the American way of dying. That was her thesis project. And so she built a "How do you want to die" booth. She spent weeks making this big, black booth and she was behind a curtain. She went into a public park every weekend for a month. And she approached people, saying, "talk to me about how you want to die." "I'm pumped talking about death." And it was amazing. You're not going to find [the instructions to do] that in a book. She was creating conversations and collecting really rich data, getting stories about people's reactions to it morbidity and their own mortality.

It goes back to the essentialist view, which is that you do these things in order to reap some reward for yourself. That you go through these steps, follow all the rules, get the end goal, send it out for an award, get acknowledged for it; and if you're really well connected, then you become famous within your field. Get on a TED Talk. There's a ladder that has been predefined.

But the intersectional piece of it and the positionality of it is that if you were coming with a certain amount of sensitivity to "who am I in the space of this question?" and "Who am I as a designer," "What am I trying to learn by doing this work?" Not how do I get famous doing it, but how do I learn something in the process of doing this, then you can be more honest and authentic about how you're asking the question and then people are more willing to talk to you.

NOTES

1. Intersectional Environmentalist,
   Instagram:@intersectionalenvironmentalist.
2. Phyllis M. Taylor Center for Social Innovation and
   Design Thinking, Tulane University, March 26, 2021,
   taylor.tulane.edu/design-thinking/breakfasts/raja-
   schaar/.
3. The Editors, "Prince and His Fashion Revolution,"
   Rolling Stone, April 22, 2016.
4. Dayton, Adrian, "The Power of Twitter to Turn
   a Terrible Superhero Film from Bad to Good:
   #releasethesnydercut," *Forbes*, March 15, 2021; and
   Twitter: #releasethesnydercut twitter.com/hashtag/
   releasethesnydercut.
5. Butler, Octavia. *Parable of the Sower* (1993) and
   Parable of the Talents (1998), New York: Four
   Walls Eight Windows. A third book, *Parable of the
   Trickster*, was incomplete at the author's death in
   2006.
6. Conant, Ericka, "With each year, California inches
   closer to Octavia Butler's science fiction," *Al Dia*,
   August 24, 2020; and Onion, Rebecca, "Why So Many
   Readers are Turning to Octavia Butler's Apocalypse
   Fiction Right Now," *Slate*, September 19, 2020.
7. Writings by Dr. Ayanna Elizabeth Johnson,
   ayanaelizabeth.com/writing
8. Burton, Jasmine, Devika Patel, Grace Landry, Sarah
   M. Anderson, and Emma Rary. "Failure of the "Gold
   Standard: The Role of a Mixed Methods Research
   Toolkit and Human-Centered Design in Transformative
   WASH." *Environmental Health Insights* 15 (2021):
   11786302211018391.
9. Myke Johns, "Refugee Relief: Tech Designers Bring New
   Toilet to Kenya," *City Cafe*, *WABE* (8:02), July 30,
   2014. wabe.org/refugee
   -relief-tech-designers-bring-new-toilet-kenya/.
10. Buzon, Darin. "Design Thinking Is a Rebrand for White
    Supremacy," *Medium*, March 2, 2020. dabuzon.medium.
    com/design-thinking-is-a-rebrand-for-white-supremacy-
    b3d31aa55831.

RESOURCES

Some of Raja's top follows: a cluster of folks who
are slightly nerdy, really fun or seem to be fun, are
passionate about sustainability, and have done a good job
at relating to people.

1. Robert Bullard, "Father of Environmental Justice" and
   Emeritus professor at Texas Southern University. Web:
   drrobertbullard.com/.
2. Ayanna Elizabeth Johnson, Marine biologist based
   in Atlanta, former co-host of *How To Save a Planet*
   podcast, Instagram: @how2saveaplanet.
3. Jasmine K. Burton, Wish for Wash. Web: jasminekburton
   .com/.
4. Chandra Farley, LinkedIn: linkedin.com/in/
   chandrafarley/.
5. The Intersectional Environmentalist, Instagram: @
   intersectionalenvironmentalist.

AFROFUTURISM
IN DESIGN

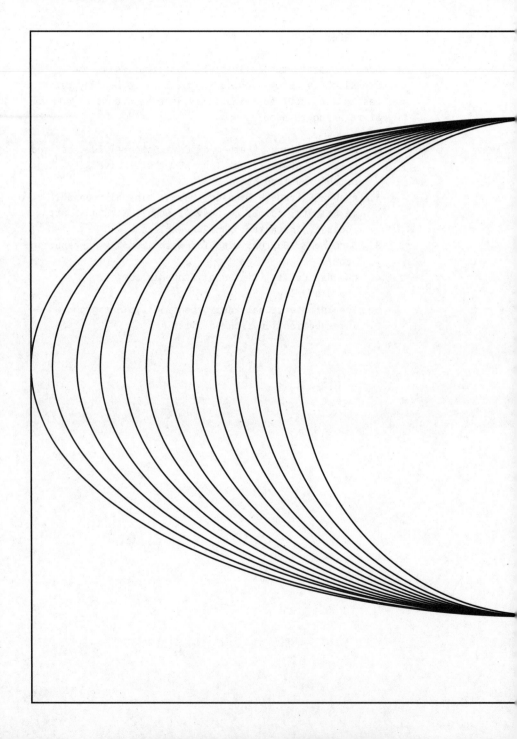

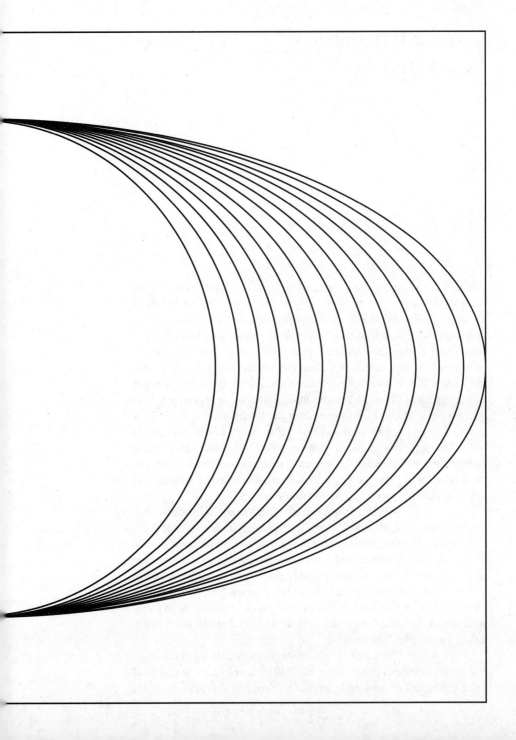

AFROFUTURISM IN DESIGN

Chapter Introduction:
Lesley Ann-Noel

While other people may have had an interest in Afrofuturism that spans decades, my own interest seems only to go back as far as the *Black Panther* movie, released in 2018. Before *Black Panther*, speculative fiction and science fiction had not drawn me in. In *Black Panther*, I, like millions of other people of the African diaspora, could finally see myself. *Black Panther* also helped me take note of other examples of diversity in sci-fi that I had not noticed before, such as the diversity of *Star Trek*, and other genres of futurism such as Chicanafuturism and Asianfuturism, and it underscored the absence of plurality in many depictions of the future.

For this section, we invited contributions from people who are doing exciting work that is connected to Afrofuturism. It is a chance to hear firsthand from Black thought leaders like Lonny Avi Brooks, Woodrow W. Winchester III, John Jennings, Adah Parris, and Folayemi Wilson, all of whom combine design, futurism, and their Black identities.

For Dr. Lonny Avi Brooks, focusing on the future empowers him to imagine, play, and reflect. Through play, Dr. Brooks uses Black storytelling and imagination to challenge oppression and expand notions of what is possible in the future. In his essay, he remarks on how members of BIPOC communities are overlooked in global futures practices, noting that less than 2 percent of professional futurists are Black or indigenous people of color. In his essay, Dr. Brooks shares how he has created a game, Afro-Rithms from the Future, which centers BIPOC imagination to reveal solution spaces for BIPOC issues.

Woodrow W. Winchester III, begins his essay by noting the disproportionate impact of the COVID-19 pandemic on communities of color, calling for new designerly ways of thinking and acting. He proposes engaging Afrofuturism to create a more inclusive technological future, through a framework called BCD (Black-centered Design). In focusing on the needs of Black people when designing technological innovations, in the view of Winchester, all people will be better served, since addressing the needs of marginalized groups will then also meet the needs of dominant groups.

John Jennings's work centers around the narratives that intersect across identity politics and popular media. Jennings opens his section pointing out the paradox in the popularity of the genre of Afrofuturism and specific works like *Black Panther*, when the reality is that this world historically devalued Black life. Jennings traces the history of Afrofuturism, and the lack of references to people of color in seminal works about speculative fiction and sci-fi. He opens his essay with a reflective quote by Sun Ra, "The Impossible attracts me because, everything's already been done, and the world didn't change." He closes the essay by challenging Black designers to be drawn to the impossible, by reimagining stories about race and mitigating the damage that these visual stories have done to Black people. He suggests that Afrofuturism can support us as we do this necessary work.

While Afrofuturism examines the future through a lens that addresses the injustice of four hundred years of oppression, which is the experience of people of African descent in the Americas, Adah Parris, a futurist and cultural innovator, prefers to use an Africanfuturist approach to create a generative and transformative framework of guiding principles for life. Africanfututurism is centered deeply in African culture and world-views and in the views of some decenters whiteness and the Western gaze more effectively than Afrofuturism.

Parris creates a framework of five guiding principles or questions for every Black designer as they move through their worlds and plan for the future. The question "what kind of ancestors do we want to be?" becomes her golden rule. She draws on her African (Igbo), Guyanese (Amerindian), Black British experiences and cultural traditions as a starting point for her design process. She asks other Black designers: how can we use our genealogical and ancestral knowledge and wisdom to our advantage?

In her work, Folayemi Wilson celebrates the Black imagination as a technology of resistance and self-determination. In her essay, we get a glimpse into the many factors that have built her version of Afrofuturism. In her youth, she engaged in practices that expanded her spiritual self and connected her to a universal consciousness, such as meditation and African cosmology. She became aware of nonlinear time as a framework for Afrofuturism; and through visits to Nigeria where she learned about Yoruba history, becoming more embedded in an African-centered worldview, and she uses this in her practice today.

The five contributors have been influenced by Afrofuturism and Africanfuturism in different ways. Winchester, Brooks, Jennings, and Parris note the absence of Black people and the general lack of representation of people of color in the field of futures. These contributors appeal to designers, and people in general, to use the generative and culturally situated nature of Afrofuturism and variations of the genre to imagine new and equitable futures and technologies, to un-design racism and oppression, and to mitigate the harm of a society that is not designed for Black people.

From Algorithms

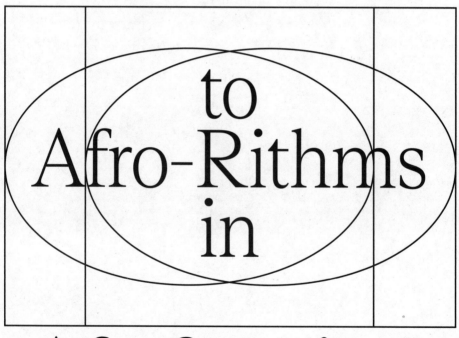

to Afro-Rithms in

Afrofuturism

LONNY AVI BROOKS

Our Black, Indigenous, and People of Color (BIPOC) communities require tools to imagine and create engaging futures. Picture never seeing yourself in visions of the future and infrequently even as Black superheroes. Less than 2 percent of professional futurists are BIPOC. Globally, futures practices rarely consider BIPOC communities unless they are tied to corporate-oriented consumerism. Future visions of healthcare traditionally have rarely addressed race and gender, instead erasing core identities along with sacred ancestral community knowledge.

Afro-Rithms From The Future, a game centering BIPOC imagination, generates artifacts from the future—amplifying community futures to reveal solution spaces for BIPOC issues. As a forecasting game, *Afro-Rithms From The Future* suggests that by changing the traditional white, patriarchal normative gaze of racism and lens through which we usually view the world, we aim to change the societal "game;" we aim to expand alternative perceptions of the world through Black and BIPOC perspectives, where Black and BIPOC futures are central and where they matter. The term *Afro-Rithms* intentionally acknowledges the leading editing role that algorithms have attained, especially on our social media platforms. We want to acknowledge the ubiquity of algorithms in our lives and ensure that Black diasporic and Africana perspectives shape and create new algorithms to expand the aperture of cultural perspectives within our digital society. *Afro-Rithms From The Future* shifts our digital lens away from one that usually reinforces and perpetuates dominant inequities, and offers new lenses that enable us to expand our range of possible and more equitable, liberating multiverses. In *Race After Technology: Abolitionist Tools For the New Jim Code*, Ruha Benjamin refers to the persistent bias in algorithms as the "new Jim Code, the employment of new technologies that reflect and reproduce existing inequities but that are promoted and perceived as more objective or progressive than the discriminatory systems of a previous era."[1]

Afro-Rithms is designed to counter the new Jim code with algorithms of liberation.

Before we describe the *Afro-Rithms* game itself, we want to provide a detailed overview of the developmental journey to create and facilitate the game with Afrofuturism in mind. In the spirit of Sankofa, the wisdom of honoring and recovering our ancestral intelligence, we seek to wake up from the colonial amnesia that was purposefully imposed upon the Black diaspora to make us forget who we are and steal our superpowers. As Amos White, the poet and entrepreneur, points out, our Vibranium, that interstellar metal that Wakanda continually mines to fuel its secret technological advancement globally, is a metaphor for the spirituals that Black slaves created to spark their imagination for an uncolonized body and mind. These spirituals served the double consciousness of our enslaved ancestors, both helping them find their own religious freedom and serving as guides, secret codes, and recipes for rebellious escapes out of slavery. Spirituals as future scenarios are the vibranium with which we can reframe and transform the narrow spheres of influence where corporate algorithms are born toward where these algorithms become reborn as *Afro-Rithms With Soul From The Future*.

Afrofuturism combines speculative and science fiction with fantasy to reexamine how the future is currently imagined, and to reconstruct futures thinking with a deeper insight into the Black experience, especially as slavery forced Africans to confront an alien world surrounded by colonial technologies.[2] Afrofuturism is born out of cruelty, and that cruelty of the white imagination was a necessary condition out of which the African diaspora had to reimagine its future. Rhetorically, Afrofuturism aims to reclaim and transform the trauma of past atrocities against the Black and Afro-queer diaspora. Think of the Middle Passage as a science fiction horror where Black people were transported from western Africa, the home planet of the Black diaspora, and where previously unseen technologies of transportation and bondage were used to dislocate and kidnap large numbers of people to a new world.[3] In this world, they had to innovate, adapt, capitulate, succumb, and rebuild their former lives and traditions. The *Black Panther* comics, for example, reflect an Afrofuturist reimagining of African futures through its superhero T'Challa and the technologically advanced and secret nation of Wakanda.[4] The white cruelty ironically served as the pathway to Afrofuturism and the imagining of more powerful futures for the Black diaspora.

Now, in the aftermath of the Age of Trump, we are confronted with a resurgence of patriarchal authority that seeks to deny and reverse advances in civil rights and restore a time where everyone knew their place in the hierarchy of white supremacy.[5] Our current present recapitulates in part the cruelty of the last centuries, and demands that we recreate stronger alternative futures. Imagining new futures can serve as a strategy to understand the nature of cruelty, and how we negotiate with cruel acts as constitutive of our greatest aspirations. As Giorgio Baruchello states, "embracing the cruel character of existence might serve itself as a precondition for any meaningful life to be lived."[6] I argue that affirming pathways that use cruelty against itself can function as a fulcrum to reduce its trauma. In this essay, I integrate Afrofuturism and game studies as a pathway and route toward supplanting cruelty and reducing the space it occupies. Specifically, I discuss the use of game jams to bring into existence new artifacts and strategies to embrace cruel truths while amplifying and developing better futures.

The game jam is an event in which game developers, made up of designers, artists, and social scientists, from amateur to professional, get together, develop a game, and release it in an extremely short period. A relatively recent phenomenon dating to 2002, game jams take:

> *an outcome that is so extraordi-*
> *narily positive you had no idea it*
> *was even possible until you achieved*
> *it . . . it was almost beyond the*
> *threshold of imagination and when you*
> *get there you are shocked to discover*
> *what you are truly capable of.*[7]

The epic win forms the pathway to rewire our minds to reframe and diminish the debilitating aspects of cruelty that constrain us.

Afrofuturist stories offer counterstrategies to cruelty. Octavia Butler's *Parable of the Sower* (1993), for example, represents an Afrofuturist tale set in the 2020s amid a dystopic backdrop of climate change, increased wealth disparity, and hypercorporate reach.[8] The protagonist of this parable, Lauren Oya Olamina, develops her gift for hyperempathy and sharing. Living in a gated community in Los Angeles, her family is attacked and murdered, leaving Lauren to form a new community born from her newfound power and religious awakening. She is a "sharer," one who senses people's pain and sensations. Her pain becomes a conduit to creating a new religion she dubs Earthseed. In this manner, the chaos of world events and the subsequent murder of Lauren's family become a call to provide a painful, new beginning and a new future. Cruelty in its traditional definition means the "callous indifference to or pleasure in causing pain and suffering" of others.[9] Baruchello states how "cruelty possesses a tragic dimension, i.e., that cruelty may only be reduced and not eliminated in toto. We might even want to avoid its extensive elimination as a desirable goal, for there may be cruelties capable of enriching life."[10]

The main character in *Parable of the Sower*, Lauren, addresses the victims and the nature of cruelty by offering a pathway toward alternative futures. She updates biblical themes by proclaiming how:

> *a victim of God may, through adapta-*
> *tion, become a partner of God. A victim*
> *of God may, through forethought and*
> *planning, become a shaper of God. Or*
> *a victim of God may, through short-*
> *sightedness and fear, Remain God's*
> *victim, God's plaything, God's prey.*[11]

Butler's is part of a lineage in the Black diasporic traditions where the cruelty of bondage and murder become portholes of redemption. In reimagining what God means in terms of an Afrofuturist perspective, we can understand the role that the nonwhite imagination can play as a pathway to new potential among cruel surroundings. Butler's tale reflects processes of a double consciousness that have inhabited Black slaves and emancipated culture for centuries; the ability to evoke and find new affordances (openings) and empowered meanings alongside cruel impositions and dislocations. W. E. B. Du Bois describes this double entendre and how it forces Black people to see themselves "through the revelations of the other world. It is a peculiar sensation, this double-consciousness, this sense of always looking at one's self through the eyes of others."[12]

Simultaneously, this cruelty allows and enables a second sight in having to create new healing psalms, rhythms, and salves from scratch, from threads of torn ancestral remembrances from the crossing of the Middle Passage.

According to Gina Neff and Peter Nagy, imagined affordances reflect the imagined uses, values, and expectations users have about technology compared with what designers intended,[13] a similar process that already reflects what the Black diaspora has had long practice in honing. For my purposes, imagined affordances enable Black people in the diaspora to strive for more within the hostile environments that have accompanied slavery and its traumatic aftermath. I expand the term here to discuss how Black people and other marginalized groups have had to embed their environment on a daily basis with imagined affordances to see and expect more from the cultural artifacts and tools than was intended by their original designers, or in the Black diasporic case, our captors and enslavers. For example, imagined affordances include Black cultural technologies such as music, where the hymns of imposed Christianity became the odes of freedom and the seeds of rebellion. Imagined affordances thus include visions for what Black people might expect from our technological landscapes, and see within them the unintended uses and values which white male engineers at major computer and media companies usually ignore.

Game design and Afrofuturist scholars argue that the design and implementation of new digital media, from game jams and Black and Queer game aesthetics to podcasts, can function as cognitive prosthetics to transform cruelty and helplessness into redemptive action and empowering futures. The resilience of the Black diaspora holds clues to building alternative futures in the midst of cruel strangers. This mental agility leads us to consider recent work of neuropolitics,[14] a "framework that allows us to reimagine culture, power, and political subjectivity in the light of our increasing knowledge about the human brain and extended mind."[15] Neuroscience research and its study of the brain offer insight into learning and memory, and into designing our organizations to support our mental development.

In defining *neuropolitics*, Jake Dunagan calls for the need "to create alternative memories of the future"[16] and exhorts us to create designer imagination environments. For the Black diaspora, this focus intersects with the soul of Black speculative history where, as Kodwo Eshun argues,

> *Afrofuturism may be characterized as a program for recovering the histories of counter-futures created in a century hostile to Afrodiasporic projection and as a space within which the critical work of manufacturing tools capable of intervention within the current political dispensation may be undertaken.*[17]

Game jams can rework our memories by creating new scenes and new futures that jam and renew positive associative pathways. They create a space in which participants can reinterpret prior memories in the service of the forgotten histories and the counter futures we aim to recover. I view game jams as a call for a futures therapy of the mind to jam epigenetics of trauma. As we stand in the twilight zone of horror, where regressive political policies reassert their ugly grip, Black speculative pathways offer more than hope. We can leverage the powerful insights of neuropolitics to provide the cognitive basis for our own liberating Afrofuturescape.

In scanning and imagining new signals to assert new empowering Afrofuturetypes, tools such as game jams can facilitate novel memories of Black alternative futures that step beyond dystopias. We call these signals *Afrofuturetypes*. Lisa Nakamura coined the term cybertype "to describe the distinctive ways that the Internet propagates, disseminates, and commodifies images of race and racism."[18] *Afrofuturetypes* extend her work to include Afrofuturist visions of new imagined Black political actors/subjects. Simultaneously, Afrofuturetypes act as a basis for critiquing current images of the future circulating as science fiction capital in popular culture. Afrofuturetypes allows us to interrogate and reimagine these images with greater nuance and with the mindful agency of Black and other marginalized groups in mind.

THE THING FROM THE FUTURE: A MINORITY REPORT 2054 EXPERIMENTAL GAME JAM SESSION

In March 2017, we held an experimental game jam session with about five predominately female and minority students and two faculty members (Ian Pollock, director of the interaction design graduate program and game jam facilitator and myself as Afrofuturist and game jam facilitator), at California State University, East Bay, located in Hayward, California. In the session, we reimagined a popular forecasting card game known as the *The Thing from the Future*.[19] Designed by Stuart Candy and Jeff Watson, *The Thing from the Future* makes imagining the future accessible to a wider audience. While the game is successful in making the future accessible and provocative, we wanted to add greater elements of the Black and minority imagination to its design, using the game as a springboard to create and repurpose board games that address Afrofuturist perspectives. In this manner, forecast gaming addresses the possibilities for intervention into the present by reflecting on possible Black futures. With four undergraduate students, one graduate student, and two professors, we hacked up *The Thing from the Future* to infuse it with the Black vernacular.

By walking through the object of the game and the topics the game cards name and offer, we transformed **The** *Thing from the Future* into **Our** *Thing from the Future* with the techno-vernacular of the Black Fantastic imprinted into the nomenclature and labels as the central focus of the card deck. *Our Thing from the Future* represents our portal, our voice and Afrofuturescape.

The object of the game is to come up with the most entertaining and thought-provoking descriptions of hypothetical objects from different near-, medium-, and long-term futures. During each round, players collectively generate a creative prompt by playing a card game. This prompt outlines the kind of future that the thing-to-be-imagined comes from, specifies what part of society or culture it belongs to, describes the type of object that it is, and suggests an emotional reaction that it might spark in an observer from the present. Players must then write a short description of an object that fits the constraints of the prompt. These descriptions are read aloud (without attribution), and players vote on which description they find the most interesting, provocative, or funny. The winner of each round keeps the cards put into play for that round, and whoever has the most cards when the game ends is declared the overall winner.[20]

Four types of cards compose *Our Thing from the Future:* Arc, Terrain, Object, and Mood. Each round, players generate a four-card creative prompt containing one of each kind of card. Based on this prompt, players will imagine a thing from the future, describe it, and sketch it. Thus, players have the chance to engage in an artistic rendering of their imagined object. We can then use player images as Afroscapes into new times and reframe how time might operate as well.

Arc cards broadly describe different kinds of possible futures. These cards contain two kinds of information. The main text of each Arc card specifies one of four generic images of alternative futures for players to imagine: Grow, Collapse, Discipline, or Transform. A time horizon—a specific segment of time projected into the future—accompanies each Arc card and scenario. Time horizons for the game include a half decade ahead, a decade in the future, a generation from now, a half century to a century ahead, to imagining a full millennium into the future.

James (Jim) Dator, director of the Hawaii Research Center for Future Studies at the University of Hawaii at Manoa, defines the Grow card as:

> *"Continued growth," the "official"*
> *view of the future of all modern*
> *governments, educational systems, and*
> *organizations. The purpose of govern-*
> *ment, education, and all aspects of*
> *life in the present and recent past,*
> *is to build a vibrant economy, and*
> *to develop the people, institutions,*
> *and technologies to keep the econ-*
> *omy growing and changing, forever.*[21]

Of all of the scenarios, Growth represents growing optimism as well. Candy and Watson condense Dator's scenario possibilities in their forecasting game *The Thing from the Future* by describing the scenario Collapse as a kind of future in which life as we know it has fallen—or is falling—apart. Discipline is a kind of future in which things are carefully managed by concerted coordination, perhaps top-down or perhaps collaboratively. Transform is a kind of future in which a profound historical transition has occurred, whether spiritual or technological in nature.

The remaining cards intend to materialize the thing from the future in more concrete terms by describing one's imagined object from the future, its context, and the mood it generates based in the present.

During our experimental session, each participating student was given a combination of the cards as an introduction to the game. Our intention was to ask ourselves what was missing from the categories and labels of subjects in the Object, Terrain, Mood, and Arc cards. Infusing and re-speaking Mood terms developed rapidly from Black sonic vernacular. Beyoncé transformed into a new card as a Mood for being unapologetic about being a Black woman while simultaneously moving through restorative steps for justice and forgiveness. Kanye West's persona represented a Mood for quixotic defiance. One African American female student suggested "sex" as a Mood, moving it from the category of Terrain.

The group of students noticed terms absent from the Terrain pile, including immigration, diaspora, race, protest, gay, lesbian, public transport, Black tax, privilege, secondary screening, diversity, rave, borders, justice, transgender, and alien abduction. Their inclusion implies different possible futures outside of a traditional male and white patriarchy, and helps to define an Afrofuturist domain that looks to the cultural periphery and marginalized groups for newfound visions.

Object terms missed vital elements of Black practices and local items, such as "handbag." One of the most prominent lyrics from Beyoncé's "Lemonade" reminds us that "the past and present merge to meet us here/what are you hidin'/why can't you see me?"[22] The handbag, with its hot sauce that becomes a baseball bat, shows unrestrained anger that, several stages later, eventually re-embraces love.

The Arc card became another terrain of contested time where we debated the game's bias toward linear conceptions of futures thinking. We shifted its standpoint to behave more similarly to principles of quantum computing and the central idea of superposition. Quantum computing represents ambiguity, the ability "to be" and "not to be" simultaneously. We found within quantum computing a powerful metaphor for reframing a conventional forecasting game into a quantum forecasting engine that fulfills the prospect of creating new memories and recovered futures—an Afrofuturescape adapting to a quantum computing state. At the core of the veiled and double consciousness of W. E. B. Du Bois's explication of Black identity[23] resides the simultaneous truth of quantum physics and its confirmation of the imaginative resilience of the Black diaspora to bring into being a myriad of forms of innovative and robust artifacts as shields against and constitutive of cruelty. Black people have always, at some level, had to act as quantum futurists, building and holding multiple truths that sought to annihilate and affirm their existence.

The hacking of *The Thing from the Future* provided a new standpoint and generated a novel game. At the end of the session, we created *Get in Front of the Fake News*, a game that pays homage to protest and incentivized peaceful demonstrations, while protecting their reportage from the online rumor mills of fake news as well as the state-sponsored espionage tactics used to dismantle democratic movements.[24] The game is in further development as a board game, to be distributed by the Multimedia Club at CSUEB. Its rules are:

1. Build a viable protest by joining pieces.
2. Spin the top to point the camera at fake news (to root it out).
3. Intercept the news camera with your protest.
4. Lose protesters if the camera does not get in front of the fake news.

In 2019, after two years of game jam and new human-computer experimentation at a communal computer research lab known as Dynamicland[25] in Oakland, California, Dr. Lonny Brooks and Eli Kosminsky launched the game *Afro-Rithms From The Future.*[26] Dynamicland's researchers describe this space as one deliberately designed to have:

> *No screens, no devices. Just ordinary physical materials—paper and clay, tokens and toy cars—brought to life by technology in the ceiling. Every scrap of paper has the capabilities of a full computer, while remaining a fully-functional scrap of paper.*[27]

We initially created a game in 2018 called *Wakandan Memories of the Future*. Players would wander through a wall sized map of the region of the fictional land of Wakanda from the Black Panther comics and film and imagine the future based on a different region of Wakanda and card prompts developed from *Our Thing from the Future*. Brooks and Kosminsky collaborated to bring Afrofuturist storytelling into a new, communal medium with the intention of helping everyone share their visions of the future: especially those who are not traditionally advantaged by technology. Several game jams and physical prototypes later, *Afro-Rithms From The Future* was born.

While showing *Afro-Rithms* at the Institute for the Future's 2019 AfroFutures Festival, Ahmed Best, co-executive producer and co-host with me on the *Afrofuturist Podcast* was asked to participate in gameplay. Bringing his background as an actor and his work on developing his theories of the emotional storytelling engine, Ahmed became the *Afro-Rithms* MC and Seer, engaging the audience and bringing out stories on a whole new level. From there, the Fathomers worked with the trio to engage new collaborators to further develop the game, including our first artist Alan Clark and graphic designer Paula Te, and to find new venues to present their work, such as the LA NeueHouse. Most recently, the group joined up with the Equitable Games Group to find a way to bring *Afro-Rithms From The Future* into organizations and schools across the country.

RADICAL FUTURES GAMING: A REPARATIONS TATTOO? I THINK YOU JUST WON THE GAME!

The year is 2030, and on a series of clandestine floating islands, the Global Afronet is weaving a tapestry of the future. Each island hosts a unique city, with a single Futurescope at its center. Citizens visit the Futurescope, an enormous structure featuring floors of research labs and art galleries, pierced through the center by a bundle of glowing wires. These wires run throughout the building, eventually converging in an orb that floats atop the building. The collective work and energy of the building diffuses through the orb, creating the perfect setting for citizens of the island to meet and collaborate on visions of the future.

As these visions are produced, they link to the network of stories created by Afro-Futurescopes across the planet, creating a colossal map for an ultimate journey through the Astro-Blackness Plane where we rise above our colonized past and see the full universe.

So begins *Afro-Rithms From The Future*. The game is designed to draw out unexpected possibilities, encourage radical reimagining, and collaboratively produce visions of diverse futures.

Its Afrofuturist imagery reflects Black-centered signals, with alternative visions we call the Black Fantastic, from Richard Iton (2008). Players sense the minor-key sensibilities generated from the underground of radical Black art. Designing a game from this perspective offers a pathway to grapple with notions of inclusion, equality, and liberation. Several Black and BIPOC artists have contributed and shaped the card deck with their pulse on the Black Fantastic of visionary images.

As a whole, the *Afro-Rithms From The Future* game expresses its values through its structure and game rules:

1. *Afro-Rithms From The Future* is a forecasting game that suggests that by changing the traditional white, patriarchal normative gaze of racism and lens through which we usually view the world, we aim to change the societal "game" to expand alternative perceptions of the world through Black and BIPOC perspectives, where Black and BIPOC futures are central and matter.
2. The term Afro-Rithms intentionally focuses on shifting the cultural lens to understand the powerful ubiquity of algorithms in our digital world(s). *Afro-Rithms From The Future* shifts the lens through which we digitally reinforce and perpetuate dominant inequities, enabling us to expand the range of possible, more equitable, liberating multiverses.
3. We not only aim to democratize the future, we intentionally anticipate democratic Anti-Racist Futures and to build resiliency for the formidable challenges to those futures.
4. A central question drives this game: How do we democratize the Future with Afro-Queer AI as the starting point to anticipate, imagine, and create liberating, inclusive futures with multiple forms of intelligences?

Fig. 1

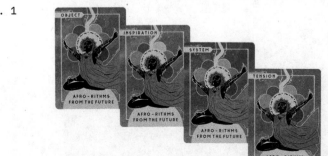

The game is a dynamic, engaging, and safe space for a community to imagine possible worlds using ordinary objects as inspirations to rethink existing organizational, institutional, and societal relationships.

During the AfroFutures Festival at IFTF, where we facilitated a group game session in March 2019, the winner of the game by declaration was a woman who imagined a tattoo that represented one's history and could be scanned to receive reparation funds to redress and heal the trauma of slavery.

Summarizing all the features of the future that the group imagined in that gameplay, Kosminsky said: "Our future has tattoos that store memories and produce reparations from one generation to the next. It has a power glove that can snap away the police. It has infinity stones, and its temperature regulated. It has a Black skirt that cannot be penetrated—it's bulletproof and reflects and amplifies the sounds in the

Fig. 2

surroundings. It has stories that induce deep empathy and self-care and naps. It deconstructs colonialism, especially for women."

The year 2020 has seen the *Afro-Rithms* team pivot to creating a digital version of the game, incorporating past card designs and content to produce an accessible and collaborative gameplay. As in the game's analog counterpart, players are dealt three different card types that help shape the universe created:

1. **Tension Cards** name values, belief systems, and phenomena that can exist on a continuum in society. Think: more or less "Ecotopia," more or less "Black Storytelling," more or less "Magic." Two tension cards will form the parameters or axes of a world that we're going to build.
2. **Inspiration Cards** look at different concepts and aspects of the contemporary world—for instance, "Queer Liberation" or "Biotechnology"—to serve as the foundation to inspire our imagined futures.
3. **Object Cards** describe the basic form of an item or institution from the future. How might "Fashion" or "Transportation" look in ten or a hundred years? Object Cards are paired with Inspiration Cards to generate ideas for **Artifacts** that populate the world described by our Tensions.

While the Minority Report Game Jam was designed to produce games with alternative voices, and visions from BIPOC voices were honored, *Afro-Rithms From The Future* seeks to suffuse our objects from the future with African and Black Diasporic soul.

CONCLUSION

Afrofuturist scholars in particular understand the history of oppressive cruelty exerted upon the Black diaspora as a pathway to the future with indigenous peoples—who have had their lands stolen and who were likewise ripped from their former "planets"—from imaginary Afro-Caribbean nation states to Australian aboriginal films to Native American science fiction seers.[28] We aim to recover counter-futures, to make new memories, and to imagine virtual, augmented, and real spaces. To navigate these tributaries, Black futures yield new, less-familiar terms where we mine for the signals comprising constellations of Afrofuturetypes that yield an expansive Afrofuturescape etched in a forecasting language that sings to us as we toil, embrace, and rise above our own metaphorical equivalents of cruelty.

NOTES

1. Benjamin, Ruha. "Race after Technology: Abolitionist Tools for the New Jim Code." *Social Forces* (2019).

2. Brooks, Lonny Avi. "Playing Minority ForeCaster in Search of Afrofuturism." *Anderson, Reynoldo, and Charles Jones. Afrofuturism 2* (2015): 149-165; Dery, Mark. "Black to the Future: Interviews with Samuel R. Delany, Greg Tate, and Tricia Rose." In *Flame Wars*, pp. 179-222. Duke University Press, 1994; Eshun, Kodwo. "Further considerations of Afrofuturism." *CR: The New Centennial Review 3*, no. 2 (2003): 287-302.

3. Gilroy, Paul. "Living Memory: A Meeting with Toni Morrison." *Small Acts: Thoughts on the Politics of Black Cultures* (1993): 175-82.

4. Coogler, Ryan, director. *Black Panther*, Coogler Marvel Studios, 2018, 134 minutes.

5. Blow, Charles M. "The Lowest White Man." *New York Times* (2018).

6. Baruchello, Giorgio. "NO PAIN, NO GAIN: The Understanding of Cruelty in Western Philosophy and Some Reflections on Personhood." *Filozofia* 65, no. 2 (2010).

7. McGonigal, Jane. *Gaming Can Make a Better World*. TED, February 2010, 19:47. https://www.ted.com/talks/jane_mcgonigal_gaming_can_ make_a_better_world (accessed October 17, 2021).

8. Butler, Octavia E. *Parable of the Sower*. Vol. 1. Open Road Media, 2012.

9. Dictionary.com, "Cruelty." https://www.google.com/search?q=Dictionary (accessed January 21, 2018).

10. Baruchello, *No Pain*, 181.

11. Butler, *Parable*, Chapter 4.

12. Du Bois, W. E. B. "The Souls of Black Folk." *W. E. B. Du Bois: Writings* (1986): 357-547.

13. Nagy, Peter, and Gina Neff. "Imagined affordance: Reconstructing a keyword for communication theory." *Social Media + Society* 1, no. 2 (2015): 2056305115603385.

14. Dunagan, Jake F. "Politics for the Neurocentric Age." Journal of *Futures Studies* 15, no. 2 (2010): 51-70.

15. Ibid.

16. Dunagan, Jake F. "The Future as a Cognitive
    Prosthetic" (Lecture). Long Term and Futures Thinking
    in Education conference, California State University,
    East Bay, July 27, 2015.
17. Eshun, Kodwo. "Further considerations of
    Afrofuturism." *CR: The New Centennial Review 3*, no. 2
    (2003): 287-302.
18. Nakamura, Lisa. *Cybertypes: Race, Ethnicity, and
    Identity on the Internet*. Routledge, 2013.
19. Candy, Stuart and Watson, Jeff. "The Thing From
    The Future," in *The APF Methods Anthology* (London:
    Association of Professional Futurists, 2015), http://
    situationlab.org/projects/ the-thing-from-the-future/
    (accessed January 21, 2018).
20. Ibid.
21. Dator, Jim. "Alternative Futures at the Manoa
    School," *Journal of Futures Studies* 14, no. 2 (2009):
    8.
22. Beyoncé, "Lemonade," 2016, Parkwood Entertainment,
    visual album.
23. Du Bois, *Souls of Black Folk*.
24. Bloom, Joshua and Martin, Waldo E. *Black Against
    Empire: The History and Politics of the Black Panther
    Party* (Berkeley: University of California Press,
    2013); Churchill, Ward and Vander Wall, Jim. *Agents
    of Repression: The FBI's Secret Wars against the
    Black Panther Party and the American Indian Movement*,
    Vol. 7 (South End Press, 2002).
25. "Dynamicland," 1: A Communal Computer, https://
    dynamicland.org/. (accessed October 17, 2021).
26. Hopkinson, Nalo. *Report from Planet Midnight* (PM
    Press, 2012); William Lempert, "Decolonizing
    Encounters of the Third Kind: Alternative Futuring
    in Native Science Fiction Film," *Visual Anthropology
    Review 30*, no. 2 (2014): 164-76.

IMAGE CREDITS

1. Afro-Rithms from the Future overview image. Created
    by the Fathomers, www.fathomers.org, a creative
    research organization that supports the production of
    our game. Image credits for the Afro-Rithms logo Alan
    Clark, https://phantomelectrik.com/. Artwork: Alan
    Clark, Graphic Design: Paula Te and Font: Grotesk by
    Frank Adebiaye of Velvtyne Open Source Type Foundry
2. Black Superheros Inspiration Card. An Inspiration card
    from the Afro-Rithms deck to imagine a future with
    more Black superheros, graphic design by Paula Te.

A Black-Centered Design Ethos:

Engaging Afrofuturism in Catalyzing More Inclusive Technological Futures

WOODROW W. WINCHESTER III

... It is important that we understand and come to terms with this now; there are technological developments in the making that could permanently affect the destiny of Black Americans, as Americans and as global citizens.

—Anthony Walton[1]

The disproportionate impact of the COVID-19 pandemic on Black communities and the continued violence against Black lives, as elucidated in protests responding to the murder of George Floyd, have made clear the pervasiveness of systemic and structural racism against Black people in the United States. While at this moment its impact on the social and moral fabrics of this country is clear, the manifestations of anti-Black racism in technological design and deployment cannot go unnoticed and unchallenged.

From evidence suggesting that many wearable heart rate trackers rely on technology that could be less reliable for users with darker skin—which negatively impacts people of color whose employers incentivize employees' use of fitness trackers with extra vacation days, better gear, or even lower health insurance premiums—to recent studies on facial recognition technologies that find that many of these systems perform poorly on Black faces, therefore "compounding the problem of racist policing practices and a deeply flawed and harmful criminal justice system," the future as imagined by Anthony Walton in his 1999 Atlantic essay, "Technology Versus African-Americans," has seemingly come to pass. Nevertheless, that future can still be changed. New ways of designerly thinking and acting are required. An explicit centering of the needs, values, and desires of Black bodies and lives in the design and development of emerging technologies is needed. Black-Centered Design (BCD), as a means by which to facilitate this centering, could offer a pathway forward.

In intention and implementation, Black-Centered Design (BCD) is not a prescriptive design methodology. Rather, BCD provides a framework by which the nuanced and pluralistic nature of the Black identity can act as an ethos for more inclusive design; enabling the complexities of marginalized identities to be seen as a positive foundation for innovation.[5] Caesar McDowell, professor of civic design within the MIT Department of Urban Studies and Planning (DUSP), has coined this philosophical approach to design as Design for the Margins.[6] McDowell, in his editorial "Diversity Is Not Enough," states that:

> The idea here is that if you design an intervention or change to work for (and with) those who are most marginalized, then you inevitably cover them and those who are in the majority. Within the structure of the United States, it is Blackness that defines the fundamental marginal group. The marginalization of Blacks is in the origin story of this country and the current politics of this country.[7]

As this author discusses in a *Fast Company* piece, BCD, as a more inclusive human-centered design approach, is underpinned by three core principles,[8] which include:

1. Engage design principles and practices that afford the explicit foregrounding of Black lives and bodies Engage design principles and practices that afford the explicit foregrounding of Black lives.
2. Seek opportunities to engage the Black community in technological design.
3. Embrace interdisciplinarity in technological design.

While tools and techniques exist that can be used to engage these principles in design (e.g., speculative design techniques such as vision concepting), the question remains of how to focus tool use to both uncover and translate relevant contextual considerations in technological design. As a design lens in providing this needed focus, Afrofuturism offers possibilities.

Traditionally viewed simply as an aesthetic, nascent conceptions of Afrofuturism (i.e., Afrofuturism 2.0) situate it at the intersections of Black cultures, imagination, liberation, and technology. As such, Afrofuturism can function as a lens for imagining more inclusive and innovative technologies just as much as it can serve as a framework for activism. This author's effort in reimagining consumer-connected fitness technologies (e.g., Fitbit devices) elucidates this approach.[9]

The goal of this more theoretical effort in offering more inclusive connected fitness devices was to center Black women in the design of these technologies. To accomplish this, Afrofuturistic arti-facts—*vision concepts*—were created with Marcel Walker, Illustrator and comic book artist, to inspire and facilitate the necessary design thinking to obtain a more holistic understanding of Black women in this context. Analogous to how concept cars are used by automotive manufacturers, the intent of the created vision concepts is to prime the design imagination and provide space, and ultimately, a place for experimentation without market-place constraints. Not meant to be considered design solutions, in their own right, the created vision concepts are thought-catalysts; providing a means to support pro-Black and, thus, more inclusive design thinking and decision-making.

Vision concepting through an Afrofuturistic lens can liberate the design imagination and offer a means by which the technology designer can begin to both grasp and galvanize with what can be described as "*values and experiences outside of mainstream technology design logics*."[10] Through engaging with Afrofuturism, the Black voice is personi-fied throughout the design narrative. This affords a more systemic contem-plation and interrogation of design outcomes and the design process. This increased reflexivity can aid in uncovering the exclusionary assumptions, implications, and impacts that often lead to anti-Black technological outcomes and implementations.

While this discussed use of vision concepting can support in foregrounding Black lives in technological design (BCD Principle 1), opportunity exists in deepening its use through more active stakeholder engagement. "So often Black people are left out of design future thinking" asserts Salome Asega in discussing her groundbreaking Iyapo Repository initiative with Ayodamola (Ayo) Okunseinde.[11] Works by Human-Computer Interaction (HCI) scholars Christina N. Harrington and Tawanna R. Dillahunt not only substantiate this assertion but offer a way forward through the development of codesign methods and tools[12] (BCD Principle 2). While design approaches and methods lie at the heart of this challenge, more work remains and is required.

The problem of exclusionary, anti-Black technologies must be viewed and addressed as a systems problem; requiring of inter-disciplinary thought and actions (BCD Principle 3). Thus, to appropriately intervene, it is necessary to understand the various political, social, and environmental forces at play within the technological ecosystem and how they connect in driving and sustaining (i.e., rewarding) prevailing exclusionary and oppressive norms, values, and beliefs. Siloed and piecemeal approaches to course-correcting the technological future as described by Anthony Walton are not sufficient.

As Antionette D. Carroll, Founder, CEO and President of Creative Reaction Lab states, "Like all systems, systems of oppression, inequality, and inequity are by design. Therefore, they can be redesigned."[13] And, this redesign challenge—a dismantling and reconstruction of the technological ecosystem—requires new approaches and framings; not only Black centered but, ultimately, Black created. In the words of Audre Lorde, "the master's tools will never dismantle the master's house."

NOTES

4. Walton, Anthony. "Technology Versus African Americans," *The Atlantic*, January 1999. https://www.theatlantic.com/magazine/archive/1999/01/technology-versus-african-americans/377392/.

5. Hailu, Ruth. "Fitbits and other wearables may not accurately track heart rates in people of color," *STAT*, July 24, 2019. https://www.statnews.com/2019/07/24/fitbit-accuracy-dark-skin/https://www.statnews.com/2019/07/24/fitbit-accuracy-dark-skin/. (accessed October 17, 2021).

6. Najibi, Alex. "Racial Discrimination in Face Recognition Technology," *Science in the News*, October 26, 2020, https://sitn.hms.harvard.edu/flash/2020/racial-discrimination-in-face-recognition-technology/. (accessed October 17, 2021).

7. Walton, "Technology." 1999.

8. Harrington, Christina, Sheena Erete, and Anne Marie Piper. "Deconstructing community-based collaborative design: Towards more equitable participatory design engagements." In *Proceedings of the ACM on Human-Computer Interaction* 3, no. CSCW 1-25. 2019.

9. McDowell, Ceasar. "Diversity Is Not Enough," MIT Faculty Newsletter 30, no. 5 (May/June 2018). http://web.mit.edu/fnl/volume/305/mcdowell.html. (accessed October 17, 2021).

10. Ibid.

11. Winchester, Woodrow W. III, "Black-Centered Design Is the Future of Business," *Fast Company*, June 8, 2020,

https://www.fastcompany.com/90513962/black-centered
-design-is-the-future-of-business. (accessed October
17, 2021).

12. Winchester, Woodrow W. III, "Afrofuturism, Inclusion,
and the Design Imagination," *Interactions* 25, no. 2
(2018): 41-45.

13. Sengers, Phoebe. "Diversifying Design Imaginations."
In *Proceedings of the 2018 Designing Interactive
Systems Conference*, 7-7. 2018.

14. Sargent, Antwaun. "Afrofuturist Museum Mines
Artifacts from the Future," *Vice*, May 22, 2016,
https://www.vice.com/en/article/8qv34x/afrofuturist
-museum-artifacts-from-the-future (accessed October
17, 2021).

15. Harrington, Christina and Dillahunt, Tawanna R.
"Eliciting Tech Futures Among Black Young Adults:
A Case Study of Remote Speculative Co-Design." In
*Proceedings of the 2021 CHI Conference on Human
Factors in Computing Systems*, 1-15. 2021.

What Type of Ancestor Do You Want to Be?

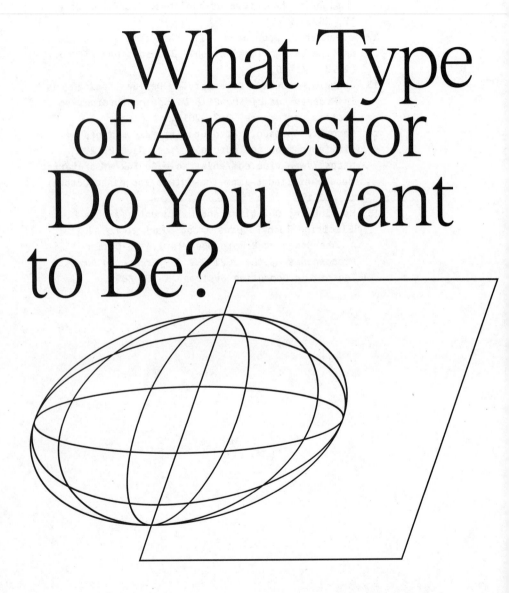

ADAH PARRIS

When asked to write this essay, I had mixed feelings. I felt a sense of pride that someone thought of me worthy to write about *The Black Experience in Design*, but there was also a creeping sense of the imposter syndrome. Am I a designer in the "true" sense of the word? Probably not, but I believe that we are all Designers, Artists, and Storytellers; it just depends on which lens we use and the value we ascribe to these labels (titles). I think that is part of the problem. There is too much emphasis placed on what something is called, by whom, and how much it is valued (often by the loudest voices and deepest pockets). What is often pushed further down the hierarchy of design needs is: What are the intended consequences *and* the unintended consequences of the design process, especially where Black and Indigenous People of Color (People of Culture[1]) are concerned?

Rather than focusing on trying to define the possible "problem" of *The Black Experience in Design*, or to quantify it, I'm going to use this chapter to introduce some guiding principles that my cofounder Marques Anderson and I have developed to explore the "anatomy of transformation" which we believe is a fundamental part of the design process from a People of Culture (PoC) perspective.

Firstly, some notes on language.

It is my belief that language, whether spoken or otherwise, has been (and is continually) used as a tool of colonization, of ideas, of knowledge, wisdom, technologies, rituals, and behaviors. The fact that it is predominantly People of Color who are defined and othered by the amount of melanin in our skin says as much as the phrase's own etymology.[2]

I recently came across the term "People of Culture" as an alternative to People of Color. Such language acknowledges our ancestral heritage *and* the historic cultural contribution that we have made to society at large. I also try to avoid using the word Indigenous or Aboriginal because the etymology of both words reveals that they were terms created to define those who had been colonized by the Europeans. We will always be on the back foot if we continue to define and categorize ourselves by the language of our original oppressors. It is a small shift in personal language and intention and some may question its efficacy but we have to start somewhere. By introducing my thought process to you, dear reader, I hope that it will encourage you to be more mindful of the language that you use. I hope that it also encourages you and others to lean in to ask questions and, hopefully, go through a process of self-reflection. These are some of the first ripples that can be created in the design and storytelling process, because to me, design is also a form of storytelling.

> *The purpose of a storyteller is not to tell you how to think but to give you questions to think upon.*
> —The Way of Kings, *Brandon Sanderson*

So, let's begin with a question.
What type of ancestor do you want to be?

GUIDING PRINCIPLE #1: HOW DO WE LEAVE THE OLD WAYS BEHIND TO CREATE NEW VALUE SYSTEMS?

The current COVID-19 pandemic has subverted the status quo.

This pandemic is forcing many in the Global North to examine our perception of our current realities and therefore our understanding of the impact of our governing -isms[3] such as nationalism, capitalism, patriarchism, digital feudalism, and spiritualism. Individuals, entrepreneurs, and business leaders are actively seeking other knowledge, wisdom, and intelligences outside their existing echo chambers and traditional problem-solving methodologies. They/we are being forced to explore the context of our existence, citizenship, kinship, and capacity to use and create new tools (technologies) to help us solve some of our fundamental human problems. Coincidentally, we have also been witnessing an exponential rise (a resurgence?) and interest in philosophies and practices such as new ageism, entheogenic (psychoactive substances, often psychedelic), and quantum consciousness, many with algorithmic and digital technology playing a significant role in the speed of adoption and the commodification of this rise. There seems to be a shift "back" toward ancestral knowledge, wisdom, and intelligence. We hear, see, and speak the language of "indigeneity," "regenessence," and "decolonization," but who is leading the narrative and for whose benefit?

We don't have to look too far back in time to recognize that many of the governing principles and doctrines that have led to the technological and innovation design processes remain those primarily based on the knowledge, insights, and wisdom of the WEIRD (western educated industrialized rich and democratic). Or, at the very least, based on cherry-picking, deliberately ignoring or outright rejecting the validity of the knowledge, wisdom, practices, and rituals of those cultures, societies and nonhuman ecologies that have traditionally been othered or seen as insignificant.

No longer are we solely dependent on the voices of the few, those brave (experimental, weird . . .) enough to challenge the status quo, the curious who wanted to help us envision potential new futures. It is interesting to note that even in the days of the emergence of speculative futures, many of the names and faces profiled were those of cisgender white men. Where were the names, narratives, and contributions of People of Culture, Afrofuturists such as Sun Ra, writers such as Octavia E. Butler, or Eastern Futurists and artists such as Tadanori Yokoo?[4]

With more access to new and emerging technologies, we are all becoming storytellers. Telling stories of the fluidity of our humanity. Gaining and adopting different perspectives on identity, culture, economics, ecosystems, and freedom, through the adoption of individual and collective rituals. This is where I think the role of a designer can come in. If this is the new landscape in which we find ourselves, what are the new rules of engagement? How do we measure success?

In November 2019, I was invited to host a series of roundtables for the Council of 90 Indigenous leaders at the World Indigenous Forum. The aim was to help them start to write their collective manifesto. People of Culture, those who have been systematically othered, were coming together to give their view of how we can and should codesign the futures that we need especially if we are to save the planet. On the top of their list was the need for a new hierarchy of needs, one that prioritizes the needs of all of the inhabitants of the earth as our base fundamental need. They placed great emphasis on the fact that we need to learn from the past and change our behavior in the present in order to have a future that we can design for.

Accepting that there is a need for a new hierarchy of needs leads us to guiding principle number 2: Breathe.

GUIDING PRINCIPLE #2:
WHAT IS OUR HYPOTHESIS CHANGE?

Traditionally we have been told that stories follow Joseph Campbell's model of the Hero's Journey, in which the hero (the cisgender, usually heteronormative, white male storytelling framework that is present in most dominant narratives in our society—just think of most of the blockbuster films out at the moment). The hero goes on a solo quest, meets the mentor, the oracle, the guru, the shaman, the one who will help to provide enlightenment and guidance for "our" Hero to be able to continue on their quest. However, our current reality (the COVID-19 pandemic) has forced many of us to realize that there is no one single wise sage coming to rescue us, to share their knowledge, wisdom, and insights to help us find our way out of this pandemic. Instead, our behavior in response to the governing mandates has led to the recognition that we all are storytellers. Now more than ever the othered voices, knowledge, and wisdom should be included in the wider cultural and societal narrative.

I believe this is where the concept of systems thinking comes into its own: "Systems thinking[5] is the ability or skill to perform problem solving in complex systems." For years, I didn't realize that I was what people call a systems thinker; I was just someone who recognized patterns and used that ability to help solve problems by noting how that same problem was addressed (and possibly solved) in another system. Subconsciously, I would start by looking to my African (Igbo), Guyanese (Amerindian), and Black British experiences and cultural traditions as a starting point for the design process. How did my upbringing and experiences of racism, of being othered, of being a lone (or minority) Black body in mostly white spaces influence my perspective of the problem? I never realized that I was doing it, as it was just my way of existing, but hindsight is a wonderful thing. Through the process of mind mapping, some new patterns and realizations began to emerge; I just needed to find a way to communicate what I was seeing.

I spent seven years mind mapping many of the patterns that emerged (and which I later recognized) across the worlds that held the most interest for me: Those of algorithmic and digital technology, spirituality, quantum mechanics, religion, and shamanism. Over that period of time my hypothesis of Cyborg Shamanism was born, to help us ask the questions needed to really explore the anatomy of human transformation as part of a bigger, wider, more diverse living system, one in which the knowledge, wisdom, rituals, and technologies of often marginalized cultures and communities are included as part of the design process and not just as research subjects for anthropologists.

Cyborg Shamanism is fluid, as it should be. It can be recognized as a series of symbiotic interconnected patterns, ideas, ideologies, rituals, behaviors, and technologies that have very similar intentions. It helps us understand and explore our relationship with ourselves, with others (including other living organisms) and with our environment. It helps us gain some form of enlightenment all in the quest to answer three questions: What does it mean to be human? What could we be capable of? How can we break out of our linear ways of thinking and being in order to codesign and cocreate inclusive, speculative, and regenerative futures? Cyborg Shamanism has also been the first stepping-stone for me to deepen that personal, professional, and systemic enquiry. To ask how we build trust and transparency in a world of instability, one in which the floor is constantly moving, especially for those of us who have been Othered. To explore how to merge the worlds of ancient wisdom, natural systems, and indigenous community practices with digital and emerging technologies. To decolonize the lives, knowledge, wisdom, experiences, and stories of the Othered. To build new narratives and replace the overreliance on the Hero's Journey as the dominant storytelling framework.

Now is the time of systemic transformation, especially for us as Black Designers. It is our time to rise to emerge from the shadows where many had been relegated, to present alternative ways of seeing, being and doing based on Othered Futurisms such as Afrofuturism (Africanfuturism[6] and Africanjujuism).

An opportunity has arisen; the COVID-19 virus is a form of technology (see my definition earlier) that has forced us as a species to explore our relationship with ourselves, with others, and with our environment in a time where many of the old rules of the game, the "old normal" are either broken or no longer exist. Whilst in this gap between the "old normal" and what comes next, we have the opportunity to make choices about our personal roles and responsibilities within shaping this new future. Design is one of the ways that we can shape that future.

For several years I've had the job title of Futurist, but I've always felt lost with it. It felt external to me, like I was trying to fit into a world and club that I didn't quite understand and would never really belong to, but I was enthusiastic. Four years later, I think that I've finally come up with a definition of Futurism that recognizes my way of being, my way of showing up, but more importantly the way that I want to be seen and recognized in the world. It's what I want to be known for.

I now believe that futurism is the ability to revisit the past, acknowledge the present, and codesign the future. My work sits at the intersection of ancient and Indigenous wisdom, natural systems, and emerging technologies, so when expanding that definition further to include living systems the phrase becomes acknowledging, valuing, and embodying the symbiotic relationship between human and nonhuman to be able to revisit the past, acknowledge the present and codesign the future.

Isn't this the basic premise of the ancestral practices and belief systems of many Peoples of Culture? It certainly rings true for me for much of my own African and Guyanese heritage. This leads me one step closer to understanding how to answer my original question, "What type of ancestor do you [I] want to be?" As Black designers, how can we use this genealogical and ancestral knowledge and wisdom to our advantage? Maybe it starts with more of us unapologetically recognizing and celebrating the value of our Blackness (or otherness) of our knowledge, wisdom, rituals, and technologies, in contrast to the usually extractive nature of the "technological discovery and invention" that we see getting lauded and funded over and over again. This, for me, is where othered Futurisms such as Afrofuturism, Africanfuturism, and Africanjujuism can, should, and, in some cases, must come in.

GUIDING PRINCIPLE #3: WHAT ARE THE TOOLS, TECHNOLOGIES, RITUALS, AND BEHAVIORS THAT CAN AND SHOULD BE INCLUDED IN THE DESIGN PROCESS TO HELP US CREATE EQUITABLE AND INCLUSIVE FUTURES?

In this current era of the Fourth (or Fifth depending on your perspective) Industrial Revolution, the word "technology" has become synonymous with digital technology. However, if we examine the etymology of the word ("technology" . . . originates from "a discourse or treatise on an art or the arts," from Greek tekhnologia "systematic treatment of an art, craft, or technique"[7]), then we can expand our perception of what constitutes a technology.

Some are choosing quantum and digital technologies (computing), plant technologies (entheogens, psychedelics, plant medicine), metaphysical technologies (sound vibrations, energy fields), or theological technologies (religion, faith, and belief systems) to explore and understand our own identities, our relationships with our environments, and how we relate to and connect with others. If we choose to accept the definition of technology as a truism, then technology is a medium, art, craft, or technique that helps us to explore and expand our curiosity, to play, to innovate, to solve problems, and to create new stories and realities.

Notice here that I include a reference to plant (ecological) and theological technologies. Some would argue that these are not technologies but for those of us who are People of Culture, this is very much in keeping with our cultural and ancestral heritage. We only need to be reminded that the concept of blockchain is not a new one to see how this can be true. Tenochtitlan was the ancient pre-Columbian Mexican city in which the ancient Mesoamericans created floating gardens called chinampas. They developed agricultural techniques that relied on small, rectangular areas of fertile arable land to grow crops on shallow lake beds. Today we would call that a decentralized distributed system, or a block-chain. It may not be in an immediately recognizable form but the intention is the same, to have a flatter, more equitable, and transparent system.

We have an opportunity not just to decolonize techno-logical innovation but also to demonstrate and prove integrating ancient wisdom, natural systems, and ancestral community practices informs and helps us to design processes leading to future innovations.

GUIDING PRINCIPLE #4: WHAT KIND OF ANCESTOR DO YOU WANT TO BE?

Having the job title Futurist is an interesting reality. People expect you to be able to have some sort of crystal ball or to be able to read the stars and predict the future. None of us can do that. However, I think it provides me with the opportunity to "world build" by leaning into the role of a speculative designer and asking some thought-provoking and seemingly existential questions. Remember, Cyborg Shamanism is delib-erately provocative to get us to think: what does it mean to be human? What could we be capable of? How can we break out of our linear ways of thinking and being to codesign and cocreate inclusive speculative and regenerative futures?

By following the guiding principles that I have already covered in this essay we are led to the next and probably the biggest ques-tion of them all.

What type of ancestor do you want to be?

This is really about the viability and sustainability of what we are designing. There is a Senegalese quote that says, "The future emerges from the past." By revisiting our past as systems thinkers and People of Culture we will be able to design speculative futures that incorporate many of the patterns, ideas, knowledge, wisdom, rituals, and technologies of our ancestry into our design processes. One example that I tend to use is the idea of 360-degree cameras. A 360-degree camera is intended to provide a 360-degree (holistic) view of a particular narrative experience. It aims to engage more than just our sense of sight but also our senses of space, time, and dimension, among others. If we look back to our past, where else can we discover an experience with a similar intention?

Cave paintings. When we first discovered cave paintings we thought that they were just markings of previous civilizations. However, as we humans began to travel and expand our knowledge of these sites around the world, we realized that they gave us a more in-depth picture of the daily lives and existence of many of our ancestors. More recent discoveries have revealed that the placing of many of those markings was not as random as first thought. Sound and music were used to complement Paleolithic art, to create holistic immersive experiences. Sound familiar?

The cave, the paintings, and the musical instruments could (by my definition) all be described as ancient forms of technology. If we fast-forward to today, then I believe we are at an opportune moment in history. We can learn from our ancestral wisdom with a deeper and more systemic understanding of their contributions to their own and future societies. But if we merge the intention of our design problems with our ever-increasing access to and understanding of the variety of technologies (digital, algorithmic, ecological, spiritual, quantum, and shamanic, to name a few), then we can take more responsibility in defining and shaping the type of ancestors that we want and *need* to be.

Maybe this is how we can start to create a more honest and inclusive understanding of the word "balance" and achieve greater states of flow as cultures, societies, and citizens of the world. This leads us to the question, "What is the future of humanity and kinship?"

GUIDING PRINCIPLE #5: KINSHIP

In Nigeria, the Igbo tribe has the concept of Mbari, a sacred ritual, a rite of passage, and a visual art form that also serves as a form of citizenship and kinship. It was used as a way of paying reverence to a particular Orisha[1] (deity, god, or goddess). It is a process that merges architecture, sculpture, bas-relief, and painting where members of the village are chosen to codesign and co-build the offering (in the form of a house). Selection was regarded as a way of demonstrating your citizenship and belief in something bigger than yourself. To the Owerri Igbo people, "Mbari is life."

So, what can we learn from this as Black designers?

The COVID-19 pandemic, coupled with the groundswell of the Black Lives Matter movement, has held a mirror up to us as a global society. We may not have liked what we saw, but we are in a fundamental moment in our history on this planet as a species. There are some key lessons that we can merge with the guiding principles that I have shared here.

They both have taught us that we can remove the many borders and boundaries that we as humans have created in order to help solve problems and design novel solutions. We need to recognize the human in each other in order to help each other meet at least our most basic needs. At some point we will all ask ourselves existential questions about the meaning, role, responsibility, and levels of power that we have.

Regardless of what we call ourselves, or are called by others—designers, futurists, storytellers, artists, activists—our ultimate goal is to create some sense of inclusion and belonging, of community, not just with other humans but with all living things. To create ideas, products, services that will have a personal, cultural, economic, technological, and ecological impact on the "us" and all inhabitants of the planet.

To do this I suggest that we recognize that we need new hierarchies of needs, to be more explicit in our shared values. We need new languages (or at least a reframing of the old ways) combined with new storytelling frameworks to create new equitable narratives. We need new and emergent hypotheses for change. We need to look to and be inclusive (not extractive) of the wisdom, knowledge, rituals, and technologies of those who have been othered, so that we can codesign the equitable, sustainable, and regenerative futures that we all proclaim to desire.

NOTES

1. urbandictionary.com/define.php?term=People%20of%20 Culture (accessed October 17, 2021).
2. wikipedia.org/wiki/Person_of_color (accessed October 17, 2021).
3. etymonline.com/word/-ism (accessed October 17, 2021).
4. Capra, F., and P. Luisi. (2014). *The Systems View of Life: A Unifying Vision*. Cambridge: Cambridge University Press.
5. Väätänen, Päivi. "Afro- versus Africanfuturism in Nnedi Okorafor's 'The Magical Negro' and 'Mother of Invention,'" *Vector*, August 31, 2019. vector-bsfa.com/2019/08/31/afro-versus-african-futurism-in-nnedi-okorafors-the-magical-negro-and-mother-of-invention/ (accessed October 28, 2021).
6. "Technology (n.)," Online Etymology Dictionary, etymonline.com/word/technology.
7. wikipedia.org/wiki/Orisha.

Black Secret Technologies

JOHN JENNINGS

The Impossible attracts me because, everything's already been done, and the world didn't change.

—Sun Ra

The cultural production mode and political aesthetic known as Afrofuturism has situated itself into the mainstream. If you scan the current media landscape, the word "Afrofuturism" is now connected to myriad symposia, university courses, and descriptions of all media forms. It has even affected politics on a municipal level with Ingrid LaFleur running for mayor of Detroit based on an Afrofuturist platform. After Ryan Coogler's 2018 blockbuster superhero film *Black Panther* decimated Hollywood's performance projections left and right, Afrofuturism has catapulted into the mainstream. It's incredible, but I do have my issues with the phenomenon. It's a very radical and paradoxical notion that an aesthetic and cultural production process that focuses on the idea of a technologically empowered Black future is so ardently embraced in a world that has historically and presently devalues and disrupts Black life.

The term Afrofuturism is attributed to cultural scholar Mark Dery, who edited a collection entitled *Flame Wars: The Discourse of Cyberculture* in 1994. In that collection, the author includes an essay/interview series called "Black to the Future." Within that text, he states:

> Speculative fiction that treats African American themes and addresses African American concerns in the context of 20th-century technoculture—and more generally, African American signification that appropriates images of technology and a prosthetically enhanced futures—might, for want of a better term, be called Afrofuturism.[1]

Dery was thinking of Afrofuturism as a type of speculative fiction, but in this definition, he also starts to posit an aesthetic. The "cyborg" (cybernetic organism) is a tried and true trope of science fiction.

It represents a being that is part machine and part human. It's hard to find a more apt allegory for what it means to be Black in America. It's double-consciousness reified into one body.

Along with the classic 2002 *Social Text* special issue journal on Afrofuturism edited by Dr. Alondra Nelson, the other artifact that influenced my thinking on Afrofuturism and Black Speculative Culture was the 1997 film by John Akomfrah, *The Last Angel of History*. The forty-five-minute documentary connects the histories of Black techno music to Black speculative cultural production, criticism, and literature. The film featured luminaries like Octavia E. Butler, Samuel R. Delany, Kodwo Eshun, Greg Tate, George Clinton, Underground Resistance, and Goldie. One of the statements that changed how I looked at my own work and its relationship to Afrofuturism came at the beginning of the documentary.

In the intro, Akomfrah introduces the concept of a time-traveling archaeologist called a "Data Thief." This Data Thief character is trying to put together the shards of creative culture throughout the African diaspora and send signals back to the future. He tells the story of a fellow Mississippian, Robert Johnson, who makes a deal with the "Devil" for a "Black secret technology" called "The Blues." It really struck me that I'd never thought of music as a type of technology. Since technology also deals with systems, ways of ordering things, and other intangible prosthetics that extend the human experience, I started to understand how music can be considered as such. My next question was: "What else can be a technology?" I came across the article "Race as Technology" by then MIT professor Beth Coleman, who essentially puts forth that, if you take away the asinine notion that race is actually a real thing that makes human beings "different" from one another, it actually acts more like a type of technology that is created for very particular reasons.[2]

I became extremely interested in this concept. It led me to create a design studio course called "Race as Science Fiction" while teaching in the Graphic Design program at the University of Buffalo SUNY. The student designers had to create projects using Afrofuturism and Black Speculative Culture as a lens or epistemology through which they could create their work. While teaching this course, I became fascinated by speculative design, an area of design discourse popularized by the British design team Anthony Dunne and Fiona Raby. Essentially, it's a type of design that involves future-casting that attempts to create design fictions in order to spark discussions about possible futures and possible effects or outcomes of those futures. Highly influenced by speculative fiction, it looks at how these fictions can stimulate questions about the conception and design of the products and experiences that will be affecting our world in the future. The speculative designer creates fictional narrative spaces for these objects and systems to exist within. So, storytelling is very much a part of this kind of design. These designed fictional worlds consist of diegetic prototypes; that is, designs that are meant to tell a story and have discussions. Their very existence is tied to starting a conversation. Dunne and Raby's book *Speculative Everything* elegantly lays out the utility of such a design practice.

In it, they state:

> *This form of design thrives on imagination and aims to open up new perspectives on what are sometimes called wicked problems, to create spaces for discussion and debate about alternative ways of being, and to inspire and encourage people's imaginations to flow freely. Design and speculations can act as a catalyst for collectively redefining our relationship to reality.*[3]

However, the glaring hole in the book is that the speculative narratives they use are all Eurocentric. There's no Octavia E. Butler, Steven Barnes, Nalo Hopkinson, or Chip Delany inspiring any thoughts about future designs. The "wicked problem" that plagues me as a Black designer is the problems of race and racism endangering, disempowering, erasing, and disrupting people of color in society.

Bruce Sterling's book *Shaping Things* talks about how design fiction "creates a story world" and generates things within that world.[4] Racism is the design fiction that has systemically changed the world and race is the deliverable that we are all still dealing with to this day. People often state that race is primarily a "social construct." My "designer brain" quite obviously wants to know where the schematics are for this construct so that we can either redesign race or un-design race.

So, I began to question what diegetic prototypes existed in Afrofuturistic stories. To my pleasant surprise, I found quite a few throughout African American literature!

In George Schuyler's 1931 farcical political satire novel *Black No More*, a Black scientist creates a chair whose technology allows Black people to turn into white people. However, their phenotypical bone structures don't change, and their complexions actually become the color of sheets or snow. Schuyler designed this diegetic prototype to poke fun at not only race but also at Black progress and the New Negro Movement, of which he was a huge critic. I also found several diegetic prototypes in the works of Amiri Baraka. In "The Pig Detector," written in 2000,[5] a device can sense the presence of off-duty cops. In Henry Dumas's short story "May the Circle Be Unbroken," which he wrote this during the Black Arts Movement in 1966, the discursive object is a musical jazz horn called the Afro-horn whose tunes are deadly to white people. I feel that this current interest is the next generation of Black speculative thought, which has always been present during times of great upheaval around Black political movements in our country. In 2015, I dubbed this new era the Black Speculative Arts Movement.

All of these explorations have caused me to think about how Black Speculation, critical making, and design all intersect. These musings have resulted in a new way of thinking about race critically through a practice I call Critical Race Design Studies. I define it as: *an interdisciplinary design practice that intersects critical race theory, speculative design, design history, and critical making to analyze and critique the effects of visual communication, graphic objects, and their associated systemic mediations of racial identity.*

This practice began with a series of questions inspired by Marshall McLuhan's *probes.* The famed media theorist created a set of rhetorical questions centered around starting conversations related to media. I called my collection of queries a *maniquesto.* It contained simple questions about visuality and race and how design sometimes is culpable in maintaining and propagating racist ideas and imagery. This way of thinking of race as a designed object has helped me reimagine my connections to design as a Black American citizen and also a critic, educator, storyteller, and graphic designer.

Race was designed around what was deemed to be an economic necessity, and it has changed the entire world on every systemic level. Its creation was intentional and now, because of a generations-long onslaught of racist propaganda, it presents itself as "natural." It is not. What it is, is one of the most effective design campaigns in history. As Black designers, we have to figure out how to reimagine the visual stories around race and discern methods to unpack the damage that the visual language of race has had not only on Black people but on *all* people. Afrofuturism can help us visualize and design new pasts and inspire new ideas around the future. In the end, I feel that should always be one of design's primary end goals.

NOTES

1. Dery, Mark, ed., "Black to the Future" in *Flame Wars: The Discourse of Cyberculture* (Durham and London: Duke University Press: 1994). 180.
2. Coleman, Beth. "Race as technology." *Camera Obscura: Feminism, Culture, and Media Studies* 24, no. 1 (2009): 177-207.
3. Dunne, Anthony and Raby, Fiona. *Speculative Everything: Design, Fiction, and Social Dreaming* (The MIT Press, 2013), 2.
4. Sterling, Bruce. *Shaping Things*. 2005.
5. Amiri Baraka, "The Pig Detector," in *Tales of the Out & the Gone: Short Stories* (New York: Akashic Books, 2009).

Dark Matter's Magic

in Design

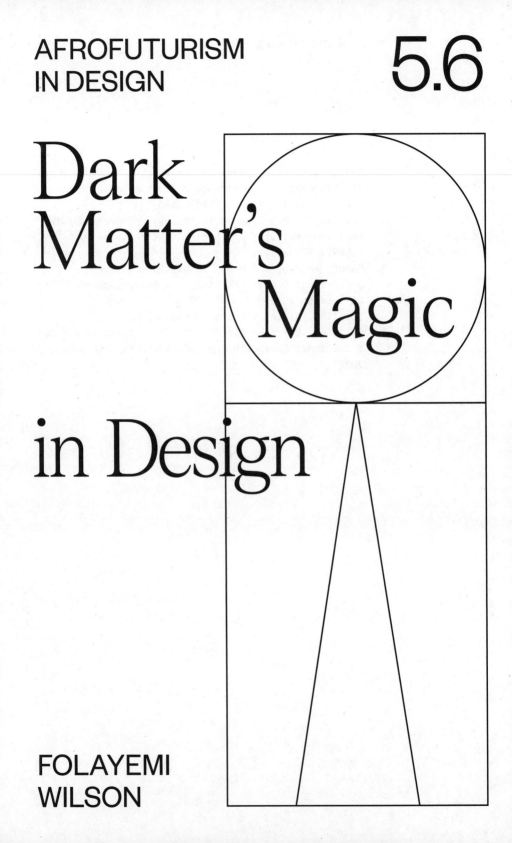

FOLAYEMI
WILSON

EDITOR'S NOTE:

This writing is adapted from an essay included in Wilson's solo exhibition catalogue *Dark Matter: Celestial Objects as Messengers of Love in These Troubled Times* (2019) and published in 2020 by Candor Arts, an independent publishing collective in Chicago that produced handmade editions to support artists and operated in Chicago from 2015 to 2021. They are now the Candor Collective. For more information about the Collective: candorcollective.info/candor-history-menu.

What follows six is more than seven.

—Yoruba proverb[1]

My first introduction to Afrofuturism was through Alice Coltrane's album *Journey to Satchidananda* (1971). Although I was not aware of the term at the time and am not sure she would have called it that, Coltrane's transcendental music, which featured Pharoah Sanders (sax and percussion), Cecil McBee (bass), and Majid Shabazz (bells and tambourine), took one on a meditative and timeless journey into a spiritual cosmos. Inspired by her studies of the teachings of Swami Satchidananda, Coltrane integrated the harp in blissful ways with what was then fairly avant-garde music.

I was a young, nerdy, somewhat hippyish adolescent around the time I discovered the album. Running the streets of 1970s Harlem in New York, one of my brothers introduced me to Black Nationalism and meditation at the National Black Theatre of Harlem (NBT)—an essential practice I maintain to this day. Ankh necklaces as markers of knowledge of an Egyptian past, and elephant hair bracelets (now banned) as African symbols of good luck were popular in the street stalls of 125th Street. Along with Samuel Weiser Books, an occult publisher near Astor Place in Greenwich Village, I frequented Lewis Michaux's National Memorial African Bookstore or the *House of Common Sense and the Home of Proper Propaganda* as Michaux referred to it, as well as the Tree of Life bookstore run by Kanya

McGee, whom we called Dr. Kanya. These were sites of Pan-Africanism, and of historical, metaphysical, and spiritual education. They attempted to counter the effects of racism, Western miseducation, social, and civic disinvestment, and crack cocaine that had been allowed to devastate many of Harlem's Black and poor inhabitants, the effects disassembling and destroying important social infrastructures and cultural economies. These sites of consciousness raising took *Black is Beautiful* pride into philosophical and intellectual territory, promoting and celebrating a Black past and a Black future's potential to overcome the oppressive forces stepping on Black people's necks. Sadly, after a long and protracted protest of resistance, both sites were closed and torn down supposedly to make way for a new state office building. With the destruction of these examples of positive Black institutional and entrepreneurial productivity, many of us felt the pain of a deliberate and organized racist conspiracy that blocked our progress. It felt so personal.

Those adolescent years introduced me to practices that expanded my sense of self and gave me spiritual agency and a connection to a universal consciousness not unlike what Coltrane was expressing in her music. I learned of nonlinear concepts of time, space, and history that form part of a spiritual and philosophical identity that imagines freedom in a Black universe and future. I learned later in my graduate studies that a central and enduring West African philosophy is that past, present, and future actually exist simultaneously. That is how I think of Afrofuturism.

In my youth, there was meditation, chanting, Kemet and Nile River studies, past-life readings, happenings, and yoga – and then there was the musician, philosopher, and poet Sun Ra, whose music, performances, and poems were as popular as the Last Poets (whom I consider the first populist rappers), who were Harlem neighbors. Much of this, along with my adventures into spirituality and African cosmology with NBT, form the basis of my introduction to Afrofuturist concepts and the human potential in the self. These philosophies transcend a corporeal present and exercise embodiments of Blackness that express a freedom that the *Black Imagination* and the *Black Fantastic*, as coined by the late scholar Richard Iton,[2] provide as a technology of resistance, self-determination, and survival.

It was through NBT that I first initiated self-taught study and design training that led to a twenty-plus-year career in graphic design and art direction, by volunteering to design the theater's posters and flyers. It was also where I took theater classes as a means to overcome an unyielding shyness, and was excited to find a community of dynamic, beautiful, and like-minded Black folx. Oh, they were so beautiful! Not only did they have a nationalist consciousness, but they also harbored a sense of spirituality that embraced the metaphysical and spiritual philosophies

Fig. 1

I had begun to explore as a young teenager through the writings of people as varied as Madame Helena P. Blavatsky, Edgar Cayce, G. I. Gurdjieff, and Kahlil Gibran. NBT's director, the former actor Barbara Ann Teer, introduced us to the growing human potential movement taking root across the country at the time among other theatrical training. Her sister Fredricka Teer, an organizational development consultant who became an important mentor, brought us to the New Age ideologies of Werner Erhard's Erhard Seminar Training (EST) where she was on the board, and to EST alumnus Leonard Orr and his Rebirthing and Actualization programs. My spiritual awakening and explorations crossed a diverse smorgasbord of cultures and various types of timeless and New Age practices.

In the summer of 1974, the theater company was awarded a grant to travel to Nigeria to research Yoruba religion and culture for a play we were developing that centered on the òrìṣà and goddess Oshun. In our play, *Soul Journey Into Truth*, this Yoruba deity of fertility and love was coming to America to deliver the masses of Black people from the devastation of the Middle Passage, racism, and oppression. I spent most of that summer with other company members in the Osogbo village compound of painter Twins Seven Seven. Twins was a flamboyant character and internationally known artist, and the only survivor of seven sets of twins. Nigeria, curiously, has one of the highest statistical instances of twin births. Twins Seven Seven had many children, and seven wives at the time (including the celebrated master adire textile artist, educator, and gallerist Chief Nike Davies-Okundaye). He seemed to enjoy hosting our zany cohort of *oyinbos*.[3] We traveled to major Nigerian cities, villages, and universities like the University of Ibadan—the country's first public university and home to famous alumni like Chinua Achebe and Wole Soyinka, whom we met. We learned about Yoruba history and culture, studied the language, participated in Yoruba ritual ceremonies, and returned as a company later in 1977 as part of the American contingent to attend and perform at Festac '77 in Lagos.[4] I was very fortunate to have a direct and meaningful experience of the Motherland, not simply the idealized one I often romanticized about back in the States.

      It was during these travels to Nigeria where I first began to understand spirituality from a deeper perspective. The African personality sees life or the potential for life in all things. Yorubas, like people of other African and ancient cultures, acknowledge a spiritual power like that of *ase*. *Ase* is a Yoruba concept that expresses "the vital principle empowering existence."[5] It can be interpreted as a life force and those who know how to access its power can harness its spiritual capacity.

      The esteemed Nigerian art historian Rowland Abiodun acknowledges that "[*ase*] is the most important religio-aesthetic phenomenon to survive transatlantic slavery almost intact."[6] I had my own particular experience with *ase* as a child sitting next to my mother in the Baptist church we belonged to. Many of the women would be inspired by the preacher's sermon as the timbre of his voice rose and the force of it made the hair on the back of our necks stand up. They would get "the spirit" or what we referred to as "gettin' happy," wail in testimony or even faint between the pews. It was very powerful; something I didn't always understand as a young child.

      In describing the manifestation of *ase* in the visual arts, Abiodun says:

> Functioning essentially as a kind of "oriki," visual art forms also carry condensed, highly charged and direct visual messages—"ase"—which are powerful and efficacious as their verbal equivalents. The visual artist uses his or her "oju-inu" (inner eye) and "oju-ona" (design consciousness)—important aesthetic attributes, to select, combine, and represent

specific colors, patterns, motifs,
and aspects of the subject matter
in order to communicate its "ase"
with the maximum visual impact.[7]

One can imagine that Picasso, Braque, and their contemporaries responded not only to what was, to them, a new ideology of aesthetics they encountered among the African sculptures and masks they found in the flea markets of Paris and the Palais du Trocadero in the early part of the twentieth century, but to the strong spiritual presence with which these enigmatic objects were imbued. The artists likely did not understand. These objects—severed from their original and spiritual functional context, now contributing to the transformation of European art and design—were originally endowed with powerful forces that traversed both living and timeless spiritual realms.

Historian William Fagg looks at the African perspective this way:

[African] cultures tend to conceive
things as four-dimensional objects
in which the fourth or time dimen-
sion is dominant and in which matter
is only a vehicle, or the outward
and visible expression, of energy or
life force. Thus it is energy and not
matter, dynamic and not static being,
which is the true nature of things.[8]

Abiodun, citing the Yoruba proverb that opens my essay, says, "We must look beyond what is easily observed if we are to understand something."[9] That is the place where Afrofuturism lives as it does in the imaginations of writers such as Octavia Butler, and in the poetry and visual art of Krista Franklin, as well as in untranslatable languages and practices in music, art, and voice—religious or spiritual, sacred or secular.

My various creative identities as an artist, designer, and maker intersect through diasporic histories. As a young designer, I had a genetic connection to *oriki* and intuitively embraced the aesthetics of twentieth-century Modernism when I began my professional career as a young art director and designer in New York in the early 1980s, albeit with a yet-unrealized academic understanding. During my graduate school studies and research in the early 2000s, I had a revelation: The aesthetics privileged in European Modernism and that of my heritage, which I presumed came from different places, actually shared the same roots.

A little less than twenty years later, my exhibition *Dark Matter: Celestial Objects as Messengers of Love in These Troubled Times*[10] pays homage to those that started me on the path to this knowledge at such a young age. The exhibition combines elements of architecture and integrates visual art, objects, sound, and video to create a celestial Afrofuturist landscape that suggests an imaginary, transplanetary Middle Passage and migration through deep space. It is an offering to encouraging forces in the universe that would have us prevail and emerge out of the shadows with love during these times of great chaos, uncertainty, upheaval, darkness, and ignorance.

In *Dark Matter*, not only are the spiritual and aesthetic legacies of Blackness enduring, but they are also part of the universe's tenable and little-understood juju.

NOTES

1. Abiodun, Rowland. "Understanding Yoruba Art and Aesthetics: the Concept of Ase," *African Arts*, July 1994, pg. 69.
2. Iton, Richard. *In Search of the Black Fantastic*, New York: Oxford University Press, 2008.
3. *Oyinbo* translates as White person or foreigner. Although Black, as Black Americans we were perceived as foreign and not culturally African.
4. Festac '77 was the second international World Black and African Festival held in Lagos, the first was held in Dakar, Senegal in 1966. It included around 16,000 participants from 56 African nations and countries of the African Diaspora.
5. Ase, (Yoruba àse). Lawal, Babatunde. "Aworan: Representing Self and Its Metaphysical Other in Yoruba Art," *Art Bulletin*, September 2001, vol. LXXXII. no.3, 498.
6. Ibid. 71.
7. Abiodun, Rowland. "Understanding Yoruba Art and Aesthetics: The Concept of Ase," African Arts, July 1994, 76. Oriki is a form of a praise poem that is meant to evoke someone's inner ase.
8. Fagg, William. "In Search of Meaning in African Art," *Primitive Art and Society*, edited by Anthony Forge,

London: Oxford University Press, 1973, 164.

9. Abiodun, Rowland. "Understanding Yoruba Art and Aesthetics: The Concept of Ase," *African Arts*, July 1994, pg. 69.

10. For more about the *Dark Matter* exhibition go to: www .fowilson.com/projects/dark-matter.

IMAGE CREDIT

1. (Installation view) Dark Matter: Celestial Objects As Messengers of Love in These Troubled Times, 2019 Hyde Park Art Center, Chicago, Illinois, Photography: Tom Van Eynde.

JOURNEYS
IN DESIGN

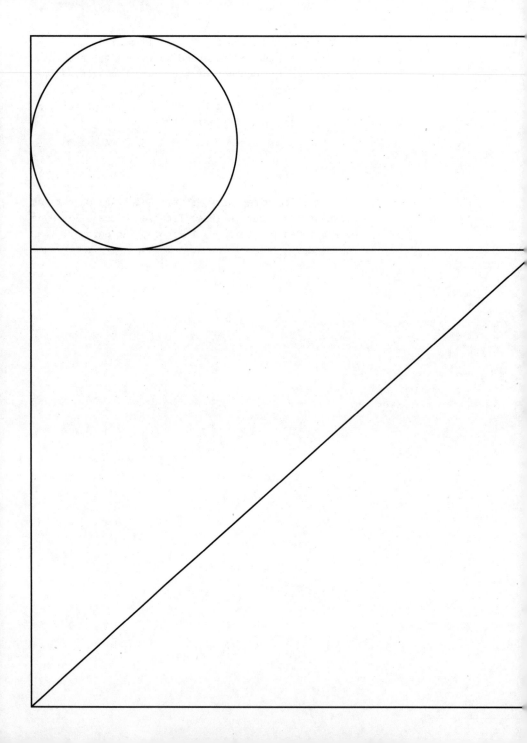

JOURNEYS IN DESIGN

6.1

Chapter Introduction:
Kelly Walters

As we have seen throughout this book, there is no singular design journey for that of a Black designer. One's entry into design is heavily influenced by a variety of factors: design training, educational background, geographic region and even cultural upbringing for instance. These aspects can influence our career path and our access within the design industry. A critical focus of this chapter is learning from designers who are looking at the bigger picture and who have mapped specific markers that influence the trajectory of Black designers. These perspectives, are aimed at highlighting the starting points, periods of transition, opportunities, anticipated barriers, and unexpected obstacles faced in the classroom or in the workplace. Regardless of the design environment, we encounter people that may inspire, guide, or discourage us from pursuing design. It is important to note when these moments play out and how they occur because they can have an impact on how we view ourselves as designers and what we think we may be capable of making. A second focus of this chapter is to hear from design creatives who are working across a spectrum of disciplines. On the pages that follow, we share a mixture of design journeys that take the form of infographics, language, imagery, self-reflective essays, and difficult conversations about race.

We open the chapter with Yocasta Lachapelle's "The Black Designer's Journey: Theory of Change." As the director of Talent at COLLINS, Lachapelle shares her evolution and "slightly random entry" into the design industry. Her essay and visual mapping highlight the barriers that prevent success for Black designers at different stages of their career. The infographic includes important actionable steps with specific outcomes

374

that are aimed at advancing mentorship, sponsorship and education for Black designers.

Forest Young continues similar themes in his essay "In Pursuit of a Prismatic Profession." Young frames his essay through four key components: representational imprinting, opening gates to support viable paths to graduation, prismatic cultures and building professional lattices. The barriers described by Lachapelle: exposure to design, lack of supportive mentorship and the difficulties in building professional networks, are echoed in Young's essay and become a recurring theme within the chapter.

As we shift to an essay by Schessa Garbutt entitled "&&&: Provoking Type," they unpack what it's like to navigate the sub-discipline of typeface design from a Black and Queer perspective. Garbutt describes how their Afrolatinx, Belizean and Southern Black experiences shape an existence in the world that is non-hierarchal and nonlinear. As they state, "I embrace my multitudes," and this provocation allows their ability to push beyond expectations of how they must practice design or exist in the world.

In "1 Word / 1 Object," the editors of *The Black Experience in Design* capture the design journey of a few of their former Black students through a selection 14 words and images. The simplicity of this visual essay is meant to draw attention to the key language that comes to mind when we think of our design journeys.

Michelle Joan Wilkinson's essay "Curating My Way into Design: A Work in Progress," describes how a constant focus in her career has been a dedication to supporting the visibility of Black narratives and challenging institutions.

In Sabine Maxine Lopez, "My Journey to Design," they discuss how multiplicity is embraced in their design practice as a means to lift up the communities they are part of.

We conclude this chapter with Shades of Noir founder, Aisha Richards, in her vulnerable and pointed conversation entitled "Moving On: Interview with White Male Academic."

Within all of these writings we see intimate reflections, efforts to uplift Black stories, and the important Black cultural artifacts that give us inspiration. I encourage the reader to see how each practitioner creates spaces for empowerment and visibility through their respective fields—from type design, architecture, curatorial practice, and corporate design practice, we see convergences of thinking that are unique yet parallel to one another.

The Black Designer's Journey: Theory of Change

YOCASTA
LACHAPELLE

I'm often asked: "What is the trajectory for Black designers into our industry?" My answer? "The same as it was in 1985." That's the year designer, historian and scholar, Cheryl D. Miller published her landmark thesis "Transcending the Problems of the Black Graphic Designer to Success in the Marketplace," identifying systemic challenges encountered by Black designers.[1] In the decades since, those issues, while acknowledged, have in many ways been exacerbated. Even current efforts to address these barriers to success remain disparate and fragmented, rather than a coordinated and deliberate systemic approach that effectively encompasses the full spectrum of a Black designer's journey. Indeed, there is no singular issue but a series of possible and inevitable obstacles Black designers face at every stage of their path into the industry.

My own journey began as a creative kid who had no idea how to channel my creativity into a viable career. It was a childhood friend, a receptionist at a production company, who recognized my talent and invited me to interview, a slightly random entry into the design industry that became an enduring career; one I largely navigated without a clear roadmap to success.

Now, I help launch careers as the Director of Talent at COLLINS, where I am responsible for talent recruitment, development, and management, including leading outreach initiatives like the COLLINS High School through College Summer Internship program.[2] Initially conceived to build early awareness about careers within design, we very quickly realized we needed to go beyond simply raising awareness. We needed to go further to figure out how to support and sustain their ability to achieve their full potential as designers.

Our experiences with our interns, coupled with Miller's profound insights to common barriers and proposed remedies, inspired us to chart young Black designers' pathways into design, and to create our program. As Miller recognized nearly four decades ago, those barriers still include lack of access and mentorship; the often prohibitive costs of higher education and experiences of "otherness" once they transitioned there. This infographic is intended not only to highlight the obstacles young Black creatives encounter at all stages of their journey, but more importantly the actions we can take as an industry, to achieve the outcomes we seek.

Like many other industries struggling with inclusion—it is a huge effort. We are trying to fix a system that is broken; one we as designers should ideally reimagine and rebuild from the ground up. Despite these challenges, we must remain committed to our efforts, learning and adding industry-wide support systems year over year to encourage recruitment and retention of Black designers. What we know is that our industry's response requires a long-term, coordinated, and systemic approach that consists of equal parts mentorship, sponsorship, *and* education—and the benefits are mutual. Design is not what we make, it's what we make possible for others. Accordingly, investing in Black design talent makes a broader and more innovative industry perspective possible.

My hope? That one day soon, through our collective action and tangible progress, my answer to the question, "What is the trajectory for Black designers in our industry?" will be: "Whatever they want it to be."

NOTES

1. Cheryl D. Miller, "Transcending the Problems of the Black Graphic Designer to Success in the Marketplace," *Thesis. Pratt Institute* (New York: Stanford Digital Repository (1985).
2. Collins Black Lives Matter statement and BIPOC educational programs, wearecollins.com/ideas/black-lives-matter-our-journey-towards-meaningful-change/.
3. Chart Footnotes: Boyington, Briana; Kerr, Emma and Wood, Sarah. "20 Years of Tuition Growth at National Universities," *U.S. News & World Report*, September 17, 2021. usnews.com/education/best-colleges/paying-for-college/articles/2017-09-20/see-20-years-of-tuition-growth-at-national-universities.
4. The Editors, "Why do students decline their dream schools?," EAB, March 23, 2017, eab.com/insights/blogs/enrollment/why-do-students-decline-their-dream-schools/.

5. Ku, Ailun, and Jessica Pliska. "Structural Racism by
    the Numbers and How to Fix It," Ozy, May 9, 2021.
    ozy.com/news-and-politics/structural-racism-by-the
    -numbers-and-how-to-fix-it/431206/.
6. Pipelines Foundation (*The Diversity Connect Report*
    2018 data), pipelines.pro/foundation.
7. Ku, "Structural Racism."
8. Crescencio, Araceli. "How Do Declining Funds for
    Art Education Affect Aspiring Artists?," Pepperdine
    University Graphic, April 16, 2019. pepperdine-
    graphic.com/how-do-declining-funds-for-art-education-
    affect-aspiring-artists/.
9. 9. Zeiser, Kristina. "Evaluating the Impact of Early
    College High Schools," American Institutes for
    Research. air.org/project/evaluating-impact-early-
    college-high-schools.
10. The Editors, "Inequality in Public School Funding:
    Key Issues & Solutions for Closing the Gap," American
    University School of Education, September 10, 2020.
    soeonline.american.edu/blog/inequality-in-public-
    school-funding.
11. National Association of Colleges & Employers,
    Internship & Co-op Report 2019. naceweb.org/
    store/2019/internship-and-co-op-report/.
12. Belli, Gina. "How Many Jobs Are Found Through
    Networking, Really?," *Payscale*, April 6, 2017.
    payscale.com/career-advice/many-jobs-found
    -networking/.

Access

PRE-COLLEGE

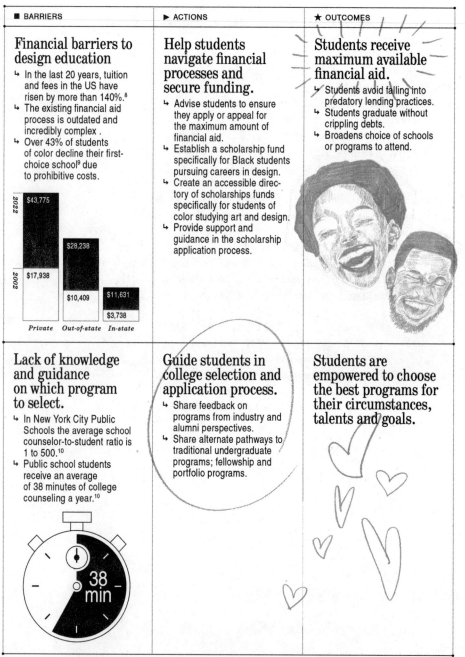

■ BARRIERS	▶ ACTIONS	★ OUTCOMES
Financial barriers to design education ↳ In the last 20 years, tuition and fees in the US have risen by more than 140%.[8] ↳ The existing financial aid process is outdated and incredibly complex. ↳ Over 43% of students of color decline their first-choice school[9] due to prohibitive costs.	**Help students navigate financial processes and secure funding.** ↳ Advise students to ensure they apply or appeal for the maximum amount of financial aid. ↳ Establish a scholarship fund specifically for Black students pursuing careers in design. ↳ Create an accessible directory of scholarships funds specifically for students of color studying art and design. ↳ Provide support and guidance in the scholarship application process.	**Students receive maximum available financial aid.** ↳ Students avoid falling into predatory lending practices. ↳ Students graduate without crippling debts. ↳ Broadens choice of schools or programs to attend.
Lack of knowledge and guidance on which program to select. ↳ In New York City Public Schools the average school counselor-to-student ratio is 1 to 500.[10] ↳ Public school students receive an average of 38 minutes of college counseling a year.[10]	**Guide students in college selection and application process.** ↳ Share feedback on programs from industry and alumni perspectives. ↳ Share alternate pathways to traditional undergraduate programs; fellowship and portfolio programs.	**Students are empowered to choose the best programs for their circumstances, talents and goals.**

Chart (Barriers, top-left):

2022 — $43,775 (Private), $28,238 (Out-of-state), $11,631 (In-state)

2002 — $17,938 (Private), $10,409 (Out-of-state), $3,738 (In-state)

Private   Out-of-state   In-state

Stopwatch: **38 min**

Development

COLLEGE

■ BARRIERS	▶ ACTIONS	★ OUTCOMES
Lack of access, network, or sponsorship to facilitate internship opportunities.	**Create opportunities for students that initiate network access and foster development.**	**Students gain industry experience and preparedness.**
↳ Summer internships are 56% more likely to result in a full-time job offer.[11]	↳ Create summer internships. ↳ Accelerate students' academic progress. ↳ Offer portfolio reviews and development. ↳ Encourage apprenticeships ↳ Produce practitioner-led workshops.	↳ Students gain greater understanding of their ideal work environment and the type of work they want to do, enabling them to tailor outreach and portfolios to those companies. ↳ Students develop greater confidence and proficiency navigating professional environments.

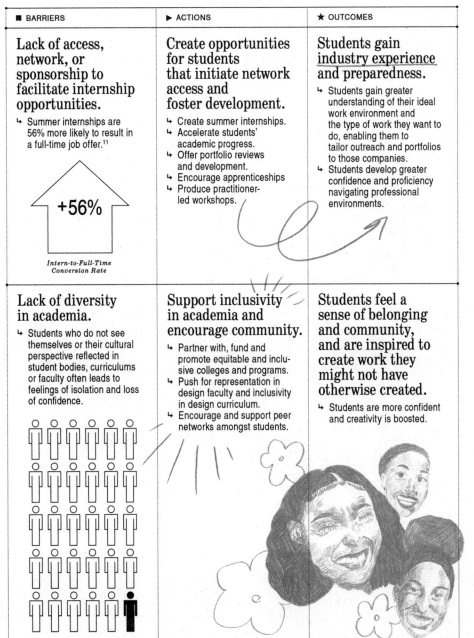

+56%

Intern-to-Full-Time Conversion Rate

Lack of diversity in academia.	**Support inclusivity in academia and encourage community.**	**Students feel a sense of belonging and community, and are inspired to create work they might not have otherwise created.**
↳ Students who do not see themselves or their cultural perspective reflected in student bodies, curriculums or faculty often leads to feelings of isolation and loss of confidence.	↳ Partner with, fund and promote equitable and inclusive colleges and programs. ↳ Push for representation in design faculty and inclusivity in design curriculum. ↳ Encourage and support peer networks amongst students.	↳ Students are more confident and creativity is boosted.

Recruitment

INDUSTRY

■ BARRIERS	▶ ACTIONS	★ OUTCOMES
Lack of network, mentorship and sponsorship to secure entry level jobs. ↳ 80% of jobs come through networks,[12] making them a vital component to industry access.	**Strengthen industry networks for students.** ↳ Share your network by fostering industry introductions and sponsorship. ↳ Provide mentorship and career counseling. ↳ Provide access to job boards and recruiters to connect students to opportunities.	**Students secure a job within the industry.**
Industries look to a few elite programs for recruitment. ↳ Elite schools boast a monopoly of our industry leaders as faculty, they also tend to have a disproportionately low % of Black students—as low as 2%. which mirrors the proportions we then see in the industry.	**Look beyond elite programs for candidates.** ↳ Actively recruit from a range of schools. ↳ Seek out equitable, inclusive and innovative programs. ↳ Support 2-year and 4-year programs as viable alternatives to traditional programs.	**Increased Black representation in design.**

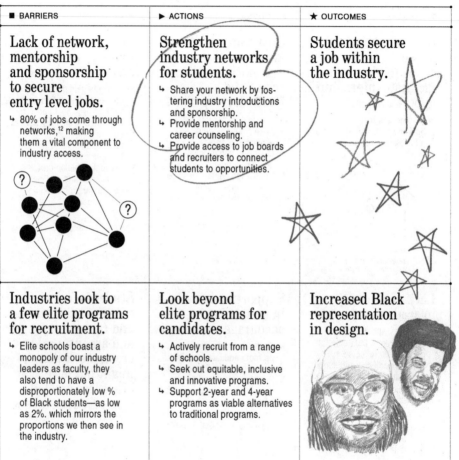

In Pursuit of a Prismatic Profession

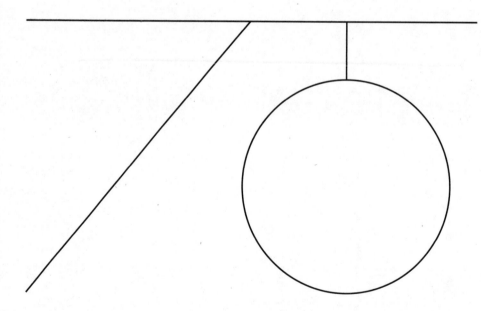

FOREST YOUNG

Blackness is the ceaselessly miraculous demonstration that there is no Black and white, just sun and shade.

—Fred Moten, New York University

Today, 3 percent of professional designers identify as Black.[1] Compare this figure to the 13 percent population estimate for African Americans from the most recent U.S. Census.[2] We observe a broken mirror. Demographers estimate that by 2045, the collective BIPOC ethnic group will overtake white Americans as the minority majority—a new majority with rising political and economic influence. By mid-century, Black power will extend beyond a revolutionary ideal to become a potent reality. Approaching this tipping point, however, it seems that as a nation we stand timidly at the foot of a daunting bridge. Will our excitement to traverse it eclipse our fear of stumbling across? How does American design resolutely embrace diversity, equity, and inclusion as its transformative point of difference?

Rising to meet this promise of a fully realized profession is also an exercise in fundamentally recalibrating it. Too many companies still uphold a scarcity argument relative to talent acquisition. Earnest actions must extend beyond incrementalism and the tallying of mere percentages. A goal is to pursue a new normal, one in which a single, colorless beam becomes prismatic. And for that, a new mechanism altogether is needed.

To clarify for the reader, I'm writing from a specific vantage point—that of my own lived experience as a Black professional designer working in the United States. I am advocating for a prismatic outcome as it transcends notions of the provider and the beneficiary, sun and shade. It is not assumptive of a future space of white-centeredness. It is brilliance, in the form of a distinct and harmonious spectrum of voices, perspectives, abilities, and histories.

The prevailing argument goes something like this: if the number of viable Black candidates is increased, diversity in the workplace will follow as a natural consequence. A key impediment in addressing a staggeringly low volume is a preconception that applicant standards would need to be lowered to fulfill a desire for greater numbers of candidates. Both the scarcity argument and standards bias are enveloped in a larger problematic and oversimplified lens—that there is a talent pipeline that is empty. Scarce metrics beget scarce metrics. To sincerely address the relative homogeneity of the design profession, we need to reframe the solution from one of scarcity, the end result of a broken career pathway, to one of professional cultivation. How, then, does a talented seventeen-year-old high school junior become a twenty-three-year-old designer?

Four anchor points drive this path forward. First, young and impressionable Black minds must see themselves within the profession. This *representational imprinting* is critical in making a design pathway visible—demonstrated by role models; it is a career trajectory that can then be mapped and emulated. Second, art education needs to surface and alleviate structural, cultural, and economic impediments to pursuing design as a course of study. It must *open the gates and support viable paths to graduation*. Third, companies must aspire to create *prismatic cultures*. Hiring can only defy tokenism when spaces are inclusive—welcoming authentic selves into the workplace, and setting candidates up for success. Lastly, a supportive *professional lattice* creates a resilient workforce and introduces new talent and networks into the field. These new connections offer a buffer and shared strategies for countering microaggressions, toxic environments, and glass ceilings; they are restorative and extend links across generations.

REPRESENTATIONAL IMPRINTING

In 2020, the absence of viable career cultivation strategies for Black designers was pronounced as our foundational reality was irrevocably shaken. We experienced our collective livelihoods set against the incendiary backdrop of a global civil rights movement and the COVID-19 pandemic. So much brokenness was visible. For BIPOC America, in particular, the coronavirus brilliantly exposed preexisting fault lines—where Black and Brown communities were disproportionately affected, just as they were called on as essential workers or persevered at demanding, high-risk service jobs to support their families. Hate crimes targeting Asian Americans spiked across all metropolitan centers. The escalated calls for civil rights were uniquely contextualized for these communities that had been ravaged by disease, and by centuries of oppressive systems. While representational advocates were visible across sports and entertainment, Black design professionals were conspicuously absent. This led Mitzi Okou to found *Where Are the Black Designers?*[3] along with Garrett Albury to promote diversity and equity, and to hold perennial design consultancies and in-house studios accountable for their complicity in amplifying a host of deleterious forces. They sought to make visible the Black designers in question, realizing that in 2020, representation had never been more vital to morale. The profession was placed under intense scrutiny. To no one's surprise, among other findings, historical professional leadership consisted of a homogenous set of actors—a cabal centered in whiteness—the former students of unchecked Eurocentrism, and the gatekeepers of entry points hiding in plain sight. For youth hoping for a telegraphic signal of "welcome"—there was none. But in peering into these deep professional fissures, we can imagine pathways for urgent remediation, and ultimately the redemption of the field. After all, the cracks are how the light gets in.

Two bright precedents highlight programmatic solutions and interventions for Black youth seeking entrée into the design profession. In Toronto, Dr. Elizabeth "Dori" Tunstall, the world's first Black dean of a design school at Ontario College of Art and Design University (OCAD), set up a mentorship program called *Blackreach*.[4] It provides a four-week summer design intensive for Black youth; attendees aged eight to twelve years are tutored on aesthetics and portfolio preparation. After all, Black students cannot gain admission into an art school without a portfolio. And if the student's high school does not offer AP Art or Architecture, in this vacuum how could we expect an inspired portfolio to emerge?

In New York City, under the visionary leadership of Caroline Baumann, the Cooper Hewitt, Smithsonian Design Museum initiated the first annual Teen Design Fair,[5] where design-enthralled teens could talk with top Black and other designers working in the fields of fashion, product design, architecture, and graphic design. Such exposure and access were valuable reminders that most designers are not public figures; their work does not usually signal Black authorship.

Both programs address, in different ways, opportunities for representational imprinting. Black youth can see themselves in Black faculty or professional mentors, better understand the bread crumbs toward success in their respective fields, and receive assistance and emotional support in preparing requisite materials for passage into the next stage of their journey—art school education.

OPEN GATES AND VIABLE PATHS TO GRADUATION

Art schools, the purveyors of design degrees, have long been equated with elite pursuits. With some schools listing annual tuition above $70,000, the risk-reward calculation is almost untenable for those whose parents cannot foot such a bill. As art schools often are tuition dependent in order to pay faculty and provide world-class facilities, they typically can't offer equivalent access to the best and brightest talent. Class asymmetries begin to dominate the dynamics of matriculation. While more affordable and culturally supportive environments exist for Black, Brown, and Indigenous students in Historically Black Colleges and Universities (HBCUs), Hispanic-serving institutions (HSIs), and Tribal Colleges and Universities (TCUs), many of these schools do not confer BFA degrees in graphic or industrial design. Further, across most of the schools' design curricula is a pedagogical gap in making visible the historical contributions of designers outside a Eurocentric canon. Educators are not incentivized to revise Eurocentric pedagogy and tunnel-visioned history due to tenure priorities, who gets elevated stature within the profession, and the successful professional placement of star students that validate the norm. In Cheryl D. Miller's landmark *Print* article "Black Designers: Missing in Action," she called out the fact that Black design students face the same challenges as their white peers—competition, accepting criticism, and asking questions with confidence. But additional pressures often prevail, including inadequate financial resources, limited guidance on navigating identity expressions and expanding the canon, and lack of emotional support from parents when pursuing a design education.[6] For many Black students who are anticipating substantial student loan debt, coupled with parental skepticism of the merits of a nontraditional educational pathway, their work begins to suffer. Even those with high school design portfolios superior to many of their incoming classmates, the work soon becomes preoccupied with being "professionally viable"—it exudes vocation over self-possession. Upon graduation, student loan debt and limited financial resources may rule out employment in vital metropolitan design hubs due to high costs of living. Those with stronger financial support may encounter a subtler and formidable barrier to entry—"cultural fit."

PRISMATIC CULTURES

Because graphic design, unlike architecture, lacks a licensing requirement, it is a profession dominated by networking and word-of-mouth referrals, and is thus particularly vulnerable to the compounding effects of cultural fit. This becomes immediately apparent for recent Black graduates who are often made to feel undesirable despite proof of academic rigor and success. Cultural fit, with its subsequent homogeneity, has become code for hermetically sealed white social contexts, including parental professional connections and art school alumni networks.

If professional design cultures are homogenous, they are not diverse. If they are diverse, they are often not inclusive. This inertia of tokenism remains un-braked, as optical diversity is much more comfortable than a sincere, systemic overhaul. In contrast to token hires, those companies aspiring to create prismatic cultures know that in order to manifest higher-performing products and visually divergent artifacts, diversity is an absolute prerequisite. Cognitively diverse teams—colleagues with divergent perspectives, ages, and physical abilities—statistically outperform homogenous teams ad infinitum. In this respect, we must reframe "Diversity, Equity & Inclusion" from quotas and obligatory contracts to creative advantage. With a greater volume of aspiring designers with varied lived experiences and vantage points, the profession at large stands to benefit exponentially. As prismatic cultures emerge as a new normal in the workplaces of tomorrow, Black design professionals will at once be more visible and have greater agency to shape the ecosystems in which they operate. To pursue a prismatic workplace is to address diversity from the demand side—we want you—versus the supply side—you are counted, but not valued.

PROFESSIONAL LATTICES

Lastly, a professional lattice can be formed between those designers who are able to traverse the precarious bridge from entry-level to managerial stations. They are the representative role models that close the loop on the cycle of cultivation. Eschewing token roles, these designers are warriors within our profession, restructuring the field as they move through it. The lattice left in their wake offers lateral pathways to rising designers when glass ceilings are impeding their progress.

In summary, the momentary existential crisis of our profession has made certain assertions abundantly clear. This X-ray exposed many models to be fundamentally flawed—such as talent scarcity arguments and standards bias rationales. The design profession benefits from plenitude. The untapped potential for the American design profession at large then lies in the cultural capital of its increasingly diverse population. If China's technological ascent was predicated largely on population scale and density, then America should see population diversity as its vital asset. The majority minority may be the catalyst for a new era of economic prosperity, free from the constraints of historical inertia. A profession, as a whole, becomes prismatic. In modifying Audrey Hepburn's maxim, to plant a Black garden is to believe in tomorrow.

NOTES

1. This figure was reported by the American Institute of Graphic Design (AIGA) in its 2019 Census report and has been widely referenced by members of the design community. As of November 2021, the report has been made unavailable for public viewing.
2. Jones, Nicholas; Marks, Rachel, and Ramirez, Roberto, and Rios-Vargas, Merarys. "Improved Race and Ethnicity Measures Reveal U.S. Population Is Much More Multiracial," *United States Census Bureau*, census.gov/library/stories/2021/08/improved-race-ethnicity-measures-reveal-united-states-population-much-more-multiracial.html.
3. Where Are the Black Designers?, watbd.org/.
4. Ontario College of Art and Design's Black OCAD U community, blackocadu.ca/bydi/.
5. Cooper Hewitt, Smithsonian Design Museum's 2018 Teen Design Fair, cooperhewitt.org/event/teen-design-fair-10-16-2018/.
6. Cheryl D. Miller, "Black Designers: Missing in Action," *Print,* Vol. 41 (1987): 58.

&&&:

Provoking
Type

SCHESSA GARBUTT

I am an identity, UX/UI, and budding type designer living and working in Inglewood, California. I grew up in Los Angeles, raised by a single mom and the city's typographic supergraphics[1]—the Hollywood sign and massive graffiti artworks on the backs and undersides of the freeways that both connect and segregate the county. As a first-generation American and college student, I grew up comfortable with standing in the doorway between identities and communities—Afrolatinx, Belizean, and Southern Black, poor at a very rich school, and genderqueer.

I have accepted and welcomed the nonhierarchical, nonlinear way that time, my mind, and my body exist and operate in the world. So far, type design seems deeply at odds with these ways of being. In my conversations with other Black designers, one person refers to type as "the country club" of design. Another "jokes" that Times New Roman and Helvetica feel like design's Confederate monuments. I knew I'd be in the belly of the beast when I entered a sub-craft that is even more white+cis than graphic design at large. But I didn't have a sense of how snakelike that beast would be until I saw it for myself.

MY WORK   In my current practice at Firebrand, I'm trying to embrace all of my identities, and am seeking out work with folks who share them. Creating in this way is deeply connected to my studio's mission of more equitable access to design for change makers of color. Especially in my recent projects, I'm pushing myself to reference less of the Eurocentric aesthetics of North American design, and turn instead toward my codesigners, to Black futurism, and to nature Herself for inspiration. I have been intentionally shifting my creative center away from whiteness and cis-masculinity. Here are some examples of how I'm doing that in my type and logotype work.

In one brand project, I worked with LA-based curanderx/healer Habló Rodriguez Diaz, who after seeing my first drafts of logo concepts, simply asked, ***"So, can we make it way more Brown, and way more Queer?"*** and in doing so gave my entire creative practice a whole new outlook. No one, in all of my time as a student or professional, had ever asked me to make something more like me, more like us. We worked together to research their/our (Mayan, Mexican, and Colombian) ancestors' aesthetics to infuse into the wordmark. We referenced the stone-carved patterns of Mayan temples, as well as Muisca (Indigenous Colombian) glyphs. Because Hablo's healing practice *is* deeply personal, and *is* about calling forth the strength and wisdom of their ancestors and teachers, it felt right that this hand-lettered "logo" was more like a sigil, a visual prayer of gratitude for their predecessors.

Fig. 1

And then I made my first font, and named it after my favorite sci-fi writer, Octavia Butler. "FCH Octavia embodies The Great Both/ And. Her aesthetic core is the retro-futurist boxy-thicc superellipse. She foretells Black femmes among the stars with her expansive counters and jetsetting crossbars. She is both organic and mechanic with her natural curves and no-nonsense, low contrast body": I wrote this description for the final presentation in my Intro to Modern Type Design BIPOC class. My femme and nonbinary classmates loved it. The white men in my life couldn't *quite* put their finger on why, but it felt like "too much going on" or they "thought it was cool, but would never use it."

I was elated that somehow it came across in the design that this type wasn't about those men, and wasn't for them.

I embrace my multitudes.
I accept your multitudes.

PROVOCATIONS   Right now I am in the yearlong certificate program at Type West. We're finishing our first term soon, and I am finding myself torn and frustrated. I'm not alone in this. The problems I

394

Fig. 2

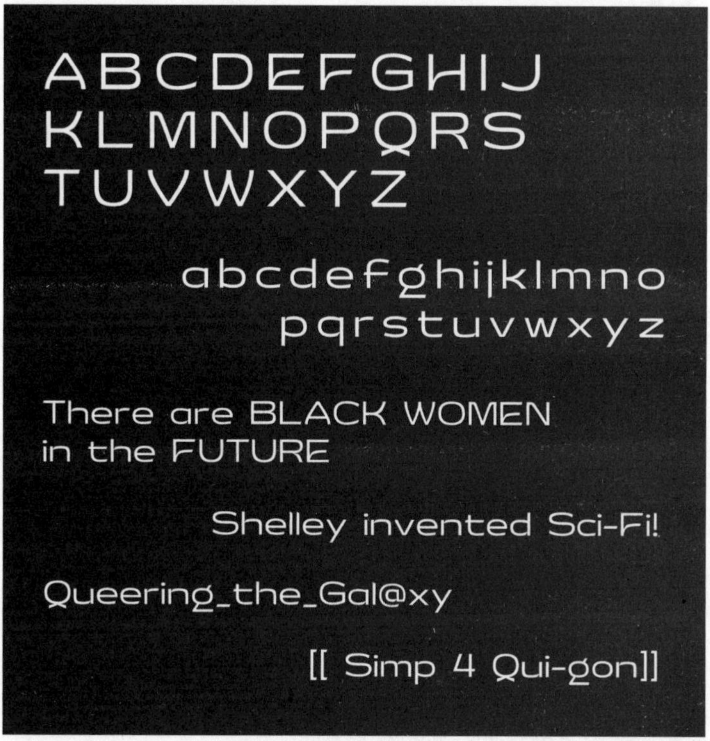

ABCDEFGHIJ
KLMNOPQRS
TUVWXYZ

abcdefghijklmno
pqrstuvwxyz

There are BLACK WOMEN
in the FUTURE

Shelley invented Sci-Fi!

Queering_the_Gal@xy

[[Simp 4 Qui-gon]]

see with our current ways of determining good from bad type have been noted by many Black designers before me. I want other Black type design students to know that they're not alone in their frustrations. My newness to the craft allows me to see it from the outside, and see the practices I do and don't want to carry forward.

I am currently doing the mental work of surveying and disentangling optical guidelines from white and Eurocentric aesthetics of type. They are a big ball of yarn. I'm not sure whether I'll end up with two separate strings or one really long one once I get all of the knots undone. Whenever a new "rule" about type design comes up, I make sure to jot it down. In their unraveling I am seeing some patterns emerge already. Here are the types of rules that sit well with me:

» Letter space is counter space. (The negative space inside of each letter should feel equal to the space between letters, if the goal is smooth reading.)
» Taper or add inktraps at the intersections of strokes so that they appear consistent in weight.

» If your stroke weight, contrast, and letter spacing are consistent, the typeface will feel cohesive.

There's a trend here—I'm responding to the way that type is perceived by (Latin alphabet-reading) brains as positive and negative space, and how to better understand the things most of our eyes do when they stare at little symbols. These feel like maxims that I can use for most any text weight typeface designed for longform and fast reading. Of course, knowing these makes me want to intentionally subvert them, especially if my goal is to slow a reader down, dazzle their eyes, or create a contemplative experience—perhaps for short or coded messages. (In a time where we're all rushing from screen to screen and content to content, I'm finding those goals and experiments more appealing in my personal practice.)

Here are some of the rules and expectations that I find myself pushing against:

» Reference old type styles and aesthetics when creating new type— the old masters (mostly white men) know better than us.
» Type is a tool that shouldn't inhibit reading; reading what is written is always more important than how it looks. (See design theory classic, "The Crystal Goblet")[2]
» Focus on making typefaces that *others* would find useful.
» "There are too many ideas in this typeface."
» "This sketch of this letter is too weird."

I like knowing these rules—and ignoring them once I hold them next to the type I want to make, the histories I want to revive, and the design futures I want to see.

Being told that a typeface is "*too much*" or "*too loud*" is an unnecessary othering of new type ideas. It sets off the same alert in my mind as when Black women and Queer folks are told that we are being too much or too loud. It's the typographic equivalent of tone policing.

"Tone it down with the volume/joy/style/hair/opinions/ language/anger—*then maybe* we'll listen to what you have to say."

"Share your opinion in these preapproved ways and channels, and then maybe we'll be comfortable enough to listen."

"Design your type to appeal to *these* mainstream tastes, and then we'll consider it good type."

I am "too much" only in that I'm made of many inter-secting Others. I am called "opinionated" only when my opinion differs from the majority and I am willing to assert it. If my being Queer and Black makes my type design choices "loud," then maybe it's type for shouting. Maybe it's type just for writing opinions that refuse to be placated. Maybe it's for representing voices that speak in other dialects. Maybe this type is speaking creole or AAVE, not MLA or "good English." Maybe this type isn't talking to you, and the conversation isn't about you.

A missing piece of the larger type design conversation is exploring new ways for BIPOC and Queer folks to talk to *ourselves*. No doubt, the essay you are reading will be typeset in something ubiquitous, because it's easier to read quickly, and because a more traditional typeface will signal "academic discourse." Type design has always been a shibboleth for certain groups and subcultures; academia is no exception. Times New Roman has become the calm, even tone at the podium, speaking "objectively." (Compare that to design for heavy metal posters: intentionally jarring, jagged, and hard to read; designed to resonate with the aesthetic preferences of the crowd it's speaking to as well.) When I want to speak primarily to a "mass market" (white) audience, or signal "friendly and chipper" I might use Arial. But if I want to speak specifically to other Black and Brown witches in Los Angeles, I'll use something a little more lively. I'll relax into myself a little bit more. I'll relax into the comfort that I'll be understood when I'm at my most exploratory, esoteric or expressing all my hyphenations at once. **My type may also embrace all its hyphenations.** *Where can I learn to embrace all of my hyphenations?*

IN THE CLASSROOM   Can white type designers (historical and present-day) teach Black and Queer folks how to talk to ourselves? How would this classroom be different with a BIPOC instructor in it?

When it comes to referencing historical designs, there are standards that should be followed *if the goal* is to make a design feel more digestible and traditional. Following conventions is a tool. Just like conventions in app interface design, conventions in type design can reduce the friction a user feels when they interact with something unfamiliar. Making sure a lowercase u doesn't have those extra serifs[3] is akin to putting the hamburger button in the top corner of the screen.

On the other hand, we must continuously acknowledge that these conventions are what white men thought would look good to other white men that they wanted to sell type to. Early metal type design-ers knew that their primary consumers were not women of color and poor people (though many American foundries used slave labor). White-owned foundries knew that their audiences were interested in rationality, symmetry, and mechanical perfection—Enlightenment ideals that they felt should be reflected in all things, including type. **Every aesthetic has an implied value system.** We can't assume that a new, more diverse generation of type designers prioritizes our values in the same way that those three hundred plus years ago did. We must each meditate on what we care about today, in the present. Expressiveness? Accessibility? (What makes a font hyperlegible is different for different audiences/media.) Intuition? Honoring our own histories, rather than reviving others'?

There's a colorful history to what much of old type had been used for. Maybe Black/Queer designers aren't interested in referencing and reviving styles that were primarily used in conquest and forced conversion, used to typeset receipts in economic systems that sold our bodies as goods, or printed in books that were used to make us forget our own religions and ancient wisdoms. This isn't to say that all of Western type history goes out the window. Ultimately, I live steeped in these traditions as part of my cultural DNA too, by virtue of living in the United States and growing up with these typefaces in this design ecosystem. I am both inside and outside the tradition, like standing in a doorway.

The answer to whether white+cis teachers can inform Black and Queer work becomes stickier when it comes to present-day type teachers. On one hand, certain optical rules are learned through instruction and practice. And if I'm working on a "mainstream" typeface, I defer to my teachers as experts. On the other hand, we value our cultural references differently. While Blackletter is seen as a precious and indispensable type reference, graffiti is painted as a "special interest" and not a part of the official American design canon (despite the fact that many letterforms used in Los Angeles tagging are descendants of Blackletter styles found in the *Speedball Text Book*).[4] I grew up surrounded by graffiti. Is it possible to remove those references from my design decisions? Should I adopt the casual classism that relegates these styles to "vernacular" or "not real design" and reject them from my personal canon? Whether I choose to use them or not, they are a part of what has shaped me as a designer.

And if I adopt my own references, will my classmates and teachers put in the work to respect or understand them well enough to be able to critique them beyond "this reminds me of graffiti"? Will they be able to say, "Hey, have you considered a K with a hooked leg instead of a straight one? Look at this and this classic LA graffiti for reference." **I have put in the work to respect and understand white type ideals, so have many other students.** There is work that I'm eager to make but hesitant to share in a formal design school context because I know it won't receive the critique and elevated conversation that it deserves. I believe that in most classrooms, the teacher can learn as much from the students as the students learn from them. **It is not good enough for teachers to admit a blind spot and/or just ignore the work in crits.** On critiquing the work of BIPOC students, Kelly Walters, offers: "Get curious. Ask lots of questions about your students' work. Then, actively listen."

VERY VERY, I explain my frustrations to Saki Mafundikwa, a pillar in
VERY VERY Black type design and author of *Afrikan Alphabets*. He tells me about his own journey back to Zimbabwean aesthetics, after working in New York alongside Hoffman and Rand, making work as elegant as theirs. "I realized I grew up surrounded by designers," he shared. "My father was a carpenter. My mother crocheted. She was making wireframes before the word was invented!" We talk about the spiritual gift that creativity is, and our mutual belief that sometimes our ancestors want to send a message through our work; and how the imaginary white art director on our shoulder sometimes stops them at the door. This conversation feels taboo for a contemporary design classroom (and so I am sharing it here in case you never hear it elsewhere). He offered me so much advice, but here are the two that I feel compelled to share with other designers and students of color/queerness:

"Make the work you need to make." Don't let anyone extinguish your flame, or keep you from expressing the messages that want to be seen through your work.

and

"With your teachers, you will have to be very very . . . very very . . . Kind." They are also learning from me, and you. This writing is an act of kindness for me. I am sharing my story, my multiplicity, my praxis here so that we can move the conversation forward.

To Saki's advice I would add: *Your energy is precious.* Whiteness will endlessly ask us to explain and re-explain our ways of being. Know that your patience and time don't have to be bottomless wells. Share what you want. Save the rest for yourself and your work. Thank you for being here.

Thank you to my mentors and peers, whose conversations nourish me and helped me clarify my thinking: Kelly Walters, Steve Jones, Tré Seals, Saki Mafundikwa, Nina Stössinger, Agyei Archer, June A. Grant, Alex Pines, Michelle Devlin and Juan Villanueva.

SCHESSA GARBUTT

NOTES

1. Say that five times fast.
2. Warde, Beatrice. "The Crystal Goblet or Why Printing Should Be Invisible," *The Crystal Goblet, Sixteen Essays on Typography*, Cleveland: World Pub. Co., 1956.
3. Aren't all serifs a little extra?
4. Check out Eric Hu's 2020 Typographics talk. In twenty minutes I learned more about my local type history than in all of my other design education. https://2020.typographics.com/schedule/eric-hu/.

IMAGE CREDITS

1. Curanderx Connections wordmark, Schessa Garbutt
2. FCH Octavia typeface, Schessa Garbutt

1 Word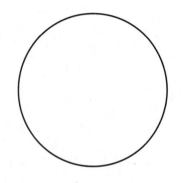

---

1 Object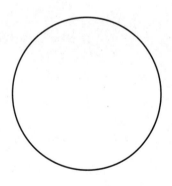

FORMER AND CURRENT
DESIGN STUDENTS

The co-editors of *The Black Experience in Design* reached out to some of their former and current Black design students during the development of this book. They wanted to learn how their students might reflect on their journey in design, what they have learned and how they have navigated the discipline. As part of this design contribution, we asked our students to select one object and one word to describe their experience.

What you see here is a lyrical mixture of objects and words that convey a range of responses to our prompt: What one word and image reflects your current journey in design? From among the graphic and product designers, researchers, illustrators, strategists, and entrepreneurs, we see revealed many intersections of thought. We see complexity and craft. We hear curiosity and critique. We see process and product. We hear histories and futures.

With these fourteen objects and words we find ourselves reflecting on the objects and words we might have submitted at different stages in our journey. We hope these fourteen provide the inspiration for your own reflections on your place in time.

The following images and words were submitted by Brian Bishop, Terrayne Brown, Eden Elam, Kgothatso Lephoko, Asha McClendon, Janel Rose Mitchell, Staicy Wairimu Ngongu, Jecori Owens-Shuler, Unique Patton, Ajay Revels, Brandon Juan Surtain, Joshua Wall, Kyra Wells and Brandon Wilburn. These designers have either graduated from or are current students from some of the following institutions: The Claremont Colleges, Cleveland State University, Louisiana State University, North Carolina State University, Parsons School of Design at The New School, School of Visual Arts, Tulane University, University Arts London: Central Saint Martins, and Washington University in St. Louis.

Communal

Brian Bishop
Brian Bishop is a Designer for and by the Global Family.

Worthwhile

Terrayne Brown

I'm a Social designer working at a studio which has an equity-centered practice which centers Black experiences, histories, identities and assets in the design process

Prolonged

Asha McClendon
Asha McClendon is a soon to be graduate of Cleveland State University
(2021) and a full-time designer at an advertising and marketing agency in
Downtown Cleveland.

Broadening

Staicy Wairimu Ngongu
Staicy Wairimu Ngongu, 22 years, born and raised in Nairobi, Kenya.
Currently completing a bachelor's degree in communication design at
Parsons Design School.

Proximity

Janel Rose Mitchell
Design can be a potent tool for communication & social transformation. My intent as an artist is to penetrate peoples intellectual boundaries; by creating from a place of purpose; saturate & shift viewers perspective; by challenging normative context; and extract love & understanding of the human condition. I hope my art does this for you & everyone that sees it.

Exploratory

Jecori Owens-Shuler
I love doing the stuff that challenges the way that things are done or are perceived.

Evolving

Unique Patton
I am an Undergrad student attending NC State University majoring in Design
Studies with a concentration in Business Administration.

Forensics

Ajay Revels

Ajay Revels is a strategic design researcher who applies systems think-ing, ecological sciences and forensic approaches to uncover the cultural assumptions embedded in complex digital systems.

Enlightening

Brandon Juan Surtain
Brandon Surtain is an architectural designer and artist. His work primarily focuses on contributing to the dignity and agency of marginalized communities.

Layered

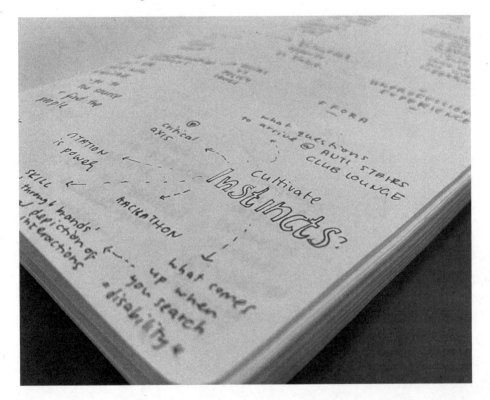

Kgothatso Lephoko

Kgothatso is a South African UX designer. She's keenly interested in the intersection of technology and local South African languages - explored in her masters thesis.

Interpretation

Kyra Wells

Kyra Wells is an alumna of Cleveland State University and works as Marketing Designer at American Greetings. Kyra actively serves Cleveland's creative community as a board member of AIGA Cleveland.

Fractal

Brandon Wilburn
I am an interactive designer at Consume and Create whose work is guided by embracing the what, considering the who and always asking why.

Inheritance

Eden Elam

Eden is a first-year Transdisciplinary Design MFA candidate at Parsons School of Design. She loves to swim, travel, and spend time with her mother.

Deconstructive

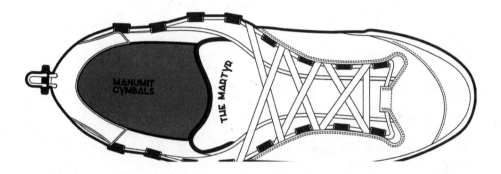

Joshua Wall
Joshua Wall is a Master Industrial Design Graduate from NC State University. He is the founder of brand/footwear design consulting company Manumit Cymbals.

Brian Bishop / Communal
Brian Bishop is a designer for and by the Global Family.

Terrayne Brown / Worthwhile
I'm a social designer working at a studio that has an equity-centered practice that centers Black experiences, histories, identities, and assets in the design process

Eden Elam / Inheritance
Eden is a first-year Transdisciplinary Design MFA candidate at Parsons School of Design. She loves to swim, travel, and spend time with her mother.

Kgothatso Lephoko / Layered
Kgothatso is a South African UX designer. She's keenly interested in the intersection of technology and local South African languages—explored in her MFA Products of Design thesis at School of Visual Arts NYC.

Asha McClendon / Prolonged
Asha McClendon is a soon-to-be graduate of Cleveland State University (2021) and a full-time designer at an advertising and marketing agency in downtown Cleveland.

Janel Rose Mitchell / Proximity
Design can be a potent tool for communication & social transformation. My intent as an artist is to penetrate peoples intellectual boundaries; by creating from a place of purpose; saturate & shift viewers perspective; by challenging normative context; and extract love & understanding of the human condition. I hope my art does this for you & everyone that sees it.

Staicy Wairimu Ngongu / Broadening
Staicy Wairimu Ngongu, twenty-two years, born and raised in Nairobi, Kenya. Currently completing a bachelor's degree in communication design at Parsons Design School.

Jecori Owens-Shuler / Exploratory
I love doing the stuff that challenges the way that things are done or are perceived.

Unique Patton / Evolving
I am an undergrad student attending NC State University majoring in Design Studies with a concentration in Business Administration.

Ajay Revels / Forensics
Ajay Revels is a strategic design researcher who applies systems thinking, ecological sciences and forensic approaches to uncover the cultural assumptions embedded in complex digital systems.

Brandon Juan Surtain / Enlightening
Brandon Surtain is an architectural designer and artist. His work primarily focuses on contributing to the dignity and agency of marginalized communities.

Joshua Wall / Deconstructive
Joshua Wall is a footwear designer. He is the founder of brand/footwear design consulting company Manumit Cymbals.

Kyra Wells / Interpretation
Kyra Wells is an alumna of Cleveland State University and works as Marketing Designer at American Greetings. Kyra actively serves Cleveland's creative community as a board member of AIGA Cleveland.

Brandon Wilburn / Fractal
I am an interactive designer at Consume and Create whose work is guided by embracing the what, considering the who, and always asking why.

Curating My Way into Design:

A Work in Progress

MICHELLE JOAN
WILKINSON

Writing about the grand opening in 2016 of the National Museum of African American History and Culture for *Disegno: The Quarterly Journal of Design*, scholar Adrienne Brown shared an unexpected finding. After describing the exterior design of the museum, the adjacent monuments, and the surrounding structures on the National Mall built by the enslaved, she explains, "What came unexpectedly was the consistent attention within the collections to the history of African American architecture and building, an aspect of the Black experience in the US that is frequently overlooked by historians and architects alike."[1]

In an essay that portends to focus on the design story of the building itself, Brown comfortably segues to examining how "[t]he emphasis on Black design precedents visible in the museum's exterior carries over to its holdings, which include objects ranging from a slave cabin to advertisements for Black housing developments."[2] Her review essay affirmed what I had hoped when I joined the museum in 2014—that architecture and design would be a legible part of the story the museum would tell, and that visitors would come away with a greater understanding and appreciation for the histories of Black people in design and building.

How I came to be an advocate for making design visible is my focus here. It is a story I have to tell myself as well, to make visible how and why design came to matter in my personal life and professional pursuits.

KIMBERLY HUGGINS: . . . What was it that sparked this transition in you?

SARA ZEWDE: . . . Most of my friends and colleagues entered into design from another creative field, but *I read my way into design*. Reading Du Bois, Lefebvre, de Certeau, and bell hooks, I just became fascinated with the spatial dimensions of this social world they're so interested in.[3]

HOW IT STARTED

I am about three years old and looking intently at a design imprinted on the walls of the house I grew up in, in Guyana, South America. The design is beautiful—glimmering greenish-gold hues against an eggshell matte surface, the outlines of a fleur-de-lis pattern catching the light flooding onto our floors and walls. I think, *This wall is magical, chameleon-like.* I move my body side to side, to see where it glimmers and when it turns static. Of course, if I am three, this is not my vocabulary. But is it my sentiment—wonder. I am a small girl encountering a large wall, but it is my wall and canvas. My space.

I had an early fascination with space and spaces, views, vistas, verandas, patterns, and designs. That fascination never left me. I took some circuitous routes to satisfy those passions. I studied literature and visual culture, not architecture and design, but I gravitated toward interpreting the spatial dimensions and design ideas represented in novels, poetry, paintings, and photography throughout my undergraduate and graduate years. I was in an interdisciplinary studies PhD program at Emory University when I first learned about the field of "cultural geography." More than a definition, the field can be described as addressing "how social groups engage with their landscapes, how people construct and make sense of their places and spaces . . . the ways that people enact identity, belonging, pleasure and difference throughout society . . . [and] the power structures that saturate these worlds."[4] Spurred by this new interest, I started a reading group on "Mapping, Space, and Culture," to gather colleagues I could engage with about new titles in the field. This was the early 1990s, and some of the authors I began reading were Peter Jackson, Neil Smith, and Doreen Massey.[5] In my courses I continued to fixate on issues of spatial representation—for example, the discussions of the "verandah" in Amitav Ghosh's *The Shadow Lines* resonated deeply with my experiences in Guyana, and were a jolt forward in recognizing that for the displaced, exiled, or immigrant, the memory of space lives in the individual's psyche. I recall writing essays exploring the longing for "home" in postcolonial literature, "cartographies of liberation" in women's narratives, and even the concept of "representin" as "a geopolitical aesthetic of rap music." I was consistent in my attention to how people navigated and remade space—not only the characters in an author's imagination, but how all people contended with belonging and how their decisions to "represent" reflected intense engagements with space and place. Some of my early scholarship took up these themes of identity formation vis-à-vis a spatial lens, "from neighborhood to nationhood" as I then called it. In retrospect, I was practicing forms of cultural geography intuited from my own experience as a child of two nations—Guyana and the United States—and as a scholar with training in **Comparative** Literature and **Interdisciplinary** Studies, two fields in which the brain is made to work at bringing in multiple perspectives and reading for intersections, overlaps, and divergences. A learned acuity to spatial environments, forged through my own experiences of movement, was enhanced by my academic training to critically examine ideas from multiple lenses. This layering became the foundation for my work to come.

HOW IT WENT   As a professor at Bard College, I continued further along this trajectory. My course "Mapping African American Literature" looked at how authors crafted the spatial worlds of their characters—did their protagonists flee, redesign, or resign themselves to the constructs imposed upon them? Texts like Jean Toomer's *Cane*, Ralph Ellison's *Invisible Man*, and Paule Marshall's *Brown Girl, Brownstones* brought students into this mode of critical thinking about the interior lives of Black people with their concomitant spatial concerns. Another course, "Women Writing the Americas," similarly moved beyond attending to representations of space, to understand the agency of women navigating, way-finding, and redesigning paths to get free of experiences that did not serve them well. What did the students think of these texts and these approaches? My sense is that they were no more or less moved by these ideas than any others in my teaching repertoire—and perhaps that is the lesson. The topics were accepted as "normal" and not something outside the box, but understood as part and parcel of how any text could be read. By the late 1990s, the "spatial turn" had made an imprint on academia, so if not on trend my thinking was at least within the realm of sanctioned scholarly approaches.

As I moved from teaching to museum work, I added this way of thinking to what I was learning about "ways of seeing" in art. By the time I became a full-fledged curator in 2007–2008, my first major exhibition at the Reginald F. Lewis Museum of Maryland African American History and Culture was *A People's Geography: The Spaces of African American Life*. As I summarized:

> From southern roads to the North Star,
> churches to barbershops, Black belts
> to the Black 'burbs, 27 visual artists
> expressed their vision of African
> American geographies through photog-
> raphy, prints, film and digital media,
> sculpture, textiles, and installation.
> The exhibition included historic maps
> and photographs, Underground Railroad
> routes, and visual and textual images

*reflecting on specific physical spaces—
slave ship, auction block, tenements,
the wilderness—as well as the internal landscapes of the imagination.*[6]

The show established ideas about Black geographies and Black space that drew from history and infused the gallery with glimpses of cultural intimacy as experienced in houses of worship (Jason Miccolo Johnson), the hair salon (Deborah Willis), and on a Baltimore stoop (Linda Day Clark). Other artists such as Terry Boddie, Stephen Marc, Sheila Pree Bright, and Roland Freeman helped frame the contours of the exhibit through works that highlighted restraint, escape, belonging, and the comforts of home. Through curatorial investigation and in three-dimensional form, I was realizing a personal goal to engage with artists who had also been exploring questions of space and place, physical structures as well as psychic landscapes. The exhibition was a turning point, marking the beginning of the period when my interior scholarly contemplations would have a more public expression and resonance through the design and built form of an exhibition space.[7]

In 2010, I began to explicitly add histories of design into my interdisciplinary research in African American and African Diaspora studies. I began by researching the design history of the house of my childhood—a concrete home in the "international style" designed and built by my grandfather in Guyana in 1954. Why did he make the design decisions he made, to build in concrete at a time when the predominant material was Guyanese timber? What did his family think of the house? Did they have the same fond memories that had stuck with me—the airy veranda, the fleur-de-lis walls, the fruit trees in the front and back yards? What was happening in the world that might have influenced his ideas, and how was his undertaking possible in 1954? Like that little girl looking up at a wondrous wall, I was again peering at an idea I wanted to better understand.

My interests were veering outside the scope of my curatorial duties at the Lewis Museum, but seemed increasingly pertinent to my personal fulfilment. Seeking to rectify that imbalance, I sought out conferences that would provide me with intellectual camaraderie and fellowships that could offer financial support for my research. I traveled to the National Archives in Guyana and the National Archives, Kew Gardens in the United Kingdom on a mixture of self-financing, crowdfunding, and research grants. I had opportunities to write about Guyana's architectural heritage using my family's history with design and building as fertile ground for a close reading of "mid-century modernisms" developed by Black craftspeople and builders. I contended that these late-colonial design histories were obscured by reliance on the terminology of "skilled laborers" to encom-

424

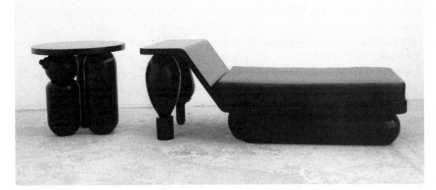

Fig. 1

Fig. 2

pass individuals like my grandfather—a proficient carpenter, draftsman, and building contractor with his own business, intellectual prowess, and decision-making power.

My curiosity was not only about the past. I was also in search of contemporary Black designers—who were they, where were they, what were they creating and designing, for whom, and why? My "vacations" were steered toward art and design fairs, including the African and African Caribbean Design Diaspora Festival in London in 2011. My experience there was a defining moment also, as I was introduced to Black designers such as Simone Brewster (Figs. 1 and 2) and Yinka Ilori. The strong narratives in their work brought design into view for me in a way that had not yet been fully exhibited or embraced in the United States for Black designers.

When I was selected as a fellow of the Center for Curatorial Leadership in 2012, I chose the Design Museum in London as the site of my one-week residency in order to shadow the museum's director, Deyan Sudjic. This appealed to me for two reasons. One, I wanted to spend time at a museum of design to get behind the scenes and understand how curatorial work played out in this setting. Two, I was impressed that the director had managed to maintain an active publishing record while leading an institution. I found his book, *The Language of Things: Understanding the World of Desirable Objects* accessible to a nonspecialist audience. The combination of having a residency within a design-focused museum and the public accessibility of the director's design writing made me identify that museum as a match for my learning.

The nuances of collecting and exhibiting design intrigued me, and I was curious about the ethics of design curation. One of my questions to Sudjic was about how one works with brands to exhibit design that is also available in the commercial marketplace. To what extent did a museum's nonprofit status present a conflict to collecting, exhibiting, and interpreting profit-driven design work? The answer was probably along

Fig. 3

Fig. 4

the lines of, "It's complicated," but it's the question that bears repeating for anyone undertaking curatorial work in this arena.

At the Lewis, I had begun trying to introduce design into my curatorial practice. My intention with the *Material Girls: Contemporary Black Women Artists* exhibition was to emphasize the inventive ways artists were attending to issues of material and use. In particular, I was looking at how generations of Black makers—male and female—birthed contemporary artists such as Joyce J. Scott, Sonya Clark, Renee Stout, Martha Jackson Jarvis, Chakaia Booker, and Maya Freelon Asante. For artists Maren Hassinger and Torkwase Dyson, I was attracted to the environmental concerns their material-driven work addressed. Dyson came the closest to introducing design as an element of the exhibition through a model structure she designed, titled *The Strategy of an Exuberant Future: Or, Reflection on a Lost Birth Certificate* (Figs. 3 and 4, 2011). The experimental prototype engaged ideas about solar powered habitation, reduction of waste, and preventing the extinction of endangered species. It was also a whimsical vessel decked out with feathers and sequined touches that intrigued and confounded visitors.

Material Girls was successful in the critical press and popular opinion, as the art itself merited . . . but I knew that curatorially, its core wasn't about design, yet. Indeed after having seen the spellbinding *The Global Africa Project* curated by Lowery Sims and Leslie King-Hammond which had opened in 2010 at the Museum of Arts and Design, I knew that a focused exhibition on design would require more sustained engagement with designers and practitioners. The questions I needed to ask would be different once the functionality of an object was an explicit imperative for its creation. The thinking about craft that I had begun with *Material Girls* was an important step, but there was more that I needed to investigate about design's delineation from art, craft, and other forms. I was up for that. I continued compiling my research file on Black designers, refining the questions that a design exhibition would pose, and conceiving of potential shows to make this work more visible.

In late 2013 I interviewed for a curatorial position at the National Museum of African American History and Culture, a forthcoming Smithsonian museum. I had solid curatorial experience under my belt that I spoke to in the interview, but I also had a passion that I needed to speak up about. I recall making a plea—more like a pitch!—for architects and designers to be well represented in the collections and exhibitions the museum was still developing. From the moment I said this, I was assured that such stories were important to the museum's leaders and curatorial staff. In fact, work was in progress to include such content. My ideas could have a home there, among the other work

I would be doing alongside colleagues.[8] That validation was stabilizing. I joined NMAAHC in March 2014, as a curator with general responsibilities in African American history and culture. In 2018, my curatorial duties became focused on architecture and design. But how did that happen?

And How Is It Going . . . ?

CALLING OUT DESIGN   When I arrived at NMAAHC, content about design and building was being integrated across several exhibitions throughout the museum. The museum's leadership, curatorial team, scholarly advisors, and focus groups had provided the contours of what stories the museum would tell. As for my role, I saw my work as making design explicit—calling design out from the shadows when needed, and making space for design on its own grounds as a recognized area for expanded collecting and exhibiting.

What do I mean by making design explicit? Despite having objects in our collections that related to design processes and professions, the significance of these objects to architectural history and design history was not always the primary reason the objects were acquired. Perhaps some of these objects were collected to illustrate stories about entrepreneurship, Black community life, or activism and social movements—and they also happened to exemplify aspects of design. For example, a newsprint poster by Emory Douglas, Minister of Culture for the Black Panther Party, may have had the following keywords assigned to it in the collections database: "Black Power," "Political Organizations," "Activism," and "Visual Arts." But not "graphic design." Understanding that, historically, many African Americans rendered their designs in anonymity, I felt compelled to identify "designers" and graphic artists whenever possible. Thus, one of my goals was to expand our collections to increase the quantity of objects and stories related to architecture and design. Another goal was to assess what was already in the collection to make sure we accurately identified the different forms of design in our holdings.

However, the first goal for everyone on staff was to get the museum ready for opening. When I joined the staff in 2014, we still had two years to go. In those two years, I cocurated and coscripted text for two inaugural exhibitions, *A Changing America: 1968 and Beyond* and *A Century in the Making: Building the National Museum of African American History and Culture*. For each, I inserted new narratives about design into the content being developed.

In the exhibition about a "changing America," we call attention to the cultural geographies that informed the post-1968 era. My cocurator William Pretzer and I specifically explore spatial dynamics in a

428

Fig 5

section titled "Shifting Landscapes," where a text panel on planned communities and subdivisions features Soul City, North Carolina. Conceptualized
by Floyd McKissick, Soul City sought to attract African Americans (and
others) to invest in developing a full-service, amenity-rich, residential and
commercial community. We were fortunate to have pamphlets about Soul
City in our collection that had not yet been slated for use in any of the
inaugural exhibitions. In addition to referencing the built landscape, the
proposed design materials featured illustrations of African Americans
engaged in all facets of the town's activities. These captivating images were
inclusive and affirming, and helped us visually present the Soul City story.

In an adjacent panel, also about planned communities,
we include images of architect Paul Revere Williams's work on the Berkeley
Square development in Las Vegas. The subdivision of 148 ranch-style
homes was recognized on the National Register of Historic Places in 2009
and remained a predominantly African American enclave into the twenty-first century.[12]

In a later section on hip-hop, we make connections to
graphic design. The initial plan was to exhibit a large Public Enemy banner
the museum had acquired and to discuss social consciousness in rap. In
our text panel for the banner, we added that front man Chuck D was a
trained graphic designer who designed his group's logo of a Black man in the
crosshairs of a gun sight. This profound image of a Black body as a target
helped us talk about racial profiling and police violence. We discuss how

being perceived as a "public enemy" continues to affect the lives of Black men and women today. Through such intentional label-writing, I sought to not only call attention to the iconic design, but also to counter the invisibility of designers by naming Chuck D as the logo's originator.[13]

For *A Century in the Making*, the exhibition was initially dedicated to documenting how the museum complied with stipulations for building on federal lands. However, with my cocurator Joanne Hyppolite, and the encouragement of founding Director Lonnie Bunch, we developed a more expansive concept that included the history of efforts to create such a national museum, the history of the site itself—adjacent to the Washington Monument—and the design inspirations for the resulting form and façade of the building. We conducted interviews with the museum's architects and other design and construction professionals that informed our script. We also included information about the design competition for the museum and reproduced images of the finalists' designs, which included several Black architects and architectural designers who led or joined multi-firm design teams. Our script for the exhibition also makes reference to the landscape architects, font designer, exhibition fabricators, and other design professionals involved in the development of the National Museum of African American History and Culture. Looking back, I recognize these curatorial interventions as formative and decisive—they paved a path for the work I had committed myself to doing, and for the role I envisioned for the museum: a space where the much-lauded design of its exterior would complement significant design-related collections, archives, and stories inside.

A CURATORIAL VISION FOR DESIGN In 2015, with work on the inaugural exhibitions nearing completion, I began to outline a curatorial vision for architecture and design at the museum. I assembled an ad hoc advisory group of scholars, curators, and designers to assist me with identifying priority names of architects and designers (historical and contemporary), collecting opportunities, and gathering resources for my collecting work.[14] I narrowed my collecting focus to architects, landscape architects, planners and urban designers, graphic designers, industrial and product designers, and designers of furniture and household objects. Other areas such as fashion and automotive design would be covered by curator colleagues.

In order to collect, curators are asked—what is the intellectual framework? In this case, I also asked myself, "What would make a collection at a museum of African American history and culture different from one at a museum focused on architecture and design or a museum with significant collections and galleries devoted to these areas?"

My museum's "African American lens" gave me a different vantage point from other curators. I knew it would be necessary to counter histories of exclusion and invisibility. But it would be even more important to tell stories that were not only oppositional, but to rightfully position architecture and design within the prism of Black life that the museum had already conceived. I also wanted to confront design on its own terms with collections that would allow us to trace a design process from ideation and fabrication to production and circulation. What were the objects, archives, documents, and digital materials that would enable the museum to exhibit processes as well as products, the unbuilt as well as ubiquitous?

By looking at design as a form of expression, decision-making, inventiveness, and ingenuity, the museum could tell stories that were not only oppositional, but to rightfully position African Americans as active agents in shaping their lives and surroundings. Furthermore, our work would reveal how African Americans have used the design professions to make contributions that are important to view through the lenses of history and culture. In writing a rationale to collect in architecture and design, I was establishing why the museum, as a whole, needed this represented through dedicated curatorial attention and support for acquisitions. In framing architecture and design as a specific collecting area, with a related mandate for exhibitions and scholarship, I was unknowingly, but perhaps instinctively, providing the contours for a new curatorial position at NMAAHC that I would come to occupy.

BUILDING COLLECTIONS   To write the collecting rationale and build a collection, I had to do research. While on work trips in 2015, I took advantage of the opportunities to visit and meet with staff at local museums with design collections. From inspecting collections displays at Smithsonian's Cooper Hewitt, National Design Museum in New York to touring the collections storage for architectural archives at the Getty Research Center, I tried to pack in as much looking and learning as possible. At the Vitra Design Museum, I saw exhibitions of contemporary Black designers and postindependence African architecture. Germane to my purposes, I was also able to go behind the scenes with the museum's collections staff to view their holdings of chairs, lighting, and all manner of design objects that were not on display. I was looking at how design was exhibited and interpreted, and also how it was housed and cared for.

This research process was fundamental for developing a curatorial approach to design at a "Black museum." I wanted to properly attribute the intellectual and artistic work of early Black makers and designers within the history of design. Likewise, I was committed to collecting from today's most innovative designers. I saw the potential for the museum's holdings to bolster global knowledge in the specialized categories of African American architectural history and African American design history, while also showing design as a site of engagement with the broader world around us.

My reading material varied. Lisa Farrington's *African American Art: A Visual and Cultural History*, Dreck Wilson's *African American Architects: A Biographical Dictionary, 1865–1945*, and Jack Travis's *African American Architects in Current Practice* were resources for identifying names and key projects. Material on Black designers was less comprehensively represented in a monograph form, but articles by Sylvia Harris, Cheryl D. Miller, and others provided starting points. In addition, I was still receiving suggestions from my advisory committee. Committee member Lowery Sims had drafted a preliminary checklist for an exhibition of Black designers that she had not yet mounted. Her list was and still is foundational for the work I do. Similarly, Michele Y. Washington connected me to several designers for potential collecting opportunities. New publications in design were also instructive, with *Design Objects for the Museum* offering accessible and informative perspectives on the collecting process and beyond.

In architectural design, our collected materials include documents, sketches, photographs, artifacts, and archival collections. Since 2017, I have been working to collect Black architects' archives in a way that speaks to the lens our museum provides. We ask: what early experiences shaped their entrance to the field? Did race or racism impact their opportunities? What projects are they most proud of? We also recognize design as a method for controlling Black mobility, Black homeownership, Black voting power, and access to anything anywhere. Design is a critical site of engagement about Black life. Thus, our collections tell stories about design achievements, discrimination and disenfranchisement, community building, and legacies left behind.

NMAAHC architect of record, Phillip Freelon, had the distinction of being the first architect represented in our architectural archives collection. Other archival collections include Norma Sklarek (the most renowned Black woman architect of the twentieth century); Harold Williams (a cofounder of the National Organization of Minority Architects); and Michael Marshall, the D.C.-based architect who designed the new student center at his alma mater, the University of the District of Columbia (UDC). These acquisitions met some of my initial goals, including to collect from architects associated with the museum, to identify and collect from trailblazers in the field, and to represent local D.C. architects in the collection—a significant focus given that the D.C. area has the highest rate of licensed Black architects per capita in the United States. Acknowledging that our collecting work in this area had commenced, in 2018 we mounted a small display, *Recent Acquisitions: Architects' Archives*, to accompany a three-day symposium on Black architects and planners.[15]

My work to build the collection in design fields beyond architecture has brought in some exciting objects as well. The museum acquired the *Dan Chair* by Michael Puryear, which enables us to tell stories about West African craft and design, the experience of the enslaved, the connection of U.S. presidents to slavery, and Japanese design traditions— all of which influenced Puryear. Sheila Bridges's *Harlem Toile* wallpaper was a must-have for its playful lampooning of African American pastimes, but we also wanted her *Hudson Valley Toile*, which speaks to Bridges's appreciation for the beauty and quirkiness of that region of New York, where she also bought a home. Black designers are inspired by the world around them, their travels, and their education. Within a museum dedicated to African American history and culture, it is crucial to say and show that not everything an artist, an architect, a designer, or anyone else Black does is or must be about "race."

Other highlights in our design collection include graphic illustrations by Andrea Pippins; episodes of *Revision Path*, a design-focused podcast hosted by Maurice Cherry; and an archival collection from graphic designer Gail Anderson. In the coming year, I look forward to acquiring significant examples of furniture and household objects from contemporary Black designers.

The goal is not only to collect, but also to highlight and publicize design. One of the ways I've focused on getting the museum's design collections to the public is through working with colleagues to prioritize objects for digitization. Once digitized, objects can become accessible online via our collections database. The more objects that are in the database, the more online learning is possible. To introduce design as a highlight of the museum's collection and connect our holdings to other design collections, we published the *Looking for Design* series in 2017. The series featured short posts about the work of Black and Latinx designers at NMAAHC and at the Cooper Hewitt, Smithsonian Design Museum.[16] In presenting a breadth of design practices—from Art Smith's jewelry to Stephen Burks' stool—*Looking for Design* has the potential to grow by taking on new collaborators and by sharing recent design acquisitions online as our collection expands.

By my fourth year working at NMAAHC, I had established a new collecting area, worked to make design explicit in my exhibitions, and begun building an online presence for architecture and design stories. When the museum determined that a curatorial position would be focused primarily on architecture and design, even I was a little surprised. I felt then, as I feel now, that my work is in progress. I wasn't sure that it had "arrived." But I also understood the symbolic cachet of this decision—if the museum envisioned itself as a leader in the interpretation of Black life, in the scholarly exchanges about African American history and culture, then dedicated curatorial attention to Black design history was a sign of value, conveying recognition in the same way I was working to call out design and identify designers. My new role would be a continuation of my existing work—essentially, I would keep doing what I'd started. Making progress on the work in progress.

CONCLUSION Perhaps slightly beyond mid-career now, I'm no longer that small girl looking intently at an ornately patterned wall. In the decades since those days, I have seen walls go up and come down, and galleries change and rearrange. What has remained, however, is that commitment to being a conduit for ideas, expression, and connection. The passions around space remain. The dedication to making design visible and recovering Black design stories is unchanged, though the tools through which I do this work will continue to adapt.

In the past year I've been working to document the visual culture of architectural ideas through a project titled *Rendering Visible*. By digitally collecting drawings, watercolors, renderings, and other architectural imagery, the project seeks to unite and make easily accessible such material for the first time, thereby providing a fuller picture of the Black architect's imagination, process, and draftsmanship. My interest in these images has shifted my curatorial perspective from thinking strictly about collecting physical materials for the museum to also focusing my sights on digitizing existing illustrations held by other institutions or individuals. I'm interested in the possibility of digitally preserving materials that may be in archives at Historically Black Colleges and Universities, in the flat files of architectural firms, or in drawers of home offices. This more expanded goal, though long-term, also feels attainable, given the right support.

A commingling of interests has always shaped my trajectory as a scholar, and the intersection of personal and professional pursuits forged my path into design curation. Sara Zewde has said that she read her way into design. I would say I am curating my way into design. A variety of experiences—family history, my own studies, teaching, and museum work—have shaped my journey. For me, curating has meant discerning and deliberating how to structure the visions we hold. It's a power and privilege. Alongside designers, design educators, and design students, I see my work as staking a claim for all of us in design fields. Let design be a space in Black life that we hold up and behold, together.

NOTES

1. Brown, Adrienne. "A History of Building," *Disegno:
    Quarterly Journal of Design*, last modified May 29,
    2020, https://medium.com/disegno-quarterly-journal
    -of-design/a-history-of-building-97397ca076bc.
2. Ibid.
3. Huggins, Kimberly, and Sara Zewde. "On the
    Foundational Spirit: W. E. B. Du Bois's Data
    Portraits," *Pairs*, Issue 1, (2021) Harvard University
    Graduate School of Design.
4. Atkinson, David, et al. *Cultural Geography: A
    Critical Dictionary of Key Concepts* (London: I. B.
    Tauris & Co Ltd.), 2005: xv.
5. A text I read during this time was Peter Jackson's
    *Maps of Meaning: An Introduction to Cultural
    Geography*, where I recall being surprised to find
    analyses of Puerto Rican life in New York City,
    which was a topic I had also explored in earlier
    research. Other books I likely consulted include Neil
    Smith's *Uneven Development: Nature, Capital, and
    the Production of Space*; Edward Soja's *Postmodern
    Geographies: The Reassertion of Space in Critical
    Social Theory*; Doreen B. Massey's *Space, Place and
    Gender*; and essays by Denis Cosgrove, David Harvey,
    and Frederic Jameson. In parallel, I was also reading
    "postcolonial" theory by Homi Bhabha, Gayatri Spivak,
    and Edward Said. My training had already exposed
    me to voices such Frantz Fanon, Aime Cesaire, bell
    hooks, Trinh T. Minha, Gloria Anzaldúa, Audre Lorde
    and other influential Black and Brown thinkers.
6. Wilkinson, Michelle Joan. "A People's Geography: The
    Spaces of African American Life." (Exhibition Notes)
    2008.
7. In conjunction with the exhibition *A People's
    Geography: The Spaces of African American Life*, I
    coordinated a panel further inspired by the recent
    release of the *Black Geographies and the Politics of
    Place* edited by Katherine McKittrick and Clyde Woods
    (2007). Book contributor Suzette Spencer was among
    the panelists.

8. Craftsmanship, building arts, and design are covered
    in galleries designated as History—"Slavery and
    Freedom Gallery," "The Era of Segregation," and
    "1968 and Beyond"; as Culture—"Cultural Expressions";
    and as Community—"Power of Place" and "Making A Way
    Out of No Way." Meanwhile, other inaugural exhibits
    across the museum include opportunities to learn
    about African Americans in fashion design, set
    design, and technical innovations.

9. "Shifting Landscapes" explored patterns of migration
    in the 1970s and 1980s, including some return
    migration to the US South and a rise in Black
    immigration from Africa and the Caribbean to the
    United States. Thus noting that this Las Vegas
    community designed by an African American had
    remained majority African American from the 1950s to
    the present was also noteworthy.

10. I employed a similar practice in regards to diaspora-
    related stories by identifying the countries of
    origin for Black immigrants and/or their children
    featured in the exhibition.

11. Early members of the Collecting Architecture and
    Design Advisory Group included Mabel O. Wilson,
    Lowery Sims, Paola Antonelli, Andrea Pippins, and
    the group grew to also include Michele Y. Washington,
    Toni Griffin, and Mark Raymond. I also looked in-
    house for advice. I consulted with the NMAAHC's team,
    including the archivist, oral historian, and digital
    assets manager regarding the collecting plan and its
    impacts. Similarly, I inquired with colleagues at
    other museums about how they approached collecting,
    storing, and exhibiting design. Through emails, phone
    calls, and later in person visits, I attempted to
    amass a network of individuals who could serve as
    resources for the work I sought to undertake at
    NMAAHC.

12. The display featured John Chase's drafting tools,
    clippings of Norma Sklarek speaking at a Howard
    University conference, correspondence between Harold
    Williams and Paul Revere Williams, reproductions
    of Michael Marshall's drawings, and marketing
    and publicity materials from J. Max Bond Jr. and

Philip Freelon, when they joined forces to create
the Freelon/Bond partnership and bid on creating a
program study for the forthcoming National Museum of
African American History and Culture.
13. *Looking for Design* was conceived as the culminating
project for Maeve Coudrelle, Summer 2017 Latino
Museum Studies Program Fellow. Courdrelle wrote the
series, with consultation with myself and Christina
de Leon, a curator at the Cooper Hewitt museum.

IMAGE CREDITS

1. Negress Chaise Lounge & Mammy Table by Simone
   Brewster, Photography by: Kevin C. Moore
2. Negress Chaise Lounge by Simone Brewster, Photography
   by: Kevin C. Moore
3. Torkwase Dyson, *The Strategy of an Exuberant Future:
   Or, Reflection on a Lost Birth Certificate*, 2011.
   Detail view from Material Girls exhibition.
4. Torkwase Dyson, *The Strategy of an Exuberant Future:
   Or, Reflection on a Lost Birth Certificate*, 2011.
   Installation view from Material Girls exhibition.
5. Collection of the Smithsonian National Museum of
   African American History and Culture, Gift from the
   Trumpauer-Mulholland Collection

My Journey to Design

SABINE MAXINE LOPEZ

I always knew I'd work for myself and make a living as a creative. What I didn't know was how or in what medium, nor did I know why. I didn't understand why I felt in my heart and soul that I needed to create. It just was. The need to create percolates within me stronger than any other human regulatory need. I've tried to deny it. Pushed it aside while working nine to five because a steady paycheck was more important. Health insurance, dental, and a 401(k) is what grown folks have. But for an artist or designer, these things can mean sacrifice. Sacrifice of your true self.

Fig. 1

After over twenty years of working for others, reporting to others, and helping them make their dreams come true, I'd had enough. It was time to take a risk and bet on myself. Time to believe that I could make a great life doing what brings me joy: creating and designing

SABINE MAXINE LOPEZ

HOW I USE
MY VOICE

Fashion and design have always been a passion of mine. Growing up in poverty all over LA County, I didn't have access to fashionable clothing. I would watch MTV videos and dream of wearing Cross Colours backwards like KrisKross, or a Tommy Hilfiger sports bra and baggy pants like Aaliyah. I yearned to wear brand-new Guess or FUBU outfits like my wealthier cousins, but I was lucky if I got any name-brand hand-me-downs. It was very clear whenever I was around these cousins that we were the poor ones. They lived in a stable home with both a mother and a father, and they all had their own bedrooms. I came to begrudgingly understand just how poor we were one Christmas when I was probably ten years old and my cousin (who was a few months younger than me) opened presents for what seemed like forever. I think I was done in about five minutes. It was one of the most painfully humbling moments in my life. That was the day I told myself I was going to do whatever I had to do to not be poor when I grew up.

As a teen, my passion for fashion grew along with my shapely body. I started to look to Erykah Badu and Lauryn Hill for fashion-spiration. Both Erykah and Lauryn had this amazing ability to mix vintage clothing with designer bohemian pieces with such ease. They oozed self-confidence, beauty, and a strong sense of who they were. I wanted to emulate that. These women allowed me to develop my own personal style and to understand that it was okay to dress differently. To be a "different" type of Black girl. I learned then how important it was for me to wear whatever I wanted because that's when I felt most like myself. It was especially important for a curvy, mixed-race, Black girl growing up (mostly) in predominantly Latin neighborhoods in Los Angeles.

The only way I could afford new stylish clothes in high school was by working a full-time job all summer, every summer. I was able to buy myself cute school clothes each year to make sure I looked fly. I often experimented with clothing by modifying pieces, cutting and sewing them into new creations. Sometimes I got looks from my high school classmates, but I simply didn't care. A cousin of mine introduced me to vintage clothing around this time. That sparked my love for vintage, and that love continues to this day! The Goodwill was and still is my go-to place for vintage pieces. There's something about flipping through rack after rack and finding something spectacular. Whenever I go with someone to Goodwill, I have to give them a bit of warning because I get laser-focused and cannot be talked to. I can't control it at all. So I really do try and go by myself as much as possible.

Now as an adult, I have come to believe that fashion is a form of art and expression. My clothing allows me to speak without me having to say a word. I'm able to create a visual representation of who I am as a person with my clothing. This is so important. It is also the reason

440

why I chose to use design on clothing as my form of social justice. For me, three design disciplines merge in perfect harmony: fashion as a platform for embodiment, graphic design as a means of communicating, and branding as a way to claim, narrate, and share my identity. With these tools I am able to create designs that are proud, affirming, and empowering. I want people to feel seen and rock everything with their own sense of pride while serving lewks for the gods!

I have been fortunate enough to see my T-shirts on people protesting in honor of Breonna Taylor. I've seen an amazing trans women rocking my designs with her beard glistening in the sun, skirt blowing in the breeze, and a powerful fist raised in the air. Looking as beautiful, powerful, proud, and radical as ever.

Fig. 2   Fig. 3

Some may think that fashion is not a place for politics or the social justice movement. However, history has proven that for certain identities, fashion has always been political. *The Scarlet Letter*, women in pants, cross-dressing, the Black Panther Party, the LGBTQ+ rainbow flag, and Black Lives Matter. These are just a few ways in which fashion, or words on clothing, have proven to be political. More than political—at times an extreme form of oppression, a visual representation of a movement, or at its absolute best . . . IDENTITY-AFFIRMING!

HOW I INFORM   It has taken me a long while to find my footing and figure out how I can best show up in the world. Through trial and error, I've learned how to best use the tools I have to create intentional, purpose-driven art. This was the birth of A Tribe Called Queer. The name was first verbalized on a car ride from Los Angeles to Oakland with my

Fig. 4   Fig. 5

wife and a friend. It is a play on one of my favorite hip-hop groups (A Tribe Called Quest) and Queerness. We were listening to A Tribe Called Quest and having one of those road trip moments where everyone is talking and laughing. I'm pretty sure my friend sitting in the backseat was braiding my hair as I drove. As soon as the name "A Tribe Called Queer" was spoken, it was as if I could literally see a light bulb turn on above my head. I remember thinking to myself, "This means something!" It is the perfect way to artic-ulate so many parts of myself. The hip-hop lover and the person who has created a tribe of Queer people around her. Every Queer person is my tribe because Queer people understand what it means to create your own family. Especially when you're cast out by your biological family. Plus, the use of the word *tribe* pays homage to my Navajo and Ute ancestors. In the car, we joked about the name some more and moved along to another topic of conversation. But I remember speaking with my wife later in the day about doing something with the name. I wasn't 100 percent sure what I would do, what I would create, but I knew something had to be done.

It took me a few weeks but on March 14, 2016, I launched an Instagram page under the moniker. For the first year or two, I used the platform as a way of promoting other Queer-owned businesses and people. I posted and shared information about other Queer people or events that were making a positive impact in the community. People responded pretty well to what I was doing. They loved my name and the Instagram page. I gained momentum over time and reached two thousand followers by January 2018. That was so exciting for me. However, the more followers I gained, the more I felt the need to shift what I was doing. While I loved sharing what was going on in my community, it became more important to use my platform and skills for a larger message, because I realized that even within my LGBTQIA+ community, I was still Other. I was *still* too much or not enough of something. I am strong, opinionated, and very real. I don't take shit from anyone because that's how my mother raised me and my six siblings to be. I'm a mixed, light-skinned Black woman. I'm weird and socially awkward at times. I'm overly analytical. I think way too much about things that matter too little. I am street smart because I had to learn how to be at a young age. I'm a survivor of sexual violence and trauma. I have a hard time understanding people who haven't had hard lives because it's all I've ever known. I've never ever felt like I truly fit in anywhere. I'm always juuuust a little bit too loud, or too Black, or not Black enough, or not Queer enough, or too fat, or not fat enough (I was once called a "Small Fat" to my face), not smart or educated enough, not talented enough, not popular enough, not political enough, not enough of a game player, or too poor, too outspoken, too powerful, or too fucking real. There's also a lot of gatekeeping happening at all times. And because of this I wanted to tear the fucking gates down.

In December 2017, I designed and released the first item for sale, which was the A Tribe Called Queer logo T-shirt. The second was the ATCQueer and ProjectQ collaborative T-shirt in April 2018. ProjectQ is a wonderful nonprofit organization founded by my wife, Madin Lopez. I worked for ProjectQ for several years and helped it really blossom into an incredible 501(c)(3) that provides free gender-affirming and self-empowering services to Queer and Trans homeless LGBTQIA+ youth.

I'm incredibly proud of every single part of my inter-sectional identities. II'm a Queer, Non-Binary, fat, pansexual, chronically ill, femme of color. The marginalization I feel within my very own community (and the world as a whole) has empowered me to advocate for myself and for others who are also marginalized. I do this by honoring us through designing clothing and accessories, hosting a podcast, blogging, hosting community events, creating collaborations with other BIPOC/QTPOC/LGBTQIA+ people, and raising funds for amazing organizations. It is paramount that my designs reflect not only what I want to say, but also what needs to be said.

```
All Power to All the People
Black Femme Power
Black Is Beautiful
Black Lives Matter
Beautiful Sissy
Femmes Can Be Thems
Gender Is an Illusion
Immigrants are the Backbone of America
```

No Terfs Club
Pro Black is not Anti White
Radical Queer
The First Pride was a Riot
Women of Color are the Backbone of America

All of these are more than statements—THEY ARE AFFIRMATIONS. Affirming to the world that we belong here. We have power. We are beautiful. We Exist. We are proud. We are radical. We matter.

We live in a day and age when huge companies run by cisgender heterosexual men in suits can slap a liberal or progressive message on a T-shirt and capitalize on other people's identities. It's important to do more than just wear a T-shirt, repost, or use the trending hashtags. People need to do the work every day to empower marginalized people. Those with resources, power, and privilege must use their access to open doors for those who are equally (and sometimes more) talented and give them a chance. The fashion industry itself is full of white women, white men, and above all there is Ms. Anna Wintour. Only recently has the industry acknowledged their lack of inclusion, and we are beginning to see what brilliance erupts when people of color are given a chance. Very few Black folks hold positions of power.

Ghanian-born Edward Enninful was the first-ever Black man appointed as editor-in-chief of *British Vogue* in 2017. Enninful, who identifies as gay and grew up working-class, still faces racism even with his current job title. In July 2021, Enninful shared an experience on his Instagram page about an incident where a security guard racially profiled him as he entered his own workplace. While this may seem like *just* a "misunderstanding" to some, it's incredibly important to comprehend how a Black person in a high-level position still gets mistreated. Black people cannot just be and do, we also always have to prove. Prove we're worthy of being seen as equal. Prove we're worthy of having a seat at the table. André Leon Talley came before Enninful, and he definitely had a seat at the table, his highest position being fashion editor. However, he never received such a position of power. Talley details the highs and lows of his career in his amazing autobiography, *The Chiffon Trenches: A Memoir*. It makes painfully clear that Anna Wintour rules the fashion world and is the final word on many things—in which case, she can easily be named the reason for the lack of color (POC) and size (plus) diversity in the world of design.

I personally find it insulting that it has taken this long to enact the minor changes we are barely beginning to see. Virgil Abloh, Olivier Rousteing, Kerby Jean-Raymond, Laquan Smith, Aurora James, Anifa Mvuemba, Christopher John Rogers, and Dapper Dan are just a few amazing Black designers. Models like Ashley Graham, Paloma Elsesser, Anita Marshall, and Akon Adicholl are beginning to break barriers with their curvaceous beauty. I really do hope the future will be far more inclusive in every sense of the word, because what we see in the world of design should reflect the actual world we live in. Our world is flourishing with so much diversity. No two people are exactly alike, nor do they have the same lived experience.

Can you imagine what things would look like if that were reflected back into the world? What a beautiful sight that would be.

IMAGE CREDITS:

1. Sabine Maxine Lopez, October 2020, Photo Credit: April Flores.
2. Miss J. Cagz at a Protest wearing a A Tribe Called Queer crop top, June 2020, Photo Credit: Miss J. Cagz
3. Edwin Chachi Camacho at a Protest wearing a A Tribe Called Queer T-shirt, June 2020, Photo Credit: Edwin Camacho.
4. Nneka Jackson models A Tribe Called Queer T-shirt, Sabine M. Lopez, Photo Credit: Sabine M. Lopez.
5. Madin Ray Lopez modeling A Tribe Called Queer T-shirt, Photo Credit: Sabine M. Lopez.

Moving On:

Interview with White Male Academic

AISHA RICHARDS

EDITOR'S NOTE:

This dialogue was originally published on June 19, 2020 by Shades of Noir (shadesofnoir.org.uk). Shades of Noir was founded in 2009 by Aisha Richards and is an independent organization that supports: curriculum design, pedagogies of social justice through representation, cultural currency and accessible knowledge.

This interview is with a white male academic within an arts subject-specific institution who studied the Inclusive Practice Unit within the first years of its design. He has chosen to be anonymized, an option available to anyone who contributed to Shades of Noir, for all sorts of reasons.

AISHA RICHARDS: It's been ages, how are you?

1:     Good thanks, I'm sorry that it's been such a long time and really you have no idea how much yours and Terry's teaching changed me.

AR: I'm assuming that the change has been positive?

1:     Yes I think positive, I'd go as far as saying maybe transformational. Really changed me and this is why I made contact. When I saw the submissions form I knew it was time to talk with you.

AR: Really, time to talk about what?

1:     To say sorry to you. Really Aisha, maybe to Terry too at a later date but to you really. I'm sorry.

AR: What are you sorry for?

1:     I'm sorry that I didn't do anything when the other students were dismissive or rude to you. This is the part that has really stayed with me, I didn't recognize these people that were so rude and aggressive toward you or myself in my silence. You not Terry. I know that I could have said something, done something and I didn't. I have been living with regret all this time.

AR: I have to say that I wasn't expecting this. I really appreciate it, it really was bad behavior and it has changed me too. I mean you saying sorry, I appreciate that too but really I am the teacher in that scenario and I have learned as a black teacher from these experiences too. Do you think that this changes anything?

1: I know that they respect, respected you but I've been thinking about this for awhile. I think that they were threatened by you, your words, and maybe even what was said in that space out loud. Do you mind me being frank?

AR: I prefer that.

1: I think student/staff relationships are complicated, but I do think that you being black and a woman suggesting prejudice at play was too much for them (us). I have gone through it in my head many times and given Terry was there presenting similar content and they were different with her, you being black can only be the reason that they/ we were different. It's hard to talk about this with you . . . it really is hard.

AR: What's hard?

1: Good question. Hmmm talking about this, not the apology. Yes talking about how I witnessed a group of academics be aggressive and target you and I did nothing, this is hard. I really, I should have made a formal complaint. I think because it was definitely bullying behavior. As the person who watched and did nothing I think I am part of the problem. This meeting is going in the Shades of Noir publication and what happened, what I witnessed needs to be there even if it's hard. I am a bit embarrassed but I had to say something.

AR: So now these years on, what would you do differently?

1: I think . . . I'd like to think that I would say something. Something like you know that you are shouting and I'm not sure that you are listening? Maybe I'd walk out? Maybe I would still be frozen in silence in the moment but make a complaint after, not wait so many years to say I am sorry? The way you handled what happened was so professional and composed but you shouldn't have to deal with that.

AR: What do you think I could or should have done differently?

1:                  Nothing. You presented facts with theory with questions. That is academia. I just think we were not ready for these facts from you.

AR: **Why these facts and why from me?**

1:                  I think that race information can feel very personal even when what you presented was national data, I witnessed this firsthand. I think many took it as you were calling them racist. As you or Terry rightly pointed out it may have been the first time a black academic was teaching us . . . I don't think this was easy for some.

AR: **OK are we still being frank?**

1:                  Yes.

AR: **Do you think their behavior was racist?**

1:                  Hmm I guess it was . . . nope I know it was and it is this that is and was hard to digest.

AR: **Would you say that to them?**

1:                  Hmmm I'm not sure. I mean . . . I said to a couple of them after that session—it was really wrong to behave like that.

AR: **If you have just said that my race impacted how they responded to me negatively, why is saying that this is racist behaviour a problem? I'm not trying to trick you and this interview will be anonymized but this I think is an important question.**

1:                  It is a really important question and I see that saying someone is racist is the right thing to do but it is hard because maybe . . . I think it will open up a conversation, maybe emotions, maybe the same aggression that you received and I don't feel equipped for this. I'm sorry. I feel embarrassed by . . . I am sorry it's just . . . I'm trying to be honest, this is the least that you deserve.

AR: **I appreciate that you are trying. Do you think I am used to dealing with racism then?**

1: Yes.

AR: **Do you think that I am used to facing racism from or by my peers?**

1: Yes and I am disgusted by this.

AR: **Do I deserve racism?**

1: No.

AR: **So then why do you protect your peers' emotions when they present racist behavior? I want you to know that I see that you are uncomfortable but you are trying to share with me openly. I need to know, scrap that . . . in fact I need you to think about who you protect and why.**

1: I understand. I really do. I don't know why. Maybe it's because I don't want to be in your position. That came out wrong. I really don't know what to say. Maybe I am protecting myself. I am not sure. This is actually what makes you an amazing teacher. You don't give answers you make everyone grapple with themselves. It is hard . . . I have tried to apply this to my teaching. It is a really powerful skill.

AR: **Can we go back a bit—you are right that I have experienced racism all my life and everywhere. In my mind most black people will have had similar experiences even when they don't think they have because it's systemic. What is still hurtful is knowing that my pain is second at least, even to people that cause me pain or harm. Does that make sense?**

1: I wish it wasn't like this and I wish that I was a better person to stand up. Look even now . . . I had hoped to be able to show you that you have made a difference to me, my life and my practice. Instead I have just pedaled backward to protect myself. I don't know what to say.

AR: **To be honest it doesn't surprise me, but you are on a journey. You chose to contact me directly to apologize and share. I appreciate that this was not easy for you. Tell me how has the unit impacted your practice? Do you need a break?**

1:              No I'm fine. Well Shades of Noir is not only on our
                reading lists but I also program some of the articles into
my teaching. I am amazed at how much it develops every year, I really don't
know how you do it. I get all students to read, think and share in class. This
has proven to be a real gateway for empathy. I also share often with my
team what I've read on the site and we talk about what it means. I think this
has made a huge difference to our understanding of our diverse student
cohorts over the years. I know . . . I know now that I'm speaking with you that
I have to do more work on me. This I guess reinforces that, that unit was a
start. You did say this . . . I don't think I really understood this at the time. A
rude awakening but maybe I need more time. This time being interviewed
. . . was more learning for me. The unit and what you and Terry taught us
in that really short time . . . as you said started something but it really isn't
enough is it? I can't believe that I'm protecting people who shouldn't be
protected to protect myself. Can you believe I am saying this?

**AR: I can unfortunately. I see it and experience it all the
                time. Look I don't want you to feel bad and I know that
you came to share and you didn't know what would be asked, neither did I,
but this is real dialogue. I appreciate that the unit informed your practice
and your thinking—this is definitely a win but there is more work to do.
In my opinion this is lifelong work so you have to decide if this is what you
are seeking. I know that you don't have to. I see many who present this
"racism is not my problem or real" all the time . . . this unfortunately isn't
a life I chose but one I have been born into. I love my blackness; I just wish
others would see what I see.**

1:              I know . . . I realize that now. I think that again talking
with you openly, opens my eyes to more. I'm feeling disappointed with
myself but maybe I have to.

**AR: I'm sorry that you feel like that. I don't want to lie to
                you. Over the many years since you were my student I
too have changed, developed, and learned a lot about people and myself.
This includes being honest and supporting the uncomfortable nature of
the honesty and I hope always that people see these moments to move
their own thinking on as I do.**

1:              You have always been honest and thoughtful. I
                absolutely respect what you do. I can only imagine how
                difficult it must be. All I know is I am trying to do better . . .

AR: It's fine as I am learning along the way. Really it's been great to see you and hear what you're up to. Thank you for coming and sharing. I appreciate your honesty.

1:     Aisha, before we end the interview I just want to say thank you. You and Terry are amazing and really the best and bravest teachers I have ever met. I reckon next time we speak I will have better answers and be moved on more. I hope that I haven't let you down.

AR: You could never let me down if you are thinking and trying. You know it's all complicated and very difficult physically and emotionally for everyone. Thank you for coming in really, fantastic to see you and hear you—you take care and I think that is a wrap.

DESIGN = ART ≠ DESIGN

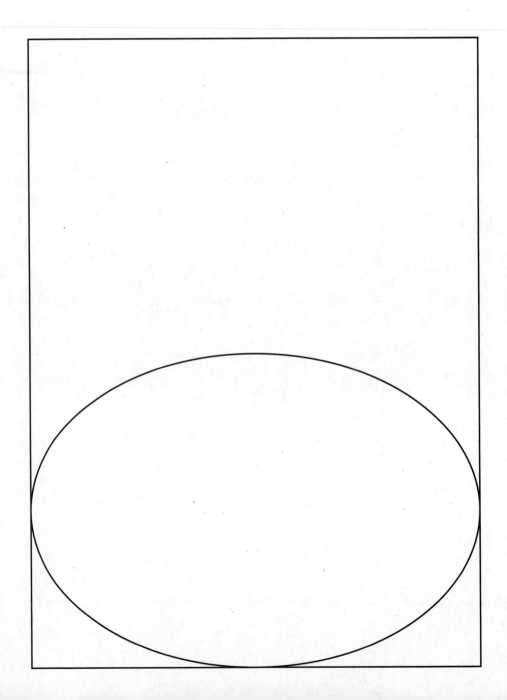

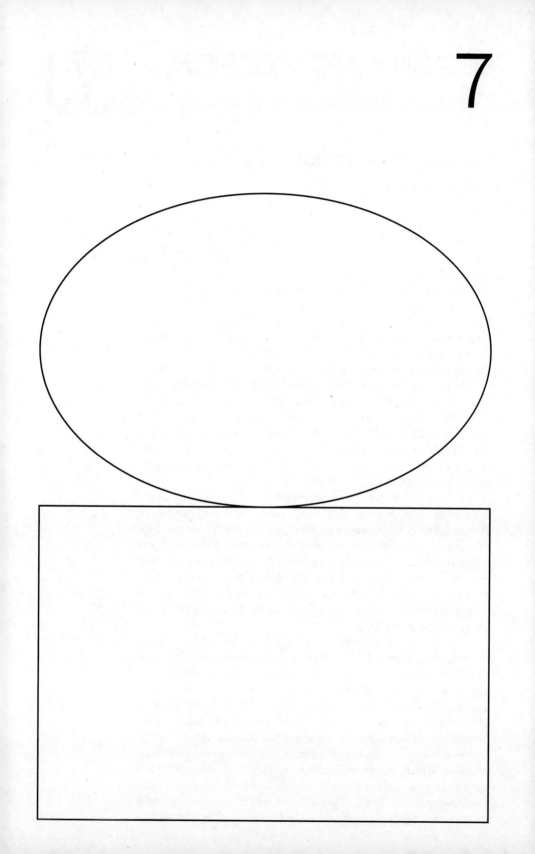

DESIGN = ART ≠ DESIGN

Chapter Introduction:
Kelly Walters

In this chapter, Design = Art ≠ Design, we attempt to map the relationship between art and design. Based on one's creative discipline, there historically has been differing opinions or interpretations on what these words mean. Some believe design can be characterized as the field that is "more professional," "about business," or "deals with clients." Whereas perceptions of art create room for a practitioner to be more "whimsical" or "free-flowing" in the making of their creative work. These "perceptions" have influenced the ways designers move through these spaces, particularly Black designers, and how their work might be positioned. While some see the absence of clearly defined distinctions between art and design, others see blurred edges if there are any edges at all. The art and design purists who uphold these separations may do so in order to create boundaries that satisfy specific creative markets or audiences. Understanding particular distinctions also creates a way for these markets to then place value on creative practitioners and the type of work they may produce.

   The reflections shared in this section explore the boundary lines between art/design and what it means for Black practitioners. Throughout the chapter we see a variety of perspectives in response to the following questions: What are the tensions between art and design? How do you know if you are an artist or a designer? What do these labels mean in design practice? What is their importance? How does design (methods, tools, ways of seeing) and art (methods, tools, ways of seeing) take form in your practice? How does Black identity and representation intersect within the space of art/design?

   We pose these questions as an entry point for discussion and an opportunity for self-reflection. The contributions in this chapter include interviews, conversations, and personal essays that highlight insights and criticisms of art and design. I engage in conversation with designers Nontsikelelo Mutiti and Cey Adams, where we explore the origin of their design practice and their understanding of art/design. These interviews offer insight into the processes that designers consider in the making of the creative works and how those works are perceived in both art and design worlds. In both conversations, understanding their audience is central to their viewpoints. Complementing these conversations is a reflective essay by designer Rick Griffith which explores a diagrammatic approach to understanding the links between art and design practice. We then transition to another discussion between creative practitioners Romi Morrison and Mimi Ọnụọha, where they describe the fluid relationship between art and design, emphasizing the real and contrived line between the two. In the last interview with Anne H. Berry and Rhea L. Combs, we understand the importance of celebrating Black artists and how it contributes to the preservation of Black narratives in culture. Across all the contributions in this chapter we hear echoes and similar parallels about how these definitions impact our design choices, methodologies, and modes of dissemination.

In Conversation:

Nontiskelelo Mutiti

& Kelly Walters

ON IMAGE MAKING,
CONCEPTUAL
PROCESS, AND THE
TOOLS OF DESIGN

I spoke with Nontsikelelo Mutiti, a Zimbabwean-born visual artist and educator on March 1, 2021. We discussed the focus of her studio practice and perspectives on design. This conversation has been edited for length and clarity.

—Kelly Walters

KELLY WALTERS: How did you get into design?

NONTISKELELO MUTITI: I had been thinking about ways to make formal connections between the images I was making and the amount of text I was writing. I was thinking about the images and the conceptual process. At that point, the text started to become an integral part of the images because the writing was becoming part of the hand-drawn sketches I was making. I was bringing texts, sometimes handwritten, sometimes Xeroxed typography from newspapers and magazines, and transferring that onto the paintings and drawings. I felt like there was another way to make things feel a little bit more connected and resolved. That's one reason why I ended up thinking about design. Inherently the discipline foregrounds really being able to activate what the meaning of the text is, by really considering what it looks like, where and how it appears, all these things are imbued with meaning. I like to work with images and consider how their scale relationship and other moments of connection can produce a kind of conversation or a healthy tension with the rest of the content. Mostly, I was not necessarily interested in graphic design. I was interested in the tools and I was interested in where design objects would go after they were made. These objects are a kind of output that could be distributed in multiples. I used to make paintings, collages and mixed media work and those would live in the gallery, but the people I wanted to be in conversation with were not coming to the gallery spaces. I really became captivated with the whole chain of stages. There's what it is made of and then what the impact is on an audience, who that audience is, and how these things can get to the audience and then the possible impact of the work.

KW: The idea that I hear as you're talking about audience, engagement, and being able to explore
the work that you're making. I think there's something compelling
about this view of how art or fine art exists. This perception of
who and what can be making for the gallery space versus who, and
what could be looking at a book that's not about the gallery or, or
some kind of object that's not for a gallery context. I'm curious, in
your practice how you navigate between worlds, how you navigate
between where your work might be living, given the audience and
given the type of object that it might be?

NM: I'm always thinking about the space on the street
level. I think about street value a lot. The things
that inspire my work, everyday objects, my experiences, combs,
beauty products, my engagement with those spaces. Beauty supply
stores, African hair braiding salons, or just getting my hair done at
home by a family member or doing my own hair. It also includes all
the other things around that such as Nollywood movies I watch when
I'd get my hair done in a salon, or the 90s movies, like *Poetic Justice*
that inform what I want to do with my hair, images of popular figures,
celebrities, all different kinds of people that we look at that I want
to emulate or some aspect of the way they presented themselves.
Those things are kind of in the communal consciousness.
I move between a lot of different geographies, so
the differences and similarities in those spaces, especially spaces
occupied by people of African descent. The things that resonated
with me from the sounds, the content of conversations, what people
are wearing, how open or closed those spaces are, what services are
available, what people are interested in looking at, or what materials
are in those spaces, what technologies are in those spaces, that's
what informs the work. I'm often thinking deeply about it because so
much is informed by those spaces, the production processes, what
the work is made up of, the kind of paper, the kind of printing, the
aesthetic often reflects that. I want the work to be able to go back
into those spaces, hair salons, beauty supply stores, bootleg CD
vendor stands, bookstores, music venues, roadside multi sellers.
Even though the work can be shown in a gallery or
museum, I'm not often thinking about that as the first venue. The
piece can be commissioned by cultural spaces, but I always know
that the work can be restaged and kind of fit even more eloquently
on the street or in someone's home. I think a lot about the way the art

market has ideas around class. Even if you are not engaging in it, you have some kind of sense or perception of how class plays into who or what is includes or excludes you.

I want the work to be accessible in terms of cost, you know? I want it to be accessible to my cousin, my niece, my friend that I'd met in the bar the night before. I want the work to be able to transfer and translate through all these slices of society. I don't want the work to feel too precious, but it must feel special because the content is important. It has so much to do with our lives.

KW: **Can you share more about what you mean by accessibility in this context?**

NM: Accessibility comes in a lot of forms. There's accessibility in terms of whether somebody can own the work. There is price point. How do you judge price point? A lot of it has to do with the materials that are used, the processes that are used, and then sometimes there's a value around the object because of who has made it. I tend to think first about the cost of materials, the costs in terms of labor, time, and shipping. I work backward and I think if I want someone to be able to buy this, what are the materials, processes, and distribution mechanisms that I can use to keep the cost down. The work can still be beautiful. The work can still be extremely deep. I think about how I can make sure that someone can still afford this? I have to work backward. Rather than making whatever I want, in whatever form I want it, then calculating the price.

Access also means looking at what the work is saying, who should be able to read and understand the meaning that's embedded in the work. Is it speaking truth for a very particular audience? The theme might only be understood by a few and it may mean that image is not for you. It might not be an image you get something out of because it's for a particular audience. I'm also thinking about access in that it's not always about just making it open for everyone. I know who I'm speaking to; I know the language and I want the work to call out to its own audience. I think people know when the work is not meant for them. I'm not speaking to the usual limitations of price point or the venue.

KW: **Is there a set of values that you are considering when you're partnering with an artist or supporting the work of another artist?**

NM: I do a lot of work on commission. That work supports other artists or different kinds of practitioners. Sometimes institutions. Sometimes it's also building work that is of our own initiative. An example of this is the work I've done with Tinashe Mushakavanhu through Black Chalk & Co. and building readingzimbabwe.com. Nobody asked us to build that literary archive online, but we knew that it was necessary work. It was also something that we needed for ourselves.

In terms of values, I cannot work outside of having a set of values. It's interesting to be asked because I've never sat down and listed the values. In a way they are given, but when people are doing work that has to do with Black liberation or when people are in a position where they are making important work that needs to be made visible because the content is something that we need or is edifying to our community (or communities), these are the kinds of projects where I feel "Yes, I can do that to work."

I have a range of skills and a range of projects come to me, but I don't have to do all of them. I definitely weigh and judge. Is this something that I'm passionate about? Is this something that I'm skilled at? Is this something that I know enough about and can build a team of people that are also concerned with the same set of ideals? I think I am very lucky to have landed in a community of practitioners who are thinking about building, you know? Who are thinking about world-building and thinking about challenging what mainstream is. Maybe we're not necessarily challenging, but preoccupied with our own narratives and what we want to see in the future.

We are on a landscape that is continuously shifting. You have to prioritize certain things at different moments. Helping individuals and particular narratives to be made visible. Working to make sure others had the vehicle wrapped around them, that would get them to where they need to be, get them into people's eyes, keep them top of mind, but now I'm thinking a lot more about depth and sustainability.

KW: How do you navigate the boundary line between
                operating within different creative industries?
Are you a designer? Are you an artist? How do these labels take
form in your practice?

NM: I have had a lot of people say to me that they don't
                understand what I'm doing. "You design books, you
design websites, you show in galleries, you get grants and you're
organizing things. What are you doing?" There's an expectation that
designers don't understand anything about the other disciplines or
that everyone should be in their own lane. Why should we cross over?
I find that so limiting and it's a fiction. There are so many artists
that do a lot of different kinds of work like Simone Leigh, Rahsida
Bumbray, Shariffa Rhodes Pitts, Xenobia Bailey, David Hammonds,
Sanford Biggers, Glen Ligon, Paul Ramirez Jonas, Ann Hamilton.
                Before I left Zimbabwe to further my education
in graphic design, I curated shows at the National Art Gallery of
Zimbabwe. I was also an art director for a couple of performances
produced by the National Ballet of Zimbabwe and theater companies.
I worked in a couple of film sets too. I'm really grateful for the
opportunities I have had to explore different modes of making. I've
loved all those collaborations. I'm definitely going to do things
tomorrow that even I don't know yet. Not everyone is that kind
of practitioner.

KW: What aspirations do you have for your practice?
                Where do you want it to go? What's next?

NM: I'm starting to build out my own studio. It's kind
                of interesting to think about formalizing some-
thing that I've been doing for many years, but has been in between a
lot of different things. I'm kind of pivoting my practice to focus more
on a studio because I feel I will have more capacity to do the kind of
supportive work that I am committed to. Setting up my own shop
means having to bring on other people that have expertise that I
need to operate at the standard I'm aiming for. You're not necessarily
taught that as an artist. Sometimes we emphasize our own work and
working on our own, but it's really exciting to think about support
structures. I am now thinking about how to have other people around

to help to keep the ship running, even if they're not attached to it full-time. I'm thinking about the financial infrastructure, including working with an accountant or having an administrative assistant, so I can focus on the creative aspects and . . . mentoring. I [am] really interested in institution building. The studio is another step in that direction. That is where my head and heart are at the moment.

In Conversation: Cey Adams

& Kelly Walters

ON DESIGN DETOURS & ARTISTIC POSSIBILITIES

EDITOR'S NOTE:

I spoke with Cey Adams, visual artist, graphic designer, and author on February 2, 2021. We discussed his evolution from the downtown graffiti movement in New York City, to the contemporary art world and his work with Def Jam Recordings. This conversation has been edited for length and clarity.

—Kelly Walters

KELLY WALTERS: **Where do we begin? You're a native New Yorker?**

CEY ADAMS: Yes. I'm a native New Yorker, born in Harlem and raised in Jamaica, Queens. Shortly after grade school and once I hit my teenage years, I was ready to explore beyond my neighborhood. I started moving around on my own independent of my parents and my brothers and sisters. I learned all the "real" action was happening downtown. This was the beginning of seeing the world, well at least NYC. I preface this by saying, independent of my parents, because for the first time I was thinking for myself. This is where I learned about creativity. My life in Queens was pretty much adolescent kid stuff, but when I was a teenager and I discovered the downtown scene, that's when I felt like I found where I belonged. That was an opportunity for me to really spread my wings and learn about music, art, culture, theater, politics, *everything*! A lot of the creative and life lessons I learned came from people older than I was. I picked up things listening to conversations at cocktail parties and art openings. This was in the mid-1970s to early 1980s and through all of it I was trying to get my bearings on who I was as an individual. I naturally already knew I was an artist, but I didn't know who I was yet.

KW: **As you were navigating who you were becoming at that time, were you being steered to kind of make certain types of artwork? Were you inspired by others around you?**

CA: No. I wasn't guided to make a specific kind of work. I didn't have a mentor or advisor to help in that way. It was more like learning from the company you keep and about making quality art. That said I was a huge fan of the Pop artists of the sixties. I read a lot of books and used that visual direction as a starting point for what my work could look like. To a certain degree, as a primary reference, I knew my art would take on the same principles of graphic design. That's been a constant thread and theme throughout my career.

KW: **What was happening in your art practice in your early twenties?**

CA: The most important years of my young career up to this point were 1980–1985. I was still a teenager in the early eighties, but I knew I needed the focus and dedication of an adult if things are going to change. It was time to get serious. My girlfriend was pregnant, and she was about to have our baby. My son was born in 1984. That was a splash of cold water on the face and a wake-up call on all fronts. Whatever I was doing had to bear fruit fast. It was time to earn a solid living since I now had real adult responsibilities. Everything shifted. There was no more goofing around with my friends and staying out late. Hustle became the name of the game. Make money, make money, make money. I had to take care of my baby. My version of hardcore hustle still went back to my fine art practice. How do I attract more collectors? How do I drum up commissioned projects? It was really about trying to figure out who my allies were. Where were the people that were supportive of what I was doing? Who's wasting my time? At this point, I decided I had to really learn about traditional graphic design. I knew I had a strong graphic sensibility through my graffiti work, but I didn't know anything technical. I didn't know the terminology. I had to think from a purely commercial perspective. I had to figure all those things out on my own. That's a really difficult thing to do when you have the confidence, but you don't have a mentor and there's no road map to follow. You're just trying to figure it out as you go along. The only thing that's certain is you know you need to get it right.

KW: **How did you begin to learn that terminology and what were the resources for you to figure that out?**

CA: First I started by focusing on myself. I asked the questions: Who am I? Who am I as an artist? Am I not a graffiti artist? Did I want to see my work exhibited in important galleries and museums? I began to study more art history. I took a close look at older

468

artists, including artists of color. It took a while to figure out what the right artistic path was. One of the things that I figured out early on was successful people surround themselves with successful people. While that's easier said than done, slowly I began to position myself in places where people could take me and my work more seriously. I ate and drank where famous artists and art dealers hung out. I was lucky enough to be one of the more talented people in the group that I ran in, so people gravitated toward me. I knew I had to conduct myself as much like a professional as I could. This meant following up on phone calls, having business cards, and looking people in the eye when you shake their hand, little things like that. It also meant having a lot of drive and determination. I had loads of confidence. I truly believed one way or another; I was going to figure things out. It's really hard talking about this now. I was one of the lucky few. Looking back, I can recall all the horrible things that happen to so many of my young friends. So much talent that was taken away too soon due to peer pressure. The endless partying, drinking and drugs. All the things that rob young people of a full life. I knew that wasn't going to be me. I was hungry! I knew I was going to make a career for myself and my family.

KW: **As you move through the 1980s, what was that like in terms of your practice, projects, and collaborations?**

CA: It all felt like hustling—constantly keeping up with working on various projects. It never felt like I had arrived, even though I thought of myself as a professional artist with great gallery representation. I didn't have a security blanket; I was always looking for new ways to expand my career. I was trying to master my style and build a visual vocabulary to become better than my peers. It was a very competitive time back then, but it was always a friendly, supportive competition. We lifted each other up, shared ideas and information. Imagine you're a Motown recording artist. You're at the best label there is, with an opportunity to put out your first (and maybe only) record. Something you've dreamed of your whole life. If you don't perform or your record doesn't sell, you are immediately put to the back of the line and you have to go back into the studio and do it all over again. That's how I remember the 1980s. I was part of an elite group of talented young (graffiti) artists that all had gallery representation, but we always did group shows. As special as I felt, I didn't feel I had the full attention of the gallery. It seemed as though the minute I blinked there was always somebody else ready to fill my slot. Very often I felt completely expendable. I had to constantly perform, perform, perform. It was a lot of pressure.

KW: **That sounds extremely competitive and cut-throat.**

CA: Yes. It was completely difficult. Oftentimes the other artists could be mean and immature. Stealing my things, fighting over work space and materials, press coverage, and gallery sales. Flashbacks of high school for sure. I had to constantly remind myself, I volunteered to be here. Like young athletes trying to make it to the NBA, I saw this as my only option to becoming a professional artist. I knew I had to keep my focus on my personal goals and block out all the negatives. I had a strong sense that things would change, new opportunities would present themselves over time.

KW: **How did your experience in the contemporary art scene differ from the more promotional design work you eventually ended up making at Def Jam?**

CA: While there is a bit of overlap between the two periods, each chapter and experience is completely different. It took me quite a few years to fully develop my studio practice. Learning which methods and ideas were the right fit for my work. Experimenting with materials, finding affordable studio space with good lighting that was close to my home. My artistic statement centered around the idea of establishing my independence as a Black artist. Building my client and fan base, one collector at a time. By comparison everything my team and I needed to start my design firm was built into the contract agreement with Def Jam. Custom built offices, computers, software packages, printers, travel and expense accounts. The album design work we made, while creatively satisfying, was just that—client-based commercial graphic design work. We had lots of freedom as long as the artist and the label were satisfied at all times. The other constant concern I had was always keeping my team happy at any cost. Very often I would go without pay or time off because someone on the team needed a raise or a few days off. Sacrifice was the first thing I learned to accept as the team leader and creative director of a small business. By 1986, a lot of what I'm talking about in the art gallery scene sort of fizzled out. People got picked up by galleries and other people didn't. Those who didn't instantly moved on. I was one of those people that said, "I have to find another way," because there were just too many bodies and it was very competitive. I say that being one of the better ones, but I just got disillusioned with the hustle. I needed a little bit more security. I needed health insurance, all of those things. I started thinking of ways that I could really take my skills and do something that I had a little bit more control over. That was really just the thinking. I'm not saying I had a blueprint. I was lucky to meet Russell Simmons and Rick Rubin when they were forming Def Jam, and I knew it at that moment. I also knew no matter how hard I would have to work, this would not be as competitive as the art world because I was competing against, in some cases, a lot of things that I could not see.

KW: **What couldn't you see?**

CA: Things that I did not know. Things I didn't get an opportunity to learn in school or at home either. For example, I didn't have a degree, so there was no way to climb the corporate ladder in a corporate company. While Def Jam was really great, a step up from there would have been to run the art department at Columbia Records. That wasn't gonna happen just because I designed the records for LL Cool J and that was my dream, to work in a more legitimate structure. We have to remember that while Def Jam seems glamorous by today's standards, it was a zoo. It was really up-and-coming, similar to that of a start-up. We were making a lot of money, but nobody had management training, nobody knew how to run a business as it relates to interacting with people. There was no HR department. You had to deal with everything, in some cases, like you were out in the street. It was difficult at times because I didn't want to feel like I was still in school. You had to figure everything out on your own, nobody pulled you to the side and said, "Listen here's the office manual, read this . . . learn that . . . go here . . ." You were just left to your own devices, you had to figure it out on your own and you had to be okay with it. There was nobody coddling you. Not to say that I thought I needed that, but I'm just saying it just wasn't there if you did need it. At that time, most of the people that got their opportunities there didn't have a college education and didn't have formal training. It was trial by fire. You learned on the job and anything goes. It just did not matter. The only thing people respect in business is money and power.

KW: **Did not having a degree impact you as you were growing and expanding in your design practice?**

CA: No. As far as I know it hasn't affected me much. That said, I'm not proud of not finishing my degree. Today I want to promote the power of finishing what you set out to accomplish. I look at myself as a positive example for young people to follow. I know I'm one of the lucky ones. I worked like a maniac; nothing was ever guaranteed. Making goals is a very important element to my success! I want to drive home the value of hard work and determination, and over time it always pays off. Everywhere you go you're measured by your past. Nobody ever said, "I graduated from the School of Hard Knocks, and life is great"! No Harvard grad ever heard, "My degree doesn't matter anymore, right?" Ivy League excellence is still what everyone in America is measured against, that along with having a serious hustle, makes all the difference in the world. Imagine: What if you don't have either? You'll constantly go through life looking over your shoulder and fighting to prove you deserve a chance. Desperately convincing people that you have what it takes to succeed. Education is what truly matters most. Our young people need to hear that more from our celebrities and influencers.

KW: **Do you think there's a difference between design and art? Are they one and the same?**

CA: When I was twenty-five, I might've been completely oblivious, but based on how I know it today I would say there is a difference. Nobody is asked to define art. People always ask: how do you define design? Design is one of these things that fits into a lot of different spaces. It could be interior, it could be furniture, it could be buildings or architecture. When you think about art—art is one of these things that ultimately people understand more. They also give the creative maker a little bit of space to experiment. Whereas with design, you look at a chair that has a funky curve, people think that's designed beyond function. Whereas art doesn't have to serve a purpose. Design has to serve a purpose. At least that's my interpretation. You can read up on this forever and make yourself crazy because there are design purists out there that will give you all kinds of definitions for what design is, but when you talk about art, it's sort of measured by high and low—the end. For me as an artist of color, I like to think that they don't get to decide for me. I get to decide what is art and what is design.

KW: **What do you think the impact has been of your Def Jam design work?**

CA: What I find so interesting about looking back at my body of work, as it relates to design, a lot of those Def Jam records are experiencing their thirtieth anniversary. Many of those artists are being inducted into the Rock & Roll Hall of Fame. They are established as cultural pioneers and specifically rock & roll pioneers. The art and design has been literally elevated because these are the designs that made them famous, as it relates to these recordings. Whether it's Notorious B.I.G., Jay-Z, LL Cool J, RUN DMC, Public Enemy: all of them. It really boggles my mind even that all of these folks that I've worked with are now considered icons and legends. So what does that mean for the work? The work has to equally be as important because if you strip that away, they have no representation. That's the thing that introduces them to the world, is that packaging, that logo design. Mary J. Blige is another one. She's got this documentary that's about to drop and I'm sitting there watching the trailer, and all I see is my logo, my logo, my logo. I'm like, that's her identity.

KW: **What do you reflect on when looking back at the legacy of your practice?**

CA: When it hit the late nineties, I decided I'd had enough of the music business and doing traditional design. Up to this point I had worked with so many amazing recording artists and designed hundreds of album covers. My career provided me with every opportunity imaginable. I achieved every goal I had set out to accomplish and so many others that I could have never envisioned. By now I was traveling all over the world, eating new foods, and studying various religions and cultures. Sharing my unique experiences with family and friends. Learning and growing beyond my limited vision of who I thought I was. Throughout my journeys I met so many wonderful and open-minded people. I was evolving as a human being. I became disillusioned with the superficial idea that success is something that is measured by how much one can acquire in this lifetime. It was time for a change. I wanted to move in another creative direction. I switched my focus to teaching young people and giving to causes that help others in need. This detour in my career led me to new possibilities. I merged everything I learned in my lifetime into one dedicated single focused art practice. All my concerns, disciplines, and passions (family, art and design, education, and philanthropy) folded into one focused creative vision. One extraordinary possibility for my future.

Design (Is) Art.

If You Want It to Be.

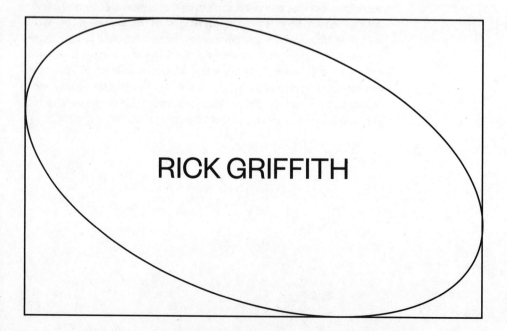

RICK GRIFFITH

I am writing for/to the person who thinks in polygons and facets, as a model for ideas that can be welded together to make vessels that hold other ideas as objects in various scales. I also write to those who do not think this way, but who will appreciate the opportunity to follow multiple ideas, in multiple time lines, with various motivations and invitations. You'll find multiples quite my thing if you follow me, and allow for lots of things to be happening at the same time. Because "things be (actually) happening," all the time.

This contribution suggests I have figured something "out." It suggests that I understand the hybrid identity of Designer/Artist and Artist/Designer making designart or artdesign. I'm not sure I understand it in a sharable way. But I do hope to shed light on the conversation's levers, pulleys, and knobs, so you can more easily navigate the space and find your own answers.

Some additional assumptions here are that (we'll agree that) the goals we share are to understand and explore the boundaries (edges) of effective communication and to make "critical" or objectively good design that might function as art. Or have a successful life negotiating with these possibilities. The reason why it's complex is because we are inside these ideas—not outside—judging and evaluating. We are inside ourselves too. Knowing whether we are capable of having an objectively useful critique of art and design is going to be quite important. It will be as important as listening to those we trust and believe for what we need to know . . . And while it is our job to be an excellent student of these affairs, it also remains our job to create the constraints and boundaries that will contribute to achieving what we want . . . in making . . . with some grace and personality intact. Designers don't always approach the making of work with these concerns but this is an important distinction between the designers who are working with independent goals and those who are in service of a commercial or institutional goal.

REFUTE THE CONTROVERSY—SOME NOTES ON
(IN) THE CONTROVERSY

I have always felt the controversy around *art* and *design* is about contrast, defining one thing against another. It is a by-product of what we have been taught about art, told to believe about the histories of artists, and what you've been guided toward (or from) by people you hardly know, who make a living in this somewhat narrow expertise. You can choose to engage in this controversy—or move through it—those who pause too long here are going to be unproductive. This conflict does not aid in the making of anything, only in the evaluation and criticism of things that are being presented for discussion. Perhaps spending time reading a biography or (better still) an autobiography of an artist would serve your inquiry better. Sensing and feeling through various works (with knowledge of the artist) is still a valid method and an honest exercise. It will also help dilute the controversy and allow for an open and vulnerable dialogue.

As infant siblings in a growing family (of ideas), art and design sleep together in one bed; as they grow, they learn to live their separate lives in separate places. Siblings in an *economy of space* that are physically and psychologically close, and, because of their maturity, they travel together emotionally, while each year they demand their own environments with particular conditions ideal to their own needs. Developing philosophies and manifestos that support their jointly tyrannical grip on the thinking person. Always hoping for maximum effect. They will diverge and converge to discover new conditions for their impulses, or new markets for their ideas. They will invent new ways of sharing and they will eventually have their own homes, each capable of hosting the other. From my view, this is hardly controversial at all. I have very close siblings and there is nothing controversial about kicking and stealing covers (blankets) from each other. It's part of the experience. *Cooperation in this regard might be overrated.*

WHAT WE KNOW **Design is quite possibly everywhere,** so ubiquitous and omnipresent, and **art is very nearly everything** done at a level that surpasses expertise. To that end, a *baker* who is called "an artist" brings honor to baking. However, when a designer is called an artist, it suggests a disconnection from materiality and medium, theme or substance. A designer's identity is somewhat connected to the idea of being rational. Being called an artist does not go far to validate the idea of rational, and as a designer I have always felt that "artist" is possibly the worst thing to be called by the wrong person. In places like Italy—where artistry and ancient visual culture are abundant—being an artist might be the least special type of person to be. And yet—I admire every one of them.

KNOW-ABOUT I wasn't mentored in capitalism or the pricing of art
VALUE. and or time/value/money, but I did learn about the
points of resistance that people develop around spending money and participating in a bulk or bargain purchase. Very little
understanding about design's (capitalistic) expressions will be useful in
understanding how art is priced or valued, and you, like me, might be frustrated trying to apply new knowledge about art, art values, production, or
sales to anything else. Particularly commercial graphic design. Try not to
be annoyed with me. I only say this so that you know they are separate
educations, taught by very differently qualified people. Early in your life,
you will have the energy and capacity to learn both; I think learning both
is the best path.

KNOW YOUR VALUE (2) KNOW YOURSELF

In my experience, art directors don't direct art very often,
but it doesn't mean they shouldn't. They mostly direct people—and mostly
direct designers. You can change that by being a designer who makes their
own *supporting art or assets*. Resist calling yourself an artist. You are a more
valuable designer, especially if you can integrate your skills with a number of
different topics or themes. I have allowed my multimedia practice to ride alongside my designer self and my curator self and my new (reluctant) writing self.
A critical part of your work as a designer is to establish
the value of (your?) art, illustration, or painting, or anything else—including
writing—for the purpose of inclusion in a design product. You must know
this before you are asked. This is the foundation of its value and your understanding. It is so critical that if it is mishandled, you will cycle backward
to it over and over again to seek clarity. Residuals will be difficult. Rights
management will be difficult. Publishing will be difficult and with that—
ensuring authorship and ownership is difficult.
Additionally, if you accept a design position with a firm
that will also include access to your talent as an illustrator, you may choose
to license your work—separately from your salary, not necessarily for more
money, but for clarity of rights to use. And it will help everyone involved
if the clients you work for require indemnity for the transfer of IP (intellectual property).

HISTORY IS MY MUSE

All art is about something. If it is elusive . . . perfect. Perhaps an experience will unlock it. It takes time, years even, to develop an artist's interest, and to inform, move, horrify, or delight your audiences. I believe that the history in our cells is the basic material of making; the muscle memory of making is a type of history that participates in our action.

The space of making and our use of languages (formal and informal vocabularies) usually grounds our experience in making, in making for audiences we understand and who understand us. And though it is a journey, the attention to pay to this often has an effect on your connection to those who are qualified to discuss your work as art. Listening is key. Blackness is a big part of it, being an immigrant is a big part of it, and having lived in other geographies has had a surreal benefit; when I say history, I mean all of it. And I honestly mean all of yours, too. To validate history is tricky. When I say tricky, I mean dangerous.

Central to graphic design, the history of typography and text creates space for some useful linguistic constructs. Yet, what the artist/designer leans into (and back from) as an impulse, as a habit, as a practice, and as an act of rebellion will have to be delicate and nuanced. This is out of respect for both the mechanisms of typography and the undeniable authority of the human hand.

This negotiation can be crippling.

We rely on connections to the history of contemporary visual culture. Art relies on knowing the difference between utility and indulgence. (Try not to see indulgence as a bad word.) Most art relies on caring for one's own psyche, and caring for one's own need to make. Impulses, even indulgences, can be good for the whole self. It may not serve in the making of works for audiences, commissions, etc. But to know one's own impulses and indulgences is good for the person—especially if these indulgences are otherwise unspeakable in various atmospheres or environments. This goes a long way to exorcise the darkness of our individual experiences and decide where the "relentless" self needs to be in order to bring the suggestion of meaning into focus.

BETWEEN THE AUTHORITY AND THE OPPORTUNITY

[Rationality v. Minimalism]
Artists who come to design often apply a polish or veneer to design, as if their understanding of design is rational; and, by contrast, their understanding of art is irrational. This is a trap. Designers sometimes

feel qualified to make rational art because of the ability to polish ideas. This is also a trap. Design polish is an extension of respectability aesthetics, cleanliness, and minimalism. Which I find deeply suspicious. The maxim "less is more" feels untrue. Less is actually less. Making minimalist work in an honest way is difficult and serious work. It always has meaning; it will always be controversial. If you do not know why you make it, it's design, not art. If you have already decided what you are making from this perspective (place), then I suggest you write about it until you are exhausted and then get to *the making* as a response to your rationale (or writing).

DEALING WITH OTHERS IN RELATION TO YOUR WORK

There will be countless critics and curators, some of whom are historians, curators, and critics of art, and some of design. Their scholarship depends on specialization. Their knowledge is not typically wide, and if they are good at what they do, they are quite deep. This puts a burden on you to be aware of the context they possess for your work. Help them by knowing your context first. It is fine if your work is intuitive; allow that intuition to develop a story in front of it and behind it. Your art history knowledge becoming—at first wide, then deep—is an important step to becoming able to write your own narrative, to tell the story of your particular output in ways that can connect to—and build upon—what people already sense, feel, or understand; and to move fluidly through new self-knowledge and actual embodied histories.

This is not a goal—this is a journey, as your knowledge grows, as your vocabulary grows, so does your work and the way you share your narrative. Do not be afraid. People of color rarely possess this knowledge, so you will have to submerge yourself in places where there are protectionist policies, where there is arrogance, and most obvious of all, where there is a policy of dismissal, rudeness, and judgment. It may not be personal; it may be a test that opens doors. Listen for the complaints of others who do not have access to gatekeepers, because they can't find them or pass their tests.

People who possess this knowledge avoid sharing it outside their already tight community of influence. Attending members-only events at institutions or curator-led events will give you insight to the community you wish to join. If you wish to be collectable, you will probably need to know some collectors. The challenge you must accept is to study alone and study in these spaces simultaneously. If you have access to a college or university, take every art history credit you can find. Then, temper it with other time lines in social studies and Africana studies if you can. All of this is only information. It is not the only history—and as you'll soon find out, your own history is quite different and quite rich even though you may not find it in these spaces.

The arbiter of good taste—in art—is less of an esteemed position and the market's acceptance of various modes—built with expertise and status, but a question of quality. The artist/designer already relies upon this question to make in any fashion, for private exploration and healing, for an expression of an idea, for the practice of making, or for the participation in the markets of art. To make without this idea is to marginalize oneself in the belief that others are more eligible to judge the work than you are. The only judgment that is required is that of the maker and the confidence that the artist/designer is aware of where and how the works participate in their lives, and how they are eligible to be discussed in any of the available areas of scholarship or criticism. If this is not resolved you will find yourself coming back to this before you can move forward.

WHO IS IN CHARGE? If you are so self-aware, the true question becomes . . . what are curators for? What is the art establishment qualified to do in the assessment of whether an artist is ready for the world, ready for the art world, and ready to share outside of their own private practice of making?

The access to contemporary art scholarship is closely guarded, there are few powerful and important jobs in this field—in the world, few qualified teachers or mentors. Even a bad education in contemporary art criticism is expensive and tightly controlled, by status and by rank, and for this reason. More perspectives from more—even laypersons—will be good for you. Curators and critics take their status seriously and spend their reputation on the artists they present. They share their clout, their audiences, and their status with the artist. What they receive is access to your story and to your work and the opportunity to place it in the context with which they create. That context is limited to what they understand.

You are actually in charge—in the biggest way.

END ESSAY. BEGIN WORK.

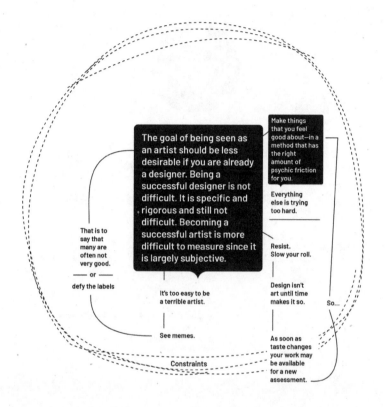

EXHIBIT 1.1   Time is a construct that makes everything fragile, for people who are goal setters, achievement-oriented persons, and those who lack patience when they get knocked back. Remember: I said be patient.

through
all of art
and
history

Ideas that
drive either
the reasoning
or the
appearance
of designed
objects

All art has been
available to become the
material of design and
continues to make itself
available at no cost
whatsoever.

Design isn't
art until time
makes it so.

And if it isn't it's
probably just
fine too.

There are still
things that
are neither
design or art.

to the designer who is
paying attention

to art history

However...

Only the first and
second acts of
making (any kind of
work) are qualified
to be art.

Concepts

EXHIBIT 1.2   Design—if it's good enough it gets to be talked about as art.

Only the first two acts of making any kind of work are qualified to be art because everything else is working too hard (see figure 1:1).

There is an area called *neither design nor art* and that place is really saying that it's not a good *representation of either thing.*

I don't say artists are not designers. Because: of course you are.

What might disqualify design to be viewed as art.

Design is not art if it -is not- -in-fact-art.

Design is not art if it has no mystery left in it.

By mystery we mean the following; friction, intrigue, question, puzzle.

There is a thing that is neither design nor art.

The maker is the arbiter of this label.

Design cannot be art if the parts are not transformed by an art concept

Bad design is not art

Nope

EXHIBIT 1.3   No one is trying to shut this down. Knowing what something is not is valuable. In the creation of constraints, definitions, assumptions and even the work itself.

In Conversation:

Mimi Ọnụọha

& Romi Morrison

ON UNSETTLING
THE EQUIVALENTS

Mimi Ọnụọha and Romi Morrison interviewed each other on May 19, 2021. They discussed their collaborative art projects and the fluid space between art and design. This conversation has been edited for length and clarity.

MIMI ỌNỤỌHA: Does design equal art? Does design not equal art?

ROMI MORRISON: I want to start by unsettling the equivalents between these two terms a little. Maybe we can frame it by what each offers to the other or what each provokes from the other. Ultimately, I think there are definitely spaces where these things overlap or trade similar visual languages and then I think there are ways in which they very dramatically depart. Each has an asset and a detriment, I think, in that regard. I'm curious about what design offers art? What art offers to design? I think both of our practices trade back and forth between those two spaces so thinking about it through offerings is kind of nice.

MỌ: I do like that. This question does come up in certain contexts more than others. Often I'm not very interested in answering it at all because there is just one very simple, straightforward answer, which is that it depends on the context. It depends on the market. It depends on where you're presenting it. Really anything that you call one of these could be presented as the other, depending on what the aims of it are, but I feel like often when people are asking this they're talking about something else, which I think you're starting to unsettle here, which is that there are these sort of aesthetic characteristics, or as you said, "offerings" or needs, that either art or design is presumed to have inherently. If we hold those in place, and we say, "Okay, that is the core and here are the assumptions of what those fields give," then yes we can say these have different aims, different needs, and often different conceptions of audience.

RM: As Black people that have to work in and between these two worlds, there is also strategy about what term you use in what space, how you present yourself in a way, depending on who's around you and how you need to be legible. I think that's why for such a long time design was a term that I used really readily. I think "artist" is also a very capacious term in a lot of ways, but I think design is even more ambiguous because it's applied in so many different contexts. Yet, it still has this strange residual air of precision or acuity. Designers are always very serious.

They're always in their monochromatic ensembles, with slightly off-color rims for their glasses. So much of this is inherited from European schools of design, especially modern design and its sleek, arid visual language. There is a seriousness that I feel is tacked onto it. It doesn't always have to justify its own value or its own credibility as much as art often has to do. This is a question of how you strategically identify yourself, depending on what space you're in, how you want to be seen, need to be seen, and what kind of role you want to play.

MỌ: **Absolutely. I think there's a sort of presumed professionalization of design. I remember a friend of mine who's an architect said that originally she wanted to be an artist, but being an architect is the acceptable way to be an artist. You're still embedded within a structure where you seem very legitimate. You can say, "Look at this degree, this isn't a joke. This is rigorous. This is work. There are standards. There are protocols. There are things that we do." Often I think there is a sense that the art world is contrasted against that, as if artists are in the wishy washy space where people are just messing around and there's nonsense, but designers have work to do.**

RM: This is where the serious creativity and making happens.

MỌ: **Exactly. Rigorous creativity is for design and foolish whimsical creativity can be passed off to art. Again, these ideas are not accurate and are over generalized and not particularly useful. However, as Black folks who are navigating these spaces, you do see these ideas and you get pushed up against them. I agree with you that there is this question where you say, okay, well, what does it mean to be—and what does it mean to call myself—a designer in this space? What does it mean to call myself an artist? What does it mean to be an artist and a designer in a space full of designers or to be in a space of people who don't care about the difference between either and to call that, to claim one or the other, that all of those have different affordances?**

I think for me, personally, it's just much easier to say I'm an artist because a lot of the structures, organizations, the residencies, the places where I show work, and the ways in which I show work, fit more into the art world. But the work itself is never about being in one of these fields. That's the thing. At the end of the day, I think the work that we are creating is informed by the practices of multiple fields, but it's not in one or the other. It then gets commodified in different ways and then presented in still other ones. That is fine. To me, the most important thing is understanding: what's the work and what's happening here? What are we trying to do? Cool, from there call it what you like.

RM: I think this is a helpful distinction between the ways that art or design are often thought about ultimately as objects versus as methods or practices. Sometimes they're considered that way, but often I feel when there's a question of "is it art or is it design," it's mostly a question of where do I place this object that's been created? Which is very different than the process of working through something and trying to place emphasis on the material as much as on what it evokes, what it performs or does afterwards, that then requires an audience or requires a viewer, it requires some kind of interaction. I feel that when I try to think about art and design, they're both very different practices depending on what kind of interaction I'm ultimately hoping to elicit, offer, or have people step into. Art and design function very differently when thinking this way.

When I am more explicitly working in a design practice, it's usually to take on the language of design, which is often about clarifying: making something more acute, axiomatic, or almost subliminal, right? It's to make something seem as if it's not designed, that has a sense of ease or is naturalized. That clarity to create these kinds of contradictions or to create spaces in which the transparency of design's visual language can be made explicit. You're making the things that aren't supposed to be visible an active part of the design language. Then it becomes really fun, especially working with maps, which we both share a deep love for. I mean the map in itself is an epistemology. It's a very clear epistemology that's being evoked and part of what makes it effective and simultaneously violent, what gives its utility is its clarity. Its clarity to demarcate borders and boundaries. To be able to visualize and ascribe whole mythologies of people and culture onto those places—that's a deeply powerful thing. Design feels like it's uni-dimensionally focused. It's very clear what the aim is. There's a path, and it's taking you onto that path very clearly. With the ways that I think about artistic practice, I'm trying to create multiple ways for someone to come into a much larger experience. Hopefully at least one of those pathways become something that's resonant or congeals in your head, to evoke a feeling that's been elicited along that journey. It isn't so discrete or didactic. It uses ambiguity in a way to unsettle something or to form a connection that previously would have been thought to be unheard of or impossible. It's a much stranger murkier kind of space. It isn't so much about the confrontation that design can offer because of its clarity as much as it is an amorphous unsettling, but in these generative ways.

MỌ: One thing that is nice, just to extend this point that you've been making, is that I think both art and design are concerned with the connotations of things. They're not just concerned with how something performs, but also with how a particular group of people will perceive it in a particular context and what that suggests. I contrast this with something like engineering, which actually should—and in the best cases, does—also have that same interest in everything around the thing that you're supposedly communicating, but at its most brittle says, well, that's unimportant. We just care about one particular metric and we can solely optimize for that. I think in both art and design, anyone who is in both of those fields has to hold a bit more of the murkiness of things. However, depending on which one you say that your work lands in, you'll be judged by the sort of ideal standards and customs of that space. Something that you just cannot get away from with design is the brief and the audience, because these two things are attached to each other. The design brief tells you what it is that you're meant to be doing. With both art and design, you're presenting some kind of information, and I use both "presenting" and "information" very broadly. With design, you have this thing where you can point to, "this is what it's meant to be," and "this is what it's meant to clarify," and "this is who it's for." I think you bringing up maps is so fantastic because I think they are such a perfect example. Maps are these artifacts that can be so many things at once. They are scientific, they're extremely artistic. They're designed objects. They're violent objects. They constantly obscure. They clarify certain things and by clarifying it, they then choose what will be obscured and that then gets erased from the process.

                Personally, I use strategies from the two worlds very differently. I try to create work in a variety of different contexts for a variety of different reasons, so it is useful to pick up and set down whatever it is, whatever I want, depending on what I'm trying to do. In some moments, I intentionally stay in the art space because of the increased murkiness compared to design, where there is no need to state so many things, even though they are still there. The fact that they are not stated doesn't mean that they're not there. The fact that you don't state it does bring in other complications. I think there's something fun to work with there, just as there's something very fun in seeing a structure supposedly be legible, but then pushing past that.

RM: While you were talking, I kept thinking about universality and its relationship to both of those spaces. In stating or not stating the design brief or the audience, I feel like design is often rhetorically spoken about as something that's situated for particular users, and simultaneously this contradictory claim to universalism through iconography and standardization.. It also has the capacity to be the metric upon which to measure universalism. There are so many universal design methods and universal design principles. It's strange that in a field that is so clear about its brief or its audience, there's still this simultaneous attachment to universalism that doesn't go away even as it's being plastically funneled to a particular user.

MQ: **It's as if the ability of design to claim a kind of, as we said, legibility or professionalism . . .**

RM: And because it's so tied to industry, very explicitly.

MQ: **I'm thinking about conversations I've had with designers and artists about this. It does seem to me that some of my designer friends are like, "Oh, but I'm creative too. You know." They're like, "I can make art as well." Which, of course you can. Then on the other side, artists, being given this sort of lovely capaciousness, that openness, the intimacy, the way that universality is not imposed on the art world in the same way that it is, I would say imposed on so much of the design world, that the assumed lack becomes, "Well, now there's no rigor." There's no standard. What does it mean? How is it even helpful? Can it even kind of scale? Similar questions. Which I think both sides are operating from a strange point of scarcity, but also of trying to prove something that doesn't really need to be proven. Again, even as we're saying this, I can still identify people who work in fields as artists and as designers who are undoing both of those. So we say all this, but this is still to say that we're speaking to a kind of core but there's so much more. There's always more space in the margins. Within that core, I do agree with you. There is a kind of freedom from the trappings of the myth of universality. I think the design world constantly is dealing with what feels like this need to show its proof of utility. This question of utility that comes up all the time. It doesn't need to. Yet, we can't not acknowledge that it does.**

RM: You just touched on standardization. I feel like we're trying to identify these things like universality, standardization, metrics, clarity, and scalability. These are things that have become for better or worse, within the vernacular and lexicon of design. Utility is often how we experience design. Right? I think in our daily lives that's often our experience with it. Which is strange because I think people probably have way more interactions and relationships with designed objects or materials than they do with anything that we would think of as art or artistic. There's a kind of intimacy that we have with the products of the design world that is a part of the design process as well. Again, because utility is so much of the focus, there are times where it can overshadow what can potentially happen within our relationships with designed objects. It becomes almost invisible. For example, I open my laptop and I start working on it. I'm not really thinking about my relationship with my laptop very much, unless I'm up at four in the morning screening something when I shouldn't be.

MỌ: **What is interesting about the two of us is that we don't fit solidly into one of these two worlds or one of any world. It's either a blessing or a curse. Something I feel like we've spoken about and I've wanted and fought for quite a bit, is this idea within the art world that the art is just in the artifact, the expression. As opposed to claiming, "Well, no. What if there's a latitude in the ways in which we can even approach thinking about a topic?" What if it's about extending what we considered to be XYZ? What if it's about creating art as this form of endurance or repetition? We talk about opening up the space to connect when you're facing the violence of the world. This is particularly important as Black artists, designers, whatever you want to call us. It feels like this framing of design versus art does rely upon the most mainstream ideas of both, as opposed to the edges of each. That edge space is far more interesting, far more blurry, and begins to look more the same. Whether people are calling that speculative design or confabulation, the space around is the more interesting thing.**

RM: I think it's interesting to think about *Noticing the Preconditions For* _____ as a way to think about the relationship between the edges or the fringes of art and design. I can see both in that project and I guess we should introduce our work together.

MO: **We've been working on this project called *Noticing the Preconditions For* _____, and it's this durational, correspondence piece in which we are looking for the traces or preconditions of the world that we want to live in, but looking for it within the world in which we're living in today.**

RM: Yes, exactly. I would say it comes in part from the proto-cols of design, at least thinking about modularity and modulation. We're each essentially creating a database, right? You have yours; I have mine as we go out and experience the world where we are trying to train ourselves to notice those preconditions, not to pass by them, but to take them in as profound moments of transformation. Even if it's just the residue of something that you desire, that's an important resonance for coming to realize the things we desire but might not know yet.. Then we struggle to put them into a form. I mean, the database that we have is a very clearly designed object. It's very axiomatic.

MO: **As we're recording those things for ourselves, we're then doing an act of translation. I notice something and then I make a short piece that's trying to communicate what I gleaned from whatever I noticed and I then send it to you. We're making that kind of translation, description, and expression really explicit in the piece too. For me, it feels like it's blurring art and design a lot more because it's subjective, it's creative. It is abstract. It's about expression. I'm still trying to communicate something to you. Ultimately I'm still trying to communicate to you something that I saw and experienced, and I'm also trying to communicate it to you in a way that doesn't close down the potential in how you might read it. I'm trying to communicate to you the potential of what I have noticed without condensing or reducing it ...**

RM: ...To something, like a designed object or an artifact, but instead something that is motivating for you to rein-terpret and to build until the project goes back and forth in this modular, explicit act of making noticing, creating, expressing, interpreting, and translating, going back and forth. So I like how it moves. I think in this kind of blurriness, along the edges, where the threads of art and design need each other, because ultimately, they're really shared languages. As we were saying before, I think how we work with those two languages, is always trying to offer a gentle unfamiliarity for how people can step into seeing the world, themselves, and their relationship to it differently. I feel like it's always trying to give people just enough to hold onto in order to take the next step into a space of discomfort.

MỌ: But there's something also quite lovely. I think
            something to stress is that both of us are doing these
noticings. We see something; we translate it into some kind of digital
artifact where it's a video. It could be audio, it could be a web, something,
it can be anything, so long as its digital. Then we send it to the other
person. That person takes that, not knowing what the original noticing
was and then engages with it, examines it, and responds to it by creating
something that then modulates upon that that changes what, what has
been sent. There is a question of not everything being given away when
I get something that you've sent me. I don't know what it is that you're
really saying.

RM: As you're describing this, I'm thinking about its relation-
            ship to Blackness beyond just identity or beyond repre-
sentation, but more into the epistemology, the critical ontologies of how
Blackness functions and what Blackness does. There are a lot of parallels,
I think, in the ways that you're describing the process right now. There is a
necessary unsettling for us, that's bringing together lots of different things
that are maybe seemingly disparate, and making new meaning from them
or remixing them in different ways, but it's always this constant orientation,
both to what has passed and to what needs to come. In a way this is not
about purity, but I think engages in the risk of modulation and of change—
of adaptability for fugitive practices.

MỌ: This feels very full circle because so much of what
            brought us into doing this whole project in the first
place was this sense of Blackness as this necessarily unsettling force.
That is absolutely indispensable, absolutely irreducible, but that within
this there are models that we can see for care and for hope in spite of
chaos and in spite of unpredictability. In spite of pain. This project has
been an enactment of that reality on so many different levels, but also a
kind of search for that at the same time. All while knowing that it is there
already, but that the thing that brings this to the surface is the practice
of searching.

RM: I think sometimes there's a frustration that I often feel
            when talking about Blackness, both in the art or in the
design world. Often the visuality of Blackness is always tied to epidermal-
ization, is always tied to the body, and then always tied to identity being
predefined. You're stepping into a situated predefined notion of how
Blackness has been articulated, but it always feels self-contained. It rarely
feels like it's leading beyond the edge, expanding or unsettling what we

think the edge or border is. It always feels very neat because it seems to be so focused on representation. That's become so loaded. I don't know what to do with it anymore.

MO: **Using representation and visibility as the two anchor points for any kind of mainstream analysis of what Blackness can be is so limiting. Certainly for the two of us and for many more people, Blackness is a destabilizing force that destabilizes so many of these notions in the first place. Not just for fun or because it makes us feel good, but because historically when it comes to the formation of this world, this globalized world, that has always been the case. How do I put it in words? Holding onto that becomes much more difficult in the face of other conceptions of Blackness that are tied to an easy reliance upon these other metrics.**

RM: Yeah. I mean it's born out of neoliberal multicultural-ism—a way of saying we can take something like Blackness or even race and we can divorce it, untangle it, or disentangle it from anything political or economic. Then representation becomes something that expresses culture. We just want to see all of these cultures together, but it doesn't fundamentally make any demands or challenge the structure or the organization of what's overwhelmingly a Western modern-ized world built on racial capitalism, that required Blackness to construct itself as coherent.

MO: **It required Blackness to construct itself, but also re-quired a kind of refusal of Blackness at the same time. That duality right there is fundamental to so much of the work that I think both of us are really interested in. It's fundamental in a high-stakes kind of way, asking "How do we live in this world?"**

RM: It's quite clear what the end point of a Western moder-nity looks like, and we're accelerating toward that pretty quickly. It looks like a complete instability with the actual natural processes of the world. That's a huge statement but I think it's very true. It should be somewhat revealing looking at industry Titans who take on this kind of hegemonic white masculinity as the saviors of Western civilization such as Elon Musk or Jeff Bezos. Their solution to the crisis of climate instability and mass extraction is that we're going to terraform another planet to extract more because this home isn't salvageable. It's completely congruent with the extractive ethos that they have profited off of so heav-ily. It should be a good indicator of not only the lack of imagination, but the refusal to shift any of those practices. Therefore, Blackness is a necessity, not even just to unsettle, but to constitute, conjure, and birth other ways of living that don't take on those same trappings. We have to figure out other ways to relate to each other, that aren't just about bloodlines or kin, but are extended into all these other relations. We have to take on different ways of looking at labor, different ways of looking at affect, and different ways of coexisting. Blackness is both used to cohere this really extremely violent constitution of the world and then simultaneously denied. In that denial, I think it has had to function alongside the violence of modernity. Blackness doesn't neatly escape racial capitalism, but it also doesn't have to absorb it or internalize it in all the same ways. This liminality is a gift.

MỌ:　　　　Absolutely. I suppose it brings us back to the place that we find ourselves in as artists, designers, whatever it is. Working in this world, working with these topics, knowing what we mean when we talk about Blackness—that we are also talking about this political economy. We're talking about the ways in which it's operated alongside different models of domination, depending on where you are. We're talking about these histories of colonization and coloniality, as we continue to inherit it today. We're talking about what it means to have to be forced to find these sustainable or just vital ways of living amidst unlivable circumstances. Continually created unlivable circumstances that are then heralded, particularly when using emerging technology as if to say, "Look, here's a brand-new novel way to do things," but actually just continues to contribute to that same degradation. Holding all of this but then existing as well in these spaces where that is very continually undercut, removed, and conformed into being something else entirely.

RM:　　　　I'm really heartened by the ways that I see particular Black scholars and thinkers move back and forth between artistic and scholarly worlds that are taking up very shared affinities for the Blackness that we're describing. They are refusing simple, neat, or innocuous reductions of Blackness as a figure to be consumed, and are really pulling from the well of a constant state of resistance and generation simultaneously. I'm thinking of the ways that Saidiya Hartman, Tina Campt, Fred Moten, and Denise Ferreira da Silva are thinkers that are really foundational to critically thinking about Blackness and [who] are being celebrated right now. That's something to recognize. It's heartening for me at the same time, as I feel really frustrated and really incensed by the ways that Blackness is just constantly reduced—particularly to make work about Blackness and then to have to appeal to institutional spaces for resources. To see how easily and how quickly what you're trying to articulate just gets plastically molded into a neoliberal multiculturalism or into something that adheres to an innocuousness of Blackness. It's really crazy how efficiently that happens.

MO: **Efficient is the word. The mechanics for that process and that kind of constant co-option are always being refined. It feels like it's refined with each generation and even more rapidly. I agree there are fantastic people who actually are getting the due they deserve. I think there are fantastic artists who have been doing this work in ways that are not so legible. I think of Simone Leigh. I think of Okwui Okpokwasili. I think there are so many people who are doing this and have been doing it for a long time and are now coming into the spotlight. I think the thing I take from what we might call the "art world," but really someone could say this is from the design world or from whatever creative world is the holding of many things at the same time. This pushback, I guess, as a response to universality, is to say, "Well, actually let's hold all of these things and they might not be congruent. Yes, these things will be co-opted, but at the same time there is something beautiful that will come through." There's a seed that continues to live and can sprout elsewhere. That does give me hope.**

In Conversation: Rhea L. Combs

&

Anne H. Berry

ON REPRESENTING EVERYDAY BLACK LIVES THROUGH FILM & PHOTOGRAPHY

I spoke with Rhea L. Combs, formerly a senior curator of Photography & Film at the Smithsonian's National Museum of African American History & Culture and currently director of Curatorial Affairs at the National Portrait Gallery in Washington, DC, about her work highlighting Black artists and the everyday lives and stories of Black people. We discussed why her role is so critical and necessary, particularly in 2021. This conversation has been edited for length and clarity.

—Anne H. Berry

ANNE H. BERRY	**From your perspective, what makes representing everyday Black life through film and photography so significant? Whether it's for Black audiences, white audiences, or mixed audiences?**
RHEA L. COMBS:	Documenting everyday experiences provides an opportunity to humanize a group of people that have historically been marginalized and left out of conversations for myriad reasons. It also allows communities to see themselves, not as some sort of extraterrestrial entity, but as critical to the fabric of society. Furthermore, those who are part of the community see themselves as they experience life. And it allows those who may be less familiar with a particular community—in my specific case, African American communities—a chance to see their humanity reflected in ways it often isn't, particularly in news, film or advertising. Historically these mainstream industries have tended to present far more reductive experiences.
	And so by presenting, either through exhibitions or design, everyday lives or experiences of people going about their lives, it offer greater passageways for communication across communities.

AHB:	**And why is it seemingly so difficult for Black people to be understood and perceived in humanizing ways?**

RLC:	It's difficult because we cannot dismiss, especially within the context of the United States, the history of Black people as enslaved and considered as property—so the narrative around Black people in this country is one that dehumanizes Black bodies. Black bodies have been perceived as expendable, and structures and systems were created to perpetuate these notions.

And as a result, the contributions of African Americans have been largely excluded from history books. Art history has definitely marginalized non-European artists who have contributed mightily to the canon. Structurally and historically, I think we really have to reimagine "when and where we entered," to borrow a phrase from scholar Paula Giddings.[1]

AHB:	**As a curator, you are shaping the narratives of how Black people are presented and represented; there's decision-making around the images you're using or how information is being introduced. You are still making aesthetic choices. So, what (if any) challenges does this create for you, whether it's on a personal or professional level? Or both?**

RLC:	Well, I think, as a Black curator who emphasizes and values the everyday, this sometimes flies in the face of museum practice and what museums want because there is often a reverence for the extraordinary, which I think sometimes creates a distance between the visitor and the work of art.

As a curator of color, I recognize there are many things happening simultaneously. In many instances, curators of color have to educate colleagues about why an idea is relevant to present at the museum. And that idea is associated with a whole host of other institutional challenges such as a lack of historical awareness surrounding the subject, funding concerns, or worry the content might challenge donors or trustees. So as a Black curator, you have a huge responsibility to justify something, educate somebody, and then prove that there is a thing such as "Black excellence." And then there is the art of presenting [the work] in such a way that is smart, nuanced, and not patronizing the artist.

There is this real tight rope that I think many Black curators have to walk as they come up with ideas, explain their aesthetic, while countering stereotypical perceptions that some people have about an artist's capability, particularly if it's someone that others don't know or have less familiarity with.

And then you have to manage frustrations when [museum staff] see someone's work and they are just kind of like, "Oh my god, this is really, really good!" As though you [as a curator] wouldn't be bringing the best to the table. There's a real set of multi-pronged, institutional, historical, and aesthetic challenges that a curator of color focused on African American art has to navigate.

It's not insurmountable, but it really does boil down to the structural problems that have been happening throughout time. And now we're in this moment where people within the museum field and other industries are having to place the mirror in front of themselves to recognize the gaping holes that have been persistent for decades. Ultimately, I think people are realizing how much more fortifying it can be when you actually engage in a multitude of different visual aesthetic conversations and experiences, as opposed to thinking that there's just one approach to something.

AHB: **It seems as though there's an underlying assumption that if we hadn't already known about these artists, if we hadn't already learned about them, or they weren't already part of the canon, they weren't worthy of consideration.**

RLC: Yes, that is absolutely correct. There's no responsibility or accountability when it comes to being informed and people will instead ask "Well, why didn't I hear (or know) about this person?" Suggesting that if they did not know about them then they must not be worth knowing.

AHB: **So why, then, is it important for Black people to be curators and creators of Black images?**

RLC: The origins of museums were another avenue for colonial entities to place their flag and demonstrate their prominence. So, on display was a country's prowess (or an individual's wealth). As a Black curator, it is about reframing that particular narrative and dismantling that unsettling history. It becomes critical for us to demonstrate what else can be considered culturally relevant. In this regard, this work becomes another social justice effort because our work can provide some essential correctives to dominant narratives that have persisted under the auspices of establishing oneself as a colonial superpower. I think it is critical [for museums] to turn the spotlight inward if we're to grow as a society. Black curators, I think, have an opportunity to expand the ways in which museums function, who the audiences are, and who a museum should be responsible to. And as a result, I think the exhibitions should reflect that.

It is not about perpetuating this idea of a dominant superpower anymore. It's about reflecting the community; it's about providing a safe space for cultural exchange versus cultural domination. And with cultural exchange, then I think Black curators really have this responsibility to, again, become visual storytellers. At the same time, they're able to engage and have visitors reflect and respond to social injustice while also looking at the beauty of what art can do. Art is essential to the way in which we understand and function in the world, and artists really shine a light on many of the contradictions and complexities and the subtle beauty that makes up a society.

AHB: **I love this idea of Black curators as a conduit for facilitating greater access and understanding. That's really beautiful . . . I'm curious to know what you think about as we look forward. What is your message to Black creatives who are following in your footsteps—or generations coming after you—about this work and what they can contribute?**

RLC: We have to know our history, obviously, but there also have been significant contributions by Black illustrators and Black creatives; Black artists always have been in these professions, so it's always important to understand and know that you're not alone. The ideas and thoughts that one might be percolating have a history and foundation that can be a launching pad to move forward.

I think that we are in a very critical and important time, a real crossroads, where institutions across genres are open to some difficult conversations. That becomes a real moment of opportunity for creatives, designers, and curators, to push boundaries and to make sure that we continue to ensure these difficult conversations occur in different spaces.

There are so many ways in which someone can take their various passions and contribute them to the work in a museum. It's not just a curator—curators don't do it alone. Museums have teams who help them bring their ideas forward. Designers, in particular, are essential to taking a concept that a curator might have and helping illuminate the idea through the environment in ways that help someone understand the story being conveyed. I think it's important for people to stay rooted and grounded in their truth, to not feel ashamed of it, and to understand that there has been a long trajectory of artists and excellence that has come from Black designers. It is important to continue to hone your craft, while truly understanding that what you have to say is unique and essential to the ways in which we better tell stories.

NOTES

1. Giddings, Paula. *When and Where I Enter*. Bantam
   Doubleday Dell Publishing Group Incorporated, 2006.

COLLECTIVE, RADICAL
& LIBERATORY
SPACES IN DESIGN

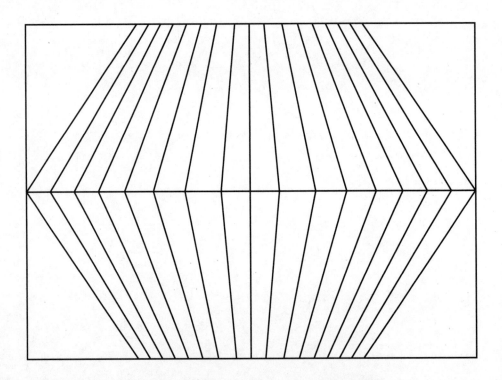

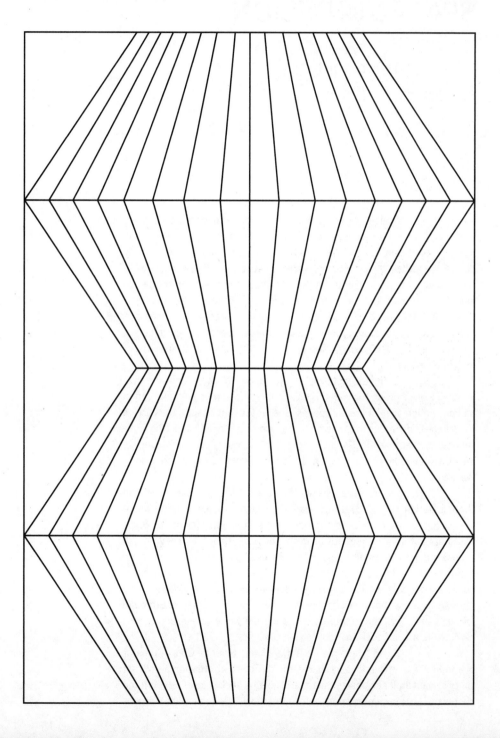

COLLECTIVE, RADICAL & LIBERATORY SPACES IN DESIGN

Chapter Introduction:
Lesley Ann-Noel

The language of design, abolition, emancipation, and liberation overlap at times. The overlap focuses on building, reconstructing, creativity, and making new visions. This section focuses on Black radical liberation by design. We invited people who have created spaces for Black creatives to thrive, despite the lack of support that they have received from the design industry. The contributors come from different corners of the world of design and have used different channels such as professional organizations, networking websites, social media groups, podcasts, design guilds, conferences, and tech camps. Two of our contributors create spaces just in their being.

In the opening essay, Lauren Williams writes a love letter to Black women and reminds us about the need for self-preservation and protection against hostile spaces. She writes that despite the carrots that these institutions may seem to offer, we do not need them (the institutions) or their carrots. We do not need to give every drop of ourselves. We do not owe them. We do not need to be validated by white adjacency. We are enough.

Terrence Moline, founder of the African American Graphic Designers (AAGD) group, takes what might be considered a controversial position and defends the need for segregated spaces for Black designers to thrive. He reminds us of the forgotten benefits of segregated spaces that provide comfort and safety and describes how his organization creates a space for people to learn and flourish within an industry and a country that holds Black people back. AAGD is a place for Black designers to grow and share without the crippling impacts of racism. It mentors through love and empathy. It is a "for us by us" space, not white-facing, and unconcerned about what goes on in white spaces.

In "Make the Path by Talking," Maurice Cherry, creator of the *Revision Path* podcast, shares the difficulty of creating a podcast that focused on Black design talent, and how he almost gave up. With the support of an unexpected sponsor (go read the article to see who), he was able to breathe new life into the project. In creating the weekly podcasts, Cherry was actually documenting Black design's present and history. He is an example to all of us: Make the history ourselves.

The Black Artist and Designers Guild (BADG) was born out of Malene Barnett's frustration with the design industry. Barnett's story, like others in the chapter, traces her own personal history and upbringing that made her love her Blackness. Barnett's feeling of invisibility in the design industry started at college and has remained with her throughout her career. Though the interior design industry comfortably appropriates African aesthetics, there is little space for Black designers. She created the Black Artists and Designers Guild as a response to the whiteness and inequitable spaces of the design industry and as a space for thriving, connection, and collaboration. The BADG aims to build visibility for Black designers who might otherwise remain invisible in the hyper whiteness of interior design.

In an essay derived from a conversation, Ari Melenciano shares how the technology festival Afrotectopia began, demonstrating, as Barnett and Moline did, how comfort with her Black identity as a youth instilled a sense of confidence and agency that has carried through her work to today. Like Barnett, Melenciano was one of the only Black students in her undergraduate and graduate programs. Afrotectopia was created as a space to celebrate creativity, experimentation with technology, and Blackness.

We close this section with powerful words from adrienne maree brown about creating transformative, liberatory, and radical spaces as designers. brown shares advice to support Black designers as they move into roles of facilitation, organizing, and activism and challenges Black designers to have grand visions of the future.

The thread that runs through these pieces is that Black designers must boldly create these spaces for themselves. These spaces need to be visionary, liberatory, and emancipatory communities for Black designers who are being ignored by the design industry.

for colored girls who feel trapped

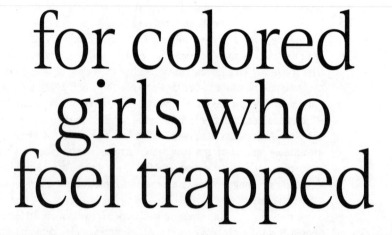

in

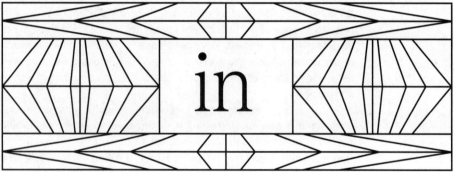

white institutions

LAUREN WILLIAMS

This is sort of a manifesto, a reminder to myself, and a love note to my past self and other Black women who give too much of themselves to institutions. Perhaps it contains a bit of poetry, if you, too, find poetic the ways my consciousness has evolved over time and the force with which it now drives me away from institutions and back to myself. Maybe it contains a bit of choreography, if you, too, find the need to ever so carefully orchestrate your movements to navigate the places that pay you to labor.

It's a play performed by one woman in several roles—the angry Black woman; the increasingly dissatisfied abolitionist; the self-conscious first-time teacher; the young(ish) artist unsure of herself and whether or not she can even call herself an artist if she's never had a practice of her own; the list goes on.

You have been stubbornly insisting, believing, inching forward within institutions that don't care about you, don't care about us, can't care for us, and won't carry us, for too long. It's time to abandon trust in an untrustworthy place.

Banging your head against its white walls is unproductive and self-harming and precisely what it wants of you. Deprive it of that pleasure; reclaim that satisfaction for yourself.

You don't owe the institution anything. It will insist, passive aggressively—and you'll believe—that you owe it for the clout, the credential, the salary, the opportunity, the adjacency to whiteness.

But, you don't.

You don't owe anything to an institution that will gleefully encourage students to insert themselves in discourses and neighborhoods to which they don't belong but can't begin to teach them to interrogate the ones from which they come or the systems of oppression in which they're complicit and by which they're shaped.

You don't owe anything to an institution that hires a magical Negro to handle its "diversity problem" when the problem in fact belongs to capitalism, extraction, and white chauvinism.

Though you'll feel like you owe it to your students, you don't owe anything to them either.

Whatever you did owe them you've paid in full. You've believed them, encouraged them, grown for them, grown with them, listened to them, learned with them. That's a gift for both of you.

There will be people there and at adjacent institutions who you appreciate, who make you feel appreciated, who make you feel like it might be worth it, who promise the job security warrants the other bullshit.

You'll thrive, at times, in ways that serve the institution but not in the ways you need yourself to. You'll realize, a bit too late, that your presence and your labor and your critiques of the institution are part of the charade.

Sometimes you'll get trashed in student evaluations; other times you'll get glowing reviews. Every single time you'll ignore the countless studies about the ways racism colors student evaluations and internalize the criticisms as points to improve on yourself. They'll hate the way you critique and, though you know it intellectually, it'll take you years to accept emotionally that it's because they've been taught to be told what to do and that your trust in their capacity to make artistic decisions themselves isn't enough to inspire it in the span of a single semester.

You'll realize that the places you struggled most were the ones where you were expected to teach and enforce the rules of a canon that you know to be flawed, limited, arbitrary, and chauvinistic in its commitment to Western, white rules and assessments of taste colored, in large part, by capital. But you've no interest in enforcing those rules, in *policing* the margins, the kerning, and the composition. You've learned, of late, that your commitment to abolition is a practice you must bring into your practice and the classroom, too; a repeated set of actions; a thing we will fail at daily and try again the next. You'll find it hard to practice that in this place.

You'll realize that the greatest service you can offer is to give students the space and the tools and the invitation to bring themselves into their work; that they cannot and should not be expected to compartmentalize them*selves* away from their creations; and that doing so will bring you the greatest joy, too.

The institution and the people in it can't begin to comprehend what you actually need; that it needs you more than you need it. It presumes to have succeeded by including you.

Remember, if nothing else, to protect your energy: hold fast, you don't need to serve on that DEI committee, beloved. What *do* you need? Find that, follow it diligently, and build the institution you want to believe in, teach in, learn through, invest in, place your hope in, place your*self* in.

The Black Student Union

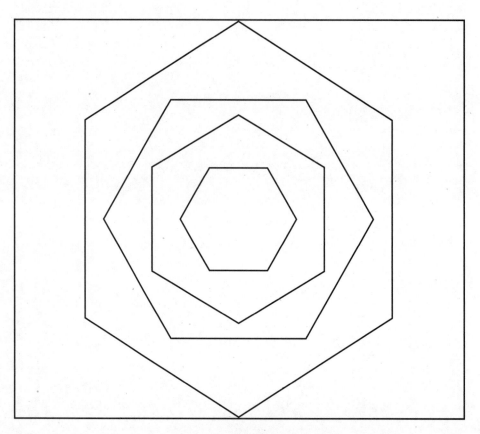

TERRENCE MOLINE

Forming a Liberatory Space for Black Creatives Is a Form of Protest, the Fulfillment of a Promise and the Only Pathway for Unapologetic Black Creativity.

ABSTRACT   As Americans of African Heritage, we have had deep existential questions about our identity and consciousness. As practitioners of the organization of space, time, and people, Black designers should continue to:

- » Practice reshaping our narrative as citizens of this young democracy.
- » Strive to make space to breathe and, through that small, essential expansion, speak our truth.
- » Find our place to hold steady ankles as we support our greatest asset: our next generation.

This article explores the continued need for segregated community and illustrates how separate and equal spaces are structured to make a difference in the lives of African American/Black (AA/Blk) visual communicators.

SON OF THE SEVENTIES   My parents are in their late seventies. I was fortunate enough to hear them talk about the troubles and triumphs of being defined as Negro or Colored.

I was also lucky to be born in a city, rich in cultural heritage and filled to its chicory-souled brim with celebrations of Blackness, improvisatory collaboration, and a strong sense of being.

As a kid, I was flabbergasted by stories of brown paper bag parties, fascinated with neighborhood gatherings, and fueled by the collaborative spirit in New Orleans that gave birth to cultural artifacts.

Though I may have had rose-colored glasses when imagining the past; I believed there was measurable value in our closeness. Through the bleaching of integration, I always wondered why, as AA/Blks we all but abandoned what was uniquely ours to blend into a society that did not have enough curiosity or care to fully embrace diversity.

While I'm aware integration ushered positive outcomes for Black progress, I feel it decimated the structures that supported Black community.

Integration impacted the development of identity for African Americans as we second-guessed our initiatives and misdirected community resources to white institutions and organizations that were finally civilized enough to allow us to have access.

THE BRIDGE ACROSS INTERSECTIONALITY

As someone who identifies as an AA/Blk, cisgender, Generation Xer, I'm aware of the opportunities I have and the obligations I owe to the shoulders who have allowed me to see new horizons.

» Reconstruction and the godfather of Black identity, W. E. B. Du Bois, and patron saint of Black PR, Ida B. Wells, had been fighting to combat cultural imperialism, single-sided narratives, and the insidious prevalence of white supremacy that seeped into all aspects of American culture, commerce and visual communication.
» The Harlem Renaissance proved what happens when the people of the African diaspora incubate ideas and unite to speak truth about the vibrant and desolate dimensions of being colored.
» The golden generation before me broke down barriers and put their bodies in the throes of physical trauma to tear through veils.
» The Black Power and Black Arts patrons proved we can define ourselves through symbolism, style, and action.

My generation of Black folks owes the ancestors appreciation, adoration, and acknowledgment.

In my familial role as a little brother, a big brother, a cousin, and an uncle, my family has expectations of me taking care of and looking out for generations after me. I find, while we all speak of standing on the shoulders of giants, we rarely discuss our place in the lineage of support.

Yes, we're standing, and our responsibility is to hoist, to uplift, to bear the weight of, and to transfer all that we have and know to build the backbone and character of Black identity.

This historical outline is a sketch that defines place and as a designer, this discovery process of self clarifies a creative brief that leaves wicked problems to be solved.

BLACK PROFESSIONAL CREATIVITY

I was on a plane to Singapore to visit a college friend and on the flight they were playing Louis Armstrong.

When I was in Paris, I stepped fresh off the Métro and was hit by a wave of American hip-hop. Travel has been eye-opening in understanding the impact of AA/Blk creativity, and it is always wonderful and sobering to think about the acceptance and disdain of our work.

Professional creativity in the Black community is suppressed, feared, misunderstood, and sometimes shunned. While history illustrates the complexities of professional creativity among AA/Blks, it is no less appalling and unfortunate because *we* do the most. Internationally, we're America's cool. We are the media makers. We are the reason for the

AMERICAN Black creativity in design-related industries has been
IDENTITY smothered, side-shoveled, and stolen. It's an odd conundrum of love and hate, embrace and disdain and the tethering of capitalism is enough to cause a whiplash of consciousness when addressing the worth of Black Creativity.

Because of these reasons, we are overburdened by imposter syndrome and, in general, lack of support and direction.

I am now an elder, and creating a shelter for Black creativity has been not only a gift bestowed by time and spirit but a responsibility mandated by applying principles learned from design to a greater purpose: Black Community Design.

ITERATIONS The design of our community has been through several
OF RADICAL iterations. Through strategic, Socratic questioning and community-led insights, our process gleaned information and paved the road to continue the radical notion of creating exclusive Black creative space: Not BIPOC. Not allied. Black.

We reclaim the right to have separate and equal spaces. On our terms. With our resources. This is a form of resistance. A conscious shunning. An unapologetic: no-thank-you.

We've been trained to chase an American idea of unity and growth through togetherness. And, through our collective intelligence, we've learned this is a false narrative. Black folks are always opening doors, reaching out to be the better people and more inclusive while consistently putting Blackness on the back burner.

We no longer need whiteness or idealized "American-ness"

» Their thought process has been tainted.
» Their institutions have failed us.
» Their leaders continue to trip and are slightly behind step on how to embrace unapologetic Blackness.

» Their ideologies have been passed down from power-hungry fathers and silently supportive mothers who knowingly benefited from centuries of Neanderthalic treatment of other humans—and it seems to be non-retractable.

While we're aware of national organizations for design, they serve their target audience, which is understandable.

Through African American Graphic Designers, we have etched out and wire-framed what works. We have designed the organization to solve our issues based on our understanding of our needs.

THE PROMISE

Thus all Art is propaganda and ever must be, despite the wailing of the purists. I stand in utter shamelessness and say that whatever art I have for writing has been used always for propaganda for gaining the right of Black folk to love and enjoy. I do not care a damn for any art that is not used for propaganda. But I do care when propaganda is confined to one side while the other is stripped and silent.

—W. E. B. Du Bois, "Criteria of Negro Art"[1]

This quote by DuBois is where we start. This is our mission, our marching orders. And no white-led or Black and white coled organizations deserve to pick up this mantle. It is our task, our birthright, our job to move this concept forward without the insistent interfering of people who want to cleanse their conscience by doing the "right thing" the wrong way.

We've studied history enough to know we are not creating anything new. What we are doing is carrying on the tradition. Since we've been in America, Black folks have always realized the need to have safe places for cultural and professional growth. From Congo Square to the NAACP.

The formation of African American Graphic Designers is in the tradition of Black institutions that address educational/vocational/professional industry-focused issues our people face in a country that has successfully prohibited our abilities to flourish.

514

Our group is the tradition of Black churches, where though we practice different religions, we've flourished from finding our own way to share joy, commune, and celebrate each other.

With the connectivity of technology and social media, I've noticed a return to Blackness, the Black community, Black ideas, and thought. An unearthing and revitalization of what we accomplished as a people.

While it may seem to make sense to approach the function of our organization from a design industry perspective it does us a disservice. This ultimately is a decision to bolster Black business, Black economy, and Black education. Our beginnings start at reconstruction as we are always building on the shoulders of giants.

Our organization is a symbol. It's a sign. A beacon of a more thoughtful approach to include diverse perspectives from rejected creative kids. We are not a monolith. We embrace all avenues of Blackness.

THE PATHWAY   *Practice, Survival, Support*
From our fourteen years of curating conversations, combing through thousands of posts, and having open dialogue through our members' media of choice. We have gathered ample insight on what factors drive success in our segregated creative community.

From interviews with members of our organization, we have learned that AAGD provides:

» Leadership without the stain of racism. Our communication is cleansed of the artifacts that cause eye rolls, lack of engagement, and isolation.
» Messages specific to our people trying to survive in professional creative industries.
» Answers to address some of the challenges of isolation associated with being a Black creative.
» Guidance on how to overcome imposter syndrome and Black cultural trauma.
» An embrace of empathy far beyond personal reasoning.
» Love and piercing critique that some people are too lazy or afraid to give to Black folks. This critique is critical to growth.
» Acknowledgment of effects of white supremacy.
» Individual care on their terms.
» Opportunities to foster stronger relationships through work.

I am a constant part of white design communities. Through interacting with those organizations and watching Diversity, Equity, Inclusion, Accessibility (DEIA) efforts fail, it has reinforced my belief in segregation before integration. We're taking a step back and redefining paths.

Ultimately, it is not our responsibility to solve the diversity problem within our industry. It is not our responsibility to help bolster white-led organizations who have consciously ignored their lack of Inclusion and who feign interest without understanding nor embracing the complexity of Black creativity.

It is our responsibility to create self-led, Black-owned, creative coalitions that put our needs first. That put our art first. That put our culture first. A place that allows Black creativity to flourish.

We are faced with complex future problems such as the decline of Black wealth and literacy, the decline of the average lifespan of Black people by three years due to COVID-19, and mass incarceration. Though we do not reject the notion of forming bridges with our allies and non-Black/BIPOC initiatives, we have to work to find harmony and justice for us.

NOTES

1. Du Bois, W. E. B. *The Crisis*, Vol. 32, October 1926: pp. 290–297.

Make
the Path by
Talking

MAURICE CHERRY

The Birth of Revision Path
The year is 2006.

At the time, I worked for a large telecommunications company as a senior web designer, and I was a full-time graduate student. Outside work, I had created a side project called the Black Weblog Awards, an annual awards event where I gave recognition to Black bloggers in several different categories.

One of the categories was "Best Blog Design," and I made that category as a way to recognize some of the fantastic visual design work being done on simple Movable Type or WordPress or Blogspot sites. I knew Black designers—friends of mine, in most instances—who were doing phenomenal work for big companies, celebrities, and professional musicians. However, they were not getting any sort of recognition for it from their peers or the design community as a whole. So while I created this category initially as a way for them to get some shine, I also wanted to do something much bigger. Design magazines and websites back then really did not feature work from Black designers, and I wanted to fill that void. Unfortunately, I had too many other responsibilities and couldn't dedicate myself to making it happen. It took seven years before the opportunity finally presented itself for me to create a platform to allow that very thing to happen—*Revision Path*.

The goal for *Revision Path* was to create an online magazine featuring weekly long-form, in-depth interviews with Black designers and other digital creatives. I wanted it to resemble some of the other online magazines of the time, but I ran into one major issue pretty quickly—finding enough Black designers to profile! I thought it would be easy at first, but also I found that sustaining a regular weekly format at the time wasn't going to work. When I set out to create *Revision Path* in this iteration, I wasn't thinking of community—I was thinking of media. And really, there was a lot of trial and error in those early days. I made it up as I went along, and I did not have any type of community support to accomplish what I wanted to do. I still managed to interview some Black designers, but the publishing frequency was not consistent, and I was not building an audience. There were many times when I wondered if I should just stop what I'm doing. But one day, I got an email from a Chicago designer who wanted to be interviewed for *Revision Path*, and that request ended up changing Revision Path's entire trajectory.

REVISION PATH 2.0: THE PODCAST

I see on your Twitter page that you are
in Atlanta. I just happen to be traveling
there next Thursday if you want to try
to schedule an interview while I'm in
town. My partner and I will be there for
about a week so I'm pretty flexible as
far as scheduling goes. Hopefully, we can
connect soon.

I had not even thought about interviewing in-person, but now I have someone who not only wants to be on *Revision Path*—my first inbound interview request!—but they were also going to be in town. Without hesitation, I said yes. However, I did not have any recording equipment! We met a few days later for lunch, and I used my mobile phone as the microphone and we recorded what became the first episode of *Revision Path*'s podcast. You can go and listen to it today! That meeting opened my eyes to how I could publish interviews faster—turn the online magazine into a podcast. And so, in March 2014, *Revision Path* relaunched as a podcast with a little over a dozen episodes.

Now I entered a whole new space—the design podcast community. At the time, there were probably around two dozen design-focused podcasts publishing regularly, including well-known shows like *Design Matters with Debbie Millman*, *99% Invisible*, and *Adventures in Design*. As the podcast went on, I would reach out to other design podcasts to introduce myself, let them know about the work that I was doing with *Revision Path*, and offered to introduce my guests to their audience so they could get additional press. (You can call that last one a bit of subversive diversity and inclusion work.) Most of my messages were ignored, and the few that did reply had very negative things to say. I was called a racist for only interviewing Black guests, and was often told by other design podcasters at the time that they didn't do "race stuff."

I also attracted the attention of AIGA, the professional association for design. I did not have a great experience with AIGA just based on my local chapter, and several people I interviewed for the podcast also spoke negatively about the organization. But after interviewing Antionette Carroll for the podcast back in 2014, I was asked to join AIGA's Diversity and Inclusion Task Force. I gladly accepted and looked forward to the opportunity to help make some change from within.

The combination of being a part of these two communities ended up putting a spotlight on *Revision Path*, and on me. It was difficult to find acceptance and fellowship in these spaces. I received some public social media backlash, although most of the harshest criticism came in private. Some people even wrote to my studio saying that I should be fired (which would be hard since I owned the studio). Eventually, this made finding guests difficult, because who wants to be a part of something that's stirring up controversy? I still managed to keep the podcast on track from week to week, even getting up to one hundred episodes, but every single episode was a fight because I felt like I wanted to quit. My design podcast peers weren't recognizing the work, and it just felt like I was doing this by myself without any support.

WHERE ARE THE BLACK DESIGNERS?

In March 2015, I had the opportunity to speak at SXSW, a multi-week event with interactive, film, and music tracks that contained panels, performances, movies, and other sorts of events. I put together a presentation along with AIGA to talk about Black designers, and to answer one of the most common questions I received since starting the platform—where are the Black designers? Because SXSW accepted my panel only three months before the event, I had to raise two thousand dollars for travel and accommodations, and I had no idea how this panel would even be received.

SPOILER ALERT: THE PRESENTATION WAS NOT WELL ATTENDED

My talk was in the farthest part of the convention center on the top floor, and it happened to be in the exhibit room right next to a talk from a popular late-night talk show host. My exhibit room ended up serving as a bit of a rest area, as some people attended just to charge their phones. Overall, there were about fifteen to twenty people in a room that could comfortably seat ten times that amount. Even with such a small turnout, I gave the presentation with the same zeal and fervor that I would if I had a packed house. And for the people who were there, I believe they were greatly impacted by the message I delivered. One of the people there happened to work for Facebook, and I was invited to the Facebook House at SXSW to talk to people there about the work that I was doing with *Revision Path* and my presentation. I was *extremely* surprised that Facebook wanted to support the platform financially. At this time, Facebook had not sponsored any podcasts before us, making us the first (if not one of the first).

What a difference a new sponsor makes! Their support somehow legitimized *Revision Path*'s work in the eyes of others. More companies flocked to *Revision Path* and also wanted to support the platform, including Hover, Creative Market, and Google. We opened a Patreon page and began to receive monthly support from listeners. Thanks to Fund Club, a community-operated project funding model, we received over eight thousand dollars in donations, which helped *Revision Path* continue to grow as a platform and a burgeoning community.

If my SXSW presentation didn't answer the question of "where are the Black designers," then this support from the design and tech communities showed that they were interested in encouraging my path to becoming the response.

IT'S NOT A SPRINT, IT'S A MARATHON

With this influx of cash, it was now time to really expand *Revision Path*. I launched a job board, I expanded *Revision Path*'s blog coverage with more writers, and I started to help support other Black design initiatives and events to get ourselves out there more into the design community. I knew *Revision Path* was making an impact, but I really felt that impact when I heard from students and educators about how they were using *Revision Path* and learning about Black designers through the interviews. These were people from all over the world too—Brazil, Australia, Nigeria, Canada, Japan . . . and of course, in the United States. At some point, *Revision Path* became more than just a weekly podcast—it was becoming curriculum right alongside other design material.

Also, it was becoming history. In 2018, I was awarded the Steven Heller Prize for Cultural Commentary by AIGA "for being a renaissance talent who works seamlessly across cultural domains, editorial lines, and multiple forms of media" and "for being the definitive leader in bringing Black designers to the public, earning [me] a permanent place in the history of design, design equity and social justice."

In 2019, *Revision Path* reached three hundred episodes and later that year became the first podcast to be inducted into the Smithsonian's National Museum of African American History and Culture. It still astounds me to think of how something as simple as talking to my peers and giving them a platform to talk about their work was now a part of history. Not just design history. Not just Black history. But capital H history.

THE PATH
CONTINUES
One of the biggest lessons that I've learned from *Revision Path* is the importance of tending to the audience that you have instead of trying to attract the audience that you want. I tried so hard in the early days of *Revision Path* to get the larger design community and other design podcasts to recognize the work that I was doing. But in doing that, I was neglecting my own audience— the day-ones who have followed me from the beginning and have been the most invested in *Revision Path*'s success. Over the years, I had to learn to run my own race and stay in my lane.

I also learned that merely celebrating yourself as a Black designer is an act of rebellion. The design industry, for what it's worth, talks a lot about diversity and inclusion and equity, but I know that these have been perennial conversations since well before my time. Instead of trying to force others to recognize the heart and depth and influences that exist within Black design, *Revision Path* allows Black designers to talk in their own words with no whitewashing, no oversight from sponsors, and no corporate controlling interests. It's just them and the microphone, and I am their intrepid field guide.

I have been very fortunate to build this platform and become a part of the design community, not to mention help connect Black designers, developers, and other digital creatives from all over the world. As we move forward, I am thankful for how technology and design allow us to build spaces like this to share conversations and to meet and reach others. Who knows what the future will bring?

Building BADG:

The Guild as a Model for Liberatory Space

MALENE BARNETT

Before starting the Black Artists + Designers Guild (BADG) in 2018, and for as long as I can remember, art has been part of my life. It helped define who I am and the impact I wanted to have on the world. But at the peak of my professional career, I hit a wall as twenty years of a successful career in carpet design had veritably taken me away from my passion. Working for and catering to clients became the vehicle through which my voice was lost, and I was removed from the core of the work that I loved so much. Pausing my design business, I realized that what I really wanted was to create a space for Black makers to thrive as a collective. From this desire, BADG was born.

Fig. 1

In fact, BADG was the culmination of a years-long journey toward discovering what it means for me to be a Black artist and exploring how my identity and heritage connects to my art and design. That inquiry led me on a journey to explore West African art, textiles, and architecture—a journey that has involved extensive reading, museum visits, and travels to West African cities, where I always made an effort to connect with Black artists and designers. During these meetings we shared experiences, ideas, and resources. I also discovered that many of my colleagues throughout the diaspora, particularly in the interiors and home furnishing industry, shared similar stories of battle fatigue, the constant anxiety we all felt from battling racism throughout our industries. After each one of these get-togethers, I would imagine a space for us to expand our imagination, collaborate, connect, and thrive as a collective all centered on Blackness.

Fig. 2   Fig. 3

The final impetus came after I saw the speaker list for a prominent industry event called "What's New, What's Next," which featured conversations with "leaders in the design industry." There was not a single Black artist or designer on a panel or moderating a talk. I said, "Enough is enough!" and decided to voice my opinion about the inequity on Instagram. The community chimed in with support and affirmation. So many of us shared the same sentiments, which could be encapsulated by the questions I had been asking myself for years:

1. Why are Black artists and designers not represented consistently in major magazines?
2. Why are we almost never awarded multimillion-dollar projects, recipients of industry awards, or invited to lead special events?
3. Why is Black culture so often appropriated but almost never at the forefront of design conversations?

BADG became a space where Black artists and design-
ers could thrive, connect, and collaborate with the creative freedom not
generally afforded to those of us who work at the behest of client demands
or with the need for validation from industry gatekeepers. Importantly,
while the organization is putatively member-driven, it is constructed in the
guild model, which means that members are partners, peers, and co-collab-
orators in the best sense. My goal was never to create a top-down structure
in which members pay dues and then receive services; but rather one in
which all members have the invitation, the right, and even the mandate to
participate with one another in the stewardship and thriving of our collective community. This is how we have defined it:

Fig. 4

Fig. 5

Fig. 6

"We aim to advance a community of Black makers, build equitable and inclusive spaces and invest in our ancestral futures."

With that promise, we launched BADG in 2018 with thirty members and grew to a hundred members in less than two years. BADG's impact has become the driving force for institutions, corporations, and individuals to address the inequities that have been long ignored. Our programs are centered on empowering our members to believe that they have the right to exercise creative freedom in their art/design practices, and encourage investment in our ancestral future. Through our initiatives we are pushing Black imagination and the industry toward equitable and inclusive spaces.

Our inaugural, collaborative initiative was a project titled Obsidian, a virtual concept house collaboratively designed by twenty-three guild members, whose mission was to empower a million Black families by sharing our collective vision for an innovative, Black-centered home of the near future. The guild model—the BADG mission—set the stage for a partnership in which we found our voices, as individual creators and as a collective. Sharing that vision with our community allowed us to feel a connection with many of our Black families who are so often left out of the conversation around what a healthy, thriving, joyful home looks and feels like. Our designers and artists reflected the African diaspora from the continent to the islands to our own backyards. They drew from the symbolism of our ancestors, including Sankofa (reaching back to the past in order for us to thrive forward); and nguzo saba's principle ujima (collective work & responsibility) as our driving force for our support and growth.

The design profession has not served Black people or our culture, but with BADG I hope to build visibility, financial equity, and spatial equity by nurturing a community of Black artists and designers who define their own creative pathways. As the guild grows, my goal is to keep us wholly centered on creating mental and physical space, alongside products and practices centered on Blackness. The challenges in our industry are great. We continue to see how the field validates whiteness in part by focusing on creating fashionable spaces and products for the select few. Barriers to entry and success have continued to dissuade Black designers from centering their values, aesthetic preferences, and lived experiences; opting instead for practices centered on European aesthetics that consciously erase Black culture. My aim for BADG is to disrupt the status quo by honoring our rootedness in ancestral practices, celebrating the many forms of Black experience from across the Black diaspora, and honoring the practices and symbolism of our diasporic experiences. We thrive as a collective, as a guild. We can make room for the many over the "one" and the past over the "first." Each of us in the guild who creates success, does so for the many and reinforces the power of the collective. These are the kinds of equitable spaces we must invest in for our future.

Fig. 7

MALENE BARNETT

IMAGE CREDITS

1. BADG members and friends attend "American Craftsmanship: The Forgotten Legacy," an event at Room & Board in Manhattan. (From left: Two friends of BADG; BADG advisor Patti Carpenter; BADG Members Cristina Casanas-Judd, General Judd, Beth Diana Smith, Everick Brown, Nina Barnieh Blair, Nina Cooke John, and Malene Barnett. Photo credit: BADG.
2. The Black Artists + Designers Guild and members are featured on Bloomingdales storefront as part of Shop for Good campaign event in 2021. Photo credit: BADG.
3. BADG mission graces an exterior wall at 4019 Sunset Blvd, Los Angeles, CA in 2020. Art by BADG member Karen Revis. Photo Courtesy of Colossal Media.
4. Black Artists + Designers Guild founder Malene Barnett responds to the lack of representation at a major industry event in 2018.
5. Founding BADG in 2018 served as a rebuke to an industry that neglected the contributions of Black professionals.
6. BADG event "Crafting A Legacy" at Neuehouse, New York City
7. BADG Members Lisa Hunt, Jomo Tariku, Leyden Lewis, Richard Beavers(not a BADG Member) Malene Barnett at Texas Contemporary Art Fair in Houston Texas. Photographer: Roswitha Vogler

Designer Profile:

Ari Melenciano

LESLEY-ANN NOEL
& ANNE H. BERRY

In conversations with Lesley-Ann Noel and Anne H. Berry, artist, designer, creative technologist, researcher, and educator Ari Melenciano discussed the ways in which her work explores relationships between design, human experiences, and technology, and serves as a creative and exploratory outlet.

Born in Miami, Florida, to parents who emigrated from the Dominican Republic, Ari Melenciano's multilayered and multiethnic background has played a significant role in her identity formation. "Being Dominican, being black, being Latina, and navigating these identities, while not knowing the language, is an interesting way to come into a culture" she says, adding, "I think language is so important because it can create cultural distance when we don't have access to it or we don't carry the language with us."

Melenciano also spent part of her childhood in New York City where her early interest in art was nurtured by her mother. "My mom would tell me about the things that I would do as a kid, including giving my art to strangers on the street. So, I grew up as an artist, I've always created." But, she says, "The work is about more than just making, it's about sharing. And I like creating spaces that help people feel good. I don't know if that was what I was attempting to do as a kid—perhaps I was simply copying what I saw others doing. Regardless, the essence of that kind of generosity is still present in my work."

Her family later moved to Prince George's (PG) county, a predominantly Black area in Maryland. Though she initially missed the grittiness and energy of New York City, she came to appreciate the atmosphere and environment PG provided: "It's a space where black people represent every socioeconomic spectrum, including the wealthiest Black people in the country." Additionally, Melenciano says, "We grew up without a scarcity mindset and the sense that blackness was very normal. There was abundance, so we felt that we had everything that everyone else had." But Ari realized after being in graduate school that explorations around critical race theory and the politics of race weren't introduced in the curriculum of her upbringing. Noting the paradox, she states, "It is interesting to grow up in a space that is so predominantly Black while, culturally, we did not have to consciously think about *how* to be Black."

In addition to an early interest in art, Melenciano also had a strong fascination with technology. "I saw technology as a tool that could really expand the possibilities of art for me. I didn't necessarily know what kind of world existed between art and technology, I just knew that people like Steve Jobs, who I heavily admired, were creating beautiful tools that people were using every single day." Her interests would eventually lead her to study abroad in Barcelona, an experience she describes as "life-changing." There, she attended a festival where she saw an outdoor installation created by Moment Factory. Recalling the way in which images projected onto architecture transformed the space and gave people inside the space a new experience with technology, Melenciano says, "I knew that I was finally seeing an example of the world that I had been searching for at the nexus of technology, art, and design. I went to grad school to study creative technology and have been mind-blown ever [since] by all the things that you can do in this field."

AFROTECTOPIA One of the key projects Melenciano has developed and put her efforts behind is Afrotectopia, a social institution focused on "building at the intersections of art, design, technology, Black culture, and activism" that she created while in graduate school at New York University: "I was really excited about the possibilities of creative tech, saw immense potential when looking at technology both critically and imaginatively with a racial lens, and wanted to make sure Black people could always see themselves in this field." Afrotectopia began as a festival, a dedicated space for people to convene. "I thought of it as an intellectual festival where people are celebrating. They are having fun but also learning. It's also very rooted in learning and sharing information. And then I continued/ extended the theme of community by creating space where people can also convene online. So, there's a physical space and an online space enabling/ facilitating constant dialogue," she says. After the first festival, seeing the amount of energy and excitement toward Afrotectopia, Melenciano realized that the concept needed to be cultivated and continued in different forms: "I could see the potential for creating more opportunities for people."

"Within this space, you see how easy it can be to work with technology—by grabbing a few of the tools and expanding on an idea, you can express yourself in really exciting ways." Additionally, she says, "Afrotectopia is about providing more access to the black community." Melenciano also reflects on personal challenges she faced at the time, including frustrations about being one of the very few Black students in the master's program, not having any mentors or professors or connections to Black people doing similar work, and "no one to look to who looked like me in the creative tech world." She was inspired to make things different for others, including younger designers coming up behind her: "For me it's always about 'how can I service my younger self?' and 'how can I make sure that other students are able to find people who look like them and whose work they admire in the creative tech world?'"

Afrotectopia, a pluralistic and interdisciplinary endeavor, has provided a path for these opportunities. Bringing people together from a variety of worlds, whether inside or outside tech, participants are able to reflect on the kind of world they want to live in as well as celebrate and share with others who look like them. Melenciano says, "Traditionally, the people being acknowledged are white. Or, the spaces that bring tech and art together are all white. So, not only is Afrotectopia a more diverse space, but it also fosters community-building, shared interests, and providing support while also thinking about the future."

A TECH CURRICULUM FOR YOUNG PEOPLE

After the first festival, Melenciano and her collaborators extended Afrotectopia into a think tank and then subsequently, a free summer camp for New York City public middle and high school students: "It was such an exciting and fun time. Every day started off with learning about different pioneers within the African diaspora, Black or African American. We would study them and then introduce technologies that would allow us to recreate their work in ways that are applicable in contemporary culture and society. For example, we created data visualizations after researching artists from the Black Arts Movement and developed stop-motion animations inspired by W. E. B. Du Bois and the ACLU's Know Your Rights campaign. The aim was to ground everyday, lived experiences in technology, and then to output something to express themselves with that technology." Among other iterations, Afrotectopia has also evolved into an alternative school for adults that presents technology through an artistic, Black, and activist lens.

Though corporate sponsorships have made it possible to offer these events for free to hundreds of participants, Melenciano concedes that the model is not sustainable over the long haul. She values the support, particularly from Google and Google's Creative Lab, where she works, but she is not driven by a business mindset. Rather, she is led by passion and creating opportunities that are "as accessible as possible."

Reflecting on Afroctectopia's development over time, Melenciano notes that watching it grow "has been a reflection of my own political and racial consciousness." During the first festival, in 2019, she was angry about the ways in which Black people were being treated. She was tired of the challenges posed by technology companies and university programs and their weak diversity track records. However, her perspective shifted during the second festival, which decentered issues around combatting whiteness and focused more squarely on Black agency: "I decided to not worry about what other people were doing. I wanted to prioritize the importance of being in an environment where Black people are looking at and celebrating one another." She adds that centering experiences via a Black lens is an aspect that she wants to maintain throughout all of the Afrotectopia programming. She also references her time in Maryland, stating "We have to operate from a place of abundance and not scarcity and blame."

Paulo Freire's pedagogical practice also inspired the format for the second festival: "For me, it was all about how to maximize the voices that were being heard. Education is not about thinking of people as containers for the knowledge that we deposit into their heads. It's about creating an opportunity for people to learn as much as they can in order to be able to express themselves." In addition to embracing the concept of students as beings with great and immense potential, Melenciano refers again to the importance of language—whether that language is geography-based or technology-based—in overcoming challenges: "Language is so important when you're engaging in radical thought and you're challenging status quos. Some of the biggest barriers are about being able to understand and articulate your experience in ways that you can communicate to others."

In 2021, Afrotectopia hosted Fractal Fete, its most ambitious undertaking to date. "We had twenty different speakers, every weekday of January, giving presentations on their work. It was such a vibrant virtual space! I had no idea how complicated the process would be, but we were able to create the opportunity to learn from a lot of really brilliant people and build a sense of community online."

FUTURE AND ON REMAINING SMALL

Afrotectopia holds a lot of potential. It is a concept that can be built out on a massive scale. However, Melenciano says that she's been frugal in her approach to this particular project. Ari has been intentional in moving slowly and carefully as she's built Afrotectopia. She also sees advantages to a steadier, less-ambitious pace: "The type of space that we're trying to cultivate is sensitive and somewhat fragile because we're processing and dealing with so much. It's for Black people, yes, but it's also open to people from a variety of different racial/ethnic backgrounds. The festivals have also been open to anyone that wants to come, while still rooted in Blackness, the practice of Blackness, and the experience of Blackness. So, there is a wide spectrum of experiences and emotions to balance."

Scaling up Afrotectopia, consequently, means changing the experience: "I'm the type of person who enjoys small intimate settings. And the energy inside the space we create has been really important." Reflecting on past programming, Melenciano has come to appreciate that more spaces that provide the same level of intimacy and support are needed. "People are bringing so much of what they need into these spaces," she says. "So, as I navigate these structures that I've created, it's also important for me to be clear about my own goals and maintain my vision. I have to balance listening and staying true to the larger values we espouse through Afrotectopia."

Melenciano says that she's also thinking a lot about how to retain smallness while simultaneously making a large impact—that is, sharing all the things that are being learned, while also keeping spaces small and special: "I study indigenous design and indigenous people and their engagement with the land as well as their development of different technologies. And I'm seeing the advantages of being more village-minded and creating things for a few people, while everyone benefits from the things created by and for those few people." She adds, "You don't have to scale or promote. There's value in creating this sacred space for people in that particular group or community at that particular time."

She acknowledges the somewhat paradoxical role she plays as a technologist working in large-scale spaces and at large institutions that are focused on building and maintaining a global presence: "There's a lot of importance and excitement in global approaches, which I definitely appreciate. But on a personal level, I'm also just trying to figure out how to design futures that are healthier and more sustainable." From her vantage point, working on a small scale makes this goal accessible and achievable.

Categorizing or labeling Melenciano's work is difficult, if not unnecessary, given the breadth of her interests—she notes, for example, that sound is "probably one of my favorite senses to tap into because it's so abstract." However, she succinctly captures the essence of what she wants to put out into the world, stating, "A lot of my work is very much about experience. And it's about creating tools that allow other people to realize their own artistry."

This Is Our Time!

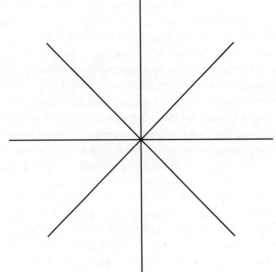

adrienne maree brown
ON DESIGN, LIBERATION, AND
TRANSFORMATION AS TOLD
TO LESLEY-ANN NOEL

This essay was created from a conversation with adrienne maree brown about her words of advice for designers in their new roles as facilitators, activists, and organizers, and creators of radical and liberatory spaces. It has been edited for length and clarity.

—Lesley-Ann Noel

I didn't realize it when I was first writing. I didn't realize how much design language is part of facilitation and creating space with other people. But it really is. Sometimes you are having a whole conversation with other people without realizing this. One of my comrades at the Emergent Strategy Ideation Institute calls herself "the architect" because she says we're designing spaces. We are building them up from the ground and from the heart.

The initial advice I would have for Black designers is to listen for the design that is the original design within you. The design that predates the trauma. The design that predates the socialization. The design that predates the shaping of Blackness as something lacking or something absent, or something less than or something plagued by suffering and struggling and pain. If you can lean into the concept of design as the sacred work of creating the world in which we share space, share lives, share the miracle—to me, that's the impetus of Black design. The focus of Black design should be to help us create the spaces where we can return to ourselves, the selves that predate whiteness, the selves that predate white supremacy, the selves that predate patriarchy, and capitalism, and all these things that have really distorted our concept of what it means to be a Black human being.

I'd also recommend that Black designers read a lot of science fiction! I think a lot of science fiction writers are designers of the future. We're really trying to think about the future. What does it look like, feel like, smell like? What does it mean to be in spaces that are green, and spaces that are equitable, and spaces that are collective and collaborative, and spaces that work for all bodies and spaces that don't require you to categorize yourself in order to enter? You know, science fiction is one of the places where all of that is getting explored. So Black designers, read science fiction! And listen underneath the trends and listen underneath the socialization for what is your unique design to bring into this world.

If as designers we read each of your books, what is the message that you'd want us to get from each one?

Each book has a special message for designers. In *Octavia's Brood*, it really is to find the lineage of those whose imaginations touch yours. For me, it's Octavia Butler. But for you, it might be other people. Don't assume that you're starting from scratch, even if you feel like a novel thinker or a novel ideator. Really identify a lineage for your own work. Then imagine inside of that.

For *Emergent Strategy*, the message is to get in the right relationship with change. I'm really interested in designs that accommodate the fact that we are constantly changing. How do we make spaces and places that actually can adapt and change with us as we grow and change?

For *Pleasure Activism*, it is reclaiming our universal right to have pleasure in our lives. And to understand that is a measure of our freedom. I'm constantly thinking about how I design spaces, movement spaces that people enjoy being a part of. So it's not all sex and drugs, although that's there too. We really have to think about pleasure. Read Audre Lorde!

In *We Will Not Cancel Us*, the message is about thinking about abolition, and what it means to create spaces that can hold our worst selves and our best selves, and space for us to grow.

Finally, in *Holding Change*, the message is that change is something that we have to intentionally hold space for. We have to hold each other in processes of change. Otherwise, it's very easy to change in ways that just put us into familiar loops, familiar behaviors, familiar shapes that serve capitalism, and that serve the elite. We all end up in jobs that we hate, and we wait for a couple of years of retirement. It's not an accident that that's what happens to most people. So really the message there is about holding changes, and asking, "How do we come together and make it easy for us to do the hard work of changing everything together?"

On the changing roles of designers from producers of artifacts to facilitators, organizers, and activists, and about feeling less uncomfortable in new roles for design.

540

I wrote *Holding Change* because I believe that everyone is not necessarily called to facilitation or mediation, but I think that everyone should have the basic skill sets. I think that our humanity would be much more intact if everyone understood what it meant to come up with an agenda together, and if everyone said something like, "Let's identify what it is we're here to do." "Let's begin by listening to the people who are here, what do we want?" Let's listen to this land. What kind of things need to be built here? What do the trees know? What do the materials know? Everything has a purpose. So, how do we create space where all of that purpose can be in a dance with each other?

Enjoying this changing role helps a lot. Relinquishing control also helps create more comfort in these new roles. One of the principles for *Holding Change* is to relinquish *your* way to find *the* way. I think that this is one of the most important pieces as a facilitator, the ability to establish: "Here's what I want to happen. Here's what I'm trying to convince, and sell and pitch everyone to do." And also to think, "How do I set that aside and see maybe there's something that can *only* come from the collective and many voices, shaping it together, that's more valuable than my singular idea?"

The collective may not be the way for everything. There might be some projects that you tell yourself, "I just want to do this one by myself!" So go do it by yourself! Don't torture everyone by pretending to collaborate. But for those things that are collaborative, for those places where many voices fit, lean into the collective. Nowadays, I think design is so much about listening to who's already there. Who are the survivors and the long-timers? I have been living in Detroit for these past twelve years. And in this space it's been important to really watch who listens and who doesn't listen. In terms of shaping the city, who sees the city as a blank canvas? And who sees it as an existing, beautiful, complex mural that's layered and has a lot to offer about what it means to live there. The best facilitators are able to be part of the container. It's not about you. It's not about your ego. It is not about performance. It's not about any of those things. It's really about relinquishing those things to be a part of the container that allows people to be their truest, most honest, most authentic selves, and to dream together.

On maintaining after making liberatory and radical spaces.

The maintenance of radical spaces, after you have made these spaces, is its own kind of work. It is being able to develop structures and systems and rhythms that everyone enjoys and understands and returns to. One of the things I think helps a lot is decentralization.

Decentralization of the vision and the practices is one of the best ways you can maintain things. Because then if the "leader" isn't there one day, everyone else already knows, "Oh, well, they didn't show up, but we know that we're here to fight for justice. And this is the thing that we're up to. And this is the agenda that we always have for these meetings. And so we're just going to continue on."

I really love co-facilitation, as a way of maintenance or shared facilitation, taking turns. It helps when different people actually are holding the space. They bring a different energy to it. The meeting is not the same meeting every single time. When other people lead, each person brings slight variations and delights from their personality. Maintenance works best when you're not tied to a particular outcome. If you try to maintain something, but it's no longer energized and no longer vibrant, it's okay to let it go. We call it "sunsetting" in movement work. It's like sunset, that organization. Just let it come to a close. Focus on maintaining the things that are vibrant and alive and that are still ready to offer things. But be also willing to let go.

It's like a breakup. Don't overstay the relationship. Don't overstay the organization. I find a lot of times people are struggling to maintain things that should be let go of, or to maintain things that are past their life cycle, you know. So you are left with these zombie projects that you're struggling to maintain. Zombies don't eat food. They don't drink water. There's no life flowing through it. So let go of what is needed to let go of. Then take turns and decentralize what's left to hold on to.

The last thing that I would add for Black designers is to really think outrageously in terms of the scale of their visions. I want to see Black designers looking at entire cityscapes, looking at entire community garden efforts, looking at entire intentional community efforts. I want them to really think on a large scale. I want them to ask themselves: "What would things look like? What would the aesthetic be if, if the nation focused on Black design? Or the foundation of a city was built on and by Black design?" I want Black designers to not just think about a building, or an object; not just to think about an interior. Practice, practice, practice! Have a really massive vision! Because I do think that this is our time.

GUIDING QUESTIONS

The guiding questions are intended to support teachers who would like to introduce the readings in class or anyone facilitating a group discussion. While they are starting points—approximately one prompt per essay—we hope you will build on them with new discussion prompts based on your own pedagogies and curricular needs.

CHAPTER 1: DESIGN PRACTICES

In 1970, **Dorothy Hayes** curated an exhibition and wrote an article for Communication Arts in which she highlighted the work of fifty Black artists and designers. Why might that have seemed necessary and/or radical at the time. What conditions of that time prompted her to create that work? To what extent did the dialogue she hoped to initiate in 1970 reshape the industry? Reflecting on the artists and designers she highlighted, are there common aesthetic or thematic patterns? What do you think Hayes hoped to say about Black art and design, Black artists and designers, or the design industries?

In A Conversation Between Dantley Davis, Darhil Crooks, and Ian Spalter on Practicing Design, **Ian Spalter** comments on how important it is to find door-openers in industry, saying "who's going to give you the opportunity to get your foot in the door? It's during this early phase that you are just trying to practice your craft, let alone master it." In design, if the trajectory of craft-building is unique to each individual, what mechanisms are in place to ensure that young designers are given opportunities to grow into their craft rather than requiring them to show up ready? In what ways do design spaces provide access for learning and growth, for young designers to practice craft with a sense of openness to each designer's learning process?

Vann Graves utilizes the metaphor of the Wall as a form of fortification throughout his career. What facets of his experience make up the bricks in his wall? Why has it been necessary for him to construct such a structure? Have you constructed a "wall" for your own fortification? What are the elements of your wall and how do they provide you with strength or comfort?

Graphic designer, illustrator, writer, and educator **Jon Key** references the four pillars of his identity—Blackness, Queerness, Southernness, and Family—each a salient facet of his work but inter-sectionalities that are often invisible to outsiders. To what extent have designers who invest in the most common tropes of marginalized iden-tities—the most visible forms of representation—actually served to further marginalize those who carry those identities? Where do you see this playing out on the visual landscape of graphic design and branding? How might being the only-of-a-kind designer on a team reinforce some of these same harms, as Black, PoC, Queer, and disabled designers are asked to oversimplify their own intersectional identities on behalf of commercial or universal principles?

Quinlin Messenger writes about stewardship as the core of design justice. How does he define stewardship in the context of architectural practice? How does it differ from leadership? How might the stewardship lens inform a critique of design in your industry? If you were to frame your practice in the context of stewardship, how might it redefine or reshape your interactions with clients, stakeholders, and communities?

In **Annika Hansteen-Izora**'s interview, they maintain that being in community is fundamental to designing authentically. Like Jon Key and June A. Grant, Hansteen-Izora sustains the argument that one's positionality informs one's perspective on the communities they are designing for, with, and within. In their view, good design is particular, not universal particularly when it aims to achieve joy or intimacy over conve-nience or consumption. How might her position on design support a view on scaling down/in over scaling up/out?

Throughout the chapter on Design Practices, the contributors offer perspectives on the successes and failures of industry. What do you see as some of the fundamental successes, and how might they be optimized to better serve Black and other PoC designers, clients, and communities? What do you see as some of the fundamental challenges or failures of industry, and what correctives are proposed here that you would like to take up in your own practice?

CHAPTER 2: DESIGN EDUCATION

Maurice Woods shares his approach to design education as an active practice: *doing* as a form of and a path to *learning*. He argues for embedded meta-lessons in activities so that, in a sense, students discover the *who*, *when*, and *why* while practicing the *what* and *how*. What do you see as the advantages or disadvantages of this approach? How might this approach appeal to young people who are unfamiliar with graphic design as a possible career path? Reflecting on the path of someone like Emory Douglas, who learned graphic design while working in a print shop, how might the industry create more opportunities for young people to learn the skills through active engagement?

Writing about "Visual Whiplash," **Colette Gaiter** compares the images of African Americans in the *Black Panther* magazine with those in *Ebony* and *Jet* magazines. What distinctions does she observe about those depictions and how they reflected attitudes about cultural Blackness in the 1960s and 70s?

Gaiter states that "visual media is ground zero for influencing how people see the world." In her essay on teaching at an HBCU, Kaleena Sales similarly references the "mere-exposure effect" (a theory developed by Robert Zajonc). Discuss what mental models for normalcy you, your students, and peers have developed based on the visual media you have experienced in your lifetime. Which of these are based on "mere" versus repeated or sustained exposure? How might a more inclusive approach to design education (as outlined by Gaiter, Sales, and Moses, in particular) shift that experience for your or future generations?

Steve Jones presents four possible scenarios Black graphic design students might experience when asked to create a self-portrait. What challenges does he identify in each scenario? In his essay, Jon Key writes about a similar experience of being critiqued for how his Queerness shows up in his work. How might the scenarios Jones names comport with the experiences of students from a range of marginalized identities? Where Colette Gaiter writes about the experience of seeing Black images across the media landscape, Jones reflects on how design educators facilitate student's ability to construct their own image. How might a design pedagogy provide spaces for students to critique and create a more representative range of visual representations and identities?

Terresa Moses shares the *Racism Untaught* framework she developed with her colleague Lisa Mercer; explaining how she has been employing the framework to unpack institutionalized racism against Black women. How might this framework apply to a curriculum in graphic design education (and the design of visual communications), industrial design education (and the design of commercial or social products), architecture (and the design of spaces and places), and digital design education (and the design of virtual or connected experiences)?

As a tool without a prescribed end, the pedagogy Moses and her colleague developed might serve as a useful foil for the Human Centered Design method. Reviewing the two frameworks, how might you evaluate the process, goals, and impacts of each? Consider your own positionality and/or the positionality of design teams who practice equity-centered or community-centered design in determining whether these methods might serve in your own practice?

Chris Rudd shares his vision for a pedagogy built around the politics of design. A core tenet of this work is the belief that design is never neutral. How does he employ his course readings and assignments to interrogate the political nature of design? How might you take ostensibly neutral artifacts of design—a spoon, a book, a bus, a housing complex, a chair—and unpack the ways in which the object itself and the ecosystem in which it interacts situates itself as political discourse?

Kaleena Sales unpacks the experience of being taught about "good" (Eurocentric) v. "bad" (Black-centric) design as a student. What are some of the examples of how a Eurocentric approach to design erases the lived experiences of Black colleagues who were raised in Black communities and shopped in Black stores? What are Black designers taught to "dislike" and "unlove" about our own personal experiences with design? Thinking about the design experiences of your own youth, how does main-stream design either erase or celebrate the experiences that you valued or cherished in your youth? How might a design education curriculum make room for students to honor their range of personal experiences without the implicit judgments of "good" versus "bad" design ideology?

Sales's essay captures her experience teaching at a Historically Black College or University (HBCU). Reviewing design curricula at HBCUs, predominantly white institutions, and international design schools, what do you see as the salient distinctions around how they handle issues of cultural positioning, the design canon, and the historically Eurocentric framings of design scholarship and practice?

Some of the book's editors and contributors have shared course syllabi. As these are all living documents, they represent a moment in time for each course, and have evolved or will evolve as faculty continue their teaching practices. How might a resource that contains course syllabi across design teaching institutions help to inform how and what is being taught, as well as how design educators might evolve their practices in solidarity with one another?

CHAPTER 3: DESIGN SCHOLARSHIP

Dr. Audrey G. Bennett argues for "the use of African fractals as a resource for the visual semantics of the communication designer's canvas." What are some of the visual references she names? How do these represent a shift in the reference points commonly used in the design education canon and design practices?

Bennett also poses this question, "How might communication designers graphically translate mathematical principles like the golden ratio and grids derived from its formula into a visual aesthetic that communicates cross-culturally?" What architectural references does she name to support her thesis about the golden ratio? How might you apply the mathematical principles she proposed to the critique or practices of graphic design, interior design, or architecture?

Nii Kommey Botchway reflects on the spiritual emptiness of Western design practices, saying, "the design we are in (as so-called 'Blacks' and in fact as humanity) is dead." How does he assess the rational v. the spiritual lens on design, particularly in the context of an Afrikan practice?

Botchway begins his essay by reflecting on his identity and the use of the framing of "Blackness." How does he self-identify? Why is the framing he uses important to his design practice? What are the key identities that you bring into your practices? How do you share these identities with colleagues, teachers/students, and clients/stakeholders? How might a practice of positionality inform your design practice?

Cheryl D. Miller muses on the critical role footnotes play in facilitating research. Using "footnote" both literally and figuratively—as Black figures and stories were often relegated to the footnotes of historical narratives—she writes about discovering Anthony, an enslaved biracial man who may have been one of the first Black graphic designers in the United States. How and where might a design scholar discover more of Anthony's history? How might the scholar Saidiya Hartman's work on critical fabulation help scholars construct a working narrative of Anthony so that we can better understand the contexts and conditions of his experience?

In her research on Free Negro Bonds, **Alicia Olushola Ajayi** shares a story about Frederick Douglass's passage out of bondage by way of his falsified papers, writing, "Douglass's narrative on the train draws a compelling illustration of how artifacts can hold immense power to sustain the abstract ideal of the institution. Once artifacts are produced by an institution, like that of a legal system, they can hold immense power to sustain the abstract ideal of the institution. The authority represented as material is so strong that the train conductor trusts the mere presence of the artifact." How does Ajayi suggest that power is instantiated in the design and materiality of the artifact? How are institutional authority and power concretized by contemporary artifacts, creating a reality that only exists because of the objects themselves? How does this translate to contemporary design, and a contemporary analysis of the artifacts designed to confer authority?

David Pilgrim relates a story from a college class in which his professor asked students to reflect on a chauffeur's cap from the Jim Crow period. How did the professor complicate the narrative of the object? In what ways did that experience inform Pilgrim's approach to collecting and interpreting artifacts? How might this perspective inform your own critical lens on design and the interpretation of objects? What primary sources might you consult in order to learn more about the history of an object? How might you work with students, peers, or colleagues to complicate the interpretation of an object that you find problematic or offensive, specifically using primary sources that provide new information or perspectives?

The essays on design scholarship offer perspectives on critical inquiry in design. What are the tools of research, inquiry, and interpretation that these scholars employed in their scholarship? What topics or questions in design scholarship interest you? What primary sources might you consult to build your critical inquiry? How might our design institutions better support scholarship and/or critical inquiries in design by Black students and scholars? What intersectional disciplines might be necessary to construct a more robust ecosystem for scholarship in the history of Black design?

CHAPTER 4: ACTIVISM, ADVOCACY, AND COMMUNITY-ENGAGED DESIGN

Mugendi K. M'Rithaa investigates the applicability of well-known community-engaged practices such as human-centered design and design thinking to the emancipatory, sustainable design agenda for the Afrikan context. What are some of the traditionally Afrikan practices that have been adapted in various Afrikan communities as a direct response to what Mugendi describes as the "greatest disruption to Afrika's progress— Imperialistic agendas emanating from Europe?"

Writing about her son Knox, **Jennifer White-Johnson** writes, "Using motherhood as an act of resistance, using it as a vehicle for my creativity allows me to stay focused on the truly important things; I don't have to plummet, I can soar," a perspective she carries into her design practice. How does resistance show up in her approach to visual ableism? How is the design community engaging—or, alternatively, not engaging— in work that is "rooted in shifting culture, co-conspiring with our disabled comrades, helping to build anti-ableist spaces, eliminating the cultural constructs of oppression that pathologize certain bodies and minds for being different?"

Michele Y. Washington reflects on the need for a biophilic approach to design, introducing this term in the context of a dignity-centered lens. How does she define biophilia, and how does the term offer a critique of historical urban design? What might a biophilic approach to an urban design project in your community look like? How might the design process differ from traditional urban planning and design? How might designers and community members collaborate with one another equitably, and how might those collaborations or roles challenge common practices? How might the biophilic approach reveal the need for redesign in your community, and how might it form the foundation for design activism?

In her essay on centering the margin, **June A. Grant** poses the question, "Can we return to the idea of designing as both qualitative and quantitative interactions that define communities?" She proposes that centering those who have historically been relegated to the margins allows us to design healthier, more thriving communities. How do her reflections on life during COVID inform her analysis? How might her framing contribute to a shift in the practices of architects and city planners? What specific steps do you think designers can (or should) take to divest from systems that perpetuate community harm and invest in multi-community design?

Both June A. Grant and Jon Key reference "minoritarianism," a view that asks what design looks like when we center those who have historically been relegated to the margins. When Grant approaches this work from an architecture and planning perspective, Key operationalizes it in graphic design. How might their perspectives serve as an argument against "Universal Design" principles? How might you construct a critical debate between Universalists and Minoritarianists in design?

In their paper on building infrastructures within organizations that center care and healing, **Sloan Leo** asserts that attaining sustainable organizational healing requires "finding justice in organizational decision-making and power sharing." How do they propose one goes about doing this? What kinds of critical shifts do organizations need to reckon with in order to attain sustainable healing and care?

In her essay reflecting on the "Preconditions to Healing," **Liz Ogbu** writes, "grieving, like cultural change, doesn't just happen. It relies on a collection of healers whose work is to tend to the wounds." What call to action does she offer artists, architects, and designers working toward healing the physical and emotional wounds caused by Spatial Injustice to do as they work toward driving cultural change? How can creative communities embrace preconditions to healing?

Raja Schaar argues that stewarding one's personal and public health, as well as the environment, might require a recalibration of our collective sense of "modernity" and a rejection of consumerist demands for the new and innovative. She writes, "repair and keeping up with old things would be better economically and environmentally." How might Schaar's argument offer a challenge for traditional product designers and contemporary cultural paradigms? How might investments in community-engaged design (as opposed to consumer-centered design) facilitate the work of environmentalism? Schaar further offers a view on the roots of environmentalism as being inherently centered in Black, Indigenous, and immigrant communities. The current environmental movement, however, presents a tension between the white and Black climate and environmental justice activists. How are environmentalist narratives rooted in Black and Indigenous practices and values reshaping the movement in the United States and worldwide? How might your own design practice embrace historically environmentalist practices or values that might have been de-centered as a result of the design industry's emphasis on innovation? How might innovation and historical practices align in your own practice?

Several essays throughout this book reference community-engaged practices, including writings by Annika Hansteen-Izora, Sabine Maxine Lopez, Ari Melenciano, and Quinlin Messenger. Based on their examples, how might you define the range of principles, frameworks, and tools that might encompass a community-centered practice? What are some of the similarities and differences among the various models? What skills does each designer bring to their practice? Where might you see new opportunities of community-engaged design where it has not yet developed a foothold? How might designers interested in this practice avert the potential for exploitation and hold themselves accountable for their impacts on communities?

CHAPTER 5: AFROFUTURISM IN DESIGN

In his essay, "From Algorithms to Afro-Rithms in Afrofuturism: Healing the Cruelty of the New Jim Code by leveraging Ancestral Intelligence," **Dr. Lonny Avi Brooks** shares a game he has created called *Afro-Rithms from the Future*, a game "centering BIPOC imagination, generates artifacts from the future—amplifying community futures to reveal solution spaces for BIPOC issues." Through the game, he positions BIPOC storytelling and futuristic thinking as a mechanism of combating oppressive traditional white patriarchal storytelling. How might positioning and centering BIPOC and Queer perspectives benefit society as a whole? In what ways is the practice of imagining new futures, particularly through gaming, beneficial for creative processes and development?

Woodrow W. Winchester III responds to the mounting disparities and anti-Black racism that exists in technology innovations by sharing Black-Centered Design, a framework centering the experiences of Black people from social, cultural, and political viewpoints. Though this framework is intended to be proactive in offering "a pathway forward," particularly when utilized through an Afrofuturism lens, how might we also use this framework to evaluate current systems of design and technology? Relatedly, how can evaluating current systems inform future thinking about building technologically inclusive futures?

Asking "What Type of Ancestor Do you Want to Be," **Adah Parris** shares a list of guiding principles she codeveloped with Marques Anderson to investigate the "anatomy of transformation" necessary for a design process rooted in a People of Culture (PoC) perspective. What are some specific, actionable ways to implement these principles into new or existing design processes? Like Dr. Brooks, Adah also references the concept of looking back in order to move forward. Identify ways in which past experiences have helped inform your decision-making in the present. How might you apply a PoC perspective framing in the future? Alternatively, consider how looking to your past—whether as an individual or as part of the collective "Other"—helps ground your positionality within design.

In "Black Secret Technologies," **John Jennings** writes about the ideas that inspired the development of his Critical Race Design Studies practice, which he defines as "an interdisciplinary design practice that intersects critical race theory, speculative design, design history, and critical making to analyze and critique the effects of visual communication, graphic objects, and their associated systemic mediations of racial identity." He also describes race/racism as one of the "most effective design campaigns in history" and ends by posing a challenge to Black designers: to interrogate the visual language around race and to reimagine/remake the way we approach visual culture. How can adopting a Critical Race Design Studies practice help us proactively respond to the damage that design has done as a result of racist propaganda? How can adopting a Critical Race Design Studies practice help us design "new ideas around the future"?

Folayemi Wilson recounts growing up in Harlem and being introduced to Afrofuturism through encounters with spiritual/ritualistic African symbols and practices that subsequently helped her develop a sense of agency. Though she draws inspiration from a variety of influences, she connects her creative/design practice with spiritual practice. Regardless of one's particular beliefs or inclinations, how might a spiritual approach (or practice) to design deepen our connection to our work? Our sense of how or what we can contribute? How might a spiritual design practice provide greater access to creative thinking and being?

CHAPTER 6: JOURNEYS IN DESIGN

Forest Young identifies four key factors that might persuade Black youth to seek careers in design: representational imprinting; open gates and viable paths to graduation; prismatic cultures; and professional lattices. How does he define each and what examples does he offer to support his overarching analysis? To what extent might any or all of these factors influence your decision to pursue or continue a career in design? How might your institution(s) incorporate these suggestions in their own programming or practices? His concept of professional latticing is a particular challenge to how design firms nurture and promote young designers, and how they conceive or create pathways toward leadership. How might job placement organizations for the design industry help to support the work of professional latticing?

Schessa Garbutt writes, "I have been intentionally shifting my creative center away from whiteness and cis-masculinity." What were some of the inspirations for that shift? In her title and in the essay, she/they reflects on the "ands" and multi-hyphenations of her/their practices. How have those "ands" shown up in their professional practice and their client collaborations?

Garbutt writes about how learning the rules of type design provokes her/them to want to consciously subvert the rules. What are some of the rules they name and what might that subversion look like? What rules of design have you consciously learned in order to dismantle or subvert them? What might that look like in your particular discipline or practice? How do you see similar subversions happening by other designers from historically marginalized backgrounds as a critique of cultural homogeneity or supremacy?

Yocasta LaChapelle visualizes the Black designer's journey in an infographic that features her proposal for a long-term, systemic approach to change. In it, she identifies barriers, actions, and outcomes over the course of a designer's journey, from high school to college to career. How does her analysis align with your own experience? Significantly, she begins with high school, when many young people are beginning to consider their career options. What systemic challenges at the high school level must design advocates or educators address in order to effect meaningful change? How might design advocates work with curriculum developers, guidance counselors, and college prep service providers to influence how young people perceive the various career options in design?

We invited students in our undergraduate and graduate design programs to share one word and one image that reflects their current journeys in design. What are the one object and one word that define your present journey in design? If you are an educator, consider assigning this exercise as a personal journal, prompting students to periodically add one image and one word that describes the current state of their journey. How might these words and images change as they move through the world and develop their practices as artists, designers, and thinkers? If students are willing to share, organize an exhibition of their favorite selections and invite an open dialogue about the themes that surface.

As a curator, **Michelle Joan Wilkinson** came to appreciate design history from the context of cultural geography and mapping. How does she describe "cultural geography?" What elements of her academic journey led her to see the importance of design artifacts in reconstructing Black narratives? How does Wilkinson use the space of the museum to reveal and share historical Black narratives through design? What specific design artifacts does she reference in her essay, and how might you similarly map the cultural geography of your own life, your family, or your community through similar artifacts?

Wilkinson writes, "Understanding that, historically, many African Americans rendered their designs in anonymity, I felt compelled to identify 'designers' as designers whenever possible." Her most recent project titled "Rendering Visible" is intended to "document the visual culture of architectural ideas." The concept of visibility is a common thread through many of the essays in the book. How is Wilkinson's work at the Museum of African American History and Culture attempting to correct the invisibilities of Blackness in the American landscape in general, and the invisibilities of Black designers in particular?

Sabine Maxine Lopez writes about integrating fashion, branding, and graphic design into her work as a form of social justice. How does her work represent a form of both personal voice and community activism? Lopez also reflects on feeling marginalized even within marginalized communities. What specific aspects of her identity does she name and how does she use her work as a designer to respond to or express those elements of her personal journey?

In her "Interview with a White Male Academic," **Aisha Richards** provokes and responds to her colleague's reflections on how racism showed up in their institution, both by students and colleagues. Richards specifically asks her colleague to consider his acts of witness and complicity. What are some of the incidents the two discuss? How might his advocacy for her at the time have altered her experience as a colleague and instructor? What does he say prevented him from speaking up? Why do you think he was willing to (or wanted to) have this conversation with Richards? What, if anything, surprised you about the conversation? If this a conversation you would want to have with a colleague? Which "side" might you find yourself on and what would you want to say?

Aisha Richards and Lauren Williams (Chapter 8) both reflect on the ways power, gender, and race in academic institutions have shaped their journeys. Williams's letter and Richards's interview seem to be in dialogue with one another. Each writer defines her own path toward liberation and healing. To what extent do you think the institutions or the individuals within it should be held responsibility for the harms they caused or perpetuated? In the context of Richards's "calling in" approach, how might institutions facilitate opportunities for individuals to reflect on their past behaviors? What might healing look like for you in the context of an institutional harm you either caused or experienced?

Many of the contributors in this chapter and throughout the book reference nontraditional entry points into design. How might community organizations, K–12 schools, and higher education (including community college) effectively facilitate the many pathways into design? To what extent can or should the industry become more aligned with nontraditional pathways into their disciplines, drawing not only from the "top" design schools but from the range of spaces where young people are defining their skills as designers? How might your own journey to design be instructive to the industry, your peers, and those who may follow?

CHAPTER 7: DESIGN = ART ≠ DESIGN

In his interview with Kelly Walters, **Cey Adams** shares some of the anxieties about being an emerging artist in the 1980s, saying, "I was part of an elite group of talented young (graffiti) artists that all had gallery representation, but we always did group shows." Why does he say he and his peers were always offered group instead of solo exhibitions at galleries? Why does he describe himself as "expendable" at this time? Why did he feel that he always had to "perform, perform, perform?" To what extent did race and contemporaneous attitudes about graffiti as an art form impact that sense of expendability and anxiety?

Adams further reflects on the transition from his art practice (graffiti and gallery work) to his design practice (client work). How did he make that transition, and what differentiated those practices for him? Reflecting on his work for Def Jam thirty years later, how does he assess its impact and legacy (perhaps in contrast to how he experienced it at the time)?

Rick Griffith asks the reader to "Refute the Controversy" between art and design. How does he frame his argument, and where might you argue with or against the points he makes?

He further offers this provocation: "Art relies on knowing the difference between utility and indulgence. (Try not to see indulgence as a bad word)." Discuss the distinctions and nuances he offers in those words. How might you examine his provocation in the context of your own practices as an artist/designer? What might indulgence mean to you?

Mimi Ọnụọha and **Romi Morrison** discuss the "not particularly useful" distinctions between art and design, saying, "Rigorous creativity is for design and the sort of foolish whimsical creativity can be passed off to art." Reflect on the distinctions they are offering here. Do you find them useful for understanding the work of artist/designers and/or your own practices? Why do Ọnụọha and Morrison find that Black folks must continue to navigate the distinctions between those spaces with intentionality? What strategies do they use to navigate each?

Nontsikelelo Mutiti speaks with Kelly Walters about seeing the street value of things and the act of navigating different geographies. How does this alertness to space inform her idea about value and values in art and design? How might this "street level" thinking inform her thoughts about the artificial distinctions between art, design, and the many disciplines she has created for and within?

Like many artist/designers in this chapter and throughout the book, Mutiti is a multi-hyphenate, transdisciplinary designer. To what extent is the experience of crossing disciplines common to Black artists and designers? Discuss the many examples of multidisciplinary artist/designers Mutiti names in her interview. What are the various ways in which they cross the boundaries of art and design disciplines?

Curator **Rhea L. Combs** argues that curatorial work often values the "extraordinary" over the "everyday." What effect does she believe that kind of emphasis has on the presentation of work by Black artists? What effect does she believe it has on audiences/viewers? What does Combs suggest are some of the correctives, and how does she address that shift in her own work?

Many of the contributors in this section reflect on the definitions of art and design, including Cey Adams, who asserts that unlike design, "Nobody is asked to define art." Reflect on your own definitions of art and design, the overlaps, connections, and divergences between the two, and how you see your own practices in the context of those terms.

Cey Adams and Nontsikelelo Mutiti both reinforce the value of taking the time to identify and understand the primary audience for your work in order to figure out where you want that work disseminated or engaged with. What lessons or guiding principles might you take from their examples?

CHAPTER 8: COLLECTIVE, RADICAL, AND LIBERATORY SPACES IN DESIGN

In **Lauren Williams**'s love letter to herself and other Black women, she cautions us to divorce ourselves from institutions that continuously take from us and yet don't really care about us—to "abandon trust in an untrustworthy place . . . deprive it of that pleasure" and focus on our own self-preservations, and figure out what we actually need to thrive in the spaces where we work. Why does Williams suggest that we reject spaces that do not serve our best interest? How do you identify spaces that affirm or exploit your existence? What does it look like to create and invest in spaces where we feel supported, seen, heard, and valued?

Terrence Moline makes a case for spaces that are "separate and equal," as embodied by the organization he founded: African American Graphic Designers. Why does he believe that segregation is necessary? In what ways might spaces like AAGD support African American/Black visual communicators in their journey and overall creative experience? How might your class thoughtfully debate his thesis?

Moline argues for designers to see themselves as not only the recipients of legacy but the "lineage of support," saying, "our responsibility is to hoist, to uplift, to bear the weight of, to transfer all that we have and know to build the backbone and character of Black identity." How might designers develop a practice that serves as a lineage of support for peers and those who may follow? What might a lineage of support look like when embedded into a professional practice?

Malene Barnett founded the Black Artists + Designers Guild to advocate for Black creatives across disciplines, providing a space of solidarity as well as challenging the status quo. Using historic guilds as a model, how does BADG purport to support the interests of Black design professionals who feel constrained by client-centered work? What are the challenges and opportunities of the guild model?

Speaking about *Afrotectopia*, **Ari Melenciano** reflects on how the initiative has changed each year. How does she say her own mindset changed, as well as the structure and programming of each year's events? Why has Melenciano focused on retaining small, intimate spaces instead of scaling up? How might institutions of higher education support initiatives like Melenciano's *Afrotectopia* or Williams' *Reconstructing Practice*, which specifically challenge the cultural supremacy of the host institutions?

Maurice Cherry writes about the challenges of creating *Revision Path*, saying that initially he was making it up as he went along, finding failure, success, and affirmation and criticism at each stage. Who were some of his early allies and how did they help to keep *Revision Path* alive? Who were some of his detractors and why? How or to what extent might race have been a principal factor in his detractors' critiques of his work? Reading about Cherry's journey and the many challenges he faced, how might we assess the degree to which prominent designers and design organizations failed to support his work in the early days but then later leveraged their relationships to him once they recognized the success of his work? Discuss how the liberatory space Cherry created represents an act of radical resistance against the demands for conformity from the design industry.

In addition to encouraging Black designers to read science fiction as a way to help engage our imaginations about what the future can be, **adrienne maree brown** addresses the need for creating spaces that help Black designers "return to ourselves, the self that predates whiteness, the self that predates white supremacy, the self that predates patriarchy, and capitalism, and all these things that have really distorted our concept of what it means to be a Black human being." In our individual or collective design practices, how can we create spaces that recognize the humanity of Black people? And what does it mean to share these spaces? With whom do we share them?

Many contributors in this section and throughout this book have written about institutions that do not serve the interests of Black designers. What are the various elements of critique that they name and how might they be addressed by some of the liberatory spaces presented here? What new pathways might be possible as a result of these proposed models?

Thinking about the range of liberatory spaces that designers have constructed, what conditions would need to be in place for you to feel liberated as a designer, learner, educator, and community member? Must liberatory spaces be scaled, scalable, or reproducible in order to be successful? How might designers participate in spaces that are exclusively created for them? What specific principles, guidelines, or practices might you take from any or all of the contributors in order to create a space that feels most liberating for you in your practice?

What are the qualities of liberatory spaces? By contrast, how might you identify the qualities of a hostile space, or a space that does not serve the best interests of historically marginalized designers? What would it take to create your own "institution" or space where you feel valued?

GLOSSARY

1619 Project was a long-form investigative journalism initiative led by *New York Times* reporter Nikole Hannah-Jones that aligns the founding of the United States with the beginning of slavery on the American continent. The project was launched in August 2019 as a multipart publication in the *Times* magazine along with live events, a podcast, and a book project. Its publication launched a years-long political debate about what constitutes the nation's founding and how society frames the role of slavery in relation to its historical narratives.

Julian Abele (1881–1950) was an architect who designed a number of prominent academic buildings, including the Widener Memorial Library at Harvard University (1912–1915), Philadelphia's Central Library (1917–1927), and the Philadelphia Museum of Art (1914–1928). He was the primary designer of the west campus of Duke University (1924–1954). Abele designed furniture, and he created (in pencil and watercolor) exquisitely detailed architectural drawings.

Laini (Sylvia) Abernathy (dates unknown) was a Chicago-based artist, designer, and activist who participated in the Black Arts Movement. She designed a number of jazz album covers, including for Sun Ra, Roscoe Mitchell, and Joseph Jarman.

African Diaspora represents the approximately 140 million people whose direct ancestors dispersed across the globe either by force (during the transatlantic slave trade between the sixteenth and nineteenth centuries) or by choice (in the modern period), bringing culture, knowledge, skills, rituals, beliefs, and aesthetic choices. The diaspora represents the heterogeneity of African-ness at its roots and in its expressions across the globe, including in the particular ways it is translated through art and design.

Afrofuturism is a multidisciplinary aesthetic movement that places African diasporic identity at the center of cultural and technological imagination, drawing from history, fantasy, science fiction, socio-geo-politics, and modern environmentalism. Among the seminal creators of Afrofuturism are Sun Ra, Octavia Butler, Renee Cox, Ytasha Womack, Nnedi Okorafor, Ikire Jones, and Selly Raby Kane

Afrikan Alphabet is a book on Afrikan typography written by Zimbabwean graphic designer Saki Mafundikwa and published in 2004.

Benjamin Banneker (1731–1806) was an almanac author, surveyor, and clock designer who used his knowledge of astronomy to map the geographical boundaries of Washington, DC, at the city's founding.

Gwendolyn Barrett (1902–1981) was an artist, writer, and journalist whose illustration work graced the July 1926 cover of *Opportunity* magazine.

Miriam Benjamin (1861–1947) was an inventor and chair designer who invented the Gong and Signal Chair, which was later adopted by the US House of Representatives and whose technology informed the design of airplane flight attendant call buttons. Benjamin received her law degree at Howard University and became a Solicitor of Patents. There is some speculation that she was also a composer.

Lerone Bennett, Jr. (1928–2018) was a Mississippi-born historian, writer, and a long-time editor at *Ebony* magazine. He wrote *Before the Mayflower: A History of Black America* (1962), a book that established 1619 as a pivotal moment in the founding of the United States. In an article he wrote for *Ebony* in 1968, he debunked the savior mythology of Abraham Lincoln, writing, "The man's character, his way with words and his assassination, together with the psychological needs of a racist society, have obscured his contradictions under a mountain of myths."

Black Arts Movement was a collective of cross-disciplinary artists and activists during the 1960s and 70s that essentially rejected the Western, white-dominant cultural canon. Among its participants were Maya Angelou, Amiri Baraka, Gwendolyn Brooks, Hoyt W. Fuller, Nikki Giovanni, Rosa Guy, Audre Lorde, Haki R. Madhubuti, Larry Neal, Dudley Randall, Ishmael Reed, and Sonia Sanchez.

Black Quantum Futurism is a Philadelphia-based artists and literary collective founded by Moor Mother (Camae Ayewa) and Rasheedah Phillips. Their work proposes "a new approach to living and experiencing reality by way of the manipulation of space-time in order to see into possible futures, and/or collapse space-time into a desired future in order to bring about that future's reality."

Thomas (Tom) Burrell (born 1939) is an advertising executive who founded the Chicago-based ad agency Burrell Communications Group (originally named Burrell McBain Advertising) in 1971. He famously stated, "I had to convince clients to understand that black people are not dark-skinned white people," and reshaped both the image of Black people in advertising and invented targeted (v. mass) marketing in the advertising business.

Octavia Butler (1947–2006) was an award-winning science fiction author born in Pasadena, California, whose seminal work, *The Parable Series* (also known as the *Earthseed Series*), published in the 1990s, featured a world struggling to survive amid religious fundamentalism, human-made environmental disaster, unsustainable wealth gap, and corporate greed. Butler continues to be read, studied, and celebrated for the depth and prescience of her work; and in 2021 NASA named a Mars rover landing site in her honor.

Elizabeth Catlett (1915–2012) was a sculptor and graphic artist born in Washington, DC but worked for much of her career in Mexico City at the Taller de Grafica Popular and later became a Mexican citizen. An activist-artist, Catlett was known as a social realist whose work remarked on and captured the lives of women, African Americans, the poor, and laborers.

Combahee River Collective (1974–1980) was a Black, lesbian, feminist, socialist, activist group named for Harriet Tubman's famous act of liberation at the Combahee River Ferry site in 1863. The founders—most notably Barbara Smith, Demita Frazier, and Beverly Smith—wrote a statement of purpose that included the assertion, "We realize that the only people who care enough about us to work consistently for our liberation are us. Our politics evolve from a healthy love for ourselves, our sisters and our community which allows us to continue our struggle and work."

David Crosthwait (1898–1976) was a Nashville-born engineer, inventor, and industrial designer who acquired thirty-nine US patents and eighty international patents for his development of air ventilation, central air-conditioning, and heat transfer systems.

Emory Douglas (born May 24, 1943) is a Michigan-born graphic designer known for his iconic print work for the Black Panther party. Douglas first learned about commercial design in a print shop before studying graphic design in college, where he joined the Black arts movement and joined creativity with activism.

W. E. B. Du Bois (February 23, 1868–August 27, 1963) was a key figure in the Harlem Renaissance—writer, publisher, lecturer, and cultural scion—DuBois has recently gained new fame for his infographics, which were compiled in 2019 into the book *W. E. B. Du Bois's Data Portraits: Visualizing Black America* that quite literally represent Black experiences in the United States through design. The book has become a seminal text for graphic design students and experienced designers alike who are constantly challenged to transform complex data in accessible visual form.

Phil Freelon (1953–2019) was a Philadelphia-born architect who led a consortium of architecture firms known as Freelon Adjaye Bond/SmithGroup. The consortium designed the National Museum of African American History and Culture. Freelon also designed the Museum of the African Diaspora (San Francisco), Amistad Research Center at Tulane University (New Orleans), Reginald F. Lewis Museum of Maryland African American History and Culture (Baltimore), Harvey B. Gantt Center for African-American Arts and Culture (Charlotte), and the National Center for Civil and Human Rights (Atlanta).

Theaster Gates (born 1973) is a Chicago-based artist, designer, activist, and educator whose work responds to the disinvestments of civic institutions in Black and impoverished communities. Among his many projects, the Stony Island Arts Bank and Rebuild Foundation have revitalized under-resourced Black communities in Chicago by centering art, design, and community space.

Chuck Harrison (1931–2018) was a Louisiana-born American industrial designer, inventor, and educator. Harrison was the first Black executive to work at Sears, Roebuck & Company where he managed the design group, making over 750 consumer products from sewing machines to Craftsman tools. Harrison actively mentored Black design students, ensuring that new generations of designers saw pathways to success for Black designers and leaders.

Dorothy Hayes (1935–2015) was an Alabama-born graphic designer who fought against racism and sexism throughout her career. Earning a degree in graphic arts from Cooper Union, Hayes was devoted to mentoring young Black designers. In 1970, she and Joyce Hopkins curated an exhibition titled, "Black Artists in Graphic Communication," which featured forty-nine young Black graphic designers. In addition to teaching and mentoring, Hayes led her own design firm, Dorothy's Door.

Thomas L. Jennings (1794–1876) was a New York–born inventor and activist whose 1821 dry-cleaning innovation earned him the first patent awarded to an African American inventor in the United States. He used the fortune he earned to fund the abolitionist movement. Later in life, he became assistant secretary for the First Annual Convention of the People of Color in Philadelphia, PA.

Caroline R. Jones (1942–2001) was a Michigan-born advertising executive who cofounded, with Frank Mingo, the Black-owned firm Mingo-Jones in 1977.

Frederick McKinley Jones (1893–1961) was a Cincinnati-born inventor, designer, and entrepreneur who held sixty-one patents and earned the National Medal of Technology (1991). Among his more notable designs are portable air cooling units, a portable X-ray machine, and movie ticket dispensers.

Marjorie Joyner (1896–1994) was a Virginia-born inventor, educator, and activist whose permanent wave technology that included a protective cap for the scalp earned her the first patent awarded to an African American woman in the United States.

Eli (Elvin Elias Lee) Kince (dates unknown) is a Cleveland-born author, educator, designer, historian, and self-taught fine artist who wrote, *Visual Puns in Design: The Pun Used as a Communication Tool*, published in 1982.

Gerald (Jerry) Lawson (1940–2011) was a Brooklyn-born electrical engineer who designed the first video game console with a removable game cartridge (the *Fairchild Channel F*) in 1976. His design was adopted by and became popularized with the Atari gaming console.

Esther Mahlangu (born November 1935) is a South African Ndebele artist from the Gauteng region, located north of Pretoria. Through her bold, geometric large scale paintings, Mahlangu has championed the preservation of her Ndebele culture, making her the first Ndebele artist to transfer the traditional Ndebele style wall paintings to canvas, exhibiting them both in South Africa and globally. Among her many accomplishments, she has painted murals and collaborated with brands including BMW and Rolls-Royce.

Noel Mayo (born 1937) is a New Jersey–born industrial designer and design educator who founded the first Black-led industrial design firm in the United States in 1964 whose clients have included NASA, the US Department of Commerce and Agriculture, IBM, and Black+Decker.

Elijah McCoy (1844–1929) was an Ontario-born inventor and engineer, who acquired fifty-seven patents including some for his innovations of the steam engine. As the child of enslaved parents who had escaped bondage via the Underground Railroad, McCoy returned to the United States as a young adult, settling in Detroit, Michigan, where he lived, worked, and developed his inventions.

Garret Morgan (1877–1963) was a Kentucky-born, Ohio-based inventor, engineer, community leader, and entrepreneur whose patents included designs for smoke hoods for firefighters, the three-light traffic signal, and a number of hair-straightening products. Morgan also founded the Black-owned newspaper, the *Cleveland Call*.

Organization of Black American Culture (1967–1992) was a Chicago-based, cross-disciplinary artist collective originally formed as Committee for the Arts by Hoyt W. Fuller, Conrad Kent Rivers, and Gerald McWorter. The members held workshops and produced a number of plays, murals, and magazines.

Jerry Pinckney (1939–2021) was a Philadelphia-born illustrator and writer of children's books who worked principally in watercolor. In 1964, he illustrated *The Adventures of Spider: West African Folktales*, the first in a lifetime of stories that centered tales and characters from across the African diaspora. He won multiple Caldecott honors, in part for his retellings of children's stories to correct the past harms of racist depictions. In his words, "I see storytelling itself as part of African American resistance."

Reynold Ruffins (1930–2020) was a cofounder of PushPin Studios. Ruffins was a New York–born and –based graphic designer, painter, and illustrator whose work can be seen in both corporate branding, as well as over a dozen children's books.

Norma Sklarek (1926–2012) was a Harlem-born architect whose work includes the US Embassy building in Tokyo, Japan (with Cesar Pelli) and Terminal One station at Los Angeles International Airport.

Richard Spikes (1878–1963) was a Dallas-born inventor, whose innovations in automotive design introduced directional signals, safety brakes, and automatic gears and transmissions to cars, trucks, and buses, earning him over ten patents. In addition to his innovations in automotive technology, he developed the pressure-dispense beer tap, which revolutionized the saloon and beer industries.

Sun Ra (1914–1993) was an experimental, Afrofuturist jazz musician born in Birmingham, Alabama, where he was originally named Herman Poole Blount. A multi-instrumentalist, Sun Ra led his band, the Arkestra, through both sonic and visual cosmic journeys across time and space.

Robert Robinson Taylor (1868–1942) was a North Carolina–born architect and designer who was the first African American student admitted to the Massachusetts Institute of Technology (MIT). Working closely with Booker T. Washington to develop the curriculum and programming for Tuskegee University, Taylor designed many of the original campus buildings. He designed several libraries, academic and administrative buildings, and a Masonic temple.

Valerie Thomas (born 1943) is a Maryland-born scientist and inventor who acquired a patent for the illusion transmitter, which has innovated the experience of 3D video games, movies, and experiences. Her invention has been used by NASA since she introduced it in 1980.

Jack Travis (born 1952) is an architect and educator born in the South Bronx, New York who designed the home of filmmaker Spike Lee, and served as architectural consultant for Lee's film *Jungle Fever*. He launched an initiative titled AC/DC (Afri-Culture/Design-Culture), now Studio Africulture, in 1994 to document, disseminate, and educate the public about the contributions of African diasporic architects and architecture.

Madame C. J. Walker (1867–1919) was a Louisiana-born inventor, entrepreneur, and activist (originally named Sarah Breedlove) who famously built her fortune designing innovative products, packaging, and marketing and advertising strategies for cosmetics and hair care products specifically targeted to African American customers.

Paul R. Williams (1894–1980) was a Los Angeles–born and based architect whose seminal works include the Theme Building at Los Angeles International Airport, LA's 28th Street YMCA, the Stanley Mosk Courthouse, the UCLA Botany Building, Woodrow Wilson High School, and several celebrity homes. His versatility as a designer meant that he could design buildings in any number of architectural styles, including Tudor Revival, French Chateau, Regency, French Country, and Mediterranean.

Ytasha Womack (dates unknown) is the Chicago-born author and filmmaker whose seminal text, *Afrofuturism: The World of Black Sci-Fi and Fantasy Culture* (2013) has contributed to new scholarship in the transdisciplinary movement.

LETTER TO FUTURE DESIGNERS: PENINA LAKER

As I sit down to write this letter, I can't help but wonder what my younger self would have found helpful, comforting even, if they came across it. And the truth is, I am not sure I have the right words to offer to the younger me about what it means to be a designer in such a challenging cultural and political climate without sounding overly dispirited.

At this particular moment in time, the world is in a period of recovery. We are attempting to prioritize healing in the wake of social injustices and a global pandemic as well as focus on the things and people that bring us joy. We are, in short, on a collective journey of self-discovery and unapologetic self-preservation. In the summer of 2020, we bore witness to the devastating effects of COVID-19 on under-resourced communities of color. We saw the injustices inflicted upon Black bodies by the police on public display. We saw thousands of American citizens across the country rise up in solidarity to protest unjust systems and institutions that have disproportionately kept Black people under oppression. We have also witnessed the power of visual and written storytelling in memorializing lives lost, capturing the frustrations of a people tired of being tired, and motivating those doing the hard work of organizing protests. The editorial team for this project knew that we needed to do our part to prevent this crucial period in American history from becoming just another painful memory for the history books. We owe it to ourselves and to *you*, future designers, to help shape whatever comes next, to take up space where our contributions and lived experiences have traditionally been excluded or misrepresented, and to be seen and heard.

So, though I struggle to find the right words to say to you, it's not for a lack of what to say but rather how to say it all. What I would like to share with you are some poignant lessons that are shared throughout this book. Namely, words of wisdom and caution, words of encouragement and affirmation, words that instill confidence and a sense of belonging, and words that will provoke and inspire. The contributors of this book have shared their journeys, their triumphs, their struggles, and their hopes and desires for a future where *you* feel valued and supported, *you* feel seen (*and see others like you*), where *you* can thrive and take a hold of *your* own narratives, and where *you* can play an active role in designing the future you dream of. The diversity of perspectives from both the Black and African Diasporic lenses will, I hope, inject a restorative sense of pride and joy in being Black designers of the future.

IT DOESN'T MATTER WHERE YOU START, BUT WHOM YOU SURROUND YOURSELF WITH

I was fortunate to stumble on the field of visual communication design while I was in college. In fact, if I hadn't mustered the courage to walk into that digital design studio elective, despite being scared of my lack of experience with computers, let alone Adobe software design programs, I am not sure I would have pursued a career in the field. Design was not an area of study that was even on my radar: I never knew what design was or what designers did. Growing up in Uganda, the professions we were guided to pursue favored career pathways in the sciences as opposed to more creative fields. When I had the opportunity to pursue a college education in the United States at a small liberal arts college in the Midwest, however, I was able to gain broader knowledge about the many disciplines outside my major.

A few minutes into that first digital design studio, all I wanted to do was quit. Everything was so foreign to me: I couldn't find the on/off button on the fancy iMac computers—why were they such a challenge to operate?—and how was mine the only one not magically working like the rest? If this is how I felt on day one, how was I going to keep up with the rest of the coursework without slowing everyone else down? I remember walking up to the instructor and asking to be excused from the class because I was overwhelmed with how little I knew and I didn't think I would be able to keep up. She encouraged me to stick around, reassured me that I would get extra help to get me on my feet, and said that there was nothing to feel embarrassed about. She reminded me that I was in college to learn and expand my knowledge of the things that seemed to be a mystery.

Over the years, it has become clear to me that finding and surrounding yourself with instructors and mentors with whom you can be vulnerable about those innermost struggles, struggles which might otherwise hinder your ability to cultivate your creative pursuits, is key to finding your footing in design. And if not your instructors, reach out to folks whose work you admire. We live in a global village where social platforms, professional networks, and dedicated spaces for Black creatives makes it easier than ever to connect. Finding your community is going to be a process, but taking the initiative to get out there and meet people is the most valuable thing you can do for yourself.

LEARN YOUR HISTORY FROM A NON-WHITE LENS

I cannot stress this enough. Do not solely rely on the references you are given in your classrooms. This will also take some work and effort on your part, but strive to expand and decolonize your education with texts that foreground the narratives of your ancestors. You will find that most of black history is filled with painful recounts of our colonial and imperialistic oppressive past, but that is not where the story ends—know that our histories also predate colonialism, where our forefathers triumphed against all odds and made lasting accomplishments to the fields of design. Reject narratives that ignore their rightful place in history. Furthermore, it's equally important that you know who you are outside the harmful racial and gendered constructs that continuously brand you as less than white people.

For most of us, our introduction to design was rooted in a Eurocentric cultural context, which is completely detached from our ancestral past and present context. As noted in this book's introduction, texts that foreground Black narratives are scarce. And this is precisely why doing our part to add to this growing body of knowledge is so important. Your foundation will be different because you have a community, past and present, to lean on.

> Those who are born on an anthill take a short time to grow tall.
> —Ghanaian proverb

You are children growing on top of an *anthill*: a repository of stories, lessons, teachings, and innovations that provides a deeper context into your past, present, and future. Our hope is that you will emerge with more confidence and a well-rounded understanding of who you are and where you come from. We hope that you will take up the mantle of sharing your experiences and uphold the tradition of boldly and proudly telling your stories, adding layer upon layer of knowledge that the world can't help but recognize.

ON WRITING & EDITING THIS BOOK: JENNIFER RITTNER & ANNE H. BERRY

Being part of the creation and development of *The Black Experience in Design: Identity, Expression, and Reflection*, has been an extraordinary journey. Beginning in the spring of 2020 with a series of conversations initiated by Anne H. Berry and a handful of collaborators and colleagues, including Penina Laker, we first considered proposing a special issue journal on the subject of Black experiences within design. This was during a period when design industries and subfields were publicly reckoning with design practices that upheld the values of white cultural supremacy and were asking the question, "Why have our industries so thoroughly under-represented Black voices?" In the wake of the national Black Lives Matter protests, there seemed to be more opportunities for Black designers to share their experiences. And as Anne and Penina brought Kelly Walters, Kareem Collie, Lesley-Ann Noel, and Jennifer Rittner into the conversation, ideas about how we might contribute to this effort grew. The more we talked, the more we began to see that the project we envisioned somehow felt too big to be contained within a single journal issue. We ran the idea by Steven Heller, who agreed that we might have a book in the making, and he generously and graciously introduced us to his colleague, Tad Crawford, at Allworth Press.

After speaking with the publisher, it became clear that a selective process was preferable to an open call, allowing us to identify contributors who represented the range of ideas we wanted to include. We had a few core tenets to guide our progress, among them a mandate to:

1. Represent a range of disciplines and practices so that designers, educators, and students would be more likely to see versions of themselves unconstrained by a single, narrow form of praxis.
2. Represent a range of identities so that readers would see and hear stories that felt familiar, surprising, honest, and complex.
3. Encourage contributors to write in ways that were true to them and not in a particular "writer's voice" or "academic style." We

wanted each contributor to feel that they were sharing the story they wanted to tell in the way they could best tell it.

4. Include contributors who expressed a desire to be included even if they didn't have time to sit down and write; and so we conducted interviews, lightly editing as needed but otherwise ensuring that their voices continued to shine through.

5. Uplift the nuance and depth represented in the contributions.

6. Produce a book that could serve as an invitation and a conversation, as opposed to a tool kit or how-to manual.

Consequently, we hope that the book inspires readers and fuels dialogue with the contributors, the editors, peers, colleagues, instructors, students, and anyone else looking to engage in conversation.

We wrote this book in the midst of the COVID-19 pandemic when we struggled with isolation that simultaneously kept us away from family and friends and tethered to monitors and screens. There were periods where we found ourselves buckling under the weight of academic research and service responsibilities while trying to adjust to pandemic life, as well as the additional work and energy necessary to support students under our care who were also struggling.

We wrote this book during a time in which three of our editors left positions in higher education, one moved into design industry, one moved to another state, one was actively applying for tenure, one lost a parent, one lost an auntie, one wrote and published another book, and another was invited to participate in additional book projects. Time seemed to be unrelenting, even as we did our best to create space to breathe, to mourn, to tend to life obligations, and to simply dream of future projects.

We wrote this book in the midst of #BLM protests that followed the unending murders of Black bodies at the hands of police.

We wrote this book in the wake of the January 6 insurrection at the United States Capitol when white supremacists tried to dismantle our functioning democracy.

We wrote this book while witnessing the impact and insidiousness of white supremacy in our industry, in real time.

Through the ongoing process of writing and editing, we met and invited dozens of colleagues to contribute. For the past year we have found ourselves unceasingly inspired by their contributions, and eager to share that work with readers. Even our colleagues who were not able to contribute, because of personal or professional conflicts, influenced us in myriad ways. We humbly acknowledge that our book would have benefited from their insights, and look forward to their many, continuing contributions to the field.

While writing this book, we found new voices, including our own.

While writing this book, we found each other.

Perhaps more than anything, the process of writing and editing this book has been an exercise in solidarity at a time when we needed it most. Despite (and perhaps because of) the challenges and obstacles, we have savored the moments of levity and the deeper conversations that helped sustain us. We affirmed and challenged each other. We respectfully disagreed. We re-prioritized and made space for one another. In the end, we believe that this imperfect process has proven that the work of solidarity is essential to our ability to thrive. Collaborating is not just making the thing *around* one another, but being informed and transformed by the process.

This beautiful, messy, imperfect, honest thing we have made represents our solidarity with one another—from the editorial team to the contributors, colleagues, and peers who have informed and inspired it. This is one more node in the ever-widening web of Black experiences in design. In our learning and scholarship, in our practices of present and future, whether we are making art as designers or design as artists, in community, as activists, and in advocacy for and with our many, intersectional communities, these are our stories.

AFTERWORD:
EDDIE OPARA

In his book, *Black and British: A Forgotten History,* the British Nigerian historian David Olusoga declares,

> From the sixteenth century onwards,
> Britain exploded like a supernova, radiating its power and influence across the
> world. Black people were placed at the
> centre of that revolution. Our history
> is global, transnational, triangular,
> and much of it is still to be written.[1]

My personal history starts with Godwin Anaememotu Opara and Teresa Waymere Jatto. My mother and father arrived in the United Kingdom at different times—at the end of the 1950s and beginning of the 1960s—as migrants coming to the "mother country" to work and for further education. This was postwar Britain. Since 1948, there had been a massive labor shortage, and Britain needed workers. At first, there was a feeling of constitutional ignorance of the government. They did not intend to bring over black students and workers from the colonies; they only favored white workers from white commonwealth dominions and war-torn Europe. This quickly subsided, common sense prevailed, and so my parents, like millions of others from the global colonies, came.

My mother and father married in 1963 and had three children, I being the youngest. Even though they were British subjects, my siblings and I were the finished articles. As children of migrants, some of you reading this will understand that failure was not an option for us. You have been blessed, given this opportunity to blossom—"Do not let us down, do not let yourself down." I struggled through lower education at a somewhat progressive Jesuit school, eventually finding my feet in graphic design, an area that I couldn't quite fully comprehend at the time. Stereotypically immigrant progenitors demand that their offspring acquire professions that are learned, somewhat profitable, and have gravitas. Luckily my father was in advertising for a short duration of time while in the UK and understood what I needed.

On the eve of my departure to the United States, as I left the shores of my birth, my father, who was a pious man, exclaimed to me that, "Design is spiritual. It's a way of life." An inspirational edict, one that I have been trying to unravel and instill in myself for the past twenty-six years. Over a quarter of a century has passed, and my faith and perception as a designer are being tested. Who am I? What do I do and what do I stand for? Where does one start? Each era presents us with challenges. But the pandemic, the upheaval in society, and our world's rapidly changing climate conjoined have inspired many of us to be more introspective. I find myself returning to my father's words—"Design is spiritual."

I was asked not too long ago to define what design is. Design is the ability to produce the desired outcome or intended result by being freed from constraints or difficulties, through the application of rational thinking, creative skill, and appraisal, thereby acquiring a transformational and progressive outcome. You would think that one's political and cultural attitudes would align to these ideas. They do not. This challenge effectively defines the experience of being a Black designer in America, and perhaps the world.

In addition to knowing what design is rationally, one needs to also know it spiritually. Why are these two subjects intertwined? Being spiritual is an experience, a belief beyond one's self, to render an individual bond to others, their well-being, and the world at large. It is the belief that there is something greater binding us all together. Using spirituality to cope with challenges in life experiences benefits our health and well-being. [2] Through spirituality, we find the tools for gaining transformational and progressive outcomes.

Design and spirituality, it seems, are not so different. In both, we are uplifted through our imaginations. Writer, educator, and design researcher Stuart Walker proposes that imagination is fundamental to both design and spirituality: "Intuitively apprehended inner sensibility that seeks meaning . . . both employ the language of metaphor, analogy, and symbolism, and both [are] spurred by sudden insight, ideas, and unexpected connections." [3]

Where the Black community has historically been perceived as the lowest common denominator through poverty, prejudice, and invisibility, imagination is the tool we collectively use to construct a higher efficacy for social development. Through design, as a form of spirituality, we reach our full potential, for both community and inner fulfillment.[4] We are a sea of hungry creative individuals, awakening to a new era, defining a better tomorrow for all-Black society. With Design, we have found our calling. With our imaginations as tuned instruments, we need to pursue a better path for our design. As Black designers, we acknowledge the urgency to take up a new mantle, one of being numinous about the work we accept and create. Determining what kind of society we want to live in, and the values we want to live by, for us to be successful, we must serve our communities; and within our communities to utilize the precise definition of what is needed, from the core of what design is—a spiritual practice.

Through a migrant's eyes, I see America as a cradle for hope and aspirations. As a migrant to these shores, I see that what it often takes is the will to leave the safe confines of home and of our studios, and **move** through and spaces that be unfamiliar. It may take us beyond the shores of the United States to experience new lands, and to migrate to places with different ideals and principles, where there are vast communities whose knowledge we need. It may take finding places where design is practiced as a form of spirituality, and where we give and receive guidance in new ways. We can follow the words of David Olusoga as we go forward, as Black designers, we are now the "[supernovas], radiating [our] power and influence across the world. Black people were placed at the centre of [this] revolution. Our history is global, transnational, triangular and much of it is still to be written."[5]

NOTES

1. Olusoga, David. *Black and British: A Forgotten History*. London: Pan Books, 2017

2. Akbari, M., and S. M. Hossaini. "The Relationship of Spiritual Health with Quality of Life, Mental Health, and Burnout: The Mediating Role of Emotional Regulation." *Iran J Psychiatry*. 2018;13(1):22-31. PMID:29892314

3. Walker, Stuart. *Design and Spirituality: A Philosophy of Material Cultures*.

4. Ibid.

5. https://www.theguardian.com/commentisfree/2016/ oct/30/what-it-means-to-be-black-in-britain-today

BIOS

Cey Adams, a New York City native, emerged from the downtown graffiti movement to exhibit alongside fellow artists Jean-Michel Basquiat and Keith Haring. He appeared in the historic 1982 PBS documentary *Style Wars*, which tracks subway graffiti in New York. Adams served as creative director for Def Jam Recordings, where he cofounded the Drawing Board, the label's in-house visual design firm, and created visual identities, album covers, logos, and advertising campaigns for Run DMC, Beastie Boys, LL Cool J, Public Enemy, Notorious B.I.G., Maroon 5, and Jay-Z.

Alicia Olushola Ajayi is an architectural designer, researcher, and writer based in NYC. After receiving a dual master's in architecture and social from Washington University in St. Louis, Alicia worked as an associate designer at MASS Design Group. She is the project developer at BlackSpace Urbanist Collective, a group of design professionals dedicated to creating and protecting Black spaces. She currently teaches architecture at Columbia University.

Malene Barnett is an artist, designer, activist, and founder of the Black Artists+Designers Guild. Her multidisciplinary studio practice and research focuses on traditions of the African diaspora and the modern black experience. Her work has been featured in many publications and commissioned globally.

> Web: malenebarnett.com
> Twitter: @malene.barnett
> LinkedIn: linkedin.com/in/malenebarnett

Ruha Benjamin is Professor of African American Studies at Princeton University, founding director of the Ida B. Wells Just Data Lab, and author of the award-winning book *Race After Technology: Abolitionist Tools for the New Jim Code* among many other publications.

Dr. Audrey G. Bennett is an inaugural University Diversity and Social Transformation professor at the University of Michigan, a former Andrew W. Mellon distinguished scholar of the University of Pretoria, South Africa, and College Art Association Professional Development fellow. Her transdisciplinary research concerns race, aesthetics, technology, and inequity regarding sustainable food, HIV/AIDS, STEM/STEAM education, and graphic design history. Her scholarly publications include "Towards an Autochthonic Black Aesthetic in Graphic Design Pedagogy."

Anne H. Berry is a writer, designer, and design educator at Cleveland State University. Her published writing includes "The Virtual Design Classroom" for *Communication Arts* magazine and "The Black Designer's Identity" for the inaugural issue of the *Recognize* anthology featuring commentary from Indigenous people and people of color. She is also cocreator of the award-winning project *Ongoing Matter: Democracy, Design, and the Mueller Report* and managing editor of *The Black Experience in Design*.

> Twitter: @annehberry, @ongoingxmatter
> Instagram: @annehberry, @ongoingxmatter
> LinkedIn: linkedin.com/in/annehberry

Nii Kommey Botchway is a design educator based in Gqeberha, South Africa, where he coordinates the Graphic Design Program at the Nelson Mandela University. His interest lies in building an appreciation and knowledge of the (Afrikan) design consciousness found within various cultures on the continent and in the Afrikan diaspora.

> Web: theafrikandesignschool.com

Dr. Lonny Avi Brooks is a professor in the Department of Communication at California State University, East Bay, where he piloted the integration of futures thinking into the communication curriculum. A leading voice of Afrofuturism 2.0, Brooks contributes to journals, conferences, and anthologies; is co-executive producer of *The Afrofuturist* podcast; lead co-organizer, Oakland, the Black Speculative Arts Movement; director, Afro-Rithms Futures Group and codesigner of the *Afro-Rithms from the Future* game envisioning Black, Indigenous, and Queer liberation; research affiliate with the Institute For The Future and a Research Fellow with the Long Now Foundation.

> Web: afrorithmsfromthefuture.org
> Twitter: @avilonny
> Instagram: @avilonny

adrienne maree brown is the author of *Grievers*, *Holding Change: The Way of Emergent Strategy Facilitation and Mediation*, *We Will Not Cancel Us and Other Dreams of Transformative Justice*, the *New York Times* bestseller *Pleasure Activism: The Politics of Feeling Good*, and the radical self/planet help book *Emergent Strategy: Shaping Change, Changing Worlds* published by AK Press in 2017. She is also the coeditor of the anthology *Octavia's Brood: Science Fiction from Social Justice Movements* with Walidah Imarisha, published by AK Press in 2015.

> Twitter: @adriennemaree
> Instagram: @adriennemareebrown

Maurice Cherry is a creative strategist, designer, podcaster, and pioneering digital creator in Atlanta, GA. He is the creator and host of *Revision Path*, a design podcast centered on Black designers, developers, and digital creatives.

> Web: mauricecherry.com
> Twitter: @mauricecherry @revisionpath
> Instagram: @revisionpath
> LinkedIn: linkedin.com/in/mauricecherry

Kareem Collie is a designer, strategist, and educator specializing in collaborative and human-centered design approaches to capture, reveal, and produce visual narratives and user experiences. He is the former Director of Design and Creativity at the Rick and Susan Sontag Center for Collaborative Creativity at The Claremont Colleges and is now a Global Design Lead at IBM Consulting.

> Web: kareemcollie.com
> LinkedIn: linkedin.com/in/kareemdcollie

Dr. Rhea L. Combs is the director of curatorial affairs at the Smithsonian's National Portrait Gallery in Washington, DC. Combs was previously at the Smithsonian's National Museum of African American History and Culture, where she served as the curator of film and photography and head of the Earl W. and Amanda Stafford Center for African American Media Arts (CAAMA). She is currently cocurating the exhibition *Regeneration: Black Cinema 1898–1971* that will open at the Academy Museum of Motion Pictures in 2022.

> Twitter: @rhea_combs

Darhil Crooks is a creative director at Apple. He previously served as *The Atlantic* magazine's creative director and oversaw redesigns of the magazine and website which were subsequently recognized by the American Society of Magazine Editors (ASME) as website of the year and magazine of the year. Prior to his time at *The Atlantic*, Crooks served as creative director at *Ebony*. where he directed the publication's first cover-to-cover redesign. He also served as art director at *Esquire* and *Men's Journal* in New York City. Crooks studied graphic design at the School of Visual Arts in New York City.

> Twitter: @darhilcrooks
> Instagram: @darhilcrooks

Dantley Davis is Twitter's chief design officer, leading design and research at the company. Prior to joining Twitter, Dantley was at Facebook where he led product design for Stories, News Feed, and Video. He spent seven years at Netflix, where he was responsible for design and product strategy for television and mobile experiences. His work transformed streaming user interfaces across the SVOD industry. Dantley received his undergraduate degree and MBA from the University of San Francisco.

Twitter: @dantley
Instagram: @dantley

Emory Douglas was the Minister of Culture for the US Black Panther Party from 1967 until the early 1980s. As the party's principal Revolutionary Artist, he art directed, designed, and was the main illustrator for the weekly Black Panther newspaper. Over 50 years later, his Black Panther images are iconic, expanding their influence on visual culture and current international liberation movements. In 2015 he was awarded the AIGA (the professional association for design) medal for "exceptional achievements, services or other contributions to the field of design and visual communication." Often working collaboratively in locations worldwide, his current work continues to advocate for "all power to the people."

Colette Gaiter is a professor in the Departments of Africana Studies and Art & Design at the University of Delaware. After working as a graphic designer, she became an educator, artist, and writer. Since 2005, she has written about former Black Panther artist Emory Douglas's work, including current international human rights activism. Her visual work and writing—for academic journals, publications, and books—always investigate creative activism.

Web: colettegaiter.com

Schessa Garbutt (they/them) is the founder and creative director at Firebrand Creative House. While their focus is brand identity design, they are also an avid writer, artist, and blossoming type designer. Schessa studied design at USC Roski and later earned a certificate in type design at Type West.

Web: firebrand.house
Twitter: @the_schessa
Instagram: @the_schessa, @firebrand.house

June A. Grant received a master's degree in Architecture from the Yale School of Architecture and her undergraduate degree from Baruch College, CUNY with a focus on International Economics and Finance with a minor in Studio/Ceramic Art. She is an architect with a long interest in the space of transactions and form. Upon leaving Steinberg Architects and AECOM, where she was a principal and associate principal, respectively, she launched blink!LAB, which is focused on new forms for occupancy and provides innovative adaptive designs that are research-supported and strategic in implementation.

> Web: blink-lab.com
> Twitter: @blinklab
> Instagram: @blinklabarchitecture

Rick Griffith is a British-born graphic designer of West Indian origin, the design director of the studio MATTER, master letterpress printer, and collagist. His works are nested in a writing practice inspired by all manner of historical contexts. MATTER, which he runs with partner Debra Johnson, is an ambidextrous design practice with a bookstore, printshop, and manufactory. His work has been widely exhibited and is represented in the permanent collections of the Denver Art Museum and Butler Library of Rare Books and Manuscripts. His work has also been celebrated by the Type Directors Club, Printmag.com, *Dwell*, and AIGA 50 Books | 50 Covers.

> Web: morematter.com, shopatmatter.com, blarp.org
> Instagram: @rickgriffith

R. Vann Graves joined the VCU Brandcenter as executive director in August 2018, bringing thirty years of creative and executive leadership experience. His work has been recognized with numerous industry awards including Cannes Lions, Grand London International Awards, a Grand Clio, and the D&AD Graphite Pencil. He has served as chief creative officer at J. Walter Thompson ATL; EVP, global executive creative director at McCann New York; VP, creative director at BBDO New York; and cofounder at FL+G. A Fulbright scholar, Vann holds degrees from Howard University, the Pratt Institute, Harvard University, and the University of Pennsylvania.

Annika Hansteen-Izora is a Brooklyn-based artist, art director, and designer across brand, web, and product, currently acting as Creative Director of *Somewhere Good*, a social start-up that's reimagining the internet. She has been featured by *The Creative Independent*, *It's Nice That*, *AIGA Eye on Design*, *Vogue*, and more.

Twitter: @annikaizora
Instagram: @annika.izora

The late **Sylvia Harris**, an American Institute of Graphic Arts medalist, was founder and principal of Citizen Research & Design. She is remembered for her pioneering approach to improving the usability of public spaces and using design to solve problems for civic agencies, universities, and hospitals. She was also creative director for the United States Census Bureau's 2000 census, which focused on encouraging more Americans, particularly underrepresented groups, to participate.

Dorothy Hayes was an American artist, graphic designer, and educator from Mobile, Alabama, and the owner of Dorothy's Door, a commercial design agency in New York. She attended Alabama State College and then moved to New York to continue her education at Pratt Institute, New York Institute of Advertising, and Cooper Union School of Art. She is known for the *Black Artist in Graphic Communication* exhibition she curated in 1970, which was among the first of its kind.

Steven Heller, cochair of The School of Visual Arts MFA Design / Designer as Entrepreneur program, is the author, coauthor or editor of over two hundred books on design and popular culture. He was art director of the *New York Times Book Review* and wrote its Visuals column and the Graphic Content column for *T Style*. He has been writing "The Daily Heller" for Printmag.com for ten years. He is the recipient of the National Design Award, AIGA Medal for Lifetime Achievement and two honorary Doctor of Arts degrees.

John Jennings is a professor of Media and Cultural Studies at the University of California at Riverside. He is coeditor of the Eisner Award–winning collection *The Blacker the Ink: Constructions of the Black Identity in Comics and Sequential Art*. Jennings is also a 2016 Nasir Jones Hip Hop Studies Fellow with the Hutchins Center at Harvard University. His current projects include the horror anthology *Box of Bones*, the coffee-table book *Black Comix Returns* (with Damian Duffy), and the Eisner-winning, Bram Stoker Award-winning, *New York Times* bestselling graphic novel adaptation of Octavia Butler's classic dark fantasy novel *Kindred*. Jennings is also founder and curator of the ABRAMS Megascope line of graphic novels.

Twitter @JlJennings
Instagram: @johnjenningsart

Steve Jones is a graphic designer, artist, and educator whose work has been exhibited locally, nationally, and internationally. His interests focus on Black icons and their representation in mass media and popular culture, identity politics, social issues and causes, and public art. He is the principal and creative director of plantain studio and currently teaches at the California College of the Arts in San Francisco, CA.

> Web: plantainstudio.com
> Instagram: @plantain_studio
> Facebook: plantainstudio
> LinkedIn: linkedin.com/in/steve-jones-573a1a1

Amos Paul Kennedy Jr. is a letterpress printer, papermaker, and builder of artist's books currently based in Detroit, MI. Kennedy uses the early technology of the letterpress printer to produce works reflecting contemporary social concerns. His chipboard posters with messages reflect his views on issues of community health, power, race, and identity. Emotionally resonant, Kennedy's work embodies passion and encourages people to think in previously unexplored ways.

> Web: kennedyprints.com
> Instagram: @kennedyprints
> Facebook: Kennedy-Prints-234464029982447

Jon Key is an art director, designer, and writer originally from Seale, Alabama. After receiving his BFA from RISD, Jon began his design career at Grey Advertising in NYC before moving on to work with such clients and institutions as HBO, Nickelodeon, the Public Theater, and the Whitney Museum. Jon has taught at MICA, Parsons, and the Lebanese American University, and is the Frank Stanton Chair in Graphic Design at Cooper Union. He is also a cofounder and design director at Codify Art, a multidisciplinary collective dedicated to creating, producing, supporting, and showcasing work by artists of color, particularly women, Queer, and trans artists of color.

> Twitter: @jonkey13
> Instagram: @jkey13

Yocasta Lachapelle is the director of talent at COLLINS, an independent strategy and brand experience design company, where she is responsible for strategic talent recruitment, growth, and retention. Yocasta has a passion for finding and nurturing creative talent. She also leads several diversity initiatives including COLLINS High School Summer Internship program, an outreach initiative to educate and inspire creatively inclined high school students in underrepresented communities to explore and consider careers within the world of design.

Penina Laker is a designer, researcher, and educator at Washington University in St. Louis. Her practice and research is centered around investigating and applying methodologies that utilize a human-centered approach to solving social problems, locally and internationally. She is currently broadening the scope and access of design education to young people in Uganda through her DesignEd workshops and *My African Aesthetic*, a podcast she cohosts.

> Twitter: @peninala
> Instagram: @myafricanaesthetic
> LinkedIn: linkedin.com/in/penina-acayo-laker
> Podcast: My African Aesthetic

Sloan Leo is an artist and the founder and CEO of FLOX Studio Inc, a community design and strategy studio working toward building a more brave, creative, and resilient social impact ecosystem. Sloan has over fifteen years of experience in strategy and community facilitation method-ologies to catalyze durable change with groups ranging from the Wikimedia Foundation to the Association of Design Professionals NY.

> Twitter: @SloanLeo1
> Instagram: @flox_studio, @therealsloanleo

renald Louissaint is a graphic designer + art director based in Brookyln, NY. He received a BFA in Graphic Design from the University of Connecticut, holds a role as a designer at Cash App, and maintains an independent free-lance practice focusing on editorial design.

Sabine Maxine Lopez (she/they) is a Queer, Black, Latinx, Nonbinary Femme from Los Angeles, California. A natural-born multi-hyphenate, Sabine dabbles in many different areas of creativity. You can find her expressing herself through design, writing, photography, fashion, and much more.

> Web: atribecalledqueer.com, sabinemaxine.com
> Instagram: @atribecalledqueer
> Twitter: @atcqueer
> Facebook: atribecalledqueer, sabinemaxinelopez

Ari Melenciano is a creative technologist at Google's Creative Lab, professor at NYU's Interactive Telecommunications Graduate Program, and founder of Afrotectopia, a social institution that is imagining, researching, and building at the nexus of new media art, design, science, and technology through a Black and Afrocentric lens. Her award-winning work has been supported and exhibited by a variety of institutions including Sundance, the New Museum's New Inc, the *New York Times*, and the Studio Museum of Harlem. She is often guest-lecturing at universities around the world.

> Web: ariciano.com, afrotectopia.org
> Instagram: ariciano

Quinlin B. Messenger is the founder and creative director of JUST Design, a studio developing and implementing strategies to spark equitable change through community engagement, sustainability, and architecture. With a bachelor's degree in architecture, and a minor in sociology and environmental studies from the University of Oregon, Quinlin has broadened his commitment to service through his adjunct professor role at Woodbury University's School of Architecture, and extends his process further by working closely with artists to facilitate conversations and experiences around race, equity, diversity, and legacy.

Dr. Cheryl D. Miller is the 2021 Cooper Hewitt National Design Award recipient, "Design Visionary" and 2021 AIGA Medalist, and serves as the inaugural 2021 Honorary IBM Design Scholar as "Eminent Luminary." She is nationally recognized for her outsized influence within the graphic design profession to end the marginalization of BIPoC designers through her civil rights activism, industry exposé trade writing, research rigor, and archival vision. She is distinguished senior lecturer, University of Texas, Austin; and board member, Vermont College of Fine Arts.

> Twitter: @cdholmesmiller
> Instagram: @cheryldmillerfineart
> LinkedIn: linkedin.com/in/cdholmesmiller

Terrence Moline is an art director, designer, and illustrator with over twenty-five years of experience creating thoughtful work for nonprofit, higher education, and social justice initiatives. Terrence is also the founder of African American Graphic Designers (AAGD.co), a collective of AA/Blk designers who collaborate while growing as a family.

Web: aagd.co
Instagram: @aagd_co
LinkedIn: linkedin.com/in/tmoline

Romi Ron Morrison is an artist, researcher, and educator. They investigate the personal, political, and spatial boundaries of race and social infrastructure within digital technologies. Using maps, data, sound, performance, and video, their installations challenge the demands of an increasingly quantified world that reduces land into property, people into digits, and knowledge into data.

Twitter: @RonMorrison_
Instagram: @elegantcollisions

Terresa Moses (she/her) is the creative director at Blackbird Revolt and an assistant professor of Graphic Design and the director of Design Justice at the University of Minnesota. She created Project Naptural and cocreated Racism Untaught. She is a PhD candidate in Social Justice Education at the University of Toronto. She serves as a core team member of AAGD and collaborator with the BLL.

Web: blackbirdrevolt.com, terresamoses.com
Twitter: @ProjectNaptural
Instagram: @projectnaptural, @blackbirdrevolt

Mugendi K. M'Rithaa is a transdisciplinary industrial designer, consultant, and professor of Industrial design at Machakos University in Kenya. He is the cofounder and chief design officer of Holos Creative Solutions, a Kenyan-based design consultancy committed to cocreating socially conscious design solutions that celebrate Afrika, Design, and Innovation. He is a founding member of the Network of Afrika Designers and former president of the World Design Organization.

Instagram: @mkmugendi
LinkedIn: linkedin.com/in/mugendi-k-m-rithaa-038a0713

Nontsikelelo Mutiti is a Zimbabwean-born visual artist and educator. She is invested in elevating the work and practices of Black peoples past, present, and future through a conceptual approach to design, publishing, archiving practices, and institution building. Mutiti holds a diploma in multimedia from the Zimbabwe Institute of Digital Arts and an MFA from the Yale School of Art, with a concentration in graphic design.

Dr. Lesley-Ann Noel focuses on equity, social justice, and the experiences of people who are often excluded from design education, research and practice. She promotes greater critical awareness among designers and design students by introducing critical theory concepts and vocabulary into the design studio e.g. through The Designer's Critical Alphabet and the Positionality Wheel.

> Web: linktr.ee/LesleyAnnNoel
> Twitter: @mamaazure
> Instagram: @lesleyannnoel
> LinkedIn: linkedin.com/in/lesleyannnoel

Liz Ogbu is a designer, urbanist, and spatial justice activist. She is an expert on engaging and transforming unjust urban environments, and uses design to address harm and catalyze healing. She's the founder and principal of Studio O, a multidisciplinary design consultancy that works at the intersection of racial and spatial justice. In addition to many other accomplishments, Liz is an IDEO.org Global Fellow, TEDWomen Speaker, Aspen Ideas Scholar, a LISC Rubinger Fellow, and one of Public Interest Design's Top 100.

> Web: lizogbu.com
> Twitter: @lizogbu

Mimi Ọnụọha is a Nigerian American artist who creates prints, installations, code, and videos about a world made to fit the form of data. Her multimedia practice uses absence and removal as lenses for investigating the power dynamics that shape collective relationships to systems that are simultaneously digital, cultural, historical, and ecological.

> Twitter: @thistimeitsmimi
> Instagram: @thistimeitsmimi

Eddie Opara is a British American designer, writer, educator and partner at the world renowned design firm Pentagram. He studied graphic design at the London College of Printing and Yale University, where he is a senior critic. He is a member of the distinguished design society, Alliance Graphique Internationale. Winner of numerous design accolades, he is author of *Color Works*, published by Rockport. He has been named one of *Fast Company*'s 100 Most Creative People in Business twice, *Adweek*'s Creative 100, and *Ebony* magazine's Power 100.

Twitter:@pentagramdesign
Instagram:@pentagramdesign
LinkedIn:https://www.linkedin.com/in/eddie-opara-3b12412

Adah Parris is a futurist, artist, activist, and chair of Mental Health First Aid England (MHFA UK). An enthusiastic curator of people, patterns, and stories, her current interest lies in the anatomy of transformation and innovation. Her work sits at the intersection of ancient wisdom, living systems, and indigenous community practices, digital and emerging technologies.

Web: linktr.ee/adahparris
Twitter: @adahparris
Instagram: @adahparris

Dr. David Pilgrim is a professor, orator, and human rights activist. He is best known as the founder and director of the Jim Crow Museum—a twenty-thousand-piece collection of racist artifacts located at Ferris State University, which uses objects of intolerance to teach about race, race relations, and racism.

Aisha Richards is Founder and current Director of Shades of Noir, The Centre for Race & Practice Based Social Justice, University of the Arts London, co-leader for the PgCert/MA Inclusive Practices Unit; an award-winning teacher and professorial candidate 2021/22.

Jennifer Rittner is a writer and educator currently serving as Visiting Assistant Professor at Parsons School of Design. She has been published in the *New York Times*, *DMI: Journal*, and *AIGA Eye on Design*; and in 2021 served as guest editor for a special issue on design & policing for *Design Museum* magazine. A daughter of women, Jennifer centers the voices of her near ancestors Bernadette, Aurea, and Dianqui in her practices.

Christopher Rudd is an instructor and lead of Community-led Design for the Chicago Design Lab at the Illinois Institute of Technology Institute of Design (ID) where his work focuses on codesigning with community stakeholders. Chris is a former Stanford Institute of Design (d.school) Civic Innovation fellow, is a community organizer, and is the founder of ChiByDesign, a black-owned and people of color-led design firm in Chicago.

Twitter: @chibydesign
Instagram: @chibydesign
LinkedIn: linkedin.com/in/christopher-rudd-225b27b5

Kaleena Sales is coauthor of the book *Extra Bold: A Feminist, Inclusive, Anti-Racist, Non-Binary Field for Graphic Designers* alongside Ellen Lupton, Jennifer Tobias, Josh Halstead, Leslie Xia, Farah Kafei, and Valentina Vergara. She is also an associate professor and chair at Tennessee State University, an HBCU in Nashville, TN. Her research centers on Black culture and aesthetics, with work featured in *Communication Arts*, Printmag.com, and *Design Observer*.

      Web: kaleenasales.design
      Instagram: @kaleenasales

Raja Schaar, IDSA, is program director and assistant professor of Product Design at Drexel University's Antoinette Westphal College of Media Arts and Design. She is an industrial designer with an extensive background in museum exhibit design who is passionate about ways design can make positive impact intersections with health, the environment, and education. She also cochairs IDSA's Diversity, Equity, and Inclusion Council.

Ian Spalter is head of Instagram Japan and former head of design at Instagram, where he leads the team responsible for all things design ranging from cross-platform app experiences to brand and identity. Ian was previously a senior UX manager at YouTube, and prior to that, director of UX & Design at Foursquare. Ian also spent four years at R/GA, where he oversaw design development projects such as the Nike+ Fuelband and Nike Running, Basketball, and Training products.

      Twitter: @ianspalter
      Instagram: @ianspalter

Kelly Walters is a designer, educator and founder of the multidisciplinary design studio Bright Polka Dot. Her ongoing design research interrogates the complexities of identity formation, systems of value, and the shared vernacular in and around Black visual culture. She is the author of *Black, Brown + Latinx Design Educators: Conversations on Design and Race* published by Princeton Architectural Press and a coeditor of *The Black Experience in Design*. Kelly is an Assistant Professor and Associate Director of the BFA Communication Design Program at Parsons School of Design at The New School in New York.

      Web: brightpolkadot.com
      Twitter: @brightpolkadot
      Instagram: @brightpolkadot

Michele Y. Washington is a design facilitator, design researcher, and design strategist who works with nonprofits, start-ups, and cultural institutions. She is currently a Columbia University A'Lelia Bundles Community Scholar and the founder of "CuriousStories Lab," a curated series of podcasts and short docs on architects and designers of color. She has an MFA in Design Criticism from the School of Visual Arts, and MS in Communications Design from Pratt Institute.

> Web: officeofmichelewashingtson.com
> Twitter: @culturalboundar, @curiousstorylab

Jennifer White-Johnson is an Afro-Latina, disabled artist, designer, educator, and activist, whose visual work explores the intersection of content and caregiving with an emphasis on redesigning ableist visual culture. She has been featured in the *Washington Post*, *New York Times*, *AfroPunk*, Google Stories, and CNN and her work is permanently archived in Libraries at the Metropolitan Museum of Art and the National Museum of Women in the Arts. She's worked within disability advocacy initiatives presenting at companies like Converse, Twitter, Amazon, Nike, and Crip Camp, and was selected as an honoree on the 2020 Diversability's D-30 Disability Impact List.

> Twitter: @jtknoxroxs
> Web: jenwhitejohnson.com, jenwhitejohnson.com/
> Kids-Solidarity-Zine-Fest-2020, jenwhitejohnson/
> Kids-Solidarity-Mini-Zine-Pack

Michelle Joan Wilkinson, PhD, is a curator at the Smithsonian Institution National Museum of African American History and Culture, where she is expanding the museum's collections in design and architecture. Wilkinson led the museum's symposium, "Shifting the Landscape: Black Architects and Planners, 1968 to Now." In 2020, she was a Loeb Fellow at the Harvard Graduate School of Design.

> Instagram: @michelleinthemix
> Twitter: @MJinthemix
> Facebook: blkgalactic

Lauren Williams (she/her) is a Detroit-based designer, organizer, researcher, and educator. She works with visual and interactive media to understand, critique, and reimagine the ways social and economic systems distribute and exercise power.

> Web: williamslaurenm.com
> Twitter: @imlwilliams
> Instagram: @ldubalicious

Folayemi (Fo) Wilson is an object and image maker whose work celebrates the Black imagination as a technology of resistance and self-determination and explores the Black Atlantic experience through sculptural and multimedia installations. She/They holds a MFA in Furniture Design from the Rhode Island School of Design with a concentration in Art History, Theory & Criticism and is associate dean of Access and Equity and Professor of Art in the College of Arts & Architecture, Penn State University.

> Web: fowilson.com, blkhausstudios.com
> Instagram: @fowilson, @blkhaus_studios

Woodrow W. Winchester III, PhD, CPEM is the director, Professional Engineering Programs for the University of Maryland, Baltimore County (UMBC). He recently launched Black Futures Design, an Afrofutures laboratory, think tank, and consultancy centered on catalyzing and amplifying inclusive and equitable approaches to new product concepting and development (NPD).

> Web: blackfuturesdesign.com
> Twitter: @woodtres
> LinkedIn: linkedin.com/in
> woodrow-winchester-iii-phd-cpem-323a375

Maurice Woods is executive director and founder of the Inneract Project (IP) whose vision is to build a global design education platform for marginalized designers of color. He received the AIGA San Francisco Fellow Award in 2016 and the Jefferson Award, and has twenty plus years of experience across brand identity, retail, exhibit, and interaction design. He currently also works full-time as a principal designer at Microsoft.

> Web: inneractproject.org
> Twitter: @dlrowseom
> LinkedIn: linkedin.com/in/mauricewoods

Forest Young leads Global Brand Design at Rivian. Prior to joining Rivian, he was the first chief creative officer at Wolff Olins—which was named Fast Company's Most Innovative Company for Design. Forest is a senior critic in graphic design at the Yale School of Art, where he is also a distinguished alumnus. His work has received numerous accolades including the ADC Black Cube.

> Twitter: @ten_ten
> Instagram: @emcray

ACKNOWLEDGMENTS

Finding the words to express appreciation to every individual who has been an integral part of the evolution of this book project is daunting. Yet, it could not have come about without the communities and networks who have provided steadfast support over the course of the last year and a half. The editorial team would like to recognize each and every one of them.

We begin by acknowledging the lands on which we and many of our contributors live and work, lands that have been stewarded for generations by peoples whose names and heritages we honor: Anishinaabeg, Apache, Carib, Comanche, Council of the Three Fires (Potawatomy, Ojibe and Odawa), Dakota, Lekawe, Lenape, Lumbee, Munsee Lenape, Khoi San, Mvskoke / Creek, Nipmuc, Ohlone, Piscataway Conoy, Quapaw, Susquehannock, Taino, Tongva, Tonkawa, Tsalaguwetiyi, Tupinamba, Waawiyaatanong, and Wyandot. Though many of our ancestors were brought to these lands against their will, and others arrived later as immigrants, migrants, and visitors, we are duty-bound to affirm that these are native lands. The work of justice includes fighting to restore lands that have been stolen by the colonial and federal governments, and to support our Indigenous, First Nations, and native brothers and sisters in their fight for sovereignty.

We also thank all of the many contributors who extended to us their time and care in the writing of their essays. Each contributor worked alone, but we could see how deeply they have all been in conversation with one another through their work. To that end, we are beyond grateful to Ruha Benjamin for her exquisite foreword, which captures so much of what we wanted this book to be about—historical context, critique, affirmation, and inspiration. So many of us have been in deep conversation with her ideas in our own teaching and practices, and it is an honor to have her engage so directly with this project. We extend an enormous thanks, as well, to design icon Emory Douglas and to our colleague Colette Gaiter whose thoughtful conversation gives this book the perspective of time and resilience. Mr. Douglas reminds us of our responsibility as educators to encourage all whose are entrusted to us, and he advises the youngest among us to never fear critique, as it will always make us stronger. To Eddie Opara, we offer a moment of quiet to honor his Afterword, which feels like a contemplative and deeply personal coda to this work. We hope to travel with you to distant shores to discover where and with whom else we might create new pathways for design. Thank you also to adrienne maree brown for offering such sage advice to young designers, and for reflecting on the intersections of her work and the many designers and activists among us. Not least, we offer light and love to the late Sylvia Harris, who has remained a source of inspiration for decades. She will never be forgotten.

      Anne would like to acknowledge Lee Roy, Beth, Joe, and Malinda Berry for their fierce love and loyalty, and the encouragement they have provided again and again over the long haul. She would also like to thank Tiffany Roman, a good friend and collaborator who helped inspire the kernel of the idea that became The Black Experience in Design, and Gary Singer for his time and for allowing us to share Sylvia Harris' words. Many thanks also goes to her colleagues Jenn Visocky O'Grady, Sarah Rutherford, and Cigdem Slankard for their advocacy as well as their care and friendship. And for the innumerable ways they have inspired, provided humor, wisdom, guidance, demonstrated patience, and simply shown kindness in the most seemingly inconsequential moments, Anne would like to acknowledge Karin Zemski Berry, John Stoltzfus, the Hostetlers and Berrys/Hawthornes, Cyleste Collins, Audrey G. Bennett, Jess Barness, Audra Buck-Coleman, Jennifer Vokoun, Michele Y. Washington, Ann McDonald, Aaris Sherin, Robin Landa, Dennis Doordan, Maria Tomasula, the late Robert Sedlack, Nikki Woods, Jason Lahr, Sarah Edmands Martin, Andre Mūrnieks, her creative family at LightBox Collective, Sarah Kingsley-Metzler, Joyce Ho, Marla Hostetter Kropf, Stephanie Hinnershitz, Ken Visocky O'Grady, Kelly Hartzler, and the staff at the Anabaptist Mennonite Biblical Seminary library. Lastly, she would like to recognize the other members of the editorial team without whom there would be no book; thank you to Kareem, Penina, and Lesley-Ann for their contributions and input, and a debt of gratitude to Jennifer and Kelly, who gave this project every ounce of energy they had to spare.

      Kareem would like to acknowledge Medina, Rayaan, and Elyas Collie, his wonderfully supportive family, for their patience and understanding on those Sundays that he hid away in the office working on The Black Experience in Design: Identity, Expression, and Reflection. He would also like to thank Anne H. Berry, Jennifer Rittner, Kelly Walters, Lesley

Ann Noel, and Penina Laker for their inspiration and collaboration. Special thanks to Anne, Jennifer, and Kelly for helping our ideas land on target and on time. Lastly, Kareem would like to offer his sincere appreciation to the contributors that he worked with: Amos Kennedy, Chris Rudd, Darhil Crooks, Dantley Davis, Ian Spalter, Jennifer White-Johnson, June A. Grant, Michele Y. Washington, Quinlin Messenger, and Vann Graves. Thank you for your time, insights, and heartfelt generosity.

Penina would like to thank her husband Kyle Laker for being her number one cheerleader—his patience and support during the writing of this book meant so much to her. She is also truly grateful to the editorial team, which been an amazing tribe to work with. The rigor with which the group seized the opportunity to elevate the all-too-often ignored narratives of Black designers has been inspiring. Special thanks to Anne H. Berry, the editorial team's fearless leader and Jennifer and Kelly for their unwavering effort to ensure that all important milestones were met. She feels lucky to have worked and learned alongside them all.

Working on this book project has given Penina a newly found sense of pride in her own African heritage. She realizes that there are so many ancestors and scholars who have paved the way for the design community to broaden the canon of design histories—there's still so much more to be done, documented, and shared. Black design history, a history that can no longer be ignored. She would like to specifically acknowledge Saki Mafundikwa, whose words continue to inspire and invoke a sense of duty to continue looking within the ancestral roots to draw inspiration for one's creative endeavors. A luta Continua!

Lesley-Ann would like to thank her son Azure for his patience during this production of this book; her parents, Kenty and Sonia for their unwavering support, her siblings Adrienne and Andre for always being available; our editorial team for its camaraderie that made researching, writing and editing this book flow so easily. She would especially like to thank Anne, Jennifer, and Kelly for their leadership throughout the process. Finally, she would like to acknowledge the large network of friends and supportive people, like Ja'Wanda Grant, Stanley Payne, Michele Y. Washington, Renata Marques Leitão, and Laura Murphy, who helped create moments of sanity in the chaos of the pandemic, co-parented, helped make community and connections or were intellectual partners on projects happening at the same time or sounding boards for ideas; without them, it would have been impossible to participate in this work.

Jennifer would like to thank the many colleagues and friends whose voices are not overtly present in this book, but whose insights and generosity informed much of how she thinks, writes, and teaches, including Sem Devillart, Ajay Revels, Liz Jackson, Lara Penin,

Aimee Guerrero, Cielo Cerezo, David Lamb, Sinclair Smith, and her many colleagues at the School of Visual Arts and Parsons School of Design. She owes a debt of gratitude to the many people who kept her sane and organized throughout the process, particularly Adrienne Hunt, Dana Dorfman, Barbara Morini, and her friends in song at UUCM. She is eternally grateful to many childhood friends with whom she has shared space, joy, resistance, and solidarity, including Charlene Coleman, Kevin Bullock, Robin Foulkes, and Michael Stauff. For their thoughtful contributions to this book, she thanks every one of the seventy writers. Collaborating with the five other editors of this book was uplifting at a time when it would have been all too easy to wallow in despair. In particular, she is grateful for the friendship and deep camaraderie of Anne H. Berry and Kelly Walters, both of whom have made working on this project joyful even at its most challenging.

There aren't words to express her love for the family of men who have supported and guided her—Robert, Alan, and Brian; and the family of women and the family of women whose legacies she hopes to carry—Dianqui, Aurea, Percilia, Lia, Viviane, Patricia; as well as her child, Theo, who showed incredible patience throughout this year. More than anything, though, Jennifer thanks her all-too-recently ancestored mother, Bernadette Maria Clemente DeSouza Rittner. Bearing witness to her experiences in the world forms the foundation of Jennifer's interrogations of design, and why we must demand the design of spaces, systems, services, and objects that see us in all of our wonderful complexity. Mamae, I could never heal your pain but I hope to honor your legacy.

Kelly would like to thank her parents Greg and Dee Walters, and her brothers Greg Jr., Colin and Sean for their endless support and encouragement during the making of *The Black Experience in Design*. In reflecting over the past year, she is amazed at all the pieces that came together in order for this book to come to life. She would also like to thank everyone who was interested in this project but was unable to participate—she has no no doubt that there will be more projects in the future where collaboration will most certainly be possible. A special thanks to Cey Adams, Schessa Garbutt, Rick Griffith, Yocasta Lachapelle, Sabine Maxine Lopez, Romi Morrison, Nontsikelolo Mutiti, Mimi Ọnụọha, Aisha Richards, Michelle Joan Wilkinson, and Forest Young for sharing your stories and being open to feedback as your contributions were shaped for this book. Your journeys and reflections on design will be an inspiration to future and current designers. Much appreciation and immense gratitude to renald Louissaint for the design of this book and working tirelessly to execute a design with care toward the content and an attention to detail. Kelly is thankful to have had another opportunity to collaborate with renald on another design project. Finally, Kelly would like to thank her coeditors,

ACKNOWLEDGMENTS

Anne H. Berry, Kareem Collie, Penina Laker, Lesley-Ann Noel, and Jennifer Rittner for uplifting and championing over seventy Black artists, designers, and creative practitioners who are reflected in this book. Kelly will be forever grateful for Anne and Jennifer's particular insight during the development of *The Black Experience in Design*. Working in partnership with them in the final push of this publication has been extremely rewarding, and Kelly has learned so much about what it means to hold space, think critically and lead with warmth, compassion and a shared commitment for advancing Black visibility in design.

The editorial team would also like to thank Steven Heller, Tad Crawford, Caroline Russomanno, Jamie McGhee, and renald Louissant, as well as the institutions and organizations that have supported our work: *Communication Arts Magazine*, California College of Art College of Art, Cleveland State University, North Carolina State University, Parsons School of Design, School of Visual Arts, Tulane University, Washington University in St. Louis, The Rick and Susan Sontag Center for Collaborative Creativity at The Claremont Colleges, and the IBM Consulting Strategic Design Team.

In closing, we are grateful not only to our Black colleagues and collaborators, but to all designers, educators, and scholars who are interrogating identity, expression, and reflections in the spaces they inhabit. While this book centers the experiences of Black designers, the work of building a more inclusive and equitable design culture is in conversation with many others who represent marginalized identities in and by design. Let's keep finding each other, having the hard conversations, and designing together.

INDEX

To access the index, enter this URL to go to the book page on the Skyhorse website:

skyhorsepublishing.com/go/9781621537854

The password protected index file download is available in the links section of the book's page.

The access password is: index.

BOOKS FROM ALLWORTH PRESS

About Design by Gordofn Salchow with Foreword by Michael Bierut and Afterword by Katherine McCoy (6⅛ × 6⅛, 208 pages, paperback, $19.99)

Becoming a Design Entrepreneur by Steven Heller and Lita Talarico (6 × 9, 208 pages, paperback, $19.99)

Brand Thinking and Other Noble Pursuits by Debbie Millman with Rob Walker (6 × 9, 336 pages, paperback, $19.95)

Citizen Designer (Second Edition) by Steven Heller and Véronique Vienne (6 × 9, 312 pages, paperback, $22.99)

Design Literacy by Steven Heller with Rick Poynor (6 × 9, 304 pages, paperback, $22.50)

Design Thinking by Thomas Lockwood (6 × 9, 304 pages, paperback, $24.95)

Designers Don't Read by Austin Howe with Fredrik Averin (5½ × 8½, 224 pages, paperback, $19.95)

The Education of a Graphic Designer by Steven Heller (6 × 9, 380 pages, paperback, $19.99)

The Elements of Graphic Design by Alex W. White (8 × 10, 224 pages, paperback, $29.95)

Graphic Design History Edited by Steven Heller and Georgette Balance (6½ × 10, 352 pages, paperback, $29.99)

Graphic Design Rants and Raves by Steven Heller (7 × 9, 200 pages, paperback, $19.99)

How to Think Like a Great Graphic Designer by Debbie Millman (6 × 9, 248 pages, paperback, $24.95)

Listening to Type by Alex W. White (8 × 10, 272 pages, paperback, $29.99)

Looking Closer 5 Edited by Michael Bierut, William Drenttel, and Steven Heller (6½ × 8⅞, 256 pages, paperback, $21.95)

POP by Steven Heller (6 × 9, 288 pages, paperback, $24.95)

Teaching Design by Meredith Davis (6 × 9, 216 pages, paperback, $24.99)

Teaching Graphic Design (Second Edition) by Steven Heller (6 × 9, 312 pages, paperback, $24.99)

Vintage Graphic Design by Steven Heller and Louis Fili (8 × 10, 208 pages, paperback, $19.99)

To see our complete catalog or to order online, please visit www.allworth.com.